Induction

Computational Models of Cognition and Perception

Editors

Jerome A. Feldman
Patrick J. Hayes
David E. Rumelhart

Parallel Distributed Processing: Explorations in the Microstructure of Cognition. Volume 1: Foundation, by David E. Rumelhart, James L. McClelland, and the PDP Research Group

Parallel Distributed Processing: Explorations in the Microstructure of Cognition. Volume 2: Psychological and Biological Models, by James L. McClelland, David E. Rumelhart, and the PDP Research Group

Neurophilosophy: Toward a Unified Science of the Mind-Brain, by Patricia Smith Churchland

Qualitative Reasoning about Physical Systems, edited by Daniel G. Bobrow

Visual Cognition, edited by Steven Pinker

Induction: Processes of Inference, Learning, and Discovery, by John H. Holland, Keith J. Holyoak, Richard E. Nisbett, and Paul R. Thagard

Production System Models of Learning and Development, edited by David Klahr

Induction
Processes of Inference, Learning, and Discovery

John H. Holland
Keith J. Holyoak
Richard E. Nisbett
Paul R. Thagard

The MIT Press
Cambridge, Massachusetts
London, England

This book was set in Baskerville by Asco Trade Typesetting Ltd., Hong Kong, and printed and bound by The Murray Printing Company in the United States of America.

Library of Congress Cataloging-in-Publication Data

Induction: processes of inference, learning, and discovery.

(Computational models of cognition and perception) Bibliography: p.
Includes index.
1. Induction (Logic). 2. Artificial intelligence. 3. Inference.
4. Learning, Psychology of. 5. Machine learning. 6. Memory.
I. Holland, John H. (John Henry), 1929–   . II. Series.
BF441.I53   1986   153   86-2811
ISBN 0-262-08160-1

We dedicate this book to four predecessors whose insights guided our collaboration:

Charles Peirce, in philosophy of science
Kurt Lewin, in social psychology
Edward Tolman, in cognitive psychology
Arthur Samuel, in artificial intelligence

Contents

4

Computational Implementations of Inductive Systems   *102*

5

Conditioning and Covariation Detection   *151*

6

Category Formation   *179*

7

Modeling the Physical and Social Worlds   *205*

10
Analogy 287

11
Scientific Discovery 320

12
Epilogue: Toward a Theory of Induction 343

Preface

Ever since Socrates taught geometry to the slave boy in Plato's *Meno*, the nature of learning has been an active topic of investigation. For centuries it was the province of philosophers, who analytically studied inductive and deductive inference. A hundred years ago, psychology began to use experimental methods to investigate learning in humans and other organisms. Still more recently, the computer has provided a research tool, engendering the field of machine learning.

Despite the diversity of methods employed, one might hope that these disciplines could offer much to each other in developing an understanding of learning. This hope led directly to this collaborative work by a computer scientist, two psychologists, and a philosopher. In 1980 we began meeting together regularly with a vague awareness that we had common concerns. Holland was working on computational models of learning, using classifier systems and genetic operators. Holyoak was conducting research on the role of analogy in problem solving and induction, and on the emergence of variability information in category learning. Nisbett had just completed a book on the limitations of inductive reasoning in humans and had begun work showing that these failures were neither as deep nor as impervious to change as he had feared. Thagard had been investigating patterns of inference in the context of the philosophy of science, and was beginning to understand them in computational terms. Our expectations of related interests quickly turned to excitement about the prospects of a collective attack on some of the problems that we had been pursuing individually.

The most tangible result is this book, which presents a framework for understanding many important facets of learning in organisms and machines, ranging in complexity from conditioning in rats to scientific discovery. The book is a genuine collaboration, in that every chapter has been reworked by at least three of us. In the end we have not accomplished the ultimate goal of a general theory of induction, capable of accounting for all kinds of knowledge change. At most we have provided a kind of holding company for theories about particular kinds of inference and learning—for example, analogy, the representation of variability and uncertainty, generalization from instances, and some aspects of classical and instrumental conditioning. But we hope that the reader will gain from our attempt to integrate the ideas of several disciplines and to construct a systematic approach to the study of induction.

Acknowledgments

If our experience is any guide, the amount of institutional and individual support necessary for the production of a book goes up as a function of the square of the number of authors.

First, the institutions. The book would never have been written were it not for the Sloan Foundation grant to the Cognitive Science Program at the University of Michigan. The foundation's support made possible the formation of that group, which is the vehicle through which we came together. Its support continued later in the form of direct subsistence of this book project.

An extremely generous grant from the System Development Foundation provided salary support for the authors during the critical year when most of the chapters received their first drafts.

Throughout the period during which the book was written, Keith Holyoak's salary was supported by a Career Development Award from the National Institute of Mental Health. Both salary support and research support were provided in generous amounts from various government agencies. These include grants from the National Science Foundation to Holland (MCS78-26016, IST80-18043, and DCR83-05830), Holyoak (BNS82-16068), Nisbett (SES82-18846 and SES85-07342), and Holyoak and Nisbett (BNS84-09198). They also include grant 1 RO1 MH38466 from the National Institute of Mental Health to Nisbett and grant 85-K-0563 from the Office of Naval Research to Nisbett.

Many people read the manuscript in earlier drafts and provided vigorous and invaluable criticism. These include Robert Abelson, Robert Axelrod, Dorritt Billman, Bruce Buchanan, Patricia Cheng, Michael Cohen, Daniel Dennett, Douglas Hofstadter, Alice Isen, John Jonides, Daniel Kahneman, Ziva Kunda, Gary Olson, Lee Ross, Marilyn Shatz, Robert Siegler, Edward Smith, and a large number of anonymous reviewers whose criticism was fully as helpful and even more vigorous!

We have had extremely able editorial assistance from Sara Free-land, Mary Jo Blahna, and Deborah Francis at the University of Michigan. Paula Niedenthal was our excellent illustrator. Harry and Betty Stanton of Bradford Books provided unusually vigorous and imaginative help in their role as publishers.

Induction

1

A Framework for Induction

The mother of a four-year-old boy, observing that he has been unusually cranky and obdurate for several days, decides that he has entered a "phase". A laboratory rat, busily pressing a lever to obtain food, hears a distinctive tone, which is followed by an electric shock. The very next time the animal hears the tone, it hesitates in its lever-pressing activity, waiting, one is tempted to say, for the other shoe to drop. A nineteenth-century scientist observes the behavior of light under several types of controlled conditions and decides that, like sound, it travels in waves through a medium.

These are all examples of *induction*, which we take to encompass all inferential processes that expand knowledge in the face of uncertainty. Understanding such processes is a central concern of philosophy, psychology, and artificial intelligence, yet little progress has been made in any of these fields. Philosophers have spent hundreds of years attempting to characterize inductive inference, yet the current research most concerned with the topic—on formal inductive logics and Bayesian decision theories—bears little relation to how people actually think. Behaviorist psychologists spent decades developing learning theories that were not fully adequate as descriptions of the inferential and learning capacities of rats and fell very far short of the mark for humans. Researchers in artificial intelligence are able to build sophisticated game players and powerful expert systems but have been largely stymied in attempts to program these systems to improve themselves. Indeed, alteration of these systems by simple *insertion* of new knowledge typically produces chaos, which can be undone only by extensive reprogramming. Induction, which has been called the "scandal of philosophy", has become the scandal of psychology and artificial intelligence as well.

In this book we propose a framework for understanding induction that is designed to overcome the limitations of previous philosophical, psychological, and computational work on the topic. A framework is not a theory: we do not offer a detailed, canonical scheme of how every type of induction is or ought to be done. But building on the insights of researchers in psychology, philosophy, and artificial intelligence, and borrowing also from disciplines ranging from biology to statistics, we have tried to develop a systematic set of principles providing coherence to a diverse set of findings on the nature of inductive processes. These principles will be used throughout the book to develop accounts of specific psychological phenomena, and their computational feasibility will be displayed through descriptions of running computer programs.

Since we are concerned with both the inductive processes of organisms, notably humans, and those of computers, we will refer to *cognitive systems* to describe the "thought processes" of everything from man to mouse to microchip. Whether we are describing organisms or prescribing for machines, it is our intent that all our assertions ultimately be rendered computational. Our description of the behavior of organisms is always in terms that we believe capable of being translated eventually into computational procedures on machines. In some cases we have achieved this computational status with running systems; in other cases our framework provides qualitative accounts that we present as the seeds for potential computational development.

Even when the qualitative aspects of our framework reach far beyond its computational grasp, our view nonetheless commits us to some quite explicit empirical predictions. For example, we will argue that (a) animal conditioning can be understood only if one assumes that rats and pigeons are capable of applying inferential rules to the relationships between events and that this practice results in the formation of a family of hypotheses to be tested by subsequent experience; (b) it is often easier to learn a complex set of interrelationships among events than to learn a single relationship between two events—hence complex categorizations will often be learned while linkages between two simple stimuli often will not; (c) many beliefs about the laws governing both the physical world and the social world are empirically wrong—and wrong in the same way and for the same reasons; (d) many aspects of inductive reasoning are statistical at base, and people's demonstrated errors in statistical reasoning are better understood as being due less to ignorance of statistical rules than to inability to code events in terms that make contact with statistical rules; (e) though people possess inductive inferential rules for statistical and causal analysis at a high level of abstraction, they possess few if any abstract rules corresponding to those of formal logic; (f) people's understanding of everyday events can be influenced by instruction in abstract inferential rules *if* such instruction includes or builds upon preexisting rules for encoding events in the special ways required by the rule system; and (g) the creative use of analogies between problems from different domains is inextricably tied to general procedures for inducing pragmatically useful categories.

Our view also commits us to some quite specific designs for computational systems intended to simulate human and animal behavior and to be capable of flexible performance and of learning from experience. Much of the basis for the more general theoretical framework we will present is derived from the *classifier systems* of Holland (1986; Holland and Reitman 1978). Classifier systems are a kind of rule-based system with general mechanisms for processing rules in parallel, for adaptive generation of new rules, and for testing the effectiveness of existing rules. These mechanisms make possible performance and learning without the "brittleness" characteristic of most expert systems in AI. A recent example of a classifier system (described in chapter 4) is to the best of our knowledge the first program to develop a working expert system from a randomly generated initial set of rules (Goldberg 1983).

Additional learning mechanisms have been studied using a program called PI, for "processes of induction" (Thagard and Holyoak 1985). In chapter 4 we describe how PI performs several kinds of induction in the context of problem solving, simulating the discovery and application of simple qualitative theories.

We now present an overview of the ideas that will play a role in subsequent discussions. Although a preliminary defense of these ideas is offered here, a fuller justification must await later chapters in which we show how numerous phenomena of inductive inference are illuminated within the general theoretical approach.

1.1 The Pragmatics of Induction

The general question we hope to answer in this book is, How can a cognitive system process environmental input and stored knowledge so as to benefit from experience? More specific versions of this question include the following: How can a system organize its experience so that it has some basis for action even in unfamiliar situations? How can a system determine that rules in its knowledge base are inadequate? How can it generate plausible new rules to replace the inadequate ones? How can it refine rules that are useful but non-optimal?

How can it use metaphor and analogy to transfer information and procedures from one domain to another?

1.1.1 The Issue of Constraints

Almost a century ago, the philosopher C. S. Peirce (in work published in 1931–1958, vol. 2., pp. 474–476) posed the fundamental problem that one must deal with if one is to address questions such as those above.

Suppose a being from some remote part of the universe, where the conditions of existence are inconceivably different from ours, to be presented with a United States Census Report—which is for us a mine of valuable inductions.... He begins, perhaps, by comparing the ratio of indebtedness to deaths by consumption in counties whose names begin with different letters of the alphabet. It is safe to say that he would find the ratio everywhere the same, and thus his inquiry would lead to nothing.... The stranger to this planet might go on for some time asking inductive questions that the Census would faithfully answer without learning anything except that certain conditions were independent of others.... Nature is a far vaster and less clearly arranged repertoire of facts than a census report; and if men had not come to it with special aptitudes for guessing right, it may well be doubted whether in the ten or twenty thousand years that they may have existed their greatest mind would have attained the amount of knowledge which is actually possessed by the lowest idiot.

In essence, Peirce raised the question of how induction can be constrained. How do people avoid generating innumerable fruitless hypotheses in their search for useful generalizations? The life expectancy of a cognitive system that devoted all its processing resources to exploring misguided inductions would be brief. Peirce's reference to "special aptitudes for guessing right" reflects his belief that constraints on induction are based on innate knowledge. Without denying the possibility that specific innate knowledge may guide induction for some organisms in some domains, our own approach will be to emphasize constraints that can be derived from the general nature of an information-processing system that pursues goals in a complex environment and receives feedback about its success in attaining its goals.

It is worth noting that the issue of constraints arises not only with respect to inductive inference but with respect to *deductive* inference as well. Deduction is typically distinguished from induction by the fact that only for the former is the truth of an inference guaranteed by the truth of the premises on which it is based (given that all men are mortal and that Socrates is a man, we can deduce with complete certainty that Socrates is mortal). The fact that an inference is a valid deduction, however, is no guarantee that it is of the slightest interest. For example, if we know that snow is white, we are free to apply a standard rule of deductive inference to conclude that "either snow is white or lions wear argyle socks." In most realistic contexts such deductions will be as worthless as they are valid. As we will see in chapter 9, the approach we advocate embraces deductive as well as inductive inference and in many ways weakens the strong distinction usually drawn between them.

Our approach assumes that the central problem of induction is to specify processing constraints that will ensure that the inferences drawn by a cognitive system will tend to be plausible and relevant to the system's goals. Which inductions should be characterized as plausible can be determined only with reference to the current knowledge of the system. Induction is thus highly context dependent, being guided by prior knowledge activated in particular situations that confront the system as it seeks to achieve its goals. *The study of induction, then, is the study of how knowledge is modified through its use.*

Because of its emphasis on the role of the system's goals and the context in which induction takes place, we characterize the theory proposed here as *pragmatic*. In contrast, most treatments of the topic have looked at purely *syntactic* aspects of induction, considering only the formal structure of the knowledge to be expanded and leaving the pragmatic aspects, those concerned with goals and problem-solving contexts, to look out for themselves. In our view, this stance has produced little insight into the way humans do, or efficient machines might, make just the inferences that are most useful. This is not to say that syntactic considerations are irrelevant; indeed, at some level they are inescapable in any computational system. Our claim is simply that pragmatic considerations are equally inescapable.

1.1.2 The Shortcomings of Syntax

Most research on induction in philosophy, psychology, and artificial intelligence has been dominated by syntactic approaches. A historical survey of the problems encountered by researchers in these fields would require a volume in itself. We must be content with a few illustrations of the related predicaments that nonpragmatic approaches have engendered. The problems that have beset purely syntactic theories serve to motivate our pragmatic approach.

Perhaps no field has been as enthralled by syntactic approaches as twentieth-century philosophy. For nineteenth-century thinkers such as Mill, "logic" meant the general study of reasoning, using methods that are quite informal. By the twentieth century, however, logic had become a highly formal, mathematical pursuit—a change due primarily to the dramatic advances in the study of deduction made by Gottlob Frege and Bertrand Russell, who showed that deduction could be characterized rigorously in axiomatic systems. In the hands of the logical-positivist movement in philosophy, which combined employment of the precise methods of the new logic with a strict empiricism, these developments naturally led to attempts to apply the same kind of rigor to the characterization of inductive inferences. The pinnacle of this new program was Carnap's *Logical Foundations of Probability* (1950), which attempted to use the formalisms of the new logic and probability theory to do for induction what Frege and Russell had done for deduction.

Improved inductive logics have since been developed by Carnap himself and by others. Many have employed the formal apparatus of Bayesian probability theory and decision theory to characterize inductive inferences (for example, Carnap and Jeffrey 1971; Salmon 1967; Kyburg 1974; Levi 1980; Horwich 1982).

Although we have no doubt that considerations of probability theory and statistical inference are often highly relevant to induction, we do not believe the primarily formal and syntactic approach to characterizing induction can succeed. The formal approach resolutely ignores the kinds of events about which the person is trying to make inferences as well as the goals that the inferences serve. In our view, it is because of its blindness to environmental and cognitive realities that the Carnapian approach to inductive reasoning has given rise to numerous paradoxes. The two that have had most influence on discussion of induction in the past thirty years are associated with the names of Carl Hempel and Nelson Goodman.

Hempel (1965), like Carnap, attempted to give a formal, syntactic account of how a generalization could be confirmed by its instances. Thus the proposition "All ravens are black" is confirmed by observations of ravens that are black. But the statement "All ravens are black" is formally equivalent to the statement "All nonblack things are nonravens." The latter proposition would be confirmed by a white shoe. Assuming that equivalent sentences are confirmed by the same instances, we get the paradoxical result that "All ravens are black" can be confirmed by a white shoe.

Goodman (1965) also showed how the Carnapian idea that inductive reasoning can be studied syntactically leads to paradox. Define "grue" as "green before time t and blue otherwise." Then observing a green emerald seems to confirm equally well both "All emeralds are green" *and* "All emeralds are grue" (assuming t is still in the future).

From a syntactic perspective it is hard to see why "All emeralds are green" is the more attractive conclusion.

In our view the raven paradox and the grue paradox are not mere problems to be solved by some refined syntactic account of induction but rather are symptoms of the fundamental inadequacy of such accounts. In chapter 8 we will attempt to resolve these paradoxes within our pragmatic framework. In essence, our approach is to deny the sufficiency of purely syntactic accounts of equivalences between inferences and to insist that sensible inferential rules take into account the kinds of things being reasoned about. Nonravens are simply not a coherent kind of thing, for pragmatic purposes, nor is grue a kind of property, except in an arbitrary world irrelevant to the goals of everyday human inference. In chapter 9 we will argue that people do not make much use of purely syntactic rules such as those found in formal logics, but instead rely on what we call "pragmatic reasoning schemas". These are clusters of inferential rules that characterize relations over general classes of object kinds, event relationships, and problem goals. These rules are quite abstract, in that they are not tied to particular content domains, but they are not so content-free as logical rules, which in our view are so highly generalized as to lose pragmatic utility for most inferential purposes.

Syntactic approaches have also been prevalent in the fields of psychology and artificial intelligence. From the early twentieth century through the 1950s the mainstream of experimental psychology was dominated by behaviorism, an approach steeped in the logical-positivist tenet of emphasizing observation over theory. Behaviorist psychologists from Watson (1924) on assumed that the laws relating reinforcement schedules to the speed of learning, or the laws that made previously neutral stimuli into aversive ones, would be quite independent of the nature of the stimuli, the reinforcement, or the organism in question. As we will see in chapter 5, these assumptions proved quite false. Cognitive psychology, which has in turn dominated experimental psychology since the 1960s, largely ignored the issue of induction until recently. Most experimental work on induction, from the early studies of Bruner, Goodnow, and Austin (1956) up to the present, has focused on the learning of artificial categories in artificial contexts, with little investigation of the impact of the learner's goals or of the role played by the nature of the categories under consideration.

Artificial intelligence is the youngest of the fields concerned with induction. With a few notable exceptions (such as Samuel 1959), workers in artificial intelligence also neglected induction until recently. Most of the work that has been done has proposed algorithms that produce generalizations from data without reference to the background knowledge or the goals that organisms have and that artificial systems ought to have (Langley, Bradshaw, and Simon 1983; Dietterich and Michalski 1983; Mitchell 1979). One of the most impressive research efforts on induction, that of Lenat (1983), has yielded programs for generating concepts and heuristics for mathematics and other domains. However, the programs all encounter the problem of "mud", which is Lenat's informal designation for uninteresting definitions and tasks. Mud sooner or later accumulates to the point that a system becomes totally involved in a round of tasks that contribute nothing to the expansion of concepts and heuristics. In our view, this is because expansion in Lenat's system is driven only by internal criteria of how "interesting" the structures are to the system, not by any external constraints having to do with their effectiveness in solving problems. In this respect the generation of mud resembles the generation of grue-like predicates.

Of course, any program is a purely syntactic entity as far as the computer is concerned. But artificial intelligence programs can simulate concern with goals and interaction with environments, using these concerns to constrain induction in the context of problem solving. The programs we describe in chapter 4 have this feature, transcending the syntactic limitations we have discussed.

In philosophy, psychology, and artificial intelligence there are other researchers who have taken a more pragmatic approach. Historically oriented philosophers of science such as Kuhn (1970) and Laudan (1977) have examined the problem-solving practice of scientists and argued that inference in scientific theories must be understood in the problem-solving context. Some cognitive psychologists, such as Tolman (1932, 1948, 1959), Lewin (1935), and Brunswik (1952), have considered how people and other organisms develop expectancies about real environments. In artificial intelligence, the checker-playing program of Samuel (1959) used goal-oriented predictions to improve its model of its opponents. The importance of integrating multiple sources of knowledge was highlighted in the speech-understanding system Hearsay-II (Erman, Hayes-Roth, Lesser, and Reddy 1980). Recent work in cognitive science, such as that of Anderson (1983), Mitchell (1982, 1983), and Rosenbloom and Newell (1986), has begun to examine the interface between goal-directed problem-solving behavior and induction of new rules. Johnson-Laird (1983) has emphasized the role of "mental models" in guiding human inference, and Schank (1982) has suggested ways in which the pragmatic context in which knowledge is acquired (for example, failures of expectations) may be used to organize knowledge in memory so as to facilitate subsequent inferences. Our framework attempts to tie together the insights of researchers such as these.

1.1.3 Knowledge, Goals, and Expectations

In our conception of the kind of processing system that can place induction in a pragmatic context, the central assumptions are that induction is (a) directed by problem-solving activity and (b) based on feedback regarding the success or failure of predictions generated by the system. The currently active goals of the system, coupled with an activated subset of the system's current store of knowledge, provide input to inferential mechanisms that generate plans and predictions about the behavior of the environment. The predictions are fed back to other inferential mechanisms along with receptor input. We use the term "receptor input" in a broad sense to include not only perceptual representations of the environment but also information about internal states of the system (for example, detection of needs or, even, contradictory inferences). A comparison of predictions and receptor input will yield information about predictive successes and failures, which will in turn trigger specific types of inductive changes in the knowledge store.

The notion of *triggering conditions* is central to our proposed framework. Particular kinds of induction are triggered by particular conditions that arise in the context of problem solving. For example, a rat in a Skinner box makes few inductive inferences so long as it is business as usual. When the rat gets shocked for the first time, however, a flurry of inductive procedures is initiated. Similarly, the mother of the four-year-old boy makes few inferences about him until his behavior changes in some respect. The way in which his behavior changes and the nature of her current inadequate understanding of him govern the occurrence and character of new inductions. The use of such triggering conditions obviates random search through the inexhaustible space of possible hypotheses. Instead, a cognitive system can direct its inductions according to its current problem situation, generating rules that are likely to be useful to it at the moment and hence possibly useful in the future as well.

1.1.4 Problem Solving and Induction

There are several important consequences of viewing induction as being closely tied to problem solving. This view implies that inferences normally will be made only about the representations that are currently active. And representations are typically active only because they characterize currently important aspects of the environment. When these representations cease to provide adequate predictions about the behavior of the environment, the system has a problem. The solution of the problem is quite likely to result in a permanent change in some of the representations, or at least in the likelihood that they will be used to represent similar environmental conditions in the future.

Our view of problem solving, while largely consistent with the theory established by Newell and Simon (1972) that now dominates the field, has some important differences of emphasis that arise from the processing assumptions we make in order to support inductive inference. Let us first consider assumptions that we share. We will treat problem solving as a process of search through a *state space*. A problem is defined by an *initial state*, one or more *goal states* to be reached, a set of *operators* that can transform one state into another, and *constraints* that an acceptable solution must meet. Problem-solving methods are procedures for selecting an appropriate sequence of operators that will succeed in transforming the initial state into a goal state through a series of steps. Some methods are highly specialized for solving problems within a particular domain (for example, a procedure for solving quadratic equations), whereas others are generalists that can be applied across a broad range of problem domains.

A handful of general methods have been described (Newell 1969), which are closely related to each other. The most representative general method is "means-ends analysis", a procedure consisting of four steps:

1) Compare the current state to the goal state and identify differences.

2) Select an operator relevant to reducing the difference.

3) Apply the operator if possible. If it cannot be applied, establish a subgoal of transforming the current state into one in which the operator *can* be applied. (Means-ends analysis is then invoked recursively to achieve the subgoal.)

4) Iterate the procedure until all differences have been eliminated (that is, the goal state has been reached) or until some failure criterion is exceeded.

It is now clear that general methods such as means-ends analysis are insufficient to account for expert problem-solving skill. Human expertise is critically dependent on specialized methods and representations of knowledge about the relevant domain. This conclusion has been supported by research on expert-novice differences in such problem domains as chess (Chase and Simon 1973) and physics (Larkin, McDermott, Simon, and Simon 1980). For the expert, solving routine problems can be viewed as a process of retrieving an appropriate "problem schema" and providing it with problem-specific parameters (Chi, Feltovich, and Glaser 1981). The problem schema will provide information about relevant problem concepts and specialized solution methods that may be applicable. At a global level, then, problem solving appears to be a process based on domain-specific knowledge, if that is available, or reliance on general methods, if it is not.

Although our own approach to problem solving overlaps in many ways with the widely accepted view sketched above, several salient differences should be noted. From our perspective, an obvious shortcoming of virtually all current problem-solving systems developed by artificial intelligence workers is that they learn nothing at all from experience. Achievement of a successful solution to a problem does not help in solving the same problem again, far less in solving a different one. Equally serious is the fact that such systems demand very specific information about the problem at hand before they can make any attempt to solve it. The problem must be well defined: the initial state, goal state, and allowable operators (associated with the differences to which they are relevant) must be fully specified. Without a clear description of the goal state, for example, it is impossible to compute the difference between it and the current state; consequently, means-ends analysis is inapplicable.

There are certainly classes of problems sufficiently well defined to meet the requirements of typical systems; theorem proving and multi-move puzzles such as the well-known "missionaries and cannibals" problem are representative examples. The trouble is that many of the problems that humans struggle with—quite often with some degree of success—fall short of the well-defined ideal. As Reitman (1964) emphasized, ill-defined problems are a variegated lot. Any of the basic components—the initial state, the goal state, the allowable operators, and the applicable constraints—may be only partially known at the outset of a solution attempt. To adapt Tolstoy's remark about happy and unhappy families, well-defined problems are all alike, but every ill-defined problem is ill-defined in its own way.

Because our main interest is in the fuzzy, ill-defined sorts of problems that abound in real life, we will augment the conventional approach to problem solving with mechanisms for seeking additional knowledge stored in memory that may clarify ill-defined problems. Rather than simply applying operators to a fixed problem representation, the representation itself may be transformed by recategorizing problem components and by retrieving associations and analogies. Such restructuring implies that search takes place not only in the space of potential "next states" along a temporal dimension but also through a space of alternative categorizations of the entities involved in the problem. This type of processing depends on the parallel activity of multiple pieces of knowledge that both compete with and complement each other in revising the problem representation. Such interactive parallelism is a hallmark of the theoretical framework for induction we will present.

1.2 *The Representation of Knowledge*

We will now introduce the major types of knowledge structures upon which we claim induction is based. The notion of a *mental model* is central to our analysis of problem solving and induction. In common with many recent theoretical treatments, we believe that cognitive systems construct models of the problem space that are then mentally "run", or manipulated to produce expectations about the environment (Craik 1943; Gentner and Stevens 1983; Johnson-Laird 1983). Induction consists of generating and revising the units from which mental models are constructed. For a variety of reasons we will take *condition-action rules* as the most important of these units. We will discuss this proposal at some length in section 1.2.2; but first we present our rationale for the notion of mental models.

1.2.1 *Mental Models*
Mental models are best introduced by contrast with the notion of a *schema*, which has been extremely influential in cognitive psychology and artificial intelligence, under that name as well as under the labels "script", "frame", and "concept" (Bartlett 1932, Piaget 1936, Minsky 1975, Schank and Abelson 1977, Rumelhart 1980). The premise underlying the schema notion is that information about the likely properties of the environment is stored in memory in clusters that can be accessed as large units and that can serve to generate plausible inferences and problem solutions. The utility and attractiveness of the schema notion, however, may have blinded investigators to some of its very real limitations.

Although schemas are valuable for chunking information together, they exact a toll in inflexibility. What is to be done with situations or things that are not neatly matched by any existing schemas? The scripts of Schank and Abelson (1977), for example, are schemas for stereotypical event sequences that provide predictive knowledge for highly regular and routine situations. When events are highly atypical for a given context, however, the script approach is quite unhelpful. A "restaurant script", for example, will not be likely to suggest the appropriate behavior to exhibit when a goat enters a restaurant. The script will not contain a slot for "goat entry" and a corresponding list of appropriate actions. The script might be of some use, but only *in combination* with other knowledge structures (for example, a rule that states, "If a threatening or obnoxious creature intrudes, then eject it or escape from it"). Scripts alone are not sufficiently flexible (as Schank 1982 has acknowledged). It is to overcome this inflexibility that we rely on the notion of a mental model.

In everyday life we are often faced with inputs that do not readily fit any prestored category representation. Often the interpretation of an input requires the simultaneous activation and integration of multiple schemas. This is evident even in such (relatively) simple cognitive tasks as the conceptual combination of word meanings. For example (to borrow a conjunction from Tversky and Kahneman 1983), it is probable that most of us have schemas for the concepts "feminist" and "bank teller". It seems far less likely, however, that we have a ready-made schema for a "feminist bank teller", even though the concept is immediately meaningful. Clearly, the meaning of the combination is somehow derived from the component schemas; but equally clearly, the resultant concept is more than a simple sum of the components. In understanding the concept we do not simply aggregate the typical properties of feminists and bank tellers, since these conflict. Rather, conceptual combination requires some process by which the default assumptions carried by the two categories can be reconciled. In chapters 3 and 4 we discuss possible mechanisms by which existing concepts can be combined to form new ones. For now we simply note that the process of conceptual combination is an example of what we mean by model construction.

The necessity for schema integration and coordination is even more apparent when we consider the kinds of procedures required to solve novel problems. A problem typically involves several elements and the relationships among them. To take a simple example, suppose we were to ask you to think of a way to support a coffee cup several inches above a surface, using a sheet of paper. A serious attempt to achieve this goal would require much more than the activation of schemas for "paper" and "cup". It seems natural to describe the ensuing problem-solving process as an attempt to generate a mental model of the problem situation. A useful resultant model might contain information about operations that can be performed with paper (such as rolling), the weight of the cup, and so on. The model can be used to generate predictions about the outcomes of potential solution attempts—that is, possibilities can be tested mentally before you risk breaking a cup in an overt solution attempt.

Although mental models are based in part on static prior knowledge, they are themselves transient, dynamic representations of particular unique situations. They exist only implicitly, corresponding to the organized, multifaceted description of the current situation and the expectations that flow from it. Despite their inherently transitory nature—indeed because of it—mental models are the major source of inductive change in long-term knowledge structures. The reason is simple. Because mental models are built by integrating knowledge in novel ways in order to achieve the system's goals, model construction provides the opportunity for new ideas to arise by recombination and as a consequence of disconfirmation of model-based predictions. Some of these ideas will be stored in long-term memory, either as modifications of existing schemas or as new unitary concepts. It is possible, for example, that in modeling the "cup and paper" problem the problem solver may induce a new potential function for paper. From such (relatively) simple examples to the triumphs of scientific discovery, the construction of mental models provides the force and direction for the process of induction.

1.2.2 Rules

Models must consist of components that can be flexibly constructed and interrelated. Our most basic epistemic building block is a condition-action *rule*, which has the form "IF such-and-such, THEN so-and-so," where the IF part is the condition and the THEN part is the action. Condition-action rules underlie much important work in artificial intelligence, including problem solvers based on the work of Newell and Simon (1972) and most expert systems (Buchanan and Shortliffe 1984). Rule-based systems have also been used as psychological models of human memory (Anderson 1976, 1983).

Such systems contain mechanisms for maintaining a set of "facts" and checking to see whether a subset of those facts can be used to instantiate the clauses of the condition, the IF part. Once the condition is matched, the system carries out the action encoded in the THEN part. If several rules have their conditions satisfied at the same time, it is typical to resolve conflicts via some priority ordering on the rules. (As will be seen, however, the need for a strict priority ordering is minimized in systems that allow multiple rules to be executed in parallel.) In general, then, the activity of a rule-based system (or *production system*) can be described in terms of a cycle with three steps: (1) matching facts against rules to determine which rules have their conditions satisfied; (2) selecting a subset (not necessarily a proper subset) of the matched rules to be executed, or "fired"; and (3) firing the selected rules to take the specified actions. In the systems we will describe, the actions of rules involve posting *messages* (some of which correspond to what we loosely referred to above as "facts"), so that a different set of rules will typically have their conditions matched on the next cycle.

We have several reasons for choosing rules as the most basic representation for inductive systems. First, their efficacy in specifying the procedures that a system must carry out has been supported by previous research. Second, condition-action rules have an attractive modularity. In a typical computer language the meaning of an instruction is context-dependent in an awkward way: its effect depends critically on its position in the sequence of instructions surrounding it. The effect of a condition-action rule, on the other hand, need not depend on the rules that surround it. In general, the procedure defined by a set of condition-action rules will be changed in moderate, recognizable ways when a new rule is added or an old rule is deleted. In contrast, an instruction added to or deleted from a procedure defined in a standard computer language usually produces chaos.

Third, and most important for our framework, sets of rules furnish structures that can readily provide mental models of the sort we propose. Rules can be used to describe *transitions* in the environment, specifying that if certain conditions hold, then certain changes in the environment will take place. A rule such as "If inflation and government spending are high, then interest rates rise" provides a basis for making predictions about future events, enabling the system to decide on a course of action. Chapter 2 describes in detail how complexes of such rules can be used to model the environment. In the absence of rules, a system would have to rely on storage, retrieval, and processing of a host of episodes and examples. For efficient operation in a changing environment, a system is much better off if it has the capacity to use rules for quick generation of expectations. Moreover, as we will see in chapter 3, rules can be coupled naturally to form sequences crucial for planning.

We distinguish between rules describing *diachronic* and *synchronic* relations in the environment. Diachronic rules, such as the one about interest rates, represent temporal transitions between environmental states. They include, but are not limited to, the repertoire of causal theories that the system holds about the environment. In contrast, synchronic relations hold atemporally between alternate descriptions of environmental states or objects. For example, we can say that Albert Einstein was a famous scientist and a musician and a man and a human and a mammal. Synchronic relations can be expressed by simple rules such as, "If X is human, then X is a mammal." One of the important uses of synchronic rules will be to recategorize elements of a problem situation.

Several important points about our concept of rules should be emphasized. First, the natural-language sense of a rule as an imperative is misleading in the present context. We assume that whether a rule is executed depends on how it fares in competition with other rules: rules are thus more like tentative suggestions than like commands. Second, our treatment differs from most rule-based systems that contain a central algorithm that chooses one rule to be fired. The fact that systems need to model complex situations leads us to propose a *limited parallelism* in which a number of rules can be fired at once. We think of rules as constituting a network of interacting, competing, not necessarily consistent hypotheses. To represent environments fraught with novelty, mental models cannot rely exclusively on precompiled structures. Flexibility can come only through the use of *combinations* of existing knowledge structures. Allowing rules to operate in parallel means that new combinations of existing rules can be used to model novel situations. New rules can be generated, moreover, by recombining elements of those that prove advantageous when simultaneously active. Novel structures thus are generated by recombining relatively small building blocks.

Rules are a natural vehicle for what we take to be the most fundamental learning mechanism: prediction-based evaluation of the knowledge store. A realistic inductive system cannot be expected to leap to optimal inductive inferences. There must be mechanisms that evaluate candidate structures, discarding some, storing others, and modifying those that already exist. The evaluation mechanism compares the predicted consequences of applying a knowledge structure with the actual outcome of that application. Condition-action rules are obviously well suited for making predictions. A rule that leads to a successful prediction should be strengthened in some way, increasing the likelihood of its use in the future; one that leads to error should be modified or discarded. Predictions about the attainment of goals will normally be the most powerful source of feedback.

In later chapters we will discuss many different methods for generating new rules and for adjusting measures of their value to the system. Evaluation of the success of rules in dealing with the environment of a system and meeting its goals will affect the *strength* of the rules; and on the basis of their joint relevance to specific situations, rules will become associated with each other.

1.2.3 Rule Clusters: Categories

Rules are our building blocks; but for efficient operation a processing system must have its rules organized in relation to each other. *Implicit* organization arises from patterns of conditions and actions: if the action of rule 1 satisfies the condition of rule 2, then the firing of rule 1 will tend to lead to the firing of rule 2. *Explicit* organization can come through pointers that are used to link rules directly together. Both implicit and explicit organizations provide data structures that constitute *clusters* of rules that are to be considered together. We will have occasion to refer to several different types of rule clusters, including categories, schemas, and default hierarchies. All of these are by now standard components of the cognitive science armamentarium.

Rules that often are activated together in the system's attempt to model its environment will eventually become associated. For example, dogs are sufficiently common objects, as well as sufficiently interesting and sufficiently distinctive objects, to ensure that people will induce a rule cluster corresponding to the category or concept "dog". Such a category may be regarded as a set of probabilistic assumptions about what features go with what other features and what consequences are to be expected given various antecedents. In chapter 6 we examine how such categories are induced. We will pay special attention to the mechanisms that facilitate learning associations among the condition portions of rules that form an interrelated set, and to the factors that encourage learning of the statistical aspects of categories.

One consequence of viewing categories as rule clusters is that it implies the possibility that, within limits, complex sets of interrelated features will be learned more readily than isolated feature co-occurrences. In general, this should be the case so long as the features are correlated with one another in a statistical sense. Learning a rule of the form "if p, then q" should be facilitated when both p and q co-occur with r more frequently than not. A focus, early in learning, on any of the relations p-q, p-r, or q-r would facilitate ultimate learning of the p-q relation. Once any feature is found to be predictive of any other, this can be used as the "entering wedge" into the set of interrelationships. Sampling of possible features to encode as the basis for rule construction therefore will not be random. In chapter 6 we show how this inductive mechanism of "focused sampling" (Billman 1983) can result in rapid learning of a set of interrelationships.

1.2.4 Default Hierarchies and Virtual Copies

The rules that constitute a category do not provide a *definition* of the category. Instead they provide a set of expectations that are taken to be true only so long as they are not contradicted by more specific information. In the absence of additional information these "default" expectations provide the best available sketch of the current situation (Minsky 1975).

Rules and rule clusters can be organized into *default hierarchies*, that is, hierarchies ordered by default expectations based on subordinate/superordinate relations among concepts. For example, knowing that something is an animal produces certain default expectations about it, but these can be overridden by more specific expectations produced by evidence that the animal is a bird. These expectations, in turn, may be overridden by still more specific expectations, such as evidence that the bird is a penguin. Categorizing something as a penguin provides a network of expectations deriving from that categorization as well as from the knowledge that penguins are birds and birds are animals, generating what Fahlman (1979) calls a "virtual copy" of the entity.

A set of rules or pointers can be used to establish synchronic relations between categories. By virtue of these connections an object linked to one category is implicitly linked to a network of categories. In Fahlman's simulation of memory, called NETL, pointers connect nodes representing the object "Clyde" and the category "elephant", which is in turn connected to "mammal". Moreover, the hierarchy is "tangled" by linking "elephant" with such categories as "herbivore": a node can have direct links to multiple superordinates. To activate the virtual copy for "Clyde", NETL propagates markers from "Clyde" over the pointers to all nodes linked to "Clyde". The term "virtual" refers to the computer scientist's distinction among three types of memory—"working memory" (information currently active in the information buffer), "long-term memory" (stored information requiring special procedures to access), and "virtual memory" (the sum of information in working memory and a portion of long-term memory that is "marked" for ready access without special information-retrieval commands). Like virtual memory, the virtual copy of "Clyde" consists of information not explicitly stored at that node but nevertheless marked for ready access.

A virtual copy amounts to an augmented default-based representation of "Clyde"—a cluster of assumptions used unless more specific information contradicts some part of it. Rather than relying on a single monolithic category to describe an object or situation, a virtual copy uses a combination of properties and relations. The system thus avoids the computationally overwhelming problem of having a node for each complex of properties, such as "George's nephew's grandmother" or "a red Saab with a flat tire". By assembling elementary parts as needed, rather than relying on anticipation of the situation by the provision of some preformed condition, the system sets combinatorics to work *for* it, rather than against it.

Fahlman's NETL is designed primarily to supply declarative information in response to queries. It does not translate information into action, nor does it learn by induction from experience. Problem solving and induction, we will claim, require the system to take a much more active role in its environment. In chapter 2 we describe how to work with default hierarchies and virtual copies in more procedurally oriented rule-based systems, and in chapter 3 we discuss the inductive generation of such structures. Many kinds of problem solving and inductive inference will be seen to depend on the judicious use of information stored in such hierarchies.

1.2.5 *Variability and Uncertainty*
Inherent in the notion of a default hierarchy is a representation of the uncertainty that exists for any system that operates in a world having a realistic degree of complexity. In general, birds fly—but only in general. In general, mammals do not fly—but only in general. Default hierarchies are a way of representing, at one level, the useful generalizations that may be drawn upon for modeling the world, and, at a lower level, those that may be drawn upon for representing crucial exceptions to those generalizations. (In appendix B to chapter 2 we justify the use of rule systems of the generalization-plus-exception type in preference to the more exhaustive, exceptionless type on the grounds of representational and computational parsimony.)

Default hierarchies are capable of representing both the uniformities and the variability that exist in the environment. This representation serves to guide the kinds of inductive change that systems are allowed to make in the face of unexpected events. To make these points clear, we will present two examples of the way people might make inferences in the face of uncertainty.

Let us suppose you are a visitor to a remote island in the Southeast Pacific. You see a bird that your informant calls a "shreeble", and it is blue. Chances are you assume that shreebles are blue. Now suppose you see a native of the island whom your informant calls a "Barrato", and he is obese. It is unlikely that you assume that Barratos are obese. Why the difference? As Mill put it, "Why is a single instance, in some cases, sufficient for a complete induction, while in others myriads of concurring instances, without a single exception known or presumed, go such a very little way towards establishing a universal proposition?" (1843/1974, p. 314).

The answer we suggest is that people store, or can readily construct, information about the variability of the kind of object in question with respect to the kind of property in question. The number of instances required before we make a generalization of a given strength is a function of such variability representations. An efficient way of representing variability is by default hierarchies. Where there are few exception levels beneath the level representing, for example, birds of various kinds together with values for their color, a generalization based on only a few cases will be automatic. Where there are many exceptions at lower levels, generalizations will be tentative and weak.

Our second example is more complex. It shows how information about variability may trigger (or fail to trigger) inductive inferences, and it shows how expectations about the probabilities of a given event are different at different levels of categorization in a default hierarchy. In our shreeble example above, the dominant levels of the relevant default hierarchies—"bird" and "tribesman"—are intuitively obvious, but this is not always the case. When there exist alternative plausible categorizations of events, these may give rise to different assumptions about variability. The converse is also true—different degrees of observed variability in the events may give rise to different categorizations of the events.

Recall the mother of the four-year-old who has been acting up lately. If the child often has periods when he acts up a lot, there will be no trigger to infer anything at all. Reggie is just being Reggie. On the other hand, if spells of acting up are relatively rare, there is a problem to be solved. The solution to the problem very much depends on recent distinctive events concerning Reggie and on the level of Mom's default hierarchy that happens to be dominant for her when she thinks about the problem. Suppose Reggie has been notably bored by nursery school of late, or suppose Reggie knows the arrival of a new baby is imminent, or suppose Mom recalls that Reggie has been showing signs of having a cold. Reggie's mom is likely to have rules available to her suggesting that acting up could be the consequence of any of these circumstances. On the other hand, suppose she happens to know that there is a phase called the "fearsome fours". This would increase the likelihood that she will focus on Reggie not as Reggie, with his particular history and circumstances, but as just another four-year-old. Which of these categorizations is chosen is a function of variability information that Reggie's mom has about Reggie, and each of these categorizations implies somewhat different expectations about the probable duration of Reggie's acting-up phase.

Systems therefore exploit information about variability in the environment in reducing their uncertainty about the environment. Default hierarchies of categories provide an effective means of representing variability.

1.3 Overview of a Framework for Induction

We have yet to do more than hint at the theoretical framework we will be presenting. A fuller treatment must await the next three chapters, which describe respectively the kind of performance system we are proposing, the inductive mechanisms that can operate within such a system, and specific computational illustrations. Nonetheless, it will be helpful to identify now the principles that underlie our approach and distinguish it from other frameworks and theories current in cognitive science.

1.3.1 Characteristics of Inductive Systems

Our framework is based on a set of guiding principles concerning the fundamental characteristics of inductive systems. These principles underlie our computational implementations and will be employed in our qualitative explanations of phenomena.

1) General knowledge can be represented by condition-action rules. These rules can vary enormously in the complexity of their conditions and actions, representing features that range from elementary perceptual ones to highly abstract categories. The immediate actions of rules consist of the posting of "messages" internal to the system.

2) Rules can represent both diachronic relations (for instance, between current and expected future states) and synchronic relations (associations and recategorizations of categories), and the two types of rules act together to generate inferences and solutions to problems. Problem solving involves both diachronic search and synchronic recategorization of elements.

3) Higher-order knowledge structures such as categories correspond to implicit or explicit clusters of rules with similar conditions. Larger structures are thus composed of more elementary building blocks. (A

realistic system must have inductive mechanisms for constructing these larger structures, a notion we refer to in chapter 4 as the "principle of inductive adequacy".)

4) Superordinate relations among categories and rules yield an emergent default hierarchy. Exceptional information about specific examples will tend to override default rules, with the consequence that imperfect default rules will be protected from disconfirmation by rules concerning exceptions.

5) A set of synchronic and diachronic rules, organized in a default hierarchy, gives rise to an emergent mental model. The mental model guides behavior and serves to generate the predictions that serve as the basis for inductive change.

6) Rules act in accord with a principle of limited parallelism. Those rules with their conditions satisfied by current messages compete to represent the current state of affairs and to guide thinking and action. But in addition to competing with each other, multiple rules will often act simultaneously to complement and support each other. Through summation of converging evidence, the system can use multiple sources of weak support to arrive at a confident conclusion.

7) Induction involves two basic classes of mechanisms: (a) mechanisms for revising parameters such as the strength of existing rules and (b) mechanisms for generating plausibly useful new rules.

8) Mechanisms for generating new rules are constrained by triggering conditions that tend to ensure that new rules are likely to be useful to the system. Most particularly, inductions are triggered in response to the consequences of the use of current knowledge, such as failed or successful predictions.

9) Induction is guided by background knowledge about the variability of classes of objects and events. It follows that a major goal of inductive systems is to learn about the variability of the environment.

In later chapters we will show how these principles constitute a framework for developing detailed processing systems and for explaining many empirical phenomena.

1.3.2 *Comparison with Alternative Approaches*

New ideas arise from recombination of the old. In the course of this book we will attempt to give substance to this piece of conventional wisdom by describing how such recombination takes place, when it takes place, what is recombined, and what is created. Our framework itself, of course, is the product of inductive mechanisms; our goal, one might say, is a theory that can account for its own origin. It should be apparent already, and will become more so as we proceed, that our framework has many ties to earlier theories of cognition. We have already sketched relationships between our proposal and notions of rules, mental models, schemas, and default hierarchies, each of which has been discussed extensively in the cognitive science literature. What is it that we believe is novel about the ideas we will be presenting?

The answer, as the reader might expect, lies in the integrative recombination of theoretical concepts. The pieces required to understand induction have lain close at hand, but certain critical relationships among these pieces have been missing. Default hierarchies have been discussed, but typically without reference to induction. Schemas and mental models have also been developed as theoretical concepts, but not as structures that emerge from combinations of rules. Rule-based systems have been in existence for almost two decades, but have generally been used for serial reasoning rather than for exploring the possibilities of parallel competition and collaboration among rules. The variability of the environment customarily has been viewed as an unfortunate pitfall for cognitive systems, rather than as a source of information to guide intelligent adaptation.

We will add more to these claims in chapter 2. There we will present a formal analysis of mental models in terms of an extension of the mathematical concept of a *morphism*. We will also show that such structures can be given a procedural representation in terms of a system of synchronic and diachronic rules that constitutes an elaborated default hierarchy. We will argue that rule-based mental models can provide both the representations used in problem solving and the basis for inductive change. The resulting synthesis, we believe, constitutes a novel set of relations among important theoretical constructs and provides a basis for understanding mechanisms of adaptation.

In order to locate our framework with respect to alternatives, it may be useful to contrast our approach briefly with two major theoretical points of view that are currently at the leading edge of cognitive theory. These are production systems and connectionist networks.

Contrast with Standard Production Systems

In their performance aspects the systems that fall within our framework have most in common with standard production systems, which are also based on the cyclic matching and execution of condition-action rules (Newell 1973; Anderson 1976, 1983). These production systems, however, allow only one rule to fire each cycle, a restriction that places severe strains on both problem solving and induction. An important part of our framework is the use of parallelism in the form of firing of multiple rules (compare Holland and Reitman 1978; Holland 1986; Rosenbloom and Newell 1986; Thibadeau, Just, and Carpenter 1982).

The restriction to firing only one rule tends to lead to sets of rules in which it is necessary to have a single rule available to handle any conceivable step in a problem situation. This in turn creates problems in dealing with novel situations that do not match any useful rule. Suppose, for example, the system contains the rule "If the goal is to identify an animal, and it barks and wags its tail, then declare it is a dog"; and suppose that an animal is heard to bark, although its tail is unseen. This observation would fail to match the rule, and unless some alternative rule is available the observation would be left unidentified.

Intuitively, however, the system ought at least to generate a conjecture: the animal *might* be a dog. To capture this intuition, partial matching is sometimes allowed (Anderson 1983): a rule may sometimes fire when only *some* of its conditions are matched. This appears to produce the intuitive result for the above example. However, allowing rules to fire when only some of their conditions are matched can have treacherous consequences. Suppose the system has the rule "If the goal is to cross a body of water, and it is about a mile wide, and you are a strong swimmer, then decide to swim across." Now imagine that our system, a lamentably weak swimmer, wants to cross a mile-wide lake. A partial match will be found, syntactically identical to that in the "animal" example (two of three conditions in the most relevant rule are satisfied). The result, sad to say, is a dramatic decrease in our system's life expectancy.

The problems created by partial matching can be avoided in a system with greater parallelism. Where there are somewhat useful general rules, such as "If an animal barks, then it is a dog," these can coexist with more valid specific rules, such as "If an animal barks and wags its tail, then it is a dog." Performance will be dominated by the more specific rule (perhaps with support from the more general rule) when the specific rule is matched; but the general rule will provide *some* information even when the specific rule does not apply. General rules will only be maintained if they are useful, however. A rule such as "If you want to cross a wide body of water, then swim across," which fails to specify a critical prerequisite for the suggested action (the ability to swim), would be weeded out by inductive mechanisms (preferably using "lookahead" rather than an overt test!). In general, novel situations can be accommodated by maintaining useful but fallible general rules (that is, rules with few conditions), as well as by providing the system with procedures for finding and using analogies, without having to resort to partial matching.

Another criticism that has been directed at standard production systems is that they treat intelligence primarily in terms of quasi-linguistic representations and inference processes akin to those associated with conscious thinking (for example, Newell and Simon 1972; Anderson 1983). Hofstadter (1985, chap. 26) has distinguished between "cognitive" and "subcognitive" approaches to the understanding of intelligence. Subcognitive approaches assume highly parallel processing of small units of information, taking place below the level of conscious awareness. Many theorists have argued that a great deal of mental processing, underlying activities ranging from early visual pattern recognition to more abstract categorization and hypothesis-generation tasks, takes place at the subcognitive level. Standard production systems, because of their seriality and their use of abstract linguistic categories in the conditions of rules, do not appear to offer a description of subcognitive processing. Needed instead are more flexible systems in which categories can emerge through inductive mechanisms without being built in by the programmer.

Contrast with Connectionist Models
A desire to represent subcognitive processes, together with considerations of neurophysiological plausibility, has fueled recent interest in "connectionist" representation schemes. Connectionist models describe mental processes in terms of activation patterns defined over nodes in a highly interconnected network (Hinton and Anderson 1981; Rumelhart, McClelland, and the PDP Research Group 1986). The nodes themselves are elementary units that do not directly map onto meaningful concepts. Information is conveyed not by particular individual units but by the statistical properties of patterns of activity over collections of units. An individual unit typically will play a role in the representation of multiple pieces of knowledge. The representation of knowledge is thus parallel and distributed over multiple units.

In a connectionist model the role of a unit in mental processing is defined by the *strength* of its connections—both excitatory and inhibitory—to other units. In this sense "the knowledge is in the connections," as connectionist theorists like to put it, rather than in static and monolithic representations of concepts. Learning, viewed within this framework, consists of the revision of connection strengths between units.

As has been the case for production systems, connectionist models are currently proliferating, and it would be premature to strictly delimit the principles embodied in connectionist schemes or to attempt to decide their eventual status relative to production systems. Connectionist models clearly have a very different flavor from prototypical production systems, and in many respects this flavor is quite consistent with the rule-based framework we are proposing. We share with connectionist models such general principles as integration of multiple sources of evidence, revision of strength parameters on the basis of feedback derived from performance, and emergence of higher-order structures from more elementary components. We assume rules can have inhibitory effects akin to the inhibitory connections postulated in network models such as those of McClelland and Rumelhart (1981).

Our framework differs from connectionism, however, in several important respects. As will be seen in chapter 3, our rule-based system has two fundamental inductive processes at its disposal: revision of the strengths of existing rules and generation of new rules. In contrast, current connectionist models learn exclusively from revision of connection strengths between elementary units. The models exhibit a property that might be termed "topological nativism": it is assumed that the entire network of potential connections between units is part of the cognitive system's neural hardware. Many of these connections may simply be latent, with zero strength; nonetheless, all learning consists of revision of the strengths of existing connections rather than the building of new ones.

This is not to say that connectionist models do not learn the equivalent of new rules; they can indeed accomplish this task by strength-revision procedures that establish new stable patterns of activation over *sets* of units. The implicit generation of a new "rule" is thus treated as the outcome of revising the strengths of a large set of innate connections. In contrast, our framework treats rule generation more as a "quantum" knowledge change than as incremental strength revision. Basic inductive mechanisms such as generalization (chapter 3) are capable of linking previously unconnected elements in a new rule that may immediately produce radical behavioral changes. We will argue in chapter 5 that even if we consider what might appear to be a rather primitive form of inductive learning—Pavlovian avoidance conditioning in rats—we can find evidence readily interpretable in terms of explicit rule generation.

The capacity to generate new rules creates the possibility that new elements representing higher-order features may be added to a system by inductive mechanisms. Such higher-order elements may be crucial in planning and sequential problem solving. Rule-based systems can provide natural descriptions of sequential behavior, whereas some connectionist models (in particular, Boltzmann machines with entirely symmetric connections) are unable to account for sequences (Ackley, Hinton, and Sejnowski 1985). More generally, we find the language of rules to be simply more convenient for describing the enormous range of inductive tasks, from classical conditioning to scientific discovery, that are performed by cognitive systems. Thus, despite our sympathy for many of the ideas that have motivated the development of connectionist models, our approach explores a different path.

1.3.3 Overview of the Book

The next two chapters fill in the framework we have sketched here. Chapter 2 provides an account of problem solving and induction in terms of mental models. There we discuss how mental models can be realized in rule-based systems. Chapter 3 provides a taxonomy of inductive procedures and shows how these can operate in a rule-based system. Chapter 4 describes how processing systems of the sort our framework implies can be constructed. We present two particular systems (more precisely, a class of systems based on classifiers, and the program PI) that have the desired modeling properties, and we describe running programs based on them. Readers more interested in discussion of empirical phenomena than in the development of computational apparatus may wish to read selectively in chapter 4.

Chapters 5–10 treat a wide range of empirical phenomena concerning inferences and learning by animals and humans. In chapter 5 we examine simple diachronic rule learning and covariation detection in humans and animals; we present a theory of conditioning based on the induction of simple default hierarchies of diachronic rules. In chapter 6 we examine category induction and synchronic rule clustering. Chapter 7 shows how people learn to model the physical and social worlds in terms of complex rule systems and default hierarchies. Chapter 8 describes several important types of knowledge that guide generalization, and chapter 9 discusses how abstract inferential rules are used and how they can be modified. In chapter 10 we describe the role of analogy in problem solving and learning. Chapter 11 shows how the discovery and use of scientific theories can be understood within the theoretical framework developed in this book. Finally, chapter 12 outlines the formal, computational, and experimental developments required for a full theory of induction.

Rule-Based Mental Models

In our framework a cognitive system represents the world with which it interacts using mental models, constructed from rules and organized into default hierarchies. In assembling a model of the current situation (often, in fact, a range of models, which are allowed to compete for the right to represent the environment), the system combines existing rules—which are themselves composed of categories and the relations that weld the categories into a structure providing associations and predictions. The assembly of a model, then, is just the simultaneous activation of a relevant set of rules. The categories are specified by the condition parts of the rules; the (synchronic) associations and predictive (diachronic) relations are specified by the action parts of the rules. The set of rules activated is the counterpart of Fahlman's virtual copy, and the activation of additional rules by rules already active is the counterpart of his propagation of markers.

The model assembled is much more complex than a default hierarchy. Any given category used by the model is likely to be a subcategory of several other activated categories, while also being a superodinate category subsuming still other activated categories. Moreover, this tangled hierarchy amounts to only the skeleton of the model. Active categories in the skeleton can activate other categories that flesh out the skeleton with associations and predictions.

The first section of this chapter provides a more rigorous characterization of mental models. The subsequent sections develop this view of the processing system, showing how models can be constructed from rules, how rules compete for the right to represent the environment, and how rules can support one another in providing a robust and coherent model of the environment.

2.1 Mental Models as Morphisms

A useful general definition of mental models must capture several features inherent in our informal descriptions. First, a model must make it possible for the system to generate predictions even though knowledge of the environment is incomplete. Second, it must be easy to refine the model as additional information is acquired without losing useful information already incorporated. Finally, the model must not make requirements on the cognitive system's processing capabilities that are infeasible computationally. In order to be parsimonious, it must make extensive use of categorization, dividing the environment up into equivalence classes. In this section we will describe a variant of the mathematical structures called *morphisms* that will provide us with a formal definition that can meet these requirements.

2.1.1 Representing the Environment

Because a mental model is the cognitive system's representation of some portion of the environment, and because the relation between the model and the environment is critical to understanding the model's role in the cognitive system, our first step must be a more precise treatment of the environment. The environment can in principle be described by a set of *states* and a *transition function* (or "next-state" function) that specifies how the states can change over time. Formally, let S be the set of states of the environment, let O be the set of outputs of the cognitive system that act upon the environment, and let T be the transition function of the environment. For the sake of technical simplicity we will treat time as moving forward in discrete units. Then according to our definitions the state of the environment at time $t + 1$, $S(t + 1)$, is given by $T[S(t), O(t)]$, where $O(t)$ is the output of the cognitive system at time t and $S(t)$ is the state of the environment at time t.

Depending on the context, the "environment" may be defined in very local terms (for instance, a chess board, pieces, and players) or as the whole of the universe, including the cognitive system itself. In many cases the environment will in fact proceed autonomously, undisturbed by actions of the cognitive system. In other words, the next state $S(t + 1)$ may be the same regardless of $O(t)$. For example, the total actions of humanity have yet to divert the evolutionary course of the star Sirius. Also note that although the transition function is defined in principle for all combinations of states and outputs, it may be unknown to either the cognitive system or outside observers. As we

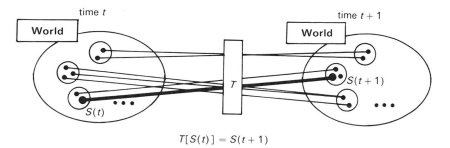

$$T[S(t)] = S(t+1)$$

Figure 2.1

Transition function. For example: T, a transition function that includes the law that fast-moving objects slow down (because of friction, say); $S(t)$, an equivalence class of objects that are "fast-moving" and satisfy the law "fast-moving" → "slow-moving"; $S(t+1)$, the same class of objects, now "slow-moving."

will see, learning a representation of the transition function is the critical goal in the construction of a mental model.

Figure 2.1 provides a simple illustration of a transition function across a single time-step. The elements in the set labeled $S(t)$ correspond to "fast-moving objects"; at time $t+1$ these elements enter the state corresponding to "slow-moving objects", in accord with a transition function T that includes the law that all fast-moving objects slow down. In this example and those that follow we assume for simplicity that the transition function is independent of any outputs from the cognitive system.

2.1.2 Levels of Approximation

Homomorphisms

Given the complexity of realistic environments and the limitations of realistic cognitive systems, it is unreasonable to expect mental models to be isomorphisms in which each unique state of the world maps onto a unique state in the model. In figure 2.1, for example, the world was divided into simple *categories* of elements, such as "slow-moving objects". In general, the cognitive system will attempt to construct various simplified models adequate for achieving certain goals. This can be accomplished by aggregating environmental states and system outputs into useful categories and ignoring details irrelevant to the purposes of the model. A faithful model based on categories, in which the mapping from elements of the world to elements of the mental model is many-to-one, is called a *homomorphism*.

Figure 2.2 illustrates a simple categorization process that provides a step toward a mental model. Simple detectors, d_1, d_2, d_3, which take

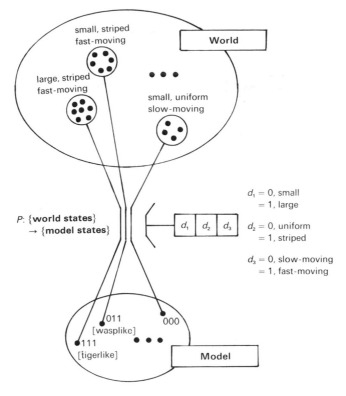

Figure 2.2
Equivalence classes induced by detectors.

on binary values, encode *properties* of states of the world. A categorization function P, defined in terms of the detected properties, maps sets of world states into a smaller number of model states. For example, all world states involving objects that are "small", "striped", and "fast-moving" (that is, "wasplike") are mapped onto a single state in the model. Thus the detectors divide the world up into equivalence classes, treating objects that the detectors do not discriminate among as equivalent.

The next step in describing a mental model is to introduce a *model transition function*, T', which is intended to mimic the transition function T operating in the world. The function T' of the model will then describe the manner in which *categories* of environmental states, coupled with *categories* of actions, lead to *categories* of subsequent states. The resulting homomorphic model is illustrated in figure 2.3. It represents the simple world transition function T of figure 2.1, as well as a categorization function P_1 that is identical to P in figure 2.2. To this structure has been added a model transition function T'_1, which takes

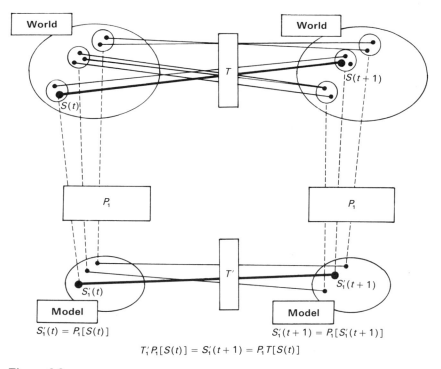

$$S_1'(t) = P_1[S(t)] \qquad\qquad S_1'(t+1) = P_1[S_1'(t+1)]$$

$$T_1' P_1[S(t)] = S_1'(t+1) = P_1 T[S(t)]$$

Figure 2.3
Homomorphism. Commutativity of the diagram $T_1' P_1 = P_1 T$ guarantees that the model can make valid predictions about the equivalence classes. For example: $S_1'(t)$, a state of the model that corresponds to all "fast-moving" objects of the world; $S_1'(t+1)$, a state of the model that corresponds to all "slow-moving" objects of the world; T_1', the model transition function, "predicts" that all "fast-moving" objects become "slow-moving" (in one time-step).

states of the model at time t, $S'(t)$, into states of the model at time $t+1$, $S'(t+1)$. As in figure 2.1, figure 2.3 illustrates a situation in which all fast-moving objects slow down, a regularity that the model captures by virtue of the categorization function P_1 and the model transition function T_1'.

A model may or may not be a valid description of the environment. A valid model, which constitutes a homomorphism, implies *commutativity of the diagram*: carrying out a transition in the environment and then determining the equivalence class of the resulting state will have the same outcome as determining the equivalence class of the initial environmental state and then carrying out the transition in the model. Specifically,

$$P[T(S(t), O(t))] = T'[P(S(t)), P(O(t))].$$

The model depicted in figure 2.3 will be valid only if all fast-moving objects in fact slow down.

Q-Morphisms

In practice, however, a model of a complex environment will typically prove to be less than completely valid. Such a situation is depicted in figure 2.4. Here the world behaves just as in the earlier illustrations, except that one element of the category of "fast-moving objects" violates the expectation that fast-moving objects will invariably slow down. Continuing the previous example, some fast-moving objects ("wasps") may not slow down in most circumstances. The level 1 model makes erroneous predictions with respect to these objects because it does not distinguish them from other members of the equivalence class.

Level 2 of the model, depicted in figure 2.4, corrects for these exceptions. We can think of the mapping P_2 as based upon additional properties that enable a distinction to be made between wasps and other objects. For example, an additional detector d_4 might encode the property "airborne", allowing P_2 to define the more specific category of "small, striped, fast-moving, airborne objects". Once this new category is available in the elaborated model, the model transition function can also be refined by the addition of T_2', which indicates that small, striped, fast-moving, airborne objects continue to move quickly, rather than slowing down.

The model depicted in figure 2.4 is a layered set of transition functions, which we will term a *quasi-homomorphism*, or simply *q-morphism*. In a q-morphism a higher layer in the model, with its broader categories, provides default expectations (such as, fast-moving objects slow down) that will be used to make predictions unless some exceptional category is signaled. An exception evokes a lower level of the model, at which a different model transition function is specified to capture the exception. The relations between level 1 and level 2 of the model in figure 2.4 can be generalized to more complex multilayered q-morphisms (see appendix 2A). For example, the level 2 model will itself admit of exceptions (striped marbles thrown through the air slow down).

2.1.3 Q-Morphisms and Induction

The process of model construction can be viewed as the progressive refinement of a q-morphism. The initial layer of the model will divide

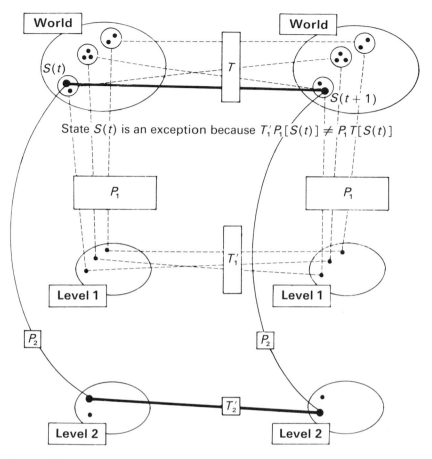

Figure 2.4

Q-morphism (defaults only). P_2 is chosen to distinguish S from other members of the equivalence class induced by P_1. Then T_2' is chosen to map the image of S under P_2 into the image of $T[S]$ under P_2. Under this arrangement the elements of level 1 serve as defaults, to be used unless the exception is detected, at which point level 2 is invoked. For example: The level 2 element might be "small, striped, fast-moving, airborne" (e.g., a "wasp") that remains "fast-moving" (i.e., it continues flying), thus contradicting rule T_1', which predicts a slowdown. T_2' compensates for this exception by predicting no slowdown in the specific case of "small, striped, fast-moving, airborne" objects.

the world into broad categories that allow approximate predictions with many exceptions. Each additional layer in the hierarchy will accommodate additional exceptions while preserving the more global regularities as default expectations. The induction process will be guided by failures of the current model. As suggested by two examples of inferential rules in table 2.1 (see section 2.2.1), failed expectations will serve as triggering conditions for the generation of new, more specialized rules. In a complex environment the process of model refinement by the cognitive system is unlikely ever to be completed. New exceptions to the current model will always be possible.

The concept of a q-morphism captures several basic aspects of a pragmatic account of the performance of cognitive systems. First, its hierarchical structure allows the system to make approximate predictions on the basis of incomplete knowledge of the environment. Second, as the model is refined, rules that represent useful probabilistic regularities can be retained as defaults. Appendix 2B demonstrates that a hierarchy of default rules with exceptions can represent knowledge more concisely (that is, with fewer total rules) than a system restricted to "exceptionless" rules.

The representation of events and event sequences at different levels of a default hierarchy is the most basic way for a system to deal with variability within a class of events. Events are treated as equivalent unless there are features—or a failed expectation—suggesting further differentiation. Thus one treats a male employee in a restaurant as a waiter unless there are signs suggesting that he is the host, the wine steward, or the busboy. For some purposes one's behavior toward persons occupying any of these roles is the same, but for many purposes the appropriate behavior is quite different. Many an adolescent embarrassment has resulted from failure to specialize the "waiter" default values.

The addition of a further layer to a default hierarchy always increases the complexity of the overall model. The justification for an addition is inherently statistical: Does the augmented model account for additional variance in the environment commensurate with the extra "degrees of freedom" required? Model construction is guided by two opposing pressures. The need for more accurate prediction favors the addition of further specialized rules, whereas the need for efficient prediction favors the addition of general rules to replace a larger number of specialized rules. As a result, the construction of a q-morphism involves generalization as well as specialization.

The usefulness of a q-morphism, it should be noted, must be defined relative to the alternatives available. If a rival model based on radically different categories (that is, a different mapping function P) is less complex and makes a broader range of predictions, the less effective model will likely be abandoned. But in the absence of such a rival even a feeble q-morphism will be preferred to no model at all.

In general, three broad classes of responses to failures of a model can be distinguished. The appropriateness of each type of response will vary with the amount of experience embodied in the failed part of the model. The first possibility is that the current model is radically invalid with respect to the portion of the environment that it is intended to predict. In this situation, which is obviously most likely to arise early in learning, failures of prediction are less the exception than the norm. The cognitive system will have little or no confidence in either its current categorization function P or its model transition function T', and the most appropriate response is to attempt to recategorize the environment (that is, find a new mapping P) and then build a new transition function.

A second possibility—and the one we will discuss most frequently —is that the exceptional states are truly exceptional. That is, the current model makes accurate predictions in many circumstances but fails in some. The most appropriate response is to preserve the current categories in the model, but with specific modifications to accommodate the states that constitute systematic exceptions to the current transition function. In particular, exceptions can be accommodated by creating a more specific category that encompasses them (that is, a refinement of the mapping P), together with a corresponding specialization of the transition function. This is the case that leads to elaboration of a q-morphism, as illustrated in figure 2.4.

The third possibility, which will characterize a relatively late stage of learning, is that it will prove increasingly difficult to construct more specific categories that predict the transition function for exceptional states more successfully than the current categories do. Although the model sometimes makes erroneous predictions, the errors are apparently unsystematic. In this situation the cognitive system may accept a probabilistic transition function. The behavior of the environment, at least relative to the discriminative capacity of the cognitive system, may have an irreducible degree of inherent variability (in statistical terms, "error variance"). In this case the most appropriate inductive response is simply to estimate the degree of uncertainty associated with the model transition function T'.

We should emphasize that in the actual operation of an inductive system the above types of responses to failures of prediction need be neither mutually exclusive nor strictly serial. At any time the system will have differential knowledge of the various aspects of the environment and hence may respond in different ways to various predictive failures.

The success of a q-morphic model is fundamentally limited by the categories available for *encoding* the environment. In our earlier example, until a category that picks out wasps has been generated in the model, it is impossible to define an adequate model transition function. The categories in the model are in turn dependent on the detectors that encode properties of the world. Without a set of detectors adequate for encoding the property "airborne", for example, other categories cannot be differentiated with respect to that property. As new properties are encoded and new categories become available, the predictive power of the model has the potential to increase.

The q-morphism notion helps to lay the groundwork for our claim in chapter 7 that people's beliefs about the laws underlying both physical and social events are often drastically wrong in an empirical sense. The rules that people induce for events are always local ones to some degree. They are learned in the context of people's attempts to develop q-morphisms for aspects of the world that are important to them and to which they are exposed with some frequency. These local contexts may be quite parochial with respect to the broader context that a scientist might examine. Thus people's rules for mechanical events are developed in a world characterized by virtually ubiquitous friction. This results in their inducing laws of motion that constitute a good q-morphism of a world with friction but that are quite mistaken in a scientific sense; they can be shown to produce errors for unfamiliar aspects of the world people actually inhabit.

The q-morphism notion is also useful in helping us to understand one kind of *incoherence*. People are not trying to develop coherent views of the world any more than they are trying to develop scientifically accurate theories. They are merely attempting to generate accurate predictions for whatever portion of the world they are focusing on at the moment. Thus their beliefs at some higher level of a default hierarchy may be quite inconsistent with their beliefs at some lower level of the hierarchy. We will see examples of this kind of incoherence in chapter 7, where we will find that people can adhere to general laws of motion that are quite incompatible with the laws of motion they endorse at one or another lower level of specificity. Consistency is no hobgoblin for the q-morphic mind.

A further use of the q-morphism concept should be noted here. Inferential mechanisms often make use of *analogy*, as we will illustrate for simple cases later in this chapter. In chapter 10 we will see that the use of analogy in problem solving and induction can be understood using the same theoretical machinery required to describe model construction in general. In essence, an analogy is a kind of second-order q-morphism, where a mental model of one domain is used to generate a mental model of another.

2.1.4 Mental Models and Problem Solving

As we have seen, a model typically preserves only some aspects of the world. What defines the appropriate degree of preservation? The answer is fundamentally pragmatic, and it highlights the link between mental models and problem solving. From the point of view of the cognitive system, relatively few environmental states have direct value to the system. The values of other states in relation to satisfaction of the system's goals must be inferred. The fundamental use of induction is to generate models of the environment that the cognitive system can use in selecting actions that will lead to environmental states with positive value. The cognitive system attempts to plan a sequence of actions that will transform the initial problematic state into a goal-satisfying state. An adequate mental model can accomplish this task by mimicking the environment up to an acceptable level of approximation. The model need only describe aspects of the environment and of the system's actions that are relevant to the attainment of goal-satisfying states.

Figure 2.5 schematizes a problem model viewed as a homomorphism. The top of the diagram, labeled "World", depicts transitions between environmental states. S_I is the problematic initial state, S_G is the state (or states) that would satisfy the goal, and $T(S(t), O(t))$ is the transition function allowing potential *sequences* of state changes that (if the problem is solvable) could transform S_I into S_G. The bottom of the diagram, labeled "Internal model", depicts corresponding elements of the problem solver's mental model of the world. As in earlier figures, the categorization function P relates elements of the world to elements of the model; in effect, P subsumes the features to which the model attends in describing the situation. S_I' corresponds to the problematic initial state. S_G' is the goal description, and $T'(S't)$, $O'(t))$ is the transition function for the model. In the context of a problem model, O' will be the set of types of operators (effector actions) relevant to goal attainment that are available to the cognitive system. In addition to mapping environmental states into representations of state categories, P will map outputs of the cognitive system into representations of categories of operators.

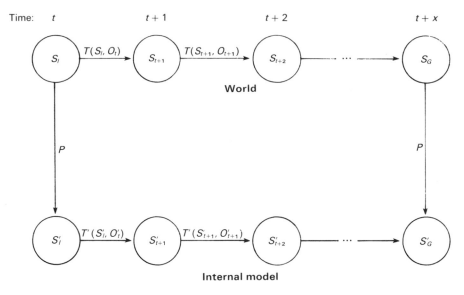

Figure 2.5
A problem model as a homomorphism.

A problem model is valid only if (1) given a model-state S_I' that corresponds to an initial (problem-specifying) state S_I, and (2) given a model-state S_G' that corresponds to a goal state S_G in the environment, then (3) any sequence of actions (operator categories) in the model, $\{O'(1), O'(2), \ldots O'(n)\}$, which transforms S_I' into S_G' in the model, describes a sequence of effector actions that will attain the goal S_G in the environment. An "ideal" problem model thus is one that describes all those elements of the world necessary and sufficient for the concrete realization of a successful solution plan. The process of induction is directed by the goal of generating mental models that increasingly approximate this ideal.

2.2 Mental Models as Rule Systems

Our abstract characterization of modeling via q-morphisms does not in itself indicate what information-processing mechanisms might be used. In this section we describe how different kinds of rules are suitable for representing q-morphisms and hence for modeling the environment. Then in the remainder of the chapter we will describe the operation of processing systems based on rules.

2.2.1 *Rules and Operating Principles*

In our rule-oriented framework the representation of the environment is formed and altered by the application of condition-action rules, which have the general form, IF (condition 1, condition 2, ... condition *n*), THEN (action). Satisfaction of the conditions depends on *matches* between the conditions and active information in memory. "Active" information, in contrast to "stored" information, is declarative knowledge currently being processed by the system. We do not assume that the information is necessarily linguistic or propositional in nature.

Active information may come directly from perceptual input, from other rules, or from a memory store containing declarative knowledge. For convenience and uniformity we can think of all such information as being in the form of *messages* (which collectively comprise a *message list*) sent from various parts of the system (the input interface, the rule processor, declarative memory, and so on) to the rule processor. The actions of matched rules determine what the system will *do*; that is, the rules incorporate procedural information. The actions of rules can include not only outward-directed actions (actions of the cognitive system on its environment) but also inward-directed actions (modifications of the system's store of knowledge).

The three major types of procedural knowledge that we focus on are *empirical rules*, *inferential rules*, and *system operating principles*. Empirical rules are the "bread and butter" performance rules of the system. They describe the environment and its likely next states. Inferential rules provide relatively domain-independent procedures for altering the general knowledge base. Operating principles are innate system-manipulation procedures that are immutable except (possibly) for the fine-tuning of parameters. Although not actually rules, they function much like inferential rules, serving both performance functions (for example, running the "bidding" system by which rules compete, as described in section 2.3) and knowledge modification functions (for example, the operation of the "bucket brigade" mechanism described in chapter 3, which apportions credit to empirical and inferential rules that operate early in a problem-solving sequence). We will now describe each of these procedural types in more detail.

Empirical Rules

Table 2.1 presents several types of empirical rules and informal examples of each. The central distinction between types of empirical rules is based on their relationship to the cognitive system's sense of subjective time. *Synchronic* rules are subjectively atemporal. They

Table 2.1   Examples of empirical rules

A. Synchronic

1. Categorical

    If an object is a dog, then it is an animal.

    If an object is a large slender dog with very long white and gold hair, then it is a collie.

    If an object is a dog, then it can bark.

2. Associative

    If an object is a dog, then activate the "cat" concept.

    If an object is a dog, then activate the "bone" concept.

B. Diachronic

1. Predictor

    If a person annoys a dog, then the dog will growl.

    If a person whistles to a dog, then the dog will come to the person.

2. Effector

    If a dog chases you, then run away.

    If a dog approaches you with its tail wagging, then pet it.

---

provide recategorizations of, and associations to, individuals and categories at a single time, as in the recategorization of an individual known to be a dog as an animal. Synchronic rules represent the kind of information typically represented in a semantic net (Fahlman 1979). They can be further subdivided into *categorical* and *associative* rules. Categorical rules provide information about hierarchical category relations. They provide the basis for determining category membership, for reclassifying concepts, and for assigning properties to them. Property assignments are treated as categorical because they are equivalent to set-membership claims ("a dog can bark" is equivalent to "a dog is included in the category of 'things that can bark'"). In contrast, associative rules relate concepts that have nonhierarchical relations ("dog" is associated with both "cat" and "bone"). Such rules simply allow one concept to remind the system of another concept by activating it in memory. This function is critical to the system's ability to reason by analogy.

In contrast to the atemporal synchronic rules, *diachronic* rules specify the manner in which the environment is expected to change over time, either autonomously or in response to outward-directed actions of the cognitive system. We divide diachronic rules into two classes: *predictor* rules, which tell the system what to expect in the future, and *effector* rules, which cause the system to act on the environment. Some predictor rules constitute explicit statements of problem-solving procedures. These have the general form "If G_D and I and O at time t, then G_D will be achieved at time $t + \Delta$," where G_D is the predicted goal achievement, I is an initial problematic state, O is an operator (that is, an action or procedure). A comparable effector rule would have the form "If G_D and I, then do O."

Inferential Rules

Whereas the function of empirical rules is to model the world, the primary function of inferential rules is to produce better empirical rules. Hence inferential rules are necessarily more abstract than empirical rules, obtaining over a broad range of content domains. Unlike logical rules of inference such as *modus ponens*, however, their domain of application need not be unrestricted; some inferential rules will concern relations, for instance, whereas others underlie reasoning about regulations. Listed below are four types of inferential rules, each with an example.

Specialization Rules

If a prediction based on a strong rule fails, then create a more specialized rule that includes a novel property associated with the failure in its condition and the observed unexpected outcome as its action.

Unusualness Rules

If a situation has an unexpected property, then be prepared to use that property in the condition of a new rule if rule generation is triggered in close proximity to the occurrence of the situation.

Law of Large Numbers Heuristics

If S is a sample providing an estimate of the distribution of property P over some population, then create a rule stating that the entire population has that distribution, with the strength of the rule varying with the size of S.

Regulation Schemas

If you have the rule "If you want to do X, then you must first do Y," then create the rule "If you do not do Y, then you cannot do X."

In chapter 3 we discuss various inferential rules for specialization that resemble the one given above. Unusualness rules play an important role in our treatment both of specialization and of several aspects of conditioning and covariation detection discussed in chapter 5.

The statement of the law of large numbers heuristic is an example of a larger set of rules reminiscent of the statistician's law of large numbers. There are many abstract inferential rules that are derivable from this principle. People can easily use some of these for reasoning about everyday problems, while others are so counterintuitive that even highly trained scientists often seem to honor them chiefly in the breach (Kahneman and Tversky 1973). Following Piaget and Inhelder (1951/1975), we will argue in chapters 8 and 9 that people induce a great many sets of statistical rules from observation of the behavior of randomizing devices. Others are taught by the culture, with the result that the adult has a fairly sophisticated statistical rule system for analyzing manifestly probabilistic events. Only sometimes, however, is this rule system invoked for understanding everyday events that seem partially deterministic and partially uncertain. We will argue that this is because everyday events are often difficult to code in such a way that statistical rules are evoked spontaneously.

The regulation schema given above should not be confused with the logical principle of contraposition, "From (if p then q), infer (if not-q then not-p)," the application of which is much more general. In chapter 9 we will see that more local inferential rules such as regulation schemas are often more central to human thinking than logical principles. We will argue that apparently deductive real-world problems are in fact solved by means of what we call *pragmatic reasoning schemas*: highly general but not purely syntactic rule systems. Regulation schemas describe patterns of normative behavior that bear upon the ways in which people solve problems in everyday life. The "permission schema" used as an example will be suggested by features of a problem indicating that Y is required in order to do X. Because people have habitual experiences of both compliance with and violation of such rules, they have a schema describing possible actions and outcomes when the permission requirement obtains. This schema allows certain inferences to be made reliably and rapidly. The permission schema also has the interesting property that when people reason in accord with it, they avoid violations of the laws of formal logic that are otherwise committed. We will argue in chapter 9 that in general when people reason in accord with the laws of formal logic, they do so not by using such laws but by using inferential schemas with results that happen to coincide with those of formal logic for the problem in question.

Some of our most controversial claims will be those made about inferential rules. The first controversial claim is simply that they exist. A number of theorists hold that there are no such rules. This position is a response to the body of evidence indicating that people are not able to make effective use of deductive rules of the kind that comprise the logic of the conditional when reasoning about abstract symbols (see, for example, a review by Evans 1982). Nevertheless, people do not normally violate the logic of the conditional when reasoning about concrete events. This has led some theorists (D'Andrade 1982; Griggs and Cox 1982) to argue that people do not possess abstract inferential rules at all, but rather reason either by comparing present experiences to memories of previous specific experiences or by employing extremely domain-specific empirical rules. In chapter 9 we will argue strongly against such a position, proposing that people possess a wide variety of abstract, relatively domain-independent inferential rules that comprise pragmatic reasoning schemas. On the other hand, we will argue that some extremely abstract inferential rules, notably those of formal logic, admit of so little application to real-world problems that people do not induce them and in fact cannot easily be taught to use them in pragmatic, everyday contexts.

The contrast between inferential and empirical rules obviously admits of borderline cases. All empirical rules yield predictions concerning useful categorizations of the environment, possible successors to the current situation, or efficacious overt actions. It is quite natural to consider such predictions to be "inferences". As the examples we have given make clear, however, the scope of typical inferential rules is far more general than that of empirical rules. They are relatively independent of specific domains of events; and as we will show later, such rules can sometimes be applied to a domain of events for which the person has never used them before. Nevertheless, there are many rules that can be understood either as empirical or as inferential rules. This is true, for example, of rules such as Piaget's conservation schema that apply over an enormous range of kinds of physical event domains. It is also true of a rule we will rely on in chapters 6 and 8 to explain why people assume that the distributions of perceptual properties and social behavior tend to be unimodal symmetric, that is, approximately normal. In a sense, the rules underlying the unimodal symmetric assumption are empirical, in that they constitute a generalization over an enormous range of content domains. On the other hand, the rules are clearly expressible in inferential form.

Operating Principles

Unlike empirical and inferential rules, operating principles are neither learnable nor teachable. They are the innate system manipulation procedures. Some operating principles are best thought of as serving to "run" the performance system. These include the procedures for calling up the relevant empirical rules for representing the environment; the bidding system by which such rules compete to construct the current representation of reality and to make predictions about future realities; and procedures that initiate action on the environment.

Other operating principles invoke some of the procedures of knowledge alteration. These procedures generate new knowledge structures and evaluate existing ones; examples to be discussed in chapters 3 and 4 include the bucket brigade and genetic algorithms in classifier systems, and the mechanisms for generalization and conceptual combination in the system PI.

2.2.2 Q-Morphisms as Rule Systems

We have described in general terms how collections of rules can constitute mental models of changing environments. Rule-based realizations of q-morphisms depend upon the close relationship between the two types of empirical rules, on the one hand, and the two basic functions required to construct a morphism, on the other. Synchronic empirical rules (more specifically, categorical synchronic rules) constitute building blocks for the categorization function P that relates states of the environment to categories of the model. Diachronic empirical rules (more specifically, predictor diachronic rules) are building blocks for the transition functions T' of the model. Both P and T' can be realized as sets of rules. It is these correspondences that make possible a process-oriented description of q-morphisms.

Before we proceed, let us briefly review the relations among default hierarchies, q-morphisms, virtual copies, and mental models. The "vertical spine" of a q-morphism can be thought of as a default hierarchy, which can be represented by categorical synchronic rules. Three additional types of rules complete the q-morphism: associative synchronic rules suggesting pragmatically important relations, diachronic predictor rules indicating next states of the environment, and diachronic effector rules telling the system what to do if the environment enters a particular state. The set of rules active at a given time corresponds to the set of marked nodes in Fahlman's (1979) NETL— the virtual copy that constitutes NETL's response to a query (that is, environmental input). The virtual copy consists of the panoply of active information NETL brings to bear on the problem. Similarly, by "mental model" we mean the organized set of simultaneously active or activatable rules affording a q-morphism. Such models are more powerful than virtual copies because they furnish expectations about future situations through diachronic rules, and associations to other relevant events through synchronic rules.

A rule-based realization of q-morphisms provides the means by which rules interact to provide synchronic and diachronic relations. In our framework, because rules can only post messages, such interactions must be mediated by messages. Thus, rule R_1 can be in a synchronic or diachronic relation to rule R_2 only if the message posted by R_1 brings about the activation of R_2. Consider, for example, a system in which R_1 is part of a cluster of rules representing the concept "cat", and R_2 represents the concept "pet". Then, in the system, "cat" will invoke "pet" only if R_1 sends a message that activates R_2; in effect, activation is *directed* from R_1 to R_2. More generally, R_1 influences the activation of R_2 only when the message posted by the action part of R_1 satisfies the condition part of R_2. We will say, then, that rule R_1 is *coupled* to rule R_2. The example just given illustrates a synchronic coupling; diachronic couplings are similarly implemented. Chapter 3 exploits this representation to present simple mechanisms for rule refinement and the inductive generation of new relations.

2.3 The Performance of Rule-Based Modeling Systems

We have now set out the ingredients necessary for describing how systems represent the environment, how they act on their representations of the environment, and how they change their representations of the environment. In order to help us think about performance, we view a system as using a *message list* to embody the information produced by the active portion of its model. The message list represents not only the most interesting portions of the environment but also predicted future states and aspects of the system itself, particularly its goals. This message list, representing self, goals, contemporary environmental states, and projected future environmental states, is similar to what the psychologist Kurt Lewin (1935; Cartwright 1951) called the "life space".

In the remainder of this chapter we will describe the performance characteristics of the type of cognitive system that our framework assumes. This description will be at a level more general than that of any particular simulation. More specific examples of modeling systems will be provided in chapters 4 and 5.

2.3.1 Competing to Represent the Environment
The messages on the message list will include the products of the action portions of empirical rules that have recently won the right to represent the environment. How do rules win this right? They do so by prevailing in a competition with one another. Four major factors

determine the outcome of the competition. These are *match, strength, specificity*, and *support*.

A condition in the condition part of rule (the IF part) is *matched* if it fits the current situation, that is, if the salient features of the environment or of some currently internally generated message correspond to the features encoded in the condition. A match is a precondition for entering the competition. Rules that do not have their condition parts matched do not earn the right even to compete. Note that we treat "match" as an all-or-none event rather than as a continuum. As noted in chapter 1, production systems using partial matching have encountered difficulties because too many misleading rules are matched. An appropriate default hierarchy provides the same kind of flexibility as does partial matching, while producing a system that is easier to manipulate and that minimizes selection of misleading rules. The criterion that only rules with fully matched conditions are candidates for firing is a major limitation on the parallelism of the activity of rules.

The mere fact that a rule's condition is matched is not sufficient for it to win the competition, however. Two events that both match the condition portion of a rule may differ enormously in their likelihood. The probability that the small black animal you just saw ducking into the alley is a ferret is extremely low, no matter how slender and humpbacked it appeared to be. The competitive advantage of a rule is thus also dependent on a factor we call its *strength*, which is a numerical measure of how well the rule has performed in the past in representing the environment and its successive states.

A third factor determining the success of a rule in the competition is its *specificity*, which corresponds to the completeness with which it describes the current situation. The rule "If X has wings, then it flies" is less specific than the rule "If X has wings that are small in relation to its body size, then it does not fly." The preference for more specific rules is an essential component of any implementation of a default hierarchy, and the importance of specificity in rule competition is therefore central to our framework. (It also plays an important role in the ACT* system of Anderson 1983.) We will argue in chapters 7 and 8, however, that in many circumstances people have *too* great a preference for specific-level information and that they often override valid and useful information at higher levels of default hierarchies in favor of dubiously valid information at the level of the specific object.

The fourth factor determining the fate of a rule in competition with others is the degree of *support* it receives from other rules. Support is a measure of how well various features of the situation add up to suggest that the rule in question is actually relevant. In general, the likelihood that the system is dealing with a python may be quite low. But as the messages describing the context begin to be suggestive of jungles, vines, and parrots, the python becomes increasingly more plausible. When a very large, very long, and wriggly object finally intrudes, it is therefore much more likely to be categorized as a python than if the previous cues had had to do with concrete, glass, and pavement (in which case what is likely to be perceived is a fire hose).

Thus, competition will favor those rules that (a) provide a description of the current situation (match), (b) have a history of past usefulness to the system (strength), (c) produce the greatest degree of completeness of description (specificity), and (d) have the greatest compatibility with other currently active information (support). Systems consistent with our framework may vary in the manner in which these factors are taken into account. One general procedure uses some factors (such as match) to screen out most rules altogether, and then compares the remaining rules on the basis of each one's *bid*, calculated by combining the other relevant factors into a single numerical quantity. The greater the bid made by a rule, the greater the probability that it is allowed to post its message.

2.3.2 Competition, Support, and Coherence
As should be clear, the kind of system we are describing is extremely parallel, in that many rules are active simultaneously. In addition, some of the active rules are in direct competition with one another. The support component of the bids made by rules is critical in preventing the kind of war of all against all that might otherwise be expected to result.

Because many rules can fire on a given cycle, it is possible that messages favoring radically different interpretations of the environmental situation will be posted. In order to avoid contradictory decisions and disjointed effector actions, the system of rule competition should tend to maintain a coherent representation of the environment, one that avoids disruptive contradictions. Questions of coherence arise, in part, because the information a system receives is usually partial or fragmented. Consider, for example, the mammalian visual system. It receives information in the form of a succession of disjointed, very localized "snapshots", each produced at the end of a saccade. These snapshots must somehow be integrated to form a coherent image of the environment. Or, at a more macroscopic level, objects in a real environment are often partially obscured or blurred (for example, an animal obscured by bushes or a pedestrian obscured by signs). The system must integrate fragments in order to obtain plausible categorizations and associations, determining which hypotheses are best supported by the fragmentary information available.

A system can never have complete information about a situation, so integrating fragmentary information is a pervasive problem that requires more than *ad hoc* solutions. The problem, translated into our rule-based framework, is to find a mechanism whereby rules activated by fragments can support rules that categorize the overall situation. Because rules must compete for activation, support naturally translates into a biasing of alternatives. We use the bidding procedure as the basis for this biasing. The support for a given rule increases in proportion to the bids of rules that send messages that match the given rule.

Consider a rule R that has its condition part satisfied by the actions (that is, messages) of one or more other rules (R's suppliers). The suppliers, by being thus *coupled* to R, are clearly relevant to R's activation. The sizes of the bids of the suppliers provide information about their relevance to the overall situation. With this in mind, the simplest way to implement the notion of support is to treat the sum of the *bids of the suppliers* as the support for R. This implies that messages serve to pass support from the rules that generated them to the rules that they match. When a rule fires, the message it generates carries support proportional to the size of its bid. When messages match the condition of a rule R on the subsequent processing cycle, the sum of their support values constitutes the support for R. Support then influences R's chances of activation by being used as a factor in determining the size of R's bid.

Support is a property that accrues to rules from other rules. It is sometimes useful, however, to think of support as being passed from rule to rule by means of the intermediary messages. If one rule gets support from another because its condition is matched by a message derived from the other's action, we can speak of the *message* getting support from the first rule and passing it along to the second. In a further generalization, since messages can enter the system from the sensory interface or from memory stores, as well as being directly generated by rules, any source of a message can be viewed as providing support for rules matched by that message. Unless there is a need to distinguish these various interpretations, we will simply use the term "support" for a continuous measure, determined by the current context of information processing, that influences the bid made by a rule.

Categorization and Implicit Representation of Probabilities

The question of coherence of information is especially relevant to categorization. Aspects of the environment are often divided into mutually exclusive categories (for example, different species of animals), and the system must determine the category membership of objects by integrating information from multiple cues. Often the available cues will be ambiguous (for example, an object that is feathered and web-footed may be either a goose or a duck) or partially contradictory (for example, the object may have the shape of a duck but be unusually large).

Ambiguity and partial contradiction are inevitable consequences of the inherent variability of the environment. It is simply the case, for example, that instances of the categories "duck" and "goose" each form a *distribution* of sizes, and that these distributions overlap. Registering a particular size for an object thus may provide partial support for classifying it in two contradictory ways. If the decision is pragmatically important (that is, if the alternative categorizations call for different subsequent actions toward the object), then it is essential for rule competition to lead to a plausible choice.

The first step in developing a categorization scheme is to have the system represent the equivalent of conditional probabilities. To a first approximation, we would like to have rules of the general form "If instance I has property P, then I is a member of category C_i with probability p_i" (for example, "If there is a moderately small black animal in the visual field, then it is a dog with probability $1/3$"). (As this example illustrates, we assume the conditions of rules may be conjunctions of multiple properties.) More generally, a superordinate category C may be partitioned into a set of mutually exclusive alternatives having an associated distribution of probabilities. Thus, if $C =$ "small black animal", the category set could be $\{C_1 =$ "dog", $C_2 =$ "cat", $C_3 =$ "squirrel", $C_4 =$ "ferret", $\ldots\}$, with a tentative distribution $\{1/3, 1/4, 1/10, 1/100, \ldots\}$. The system should use this distribution to make judgments about individual instances of C; and as the system accumulates experience, inductive mechanisms should revise the probabilities to accord with observed frequencies.

Suppose that we defined a rule for each pairing of the superordinate C and a subcategory C_i (for example, "If I is a small black animal, then it is a dog"). Since all the rules in this set have the same condition, their specificities are equal. Assume for the moment that no other relevant rules are active, so that support is also equated. Then the relative size of the bid made by each rule in the set would depend on its strength alone. If we assume an appropriate decision rule (the probability that a rule will win the competition might, for instance, be proportional to the ratio of its bid to the sum of bids made by all matched rules), it follows that on average the probability of each rule posting its message will be proportional to its relative strength. If the strength of each rule were in turn proportional to the probability p_i associated with category C_i, it follows that the probability of posting each of the messages C_i would be proportional to the conditional probability of C_i given C.

As we will see in chapter 3, the operation of the basic mechanisms for strength revision will, under a broad range of conditions, tend to refine strength values to be proportional to the rule's probability of success. Thus the strength parameter will implicitly define a probability distribution over a set of rules with a common condition. This can be done not only for discrete properties, as in the example above, but also for continuous properties such as size. For example, the equivalent of a rough histogram for the size of dogs could be represented by a small number of rules (perhaps six to eight), each specifying a "size category", with strength proportional to the estimated likelihood that a dog is of the stated size: "If an instance is a dog, then its size value is ⟨moderate value⟩" (strength medium); "If an instance is a dog, then its size value is ⟨very large value⟩" (strength low); and so on. We will show in chapter 6 that people do induce the equivalent of such histograms representing the properties underlying perceptual categories. In chapter 8 we will show that similar histograms are induced for social distributions. We will also demonstrate that the information in these histograms is critical for guiding generalizations about new objects identified as belonging to the category.

Support Summation

When a message is posted, it is given a support value proportional to the bid of the rule that posted it. In the previous section we considered only the manner in which sets of rules with identical conditions generate a distribution of support levels over their associated messages. The key to flexible categorization is that a message (and hence the rules it subsequently matches) can receive support from multiple rules with different conditions. If we assume that multiple sources of support will sum, it follows that a number of rules, no one of which offers conclusive evidence discriminating among competing hypotheses, can act in concert to produce a clearcut decision.

Figure 2.6 indicates the rules involved in a simple categorization decision, using network notation. Beginning at the top of Figure 2.6, each node at the initiating end of an arrow represents the condition of

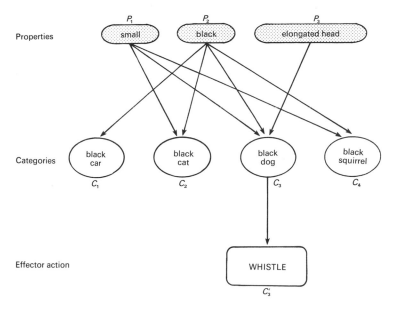

Figure 2.6
A set of property-to-category rules for use in classification.

a rule, the action of which is to send a message supporting the condition of a rule represented by the node pointed to by the arrow. Thus the P_i are properties (possibly conjunctive) that form the conditions of rules supporting various categories C_i. The categories C_i are in turn each the conditions of rules, the actions of which are to perform category-specific effector actions, C_i', which depend on the categorization decision (for example, responding by whistling to summon a dog).

In figure 2.6 each of the C_i nodes is supported by at least one rule. Three rules are passing support to C_3, however, whereas none of the remaining C_i is supported by more than two rules. Assuming the strengths of the rules with P_i conditions are approximately equal, it follows that greater total support will accrue to C_3 than to its competitors. Accordingly, the rule with the overt response C_3' as its action will tend to outbid its competitors and dominate as the system's primary effector output.

Classifications (and even overt responses) may or may not be mutually exclusive. When categories are not mutually exclusive, the corresponding rules may be simultaneously active, so that, for example, a particular small black animal might be categorized both as a "dog" and as a "pet". Overt responses that are not mutually exclusive can

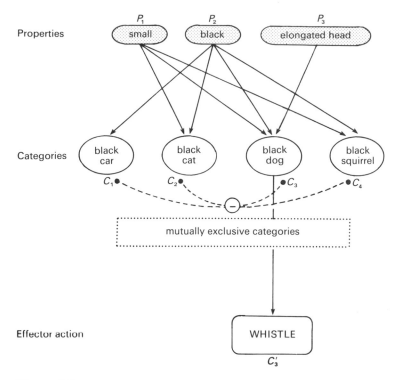

Properties

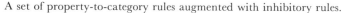

Categories

Effector action

Figure 2.7
A set of property-to-category rules augmented with inhibitory rules.

be carried out simultaneously, as, for example, turning one's head while moving forward. In other cases, however, the alternative classifications are in fact mutually exclusive. As we will see in chapter 6, inductive mechanisms tend to mark categories as mutually exclusive when they serve as the conditions of rules that produce overt conflict. For example, if an animal were simultaneously classified as a dog and as a wolf, the system might vacillate between approach and flight.

In such cases it is desirable to establish rules that effectively inhibit competing rules that would produce overtly competing responses. One way in which this can be accomplished is by allowing conditions that are *not* satisfied when certain messages are posted. In figure 2.7 the rules represented in figure 2.6 are supplemented by inhibitory rules (the dashed arrows) directly linking the C_i nodes. For example, the inhibitory rule "If instance I is a member of C_3, then it is not a member of C_1," can be rendered by the two-condition rule "If I matches the condition for C_3 and there is no message indicating C_1 is active, then send a message indicating the activation of C_3." The conditioning simulation presented in chapter 5 will illustrate a simple treatment of inhibition.

Such "lateral inhibition" between alternative categorizations is similar to mechanisms that have been included in connectionist models of recognition and categorization (McClelland and Rumelhart 1981). Support summation provides a mechanism for the flexible integration of partial information that has implications not only for categorization (discussed further in chapter 6) but also for the identification of plausible analogies (chapter 10).

Encoding

We are now in a position to define our concept of *encoding*, which we will draw on repeatedly in explanation of people's ability to apply or learn certain rules. The encoding of an object may be identified with the set of categories applied to it. Thus a small, black animal is an object to which the categories "small", "black", and "animal" have been applied simultaneously. This particular encoding is, of course, so general as to be of little use for most pragmatic purposes. More specific categories distinguishing "dog" ("elongated head"), "cat" ("round head"), and so on allow the activation of more specific rules relevant to the additional distinctions.

It is important to bear these homely observations in mind as we consider why it is that people are unable to apply certain rules to certain kinds of events. In order to be able to apply a given rule to an object or relationship, one must be able to encode the object or relationship in such a way that the resulting categories call up the rule. For example, we will see in chapter 7 that younger children often cannot learn about the rules underlying the behavior of balance beams even after observing their behavior over a wide variety of conditions (Siegler 1983a). This is apparently the case because younger children simply do not encode the distance of objects from the fulcrum. When children are encouraged to note the distance factor in static illustrations of balance beams and subsequently are shown the behavior of balance beams, they induce the rules underlying their behavior almost as well as older children.

A similar observation applies to people's ability to apply inferential rules, notably statistical rules. We will show in chapters 7 and 8 that people often fail to apply statistical rules to certain kinds of events, notably social events—rules that they apply with ease to other kinds of events, notably the behavior of randomizing devices and sports events. We will argue that this is because people do not encode some events in such a way that their variability can be assessed; and variability assessment is a prerequisite of the ability to apply statistical rules. In chapter 9 we will show that people can be taught to encode events in such a way that they can make use of inferential rules that would otherwise be inaccessible.

2.3.3 Directed versus Automatic Spreading Activation

In the previous two sections we described how systems represent and solve problems by processes akin to "spreading activation", where activation corresponds to the propagation and summation of support for rules. There are, however, some important differences between our view and the common form of spreading activation postulated by a number of theorists in psychology. We argue that the empirical evidence concerning spreading activation is more consistent with our view than with a leading alternative.

Anderson (1983) postulates a process of spreading activation through the semantic network that is entirely independent of the execution of rules. Indeed, spreading activation is assumed to proceed independently of *all* other processes by virtue of being *automatic*. This conception of automatic spreading activation is by no means unique to Anderson's theory. Collins and Loftus (1975) made spreading activation a central element of their theory of the retrieval of conceptual knowledge, and the notion found support in the theories of automatic processing proposed by Posner and Snyder (1975) and Schneider and Shiffrin (1977; Shiffrin and Schneider 1977). Spreading activation typically is assumed to have four properties: (1) once one concept is activated in memory, activation inevitably spreads to those concepts directly associated with it semantically; (2) the process requires no processing capacity and hence will not suffer interference from any concurrent cognitive process; (3) activation continues spreading from the initial associates to *their* associates, and so on indefinitely (although the amount of activation transmitted may decline with the number of nodes intervening between the "source" concept and its remote associates); and (4) the entire process is extremely rapid. Anderson's 1983 version of his system ACT predicts that activation spreads throughout the network virtually instantaneously (in less than 40 milliseconds).

The central empirical evidence relevant to the activation of concepts comes from the *lexical decision* paradigm originated by Meyer and Schvaneveldt (1971). Subjects are presented with strings of letters and are timed as they decide whether or not each string is a word. It has been found that a word judgment is made more quickly if the word is preceded by a related rather than an unrelated word. For example, subjects determine that *doctor* is a word more quickly if it is preceded by *nurse* than if it is preceded by *moose*. This priming effect indicates that activation of a word triggers activation of closely associated words. Such priming of semantic associates occurs very rapidly, even when subjects do not expect related words (Fischler 1977; Neely 1977) and (most spectacularly) when the priming word is presented so briefly that it cannot be consciously perceived (Fowler, Wolford, Slade, and Tassinary 1981; Marcel 1983). In short, the evidence for the first putative property of spreading activation— inevitable activation of immediately associated concepts—is very strong.

The other properties, however, are much less firmly established. There does not seem to be any clear evidence regarding the issue of whether spreading activation and other concurrent processes interfere with each other. There is growing evidence, however, that *no* cognitive process beyond peripheral perceptual processing is entirely "capacity-free" (Cheng 1985). For example, Paap and Ogden (1981) demonstrated that letter encoding, which was previously thought to meet this criterion, in fact does not. We therefore find the second assumed property of spreading activation suspect.

The third property—the continued spreading of activation to remote associates of the "source" concept—is perhaps the most basic in terms of the neural metaphor underlying the concept of spreading activation, since "spreading" activation obviously ought to spread. Surprisingly, it has only recently been tested. De Groot (1983) selected triplets of words such as *bull-cow-milk*, in which the first word is closely associated with the second and the second with the third, but the first has no direct association with the third. She then used the first word (here, *bull*) as a prime for its second-order associate, the third word (*milk*). If activation continues to spread from concept to concept, as the standard view of spreading activation assumes, some facilitation should be observed. Yet de Groot's extensive series of experiments failed to reveal any second-order priming effects. The results of this empirical test of the continued spread of activation were thus quite negative.

The fourth property—rapid rate of activation—clearly holds for activation of first-order associates but is severely qualified by de Groot's results. It seems that beyond the few immediate associates of a concept, the spread of activation—unless it is relevant to the system's current goals—typically stops dead in its tracks.

This battery of evidence against *automatic* spreading activation actually fits comfortably within our framework. From our perspective, the spread of activation from concept to concept is under the control of rules, their corresponding support levels, and their attendant competitive interactions (see also Thibadeau, Just, and Carpenter 1982). It depends greatly upon the building blocks (rules) held in common by the different concepts involved, including those specifying the goal. Thus, *bull* holds many building blocks in common with *cow* (such as four-leggedness, hair, horns, similar size) but few in common with *milk*. *Cow*, on the other hand, has the very special association of being a *producer* of *milk*, something largely irrelevant to our concept of *bull*.

In contrast with rule-directed spread of activation, automatic spreading activation would constitute a blind, maladaptive retrieval process. To think of *cow* as an immediate associate of *bull* is likely to retrieve useful additional information, but to think also of *milk* (in the absence of a cow) is likely to be a diversion. Anderson (1983) argues that automatic spreading activation must be independent of the execution of rules because the system would otherwise be too slow, due to competition between rules dealing with activation and all the rules required to perform other functions. This objection is indeed telling for ACT* and other production systems that allow only a single rule to be executed on each processing cycle. By virtue of their parallelism, however, systems of the sort we propose avoid this extreme bottleneck.

We will see in later discussions of analogy and scientific discovery how the kind of directed spreading activation we propose helps to make sense of some of the most creative human thought processes.

2.4 *Illustration of the Performance of a Modeling System*

We are now ready for an illustration of a simple modeling system. We will capture an episode in the life of a developing cognitive system—a three-year-old girl who lives in the more northerly reaches of North America. There she has seen the usual complement of domestic animals, such as dogs and cats. In addition, she has seen more exotic animals, such as woodchucks, otters, and ferrets. For dwellers in other regions, we note that most of the squirrels in her part of the world are black.

As the curtain rises on Jennifer, she is wandering around the family summer cottage on a morning in June. Having just slept, eaten, and fought with her older brother, her primary goal is to EXPLORE the environment, with subgoals of PICKING UP interesting portions of it, INGESTING them, SHOWING them to her father, and WITHHOLDING them from her brother.

As luck would have it, something interesting appears in the middle

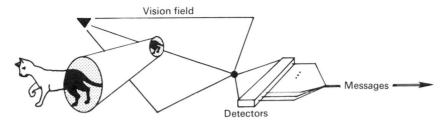

Figure 2.8
Input from the environment.

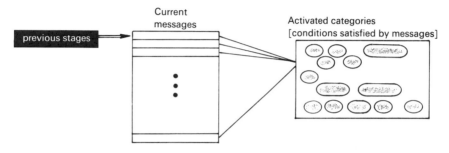

Figure 2.9
Activation of categories by messages.

distance. It is small, black, moving, obviously an animal. But what kind of animal?

For purposes of illustration of the effector portion of the system, we assume that Jennifer first catches sight of the rear end of the animal (figure 2.8). Prior to additional saccadic eye movements, she sees only enough to establish that the object in her visual field is small and black, has a long axis in the horizontal orientation, and is an animal. These messages from the input interface determine which categories will be activated by matched rules (figure 2.9). Since Jennifer has no fear of animals yet, these facts are sufficient to establish an immediate goal (a subgoal of EXPLORE) of getting close to the object (figure 2.10).

Jennifer has not yet categorized the animal with sufficient precision to tell her how to go about getting close, and we will now see how she goes about doing that. We may assume that in Jennifer's world, at least in her outside world, dogs are more common than cats, which are more common than squirrels, which are more common than ferrets. These facts are represented in figure 2.11 by specific strength values that might capture the likelihood of the object being a dog, cat,

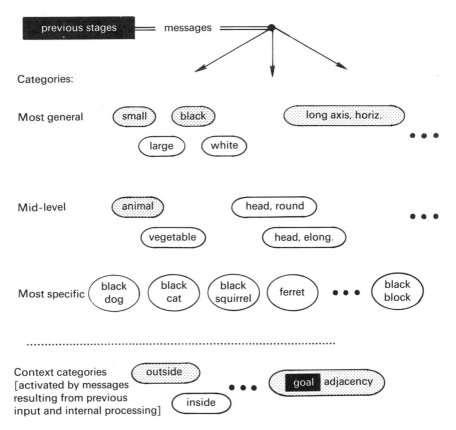

Figure 2.10
Encoding. At this stage the object is encoded as "small, black, long-axis horizontal, animal".

squirrel, or ferret, given the messages from the input interface and the context. (These strength values are not to be interpreted as probabilities in any exact sense.)

For purposes of illustration, we assume that the messages from the input interface are all equally compatible with all four animal possibilities. This is illustrated by setting the support value equal to 20 for each animal. The bottom portion of figure 2.11 shows the bids made for each categorization. (For simplicity we show support and strength as being added together to comprise the bid, but a more realistic treatment, especially one intended to be consistent with some particular statistical theory, would probably make these values multiplicative.)

Figure 2.11 shows that although the tentative categorization is "dog", it does not reach some implicit confirmation threshold (see Siegler and Shrager 1984). The confirmation threshold can be repre-

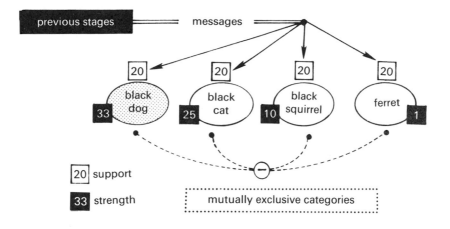

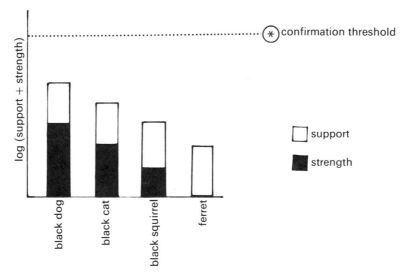

Bids
[histogram of implicit probabilities]

Figure 2.11

Competition for object specification.

⊛ At this stage the preferred interpretation is "black dog". An internal monitor issues a message with a ⌐ *conf* tag, however, because all bids are less than a triggering hold, the *confirmation threshold*.

sented implicitly by the activation of a rule that calls for seeking further information rather than making one of the competing categorizations. If the threshold is not reached, the system sends a message to that effect and initates effector actions designed to gain more information pertinent to categorization. In this case simply moving the eyes forward along the animal's horizontal axis is the first step to be taken (figure 2.12). This action produces new information to the effect that the animal has a round (rather than oblong) head (figure 2.13). This information results in an additional encoding in the form of the newly activated category "round head" (figure 2.14).

The new category adds substantial support to both the "cat" and the "squirrel" category. Since the "cat" category has greater prior strength, however, and since the new support and strength values combined exceed the current confirmation threshold requirement, the system issues a message confirming membership in the category (figure 2.15).

This is not the end of the story for Jennifer, however. She now is a system with a problem. She nccds to gct close to that cat. And before she does so, she will have learned some interesting things about her world. We will continue to follow Jennifer's escapades in the next chapter, as we turn to the core topics of our book.

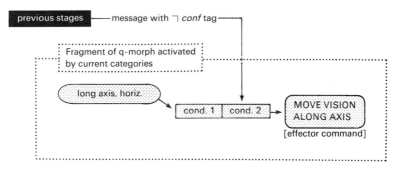

Figure 2.12
Act to confirm.

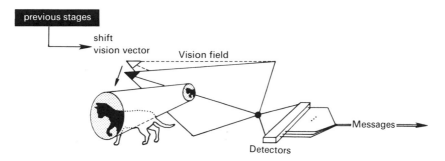

Figure 2.13
New input from environment.

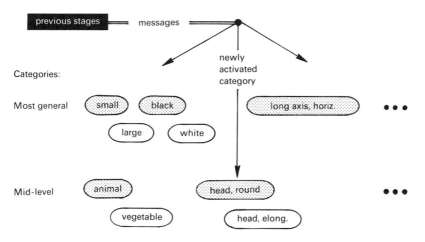

Figure 2.14
Revised encoding. At this stage the object is encoded as "small, black, long-axis horizontal, round head, animal".

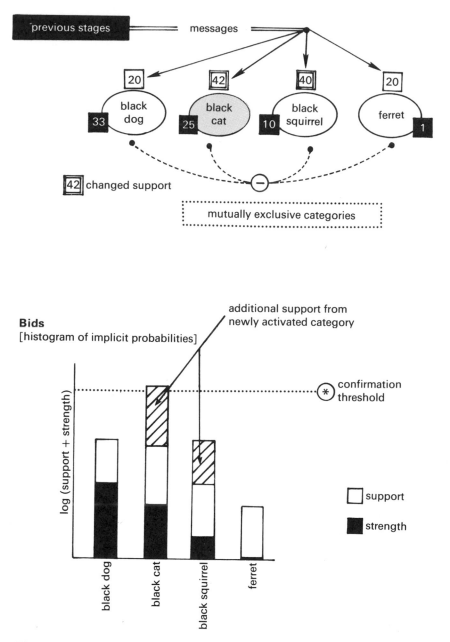

Figure 2.15
Object specification.

⊛ At this stage the preferred interpretation is "black cat". An internal monitor issues a message with a *conf* tag because there is a bid above the *confirmation threshold*.

Appendix 2A Generalized Definition of Q-Morphisms

The full variety of q-morphisms can be defined precisely as follows. The q-morphism can have any finite number of layers r. For each layer j, $1 < j < r$, there is a map P_j that aggregates the set of world states W into the model states M_j assigned to that level, $P_j: W \to M_j$. There will be one new state in the model for each equivalence class in W induced by P_j. P_j is usually a partial map defined only for some elements of W (the "exceptions")—that is, it only selects certain subsets of W. The construction of the model is cumulative, so we define a function P_j^* that subsumes the total structure up to level j. We do this for any level j by using the cumulative map from the previous level, P_{j-1}^*, along with the "local" map for the current level, P_j. Letting w be an arbitrary world state, and letting m and m' be distinct model states from M_j at level j, we proceed as follows:

1) If $P_{j-1}^*(w) = m'$ and $P_j(w) = m$,   then $P_j^*(w) = P_j(w) = m$; that is, the new "exception" overrides the old "default".

2) Otherwise, $P_j^*(w) = P_{j-1}^*(w)$; that is, when P_j does *not* supply a new image, the old one is used.

We start the process by setting $P_1^* = P_1$. For simplicity and completeness we require P_1 to map *every* element of W into some element of M_1—that is, the equivalence classes inducted by P_1 partition W.

  We define the total set of states of the q-morphism up to level j, Q_j, by adding the model states from the current level, M_j, to the cumulative set of states from the previous level, $Q_j = M_j \cup Q_{j-1}$. For certain states of the world the transition function T_j' will make a valid prediction; that is, for such states T_j' will satisfy the conditions for a homomorphism,

$$T_j' P_j^*(w) = P_j^* T(w).$$

Define W_j^* to be the set of world states for which the q-morphism makes correct predictions at level j. Then the layered set of model transition functions $\{T_1', \ldots T_j', \ldots T_r'\}$ is a *q-morphism* if, for every level j, $1 < j < r$, the set of states W_j^* yielding correct predictions *properly* includes the corresponding set of states W_{j-1}^* from the preceding level. In short, each layer added to the model adds to its ability to make correct predictions. The successive layers of the q-morphism constitute a *default hierarchy* in which Q_{j-1} is the *default set* for Q_j and Q_j is the *exception set* for Q_{j-1}.

Appendix 2B The Economy of Defaults and Exceptions: The Parsimony of Q-Morphisms

Consider, first, a homomorphic model of the environment based upon a set of k binary detectors. The model is specified by two maps:

1) a mapping P from the world states W to a set M of 2^k model states, one model state for each k-tuple of detector readings;

2) a transition function T'_M providing commutativity of the diagram.

For the purposes of this argument, we will assume that there is no simpler homomorphic model using some subset of the k binary detectors; that is, any model using fewer of the binary detectors fails to meet the "commutativity of the diagram" requirement and hence produces errors. A straightforward rendering of T'_M in terms of rules then requires one condition-action pair for each state of the model. That is, for each s in M there is a rule $s \rightarrow s'$ that provides the transition $T'_M(s) = s'$. Because there are 2^k states, 2^k rules are required to implement T'_M.

Consider, next, a nontrivial q-morphism model based on the same set of detectors. Let the level 1 map P_1 be based on $k_1 < k$ detectors. Consider a particular rule C in the representation of the transition function T'_1. The condition for C actually responds to 2^{k-k_1} distinct k-tuples of detector values. That is, the rule responds to 2^{k-k_1} distinct states of the detailed model (P_1 induces equivalence classes in the detailed homomorphic model). Because we are dealing with a q-morphism, C will provide the correct transition, the one specified by the homomorphic transition function T'_M, for only a proportion of $d < 1$ of the 2^{k-k_1} states satisfying its condition. These errors must be corrected by "exceptions" specified by deeper levels of the q-morphism. In the worst case each of the errors will have to be corrected by rules involving all k detectors. The rule C together with the $(1-d)(2^{k-k_1})$ k-detector exceptions then yields the same transitions as the set of 2^{k-k_1} rules from the homomorphic model. In other words, $(1-d)(2^{k-k_1}) + 1$ rules of the q-morphism replace 2^{k-k_1} rules of the homomorphic model, a saving of $d(2^{k-k_1}) - 1$ rules.

As an example, let the homomorphic model use 10 detectors ($k = 10$), let layer 1 of the q-morphism be based on the values of 5 detectors, ($k_1 = 5$), and let the rule C be correct only half the time ($d = 0.5$). Then, at worst, the q-morphism requires 17 rules to accomplish the same transitions as 32 rules from the homomorphic model, a saving of 15 rules. If all rules in the q-morphism have error rates no higher than C, then the q-morphism model would use at most 17/32 as many rules as the homomorphic model.

Because the number of rules required to "cover" a given set of states increases exponentially with the number of detector values specified in their condition parts, the savings of a q-morphism increase dramatically as the number of layers increases. For example, consider a q-morphism in which the highest level uses 2^{k_1} rules based on k_1 detectors, and each successive layer uses rules employing k_1 additional detector values to correct for exceptions in the previous layer. Let rules at each level, except the deepest level, be correct over at least a proportion d of the instances satisfying them. (We assume the rules at the deepest level deal correctly with individual states of a homomorphic image, as in the earlier example.) Let the q-morphism involve n layers so that the deepest level involves nk_1 detectors. Then, following an argument that parallels the one above, we see that the q-morphism requires at most $\Sigma_j(1 - d)^{j-1}2^{jk_1}$ rules to specify the same transition function as would be specified by 2^{nk_1} rules in the detailed model. For a 5-layer model ($n = 5$) with 2 additional detectors being used in each successive layer ($k_1 = 2$), and an error rate of 0.5 ($d = 0.5$), the q-morphism requires less than 124 rules whereas the direct presentation of the homomorphic model would require 1,024 rules. For a still larger model, $n = 10$, under the same conditions, $k = 2$, $d = 0.5$, the q-morphism requires 4,092 rules compared to over 1,000,000 rules required for direct presentation.

The q-morphism offers still greater parsimony if the corresponding model simply ignores some of the rarer exceptions, permitting a (low) error rate under such circumstances. Since models of real situations will almost always be prone to error, no matter how refined, the model-building process can concentrate on building exception rules for costly errors only, with still further savings in the number of rules required.

3

Modification of Rules

We come at last to the core of induction—the creation and modification of knowledge structures. In this chapter we will define inductive procedures in relation to the performance mechanisms discussed in the previous chapter and introduce them in terms general enough to encompass both the computational procedures discussed in chapter 4 and the empirical phenomena discussed in chapters 5–10.

The inductive mechanisms must accomplish three difficult, interrelated tasks. They must (1) evaluate the system's rules as instruments for goal attainment, improving them where possible and favoring the better ones in application; (2) generate plausibly useful new rules that are capable of extracting and exploiting regularities in experience; and (3) provide associations between and clusterings among rules in order to create larger knowledge structures leading to efficient modeling of the environment. In carrying out these tasks, inductive mechanisms rely upon feedback concerning predictions about the environment. Induction is not simply something the cognitive system does to occupy its idle moments, nor does it have the character of undirected inference making or random combination of ideas. Rather, induction is a problem-directed activity, executed in response to specific system objectives such as seeking plausible explanations for an unexpected outcome. In a rule-based system there are only two fundamental types of inductive change: the refinement of existing rules and the generation of new ones. These correspond to the first two tasks listed above. The third task, the generation of larger knowledge structures, must be accomplished by a combination of rule generation and rule refinement, serving to cluster related rules together. In addition to these self-initiated activities, it is possible to insert new rules from the outside. In the case of organisms this is called education. At the end of this chapter we will compare the functioning of inserted rules with that of induced rules.

As we discuss inductive mechanisms, it is important to keep in mind our overall picture of the way the cognitive system functions. The system is continually engaged in pursuing its goals, in the course of which problem elements are constantly being recategorized and predictions are constantly being generated. As part of this process, various triggering conditions initiate inductive changes in the system's rules. Unexpected outcomes provide problems that the system solves by creating new rules as hypotheses. Concepts with shared properties are activated, thus providing analogies for use in problem solving and rule generation. Covariations among salient and goal-relevant stimuli are being learned; new categories are being formed, and implicit statistical parameters are being revised.

At one level the major task of the system may be described as reducing uncertainty about the environment. In order to accomplish this, the system must learn about the variability characteristic of various properties and relationships, gaining knowledge of what falls inside the range of permissible variation for a category and what falls outside, in the region of the unclassifiable or intrinsically uncertain. Two different aspects of knowledge representation capture variability information. First, differences in expectations that can be related to categories at different levels of generality are reflected directly in the organization of the default hierarchy. Some of the induction mechanisms to be described in this chapter, especially those that perform specialization and generalization, provide the basis for the acquisition of default hierarchies. Second, variability within a level of categorization can be captured by sets of rules of varying strengths that relate properties of instances to category membership, providing an implicit probability distribution. Mechanisms for strength revision, which serve to refine rules, thus also mediate the induction of variability information.

This chapter is organized in terms of the two broad types of self-initiated inductive procedures, namely, rule refinement and rule generation. Some of the mechanisms we discuss have been implemented at the level of subcognitive computational procedures, and some at the cognitive level, while still others have the status of hypothetical constructs proposed to explain empirical psychological phenomena. The ultimate and still very distant goal of our research program is to have all mechanisms implemented computationally and well demonstrated empirically.

3.1 Refinement of Rules

3.1.1 Apportionment of Credit

A difficult and pervasive inductive task facing any system operating in a complex environment is the *apportionment of credit*. Somehow the system must identify and reward the rules responsible for its successes. The task is difficult because many rules may act simultaneously and because in complex environments overt rewards are rare; the system's behavior is mostly "stage setting" that makes possible later successes. It is easy to determine that a triple jump in checkers is a useful maneuver, but it is much harder to determine which earlier actions made the jump possible. This conundrum can be solved if we follow Samuel (1959) and require that revisions be based on feedback concerning model-generated predictions. In our view, reinforcement does not automatically "stamp in" behaviors, as traditional behaviorist theories of learning would have it; it provides feedback about the relevance of the various predictions to goal attainment. We will support this claim in chapter 5 by applying our framework to account for inductive phenomena observed in the cognitive systems most studied by behaviorists—rats and pigeons.

For rule-based systems the apportionment-of-credit task involves determining which rules in a sequence of active rules have played an important role in determining an eventual success. The key to inducing useful q-morphic models as experience accumulates is the strengthening of rules that repeatedly contribute to success. The context dependence of such rules is a critical element in this process. When a rule is activated because its condition part is satisfied, there is a tacit prediction that its action will contribute to a positive outcome. If we attach a strength parameter to the rule, as described in chapter 2, then higher strength should indicate a more confident prediction. Failure of the outcome to occur will generate feedback indicating the rule has been overvalued. The system's inductive mechanisms should then reduce the rule's strength parameter on the basis of this feedback. Conversely, if a rule produces a correct prediction, its strength should be increased. The proliferation of redundant rules (multiple rules that make the same prediction under the same circumstances) can be inhibited by forcing all active claimants to share the payoff (or the payoff can even be restricted to the highest bidder). In any case, the key problem of propagating reward and punishment back to earlier-acting rules must still be dealt with.

Rule competition, as embodied in the bidding process described in chapter 2, has a direct bearing on the revision of rule strength. A system can never have an absolute assurance that any of its rules is correct. The perpetual novelty of the environment, combined with an inevitably limited sampling of that environment, leaves a residue of uncertainty. Each rule serves, in effect, as a hypothesis that has been more or less confirmed. The higher the strength of the rule, the greater the confirmation, if the inductive mechanisms for modifying strength are doing their job. Under such uncertainty the system should continue to allocate trials to alternative hypotheses (see, for example, Holland 1975, chap. 5), revising confirmations on the basis of outcomes. One way to allow variability in responses, used in the model described in chapter 5, is to make the bid of a rule a stochastic function of its strength, so that the rule with highest strength will not always place the highest bid. While the strengthening of successful rules will inevitably bias the system toward the familiar and away from the innovative, yielding such phenomena as "set" and "functional fixedness" (Duncker 1945; Luchins 1942), novel responses will not be entirely precluded.

3.1.2 Coupling and the Bucket Brigade Algorithm

We distinguish between *local* and *nonlocal* techniques for apportioning credit. Local techniques strengthen rules directly, without requiring memory of parts of the history of the system. Some nonlocal techniques are described in section 3.1.4; here we concentrate on one local algorithm that avoids the storage costs of keeping track of sequences of rules. The algorithm has been implemented in classifier systems. In chapter 5 we will argue that an analogous procedure of rule refinement is used by organisms.

As we described in chapter 2, rules place bids for opportunities to post their messages. The bid of a rule is a function of its strength, the specificity of its conditions, and the support it receives from the messages that match it. If a rule has its bid accepted, its message carries support in proportion to the size of its bid. Support has immediate consequences for further rule processing, since it affects the bids of rules on the next processing cycle. Bids are used for another purpose by the bucket brigade algorithm, an inductive operating principle that apportions credit by altering rule strengths on the basis of current bids. Changes in strength affect the performance of the system over a longer time span than do changes in support.

Rule Coupling

In order to understand the bucket brigade algorithm, it is necessary to examine the manner in which rules can be associated to produce organized sequential activity. As in chapter 2, we describe one rule as being *coupled* to another if the action part of the first rule generates a message that satisfies one or more conditions in the condition part of the second. As a result, when the first rule is active on a given time-step, the second tends to become active on the next time-step. Rule coupling is illustrated in figure 3.1. In part (a), rule 1 will be coupled to rule 2 if some component of the message sent by rule 1, termed the *tag*, satisfies the condition of rule 2. (Tags and coupling will be discussed in more detail in chapter 4 in relation to classifier systems.) Part (b) depicts a slightly more complex example in which activation of rule 1 is contingent on a particular input from the environment, and the message posted by rule 1 potentially matches one of the two conditions required by rule 2, with the environment on the next time-step providing a match to the remaining condition. For example, rule 1 might be "IF (1) there is a dog in view and (2) the goal is to summon the dog, THEN whistle," and rule 2 might be "IF (1) there is a dog in view and (2) someone whistles, THEN the dog approaches." (See figure 3.5 for a less "linguistic" version of these rules.)

Such coupled rule sequences are crucial to the development of plans. The generation of couplings will be discussed in section 3.3.2; here we will describe the manner in which coupling allows the revision of the strength values of early-acting rules in a coupled sequence that leads to goal attainment.

Bucket Brigade Algorithm

The bucket brigade algorithm for strength revision is best described in terms of an economic analogy. The algorithm treats each rule in a coupled sequence as a kind of "middleman" in a complex economy. As a middleman, a rule deals only with its "suppliers"—the rules sending messages satisfying its conditions—and its "consumers"—the rules with conditions satisfied by the messages the middleman sends. Whenever a rule wins a bidding competition, it initiates a transaction in which it pays out part of its strength to its suppliers. As one of the winners of the competition, it becomes active, serving as a supplier to its consumers and receiving payments from them in turn. Under this arrangement the rule's strength is a kind of capital that measures its ability to turn a "profit". If a rule receives more from its consumers than it paid out, it has made a profit; that is, its strength has increased. The operation of the bucket brigade is illustrated in figure 3.2.

A rule is likely to be profitable only if its consumers, in their local transactions, are also (on the average) profitable. The consumers, in

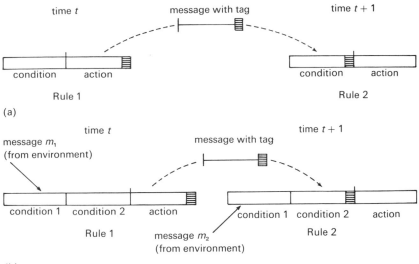

Figure 3.1

Coupled rules (diachronic pointing).

(a) Coupling between single-condition rules. When rule 1 is activated, it posts a message that satisfies the condition of rule 2. This is typically accomplished by having the condition of rule 2 satisfied only by messages with a particular tag (in the diagram, a suffix).

(b) Coupling between two-condition rules. In this example condition 1 of rule 1 is satisfied by message m_1 from the environment, while condition 1 of rule 2 is satisfied by message m_2 from the environment. As a result of the coupling, rule 2 will be satisfied only when rule 1 has been activated on the previous time-step *and* the environment has made a transition from a state giving rise to message m_1 to a state giving rise to message m_2.

Coupled two-condition rules provide a simple way of modeling causal relations in the environment. They provide a "bridge" whereby apportionment of credit algorithms, such as the bucket brigade algorithm, strengthen verified relations.

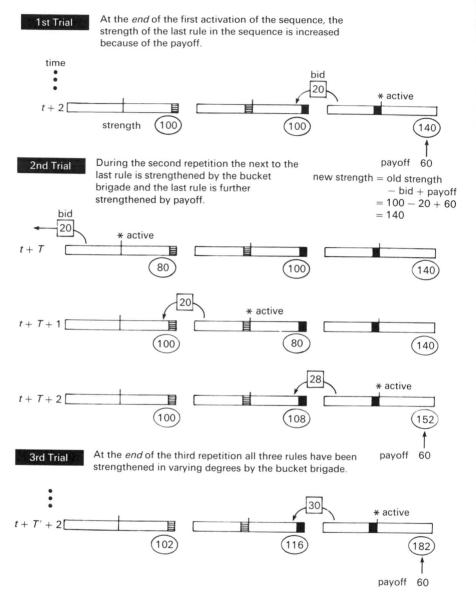

1st Trial   At the *end* of the first activation of the sequence, the strength of the last rule in the sequence is increased because of the payoff.

time

$t + 2$

strength 100   100   140

payoff 60

2nd Trial   During the second repetition the next to the last rule is strengthened by the bucket brigade and the last rule is further strengthened by payoff.

new strength = old strength
− bid + payoff
= 100 − 20 + 60
= 140

bid 20

$t + T$

* active

80   100   140

20

* active

$t + T + 1$

100   80   140

28

* active

$t + T + 2$

100   108   152

payoff 60

3rd Trial   At the *end* of the third repetition all three rules have been strengthened in varying degrees by the bucket brigade.

30

* active

$t + T' + 2$

102   116   182

payoff 60

Figure 3.2
The effect of the bucket brigade when a coupled sequence of rules is repeatedly activated. All rules start with strength 100 and bids are all 0.2 (strength).

turn, will be profitable only if *their* consumers are profitable. The resulting chains of consumers lead to the ultimate consumers—the rules that directly attain goals and receive payoff directly from the environment. When payoff occurs, it is added to the strengths of all rules active at that time. A rule that regularly attains payoff when activated is of course profitable. The profitability of other rules depends upon their being coupled into sequences leading to these profitable ultimate consumers. The bucket brigade ensures that early-acting, "stage setting" rules eventually receive credit if they are coupled into (correlated with) sequences that on average lead to payoff.

If a rule sequence is faulty, the final rule in the sequence loses strength, and the sequence will begin to disintegrate, over time, from the final rule backward through its chain of precursors. As soon as a rule's strength has decreased to the point where it loses in the bidding process, some competing rule will get a chance to act as a replacement. If the competing rule is more useful than the one displaced, a revised rule sequence will begin to form using the new rule. The bucket brigade algorithm thus searches out and repairs "weak links" through its pervasive local application.

Whenever rules are coupled into larger hierarchical knowledge structures, the bucket brigade algorithm is still more powerful than the description so far would suggest. An abstract diachronic rule of the general form "If the goal is G, and the procedure PR is executed, then G will be achieved" may be active throughout the time interval over which the individual rules comprising PR are executed. Since *all* rules active at the time of payoff (the acquisition of G) have their strength increased, both the abstract rule and the final specific rules in the sequence that specifies PR gain strength immediately. On the very next trial of procedure PR, the initially active rules in PR, acting as suppliers to the abstract rule (via the condition "if the procedure PR is executed"), will have their strengths substantially increased under the bucket brigade, because of the abstract rule's increased strength. This increase in strength supplied by the abstract rule circumvents the need to backchain strength through the intervening steps in PR, a process that would require repeated encounters with the sequence leading to G. Similar benefits are provided by abstract rules that specify subgoals. The discussion of classifier systems in chapter 4 provides detailed examples of the operation of the bucket brigade.

3.1.3 Explicit Prediction-Based Revision

The bucket brigade is not the only possible local method of apportionment of credit. A more direct local strength adjustment might be based on overt predicitions. The predictions made by predictor rules can be recorded and then matched against subsequent inputs from the environment, with correct predictions increasing the strength of the relevant rules.

We will not provide a full computational illustration of the operation of direct prediction-based revision, but we will argue in chapter 5 that there is adequate evidence of the existence of prediction-based revision even in organisms such as the rat. Such phenomena as "latent learning", to be described in chapter 5, provide evidence that animals learn simply by testing predictions, even in the absence of overt reward. Revision of rules on the basis of their predictive success is also the key to humans' ability to learn complex categories with minimal feedback, a phenomenon to be discussed in chapter 6.

3.1.4 Causal Analysis: Nonlocal Techniques of Rule Refinement

The bucket brigade algorithm can exploit hierarchical relations among rules to assign credit to early rules in a series. Neither the bucket brigade algorithm nor prediction-based mechanisms can pinpoint, however, the "plausible cause" of a faulty outcome that follows from a long rule sequence. Especially if the weak link is temporally remote from the state that generates the feedback, a great deal of trial and error may ensue before the "bad" rule is successfully replaced and the sequence rebuilt. In contrast, human intelligence often can pinpoint quickly the probable cause of a negative outcome in a temporally remote precursor.

The major reason people can pinpoint the offending rule is that they often have "models of their models," so to speak. That is to say, people often have an idea of the rules they are using to represent the environment and of the predictions made by those rules. (It is partly for this reason that we include the system's representation of itself in its model of the world.) Thus people generally have a linguistic representation of the rules they use to model, for example, the behavior of machines. When one rewinds a gadget's gizmo in the belief that this will serve to restart it, and it doesn't restart it, one thinks to oneself, "Huh, I thought rewinding the gizmo would restart that gadget; maybe it doesn't always ... or maybe the gadget's broken." The effective result of such a chain of reasoning is that the rule that gizmo rewinding restarts gadgets is weakened.

In contrast to the subcognitive bucket brigade, inferential rule-based changes in rule strength tend to require only one trial of expectation-plus-disconfirmation to produce substantial change in rule strength. The price of this one-trial learning, unless the causal sequence is short and nonbranching, is substantial processing and storage. In addition, one's model of one's model must be accurate or the resulting changes, though rapid, will be in error. Nisbett and Wilson (1977) have shown that peoples' beliefs about the rules that produced their judgments and expectations can be quite wrong. This seems to be particularly true for judgments about social objects and for evaluative judgments. For example, people's judgments about the quality of consumer goods are affected by the order in which they examine them, with later-examined objects being preferred to early-examined objects. But people do not know this about themselves. Thus we might expect that when one subsequently finds that one has overevaluated an object examined late in a series, one will not be able to trace the failing back to its position in the sequence of examination because one has no representation of the role of position effects in judgment.

The process of trouble-shooting the sources of failures is a kind of causal analysis. It depends both on empirical rules about causal sequences and on inferential rules that constitute heuristics for identifying plausible causes. The latter heuristics have been called "causal schemas" by Kelley (1972, 1973). In our terminology causal schemas are one kind of pragmatic reasoning schema (see chapter 9).

Causal analysis can be aided by the structure of goal hierarchies (Anderson 1983). If a goal cannot be achieved, and one or more of the subgoals it dominates failed to be reached, the cause of the higher-level failure can be attributed to the inadequacy either of the rule sequences invoked during the lower-level solution attempt or of the rule that generated the unattainable subgoal. Other aspects of a problem representation can also aid in causal analysis. As a solution plan is developed, the rules corresponding to operators required to carry out the plan may be explicitly stored as a sequence attached to the problem concept. If the solution plan fails when it is attempted, an inferential rule might identify the "weakest link" in the planned rule sequence simply by picking the one with the lowest strength value. The suspect rule could then be directly weakened (rather than the system's relying solely on the bucket brigade), allowing a competitor to replace it on the next planning attempt. In addition, once a solution plan has been generated, rules that led away from the eventual solution path during the process of plan generation can be weakened (Sleeman, Langley, and Mitchell 1982; Langley 1985).

Causal analysis is involved in the *generation* of new rules, as well as in strength revision. In the next section we will show how causal analysis can be used to trigger the generation of new, more specialized rules.

3.2 *Constraints on Rule Generation*

Procedures for refining existing rules, though important, are inherently limited to rules already in place. If these rules are inadequate in important ways—categories missing or wrong, coupling missing or wrong, and the like—no amount of refinement will make up the deficit. The only remedy is a set of inductive mechanisms that can generate new rules to enter into competition with existing ones. The investigation of mechanisms for generating plausible new rules is perhaps the richest domain to be explored within the framework of inductive rule-based systems. As we argued in chapter 1, this is a line of theoretical development that rule-based approaches seem more likely to facilitate than the connectionist perspective, which so far has shown itself best qualified to deal with strength-revision phenomena. Although we will describe a broad range of potential mechanisms for rule generation as systematically as possible, we do not claim to have provided an exhaustive taxonomy. Our intent here is to illustrate some directions for theoretical development that strike us as promising, many of which will be discussed further in later chapters. Before we examine particular forms of rule generation, however, we will discuss some general constraints and barriers that influence the generation process.

3.2.1 *The Requirement of Gracefulness*
We must emphasize the role of competition and the importance of graceful insertion of new rules into the cognitive system. Because of competition, the rules generated by the inductive mechanisms need not be universally correct, and the mechanisms themselves need not be very efficient. Q-morphisms are designed to absorb successive refinements. The search is not for optimal rules but rather for rules that often produce satisfactory results, as in the *satisficing* of Simon (1956). Computationally overwhelming requirements for global consistency of rules and their predictions are avoided. Rules that do not improve performance are gradually eliminated by the refinement process. And all of this goes on without affecting system performance in well-practiced areas where strong rules dominate the competition.

This property of *gracefulness* is vital for inductive systems that are to operate in realistic, complex environments. The first step in assuring gracefulness is the requirement that newly generated rules displace weak rules rather than closely related ("parent") rules. This contrasts with most optimization procedures, which search outward from the current "best", replacing it in the process. Because parent rules typically are strong rules, they will tend to remain in control of the situations in which they acquired their strength. New rules get a chance, typically, in situations where none of the high-strength rules have their conditions satisfied. That is, new rules are tried in situations where the system does not know what to do. The generation of new rules is triggered by just such situations for just this purpose. The new rules fill new "niches" corresponding to domains in which the system has inadequate sets of rules, as revealed by its inability to make reliable predictions.

Parallelism—using combinations of simultaneously active rules to determine action—provides a second element assuring gracefulness. Because of the combination of support and competition, it will be rare that any single rule is critical to determining performance. Thus a new rule may bias performance and occasionally deflect it, but the initial effect of such rules usually will be minor except where the system is "lost". A further increment to gracefulness is gained because a given rule usually serves as a component in a variety of situations. When it proves inadequate in a particular situation, this serves as a trigger for the generation of variants (exceptions), with the natural emergence of a robust default hierarchy as a result.

Overall, the system of competing rules undergoing continual revision is much like an ecology. There are niches, adaptations exploiting them, and shifting hierarchies of interaction that yield great resilience under typical variations. At the same time such systems can undergo vast revisions when sufficiently unusual and disruptive stimuli occur (as, for example, in ecological "crashes" and Kuhn's 1962 "scientific revolutions").

3.2.2 System Constraints and Environmental Barriers

Any account of rule generation must address Peirce's problem of generating *plausible* new rules. The space of *possible* rules is effectively infinite, and the islands of potential utility are widely scattered. Upon sneezing three times in rapid succession while your foot is adjacent to a gray pebble with a red stripe, why do you not entertain the hypothesis "If you see a pebble with a red stripe, then you sneeze three times"? Contrary to the evolutionary epistemology of Campbell (1974a, 1974b), something simultaneously much more constrained and much more powerful than random "mutation" of existing rules is essential.

The problem of constraining hypothesis formation is presented in high relief in artificial intelligence research. Algorithms can be written to generate a profusion of hypotheses, far more than have a chance of being useful in realistic contexts. On the other hand, psychological research suggests that organisms are too limited in their ability to generate hypotheses. Animals and people often do not generate rules that are important to effective functioning. In fact, as we will see in chapter 5, they sometimes will not generate rules that are essential to their survival. A theory of rule generation should explain why it is that important rules are sometimes not generated by real systems.

In this section we will explore some of the constraints on rule generation and some of the barriers to rule generation. The constraints that we will discuss limit rule generation, but they should not be thought of as impediments. On the contrary, the system gains inductive power by virtue of being constrained to generate mostly hypotheses that are likely to be useful. The barriers that we will discuss, however, are just that—environmental or system impediments to the generation of useful hypotheses.

Triggering Conditions

As we have emphasized repeatedly, the application of inductive mechanisms can be valuably constrained by means of triggering conditions. Two important kinds of triggering conditions are the failure of a prediction and the occurrence of some unusual event. In the case of a failed expectation, the mechanism triggered will be specific to the difficulty, generating rules that are plausible repairs or additions to the active model (compare Brown and Van Lehn 1980). The techniques of causal analysis discussed in section 3.1.4 can be called upon not merely to change the strength of rules but, by modifying related rules at some higher level of generality, to generate new ones. Our principle of directed activation suggests that the system usually will not go too far afield in generating these new rules. The candidates will tend to be close associates to rules and messages that are currently active.

Similar constraints apply to the case of an unexpected event that is merely unusual but does not contradict the currently active model. If no general rules can be found to render the unexpected event explicable, the unusualness heuristic may generate a limited range of new rules constituting hypotheses to accommodate the event. (See Salzberg 1985 for an application of an unusualness heuristic in machine learning.)

Returning to our example of the pebble and the sneezes, we see that the pebble-sneeze rule is not likely to be generated because there are no special conditions to trigger it. Neither the pebble nor the sneezes are likely to be prominent in the system's goal-directed model of its environment. Moreover, no expectation generated by the model has failed. And although the sneezes might be categorized as an unusual event, the improbability that a representation of the pebble will be active when they occur makes it unlikely that an association of sneezes and pebbles will be formed. Even if a representation is active—perhaps because the sneezer is a student of rocks—the causal theories of any system not born yesterday will preclude rule candidates linking pebbles with sneezes. In chapter 5 we will see that unusual events that in fact are predictive of subsequent goal-relevant events will sometimes not find their way into an animal's hypothesis about its environment. This is likely to occur precisely when the animal's prior history gives it no reason to assume that unusual events of the kind in question could predict the kind of goal-relevant event in question.

Guidance from Inferential Rules
Triggering conditions enormously constrain the range of candidate rules that might be generated, but not all of the candidates will be sufficiently warranted to add to the system. Additional constraints are provided by higher-order inferential rules, which are domain-independent techniques for generating empirical rules.

The unusualness inferential rule operates throughout the animal kingdom. But people, and probably animals as well, also have a variety of inferential rules of a statistical nature that constrain rule generation. At the most basic level, category formation is guided by highly general rules about the expected distribution of properties across the category. As we will show in chapters 6 and 8, people have strong expectations that properties are distributed symmetrically around a single mode. Thus the observation of a single value for a property usually results in the assumption that the value deviates from the central tendency of the property by some unknown amount. Observation of several values creates a presumption that the values are best regarded as points on a unimodal symmetric distribution.

In chapters 8 and 9 we will show that people's assumptions about the distribution of properties for a given kind of object govern the degree of generalization that they will engage in given the observation of a new value for a property or given the observation of a value for a new property. The family of rules governing generalization includes close relatives of the statistician's law of large numbers.

In chapter 9 we will also discuss nonstatistical inferential rules that guide people's inductions. These include Harold Kelley's "causal schemas"—general rules for reasoning about classes of causal relations, such as multiple-versus-single causality and deterministic-versus-probabilistic causality—and "pragmatic reasoning schemas" for reasoning about recurring types of relations in the social world, such as permissions and obligations.

Recombination

Inferential rules do not operate on randomly selected structures. Instead they exploit the combinatoric advantages of building blocks and hierarchies, composing new structures through the *recombination* of old ones.

The idea underlying procedures for recombination is that the most useful parts of existing units can be extracted and recombined in novel ways. There are two basic sources for new rules, namely, inputs from the environment, which can exhibit novel combinations of properties and relations, and existing structures, which can be transformed or combined, serving as sources of tested building blocks. Recombination can operate at different levels. Parts of the conditions and actions of individual rules can be recombined to form new rules, as can entire conditions and actions. Moreover, if rules are organized into sets— either implicitly via rule couplings, as in classifier systems, or more explicitly by the formation of "concepts", as in the system PI (see chapter 4)—then the rules in different sets can be recombined to generate new concepts. In addition, analogical mappings can be used to generate new rules by transforming old ones.

Clearly, any scheme for the recombination of building blocks depends on techniques for identifying those building blocks that are the most likely to generate plausibly useful new structures. In the case of recombinations of existing rules, rules that have achieved high strength under appropriate mechanisms for apportionment of credit are the most promising sources of building blocks for new rules. In addition, however, it is desirable to select the most appropriate *components* of rules of relatively high strength. This selection process is accomplished in classifier systems by "genetic operators" that combine the components of existing rules to form new ones. Such operators will be described in chapter 4. The recombination techniques described there and in the present chapter use three methods to constrain rule generation: (1) strong rules and important messages are preferred sources of components for new rules; (2) rules and messages active at the same time are most likely to be recombined; and (3) new rules are created from existing ones by specific adaptive types of transformations.

Point (1) above will be illustrated in chapter 6 when we discuss the role of "focused sampling" in category formation. Features present in rules that are proving predictive are preferred as candidates for inclusion in the condition or action portions of potential new rules. Sampling of features in a feature-rich environment is thus constrained in a highly useful way—useful, that is, so long as the features included in predictive rules are in fact present in others that would prove predictive as well. This is of course the case for most concepts and categories. Sometimes features occurring in the condition or action of one rule will be completely predictive of features occurring in another. More typically, features will merely be statistically correlated. But even in the latter case, as we will see, the principle of focused sampling can be a great aid to category formation.

Point (2), that recombination favors simultaneously active rules and messages, will be important to remember as we discuss the animal conditioning literature in chapter 5. We will present evidence there showing that animals can often learn simple diachronic rules extremely rapidly, sometimes in as few as one or two trials. It should be borne in mind that such impressive learning capacities are heavily restricted to the temporal parameters of the learning situation. In our terminology, when the predictive message is not active at the same time-step as the to-be-predicted event, then learning will not take place. For animals (and often for people) the temporal decay can be quite rapid. Learning may be retarded or may not even occur when events are separated by more than two or three seconds.

Point (3), concerning the production of adaptive recombinations, recapitulates our earlier assertion about the role of prior causal theories in ruling out generalizations such as those concerning pebbles and sneezes. Many new rules will tend to be specializations of preexisting general ones. This constraint is an enormous advantage in an orderly and familiar universe. It can of course be a disadvatage when nature (or more likely an experimental psychologist) sets up strange contingencies between events. It can also be a disadvantage when the general rule is too strong relative to the noise and uncertainty inherent in the available information. Under these conditions both animals, as we will see in chapter 5, and humans, as we will see in chapters 6 and 7, will generate specializations of a strong rule but will be unable to disconfirm it.

Impediments to Rule Generation

The constraints just discussed put limitations on what rules are formed, but they actually make rule generation more powerful in any realistic world, since they guide exploration of the effectively infinite space of rules. But there are also limitations of a different kind that hinder systems in their attempts to form plausible and useful rules.

We alluded to a particularly important barrier in our discussion of recombination. Normally, only messages that are currently active stand a chance of being used in the generation of new conditions for rules. We will review evidence that shows that, at least for relatively arbitrary stimuli such as lights and tones, the representation of a stimulus decays very rapidly. Thus it may never become a candidate for incorporation in a new rule, even though it perfectly predicts some subsequent goal-relevant event. This severely limits the learning of diachronic rules. Only if an event is represented at some higher level of the default-hierarchy representation of the overall situation is it likely to be a candidate for rule formation, unless the event it signals follows very rapidly.

A second type of barrier to effective rule generation is the failure to encode events. Events that are not encoded cannot become candidates for inclusion in a rule, no matter how perfectly they predict, and no matter how important the event predicted. We will provide substantial evidence of the importance of encoding in chapter 7, where we will discuss the finding that younger children often do not learn rules about the behavior of balance beams that include the factor of the distance of the weight from the center of the fulcrum. In chapter 8 we will show that people often do not apply statistical rules to events that require them, not because they lack the rule but because they lack the ability to code the events in such a way that the rule can be applied. In chapter 9 we will present evidence that people often can be helped to apply statistical rules merely by training in the relevant encoding.

Finally, perhaps the most important general barrier to learning all the rules that would be beneficial is the fact that the statistical associations between candidate events are simply too low to allow for detection of their covariation. We will present evidence in chapters 5 and 6 that, especially for events for which animals and people are unprepared by prior theories to see an association, covariation detection capacities are sufficiently bounded that important associations may never be discovered. This is true for the learning of both synchronic and diachronic rules.

3.3 Generation of New Rules

We are now prepared to discuss the major types of knowledge modification in light of the requirements and constraints we have identified. In terms of our framework, the natural way to organize this topic is to distinguish among mechanisms for generalization and specialization, for associating related rules, for category formation, and for analogy.

These mechanisms are ordered with respect to their inherent complexity, but any such classification is somewhat arbitrary. Virtually all inductive inferences may be regarded in one sense as either generalizations or specializations. This is true even for a rule that an animal might learn in a conditioning experiment, such as "if tone, then expect shock." As we will see, the commitment implied by such a rule to the expectation that another tone will be followed by another shock is tantamount to a generalization. In addition, given a prior rule describing the effector action appropriate to shock ("If shock, then suppress bar pressing"), the two rules will naturally be associated, or coupled, in a two-rule sequence. Category formation is a relatively complex form of generalization. It typically involves both the generation of novel rules and the clustering and strength revision of existing ones. Again though, even simple conditioning can be regarded as involving category formation. The tone, once it gains meaning as a signaler of shock, is well understood as belonging to several categories—the category of tones that signal shock, the category of events that signal danger, and so on. Finally, analogy, as it arises in the most sophisticated types of human reasoning, is perhaps the most complex type of knowledge modification procedure. At this level it usually involves a substantial amount of generalization and specialization and depends also on the application or formation of several categories. On the other hand, there is a sense in which even the rat in a conditioning experiment is engaged in detecting analogies. The tone must be perceived as analogous to another tone (perhaps of a different intensity and frequency), the Skinner box in which it is busily pressing a lever for food must be perceived as analogous to the conditioning chamber where the tone and shock were paired, and so on.

Thus our distinctions among types of rule modification are arbitrary to a degree, but only to a degree. As we will see, different issues, having to do with the nature and complexity of the mechanisms underlying rule modification, the importance of variability (and of the way variability is treated), and the role played by inferential rules, arise for the different types of rule modification.

3.3.1 Generalization and Specialization

As systems proceed along their inferential paths, they perform inductive housekeeping chores having to do with the modification of default hierarchies. The fundamental operations are generalization and specialization of existing rules. We will focus on two kinds of generalization that are particularly important in rule-based systems. The first is *condition-simplifying* generalization, which makes an existing rule more general by dropping or ignoring part of its condition. The second is *instance-based* generalization, in which a brand new rule is produced by associating two or more features found in examples. We will then go on to discuss specialization, and at the end of this section we will discuss generalizations produced by a process of *abduction* specifically for the purpose of explaining unexpected events. For a similar but more comprehensive taxonomy of generalization, see Dietterich and Michalski (1983).

Condition-Simplifying Generalization
The most elementary form of condition-simplifying generalization is the simple deletion of part of a rule's condition. The rule "If X has wings and X is brown, then X can fly" can be made more general by dropping the clause that X is brown, producing the rule "If X has wings, then X can fly." A less precipitate kind of condition-simplifying generalization relies on having two or more similar rules and taking the *intersection* of their conditions (compare the "interference matching" of Hayes-Roth and McDermott 1978). In taking the intersection of two conditions, requirements not held in common are treated as details to be ignored. The resulting condition is satisfied by any situation that would have satisfied *any* of the conditions intersected. As a simple example, consider the intersection of the two rules "If X is large-winged, brown, and feathered, then X can fly" and "If X is small-winged, brightly colored, and feathered, then X can fly." The result is "If X is feathered, then X can fly." In chapter 4 we will see how kinds of condition-simplifying generalization are produced by the genetic operators in classifier systems and by the inductive mechanisms of the system PI.

An appropriate triggering condition for condition-simplifying generalization is the joint activation of rules with the same actions and nearly the same conditions. The generalized rule formed under this condition is, of course, only a candidate generalization. If it yields correct predictions over the enlarged range, it will accumulate strength more rapidly than the more specific, less frequently activated original rules from which it was formed. In that case the originals will not serve as exceptions, because they do not correct mistakes of the more general rule. Otherwise, the new generalization may weaken to the point of being displaced, or it may arrive at some equilibrium with the more specific rules, serving as an addition to the default hierarchy.

Instance-Based Generalization

A second kind of generalization proceeds not from rules but from examples. The classic illustration is the inference that all swans are white based on a few instances of objects that are swans and white. Philosophers since Aristotle have been greatly concerned with this kind of generalization, most recently under the heading of "confirmation theory" (Hempel 1965); and it has been the focus of much recent work in artificial intelligence (for example, Winston 1975; Mitchell 1977, 1979). Here is a simple example. From the instances

Fido is a dog. Fido barks.
Rover is a dog. Rover barks.

we might generalize

If X is a dog, then X barks.

In the machine-learning literature this is often called "generalization by adding variables", because in the new rule that is produced the variable "X" replaces the constants "Fido" and "Rover" that appeared in the instances. This term, however, presupposes a representation rich enough to contain variables, so we prefer the more encompassing term "instance-based".

This kind of generalization can be triggered by messages describing instances with similar properties: since both Fido and Rover are dogs that bark, it may be that all dogs bark. The rules so formed are of course only candidates and must survive in competition with other rules; exceptions will weaken them. At higher ("linguistic") levels it may be possible to check explicitly whether generalization is warranted. The discussion of PI in chapter 4 describes how PI checks for counterexamples (knowledge of dogs that don't bark) and sufficiency of the number of instances (given background knowledge about variability) before carrying out generalizations. In chapter 8 we will discuss instance-based generalization in considerable detail, emphasizing the manner in which it takes into account relations of relevant concepts in the default hierarchy, as well as background knowledge about variability. The basic point we will make is that this sort of generalization must take into account the known variability of the *kind* of object in question with respect to the *kind* of property about which a generalization is contemplated. All swans will be presumed to be white on the basis of a few white examples only if the individual believes that all birds of a kind have the same color, or all shore birds, or all non-jungle birds. Such generalizations are thus intimately related to the manner in which instances are categorized and the manner in which variability is assessed. We intend to show that this dependence upon kinds and contexts defeats purely syntactic accounts of generalization.

Specialization

Once some reasonably strong rules have developed in the system by generalization or other means, other techniques can be used to refine the emerging default hierarchy. The need to have useful rules to model the environment propels the system to generalize, but the rules may later produce erroneous predictions. It would be wasteful simply to abandon the old rules, however, since the accumulated knowledge can be augmented by a specialization that produces an exception rule.

When a rule is identified as the source of a failed prediction (say, by a large loss under the bucket brigade or by causal analysis), the failure is often the result of an overgeneralization. The rule's condition is satisfied by the situation, but the result of the rule's action is not that predicted by the model. For example, the condition of the rule "If X is an animal with wings, then X can fly" may be satisfied by the appearance of a penguin, yielding the expectation that it will take to the air if chased. A subsequent chase discredits this prediction, yielding an "explanation" problem. Technically, the rule's condition treats the situation as the member of a particular equivalence class, but the transition invoked by the q-morphism does not satisfy the requirements for a homomorphism: the model does not preserve relations that exist in the world. This is exactly the situation in which we want to generate an exception rule that redefines the q-morphism.

A new rule is built from the existing one by (a) augmenting the condition of the existing rule with additional "unusual" properties of the failure context and (b) substituting the unexpected outcome as the action of the new rule. In the example above, the properties of the penguin not predicted by its classification as a bird (its unusual shape and locomotion—its "penguinhood") are likely to be used as the predictors of flightlessness. At the same time, a modified default rule may be created from the parent default rule by augmenting the condition of the existing rule with the complement of the properties used in the condition of the specialization. (For example, "If X is an animal with wings and not pudgy and waddling, then X can fly.") The modified default rule, when formed, serves the purpose of protecting a good generalization from buffeting by what would otherwise be frequent predictive failures. Specialization thus illustrates the operation of the unusualness heuristic.

Abduction

The unusualness rule for specialization is an example of induction in the service of explanation, in which a new empirical rule is created to render predictable what would otherwise be mysterious. More generally, there is a kind of inference to explanatory hypotheses that Peirce (1931–1958) called "abduction". Abduction is pervasive in human thinking, in applications as diverse as solving crimes, diagnosing illnesses, and accounting for people's behavior. A doctor will hypothesize that a patient has a certain disease, because that is the best explanation of the observed symptoms. You conjecture that a friend of yours tends to get irritable when overworked, because that would explain recent irascibility. In both these cases there is a puzzling set of facts to be explained, and a hypothesis constructed to account for them. As we will describe in more detail in chapter 11, the discovery and justification of scientific theories is also often the result of abduction.

One important type of abduction involves the triggering of a new generalization. Suppose an artist acquaintance is late for a meeting. You may form the general rule that artists are usually late, because that rule plus the fact that the tardy acquaintance is a painter would provide an explanation of the lateness. The motive for generalization here is not just to summarize knowledge about a number of instances, as in our earlier discussion of instance-based generalization, but to produce an explanation. Abduction will often require search through the default hierarchy of relevant concepts to find the most appropriate explanatory hypothesis, as in the example in chapter 1 of a mother trying to explain the behavior of a troublesome four-year-old. Such a search will also be guided by the variability of instances at a given level of the hierarchy. This type of abduction can be considered a kind of instance-based generalization triggered by an explanation problem.

Abduction generates explanatory hypotheses, but many of these can be expected to be weak or wrong. The most powerful mechanism for ensuring that a hypothesis is not arbitrary is to arrive at it by *multiple* abductions, showing that it explains a variety of facts. The discussion of PI in chapter 4 will describe multiple abductions, and it will give details about triggering conditions for abduction. Chapter 11 will show how this kind of reasoning plays a major role in the justification, as well as the discovery, of scientific theories.

3.3.2 *Generating Rule Associations*

The default hierarchy—the skeleton of a q-morphism—must be fleshed out with the associations and predictions (the synchronic and diachronic relations) that provide the combinatorial possibilities for handling the perpetual novelty of the environment. Section 2.2.2 of chapter 2 makes the point that in a message-passing rule-based system these relations can only be implemented by providing associations and interactions between rules. Indeed, the very basis of our approach—the treatment of concepts as clusters of rules—depends upon providing mutual interactions between rules. As described in section 3.1.2 of the present chapter, these interactions are provided by rule coupling. Coupling implements associations, clusters, and bucket brigades in a message-passing system. The inductive procedures that generate couplings in response to observed covariations and temporal relations thus have a central role in the induction of models.

Operating principles that provide coupling are triggered when strong, uncoupled rules are active in the same context or in close temporal order. Under this operating principle, when a strong rule is activated in the context of other strong rules, it gives rise to "offspring" rules that are more tightly coupled to the context rules. For example, if previously unassociated, well-established categories are paired—"light" and "shock", "cat" and "pet"—then the corresponding strong rules will be coupled by this operating principle. (The effect is similar to Hebb's 1949 synapse rule, in which connections between neurons that covary are strengthened.) The rationale for this kind of triggering condition is simply the observation that in a parallel system rules active in the same context are often mutually relevant (synchronic relations), and rules active in close temporal order often reflect causal connections (diachronic relations).

The offspring of this operation act only as tentative hypotheses. They will survive only if they prove useful to the system. Because coupled rules provide bridges for the bucket brigade, their strengths will be steadily refined to reflect usefulness. Ultimately, only synchronic or diachronic couplings that help attain goals (payoff) will be retained.

Diachronic Sequences

It might seem that the requirement of close temporal proximity would be too restrictive, making no provision for coupling between events well separated in time. Yet even the simple triggering condition just described can accomplish this. Consider a rule R_1 that remains continuously active over some considerable interval T. R_1 serves, in effect, as a "trace" of the event E_1 that activated it. Now let another event E_2 cause the activation of a strong rule R_2 during the interval T. Because R_1 is still active at the time E_2 activates R_2, the triggering condition already described provides coupled offspring with R_1 and R_2 as parents. The first offspring rule will be activated by E_1, and it will be coupled to a new rule that immediately activates the part of the model activated by R_2. E_1, in effect, causes an immediate "prediction" of E_2, even though E_2 occurred at some distance from E_1 in time. (The next chapter, in section 4.1.8, provides more detail about this process.) If there is a causal connection between E_1 and E_2, then the coupled offspring will thrive and become a permanent component of the system's q-morphisms.

There is a particular application that illustrates this procedure and shows its power. The procedure is initiated by the unusualness heuristic. Let us define an "unusual event" as any event not predicted by the activation of some rules in the system. Assume that any time an unusual event E_1 occurs, a strong rule R_1 is activated, as in the previous paragraph. (That is, the system has a built-in "detector" that is activated when the "unusual event" criterion is satisfied; R_1's condition is satisfied when this detector is activated.) Let E_2 be a second unusual event that follows E_1 at some distance in time. For example, E_1 could be "ingestion of an unusual food" and E_2 could be "sickness". (The persistence in animals of trace activations from an unusual taste is well known; see, for example, Garcia, McGowan, Ervin, and Koelling 1968.) The resulting coupled offspring rules can serve as the starting point for a variety of rules based on the hypothesized diachronic relation. This is a powerful heuristic used throughout the animal kingdom, often leading to useful adaptations. It can also sometimes lead to "superstitions", such as "I don't eat asparagus because it once made me really sick."

As a further example, consider the induction of a "plan hierarchy". Suppose that at the most general level there exists a rule or cluster of rules R_1 that suggests a way the system can attain some current goal ("If I get to my car, then I can eat at home"). R_1 remains active until the outcome is achieved (or abandoned). In other words, R_1 marks or characterizes the epoch during which the system is trying to execute the corresponding plan. There will be other rules in the system that can be combined to implement a somewhat detailed version of the plan. ("Go to the carport to get the car." "Turn left on leaving the carport.") The coupling procedure acts over time to couple these elements to R_1 (or its offspring), subject to the usual selection under competition. Thus, R_1 corresponds to a sketch that is filled in by the more specific rules. Because of the coupling, R_1 supports rules that are useful alternatives for filling in the sketch. As a result, support spreads in a directed fashion from the sketch, selecting plausible alternatives from a plethora of possibilities. Even a small number of rules can be combined in a great variety of ways to meet the constraints of a given application. ("If I leave the building by the rear door, then I can stop at the druggist on the way to the car.") The more detailed rules can, in turn, serve the same role as R_1, being implemented by still more detailed rules. Thus, over time, the coupling procedure develops plan hierarchies in much the same way that the other inductive procedures develop default hierarchies.

The interactions among coupling, strength, and support can be quite complex. Consider the case of a strong rule that begins to fail as the result of a change in the environment (for example, a rat no longer receives food when it presses a lever, after being consistently trained to the situation "If the lever is pressed, then food will be obtained"). The rule will lose strength under the apportionment-of-credit operating principle. However, its strength will decrease only to the point that it no longer determines behavior by winning against its competitors. Further losses will come much more slowly because the rule, when losing the competition, no longer pays bids to its suppliers. The rule will still be strongly coupled to and supported by salient perceptual cues (such as the lever). Accordingly, the rule, which summarizes experience over many trials, remains in the system for a considerable time as an insurance policy against a reversion of the environment to its old ways. (In the case of the rat, an "accidental" press of the lever that once more releases food will be quickly exploited, because the rule will not have to be "relearned"—an observation verified in countless experiments.)

Rule Clusters

Another important type of rule coupling is involved in developing categories, the topic of the next section and of chapter 6. We equate a category with a cluster of associated rules. This representation affords several advantages for the induction and refinement of categories: (1) a given rule can serve as a building block for multiple categories; (2) categories can be compared in terms of the rules and parts of rules held in common; and (3) there is no need to posit complex, monolithic categories for every conceivable situation (the "red Saab with a flat tire" problem).

The induction of rule clusters is based on the generation of synchronic couplings among rules. Clusters will emerge incidentally from the operation of the coupling procedures discussed above. Rules form a cluster when their conditions share some common component, or tag (see section 3.1.2). Any rule that produces this tag as part of its action will thereby be coupled to the entire cluster of rules that respond to messages with the tag. The tag serves as an "address" for the cluster. Looked at another way, the tag becomes a kind of label for the cluster of rules—an incipient symbol for the corresponding category. The category-as-rule-cluster may simply exist implicitly, defined by the shared tag in the conditions of the clustered rules, or an operating principle might explicitly identify the cluster on the basis of the shared components (see chapter 4). The processes of selection and recombination that we have described will tend to generate new rules that include the tag shared by strong current rules that become active together, thus extending the cluster and hence developing a richer category representation.

3.3.3 Category Formation

As systems proceed in problem solving and inference making, they are constantly creating and revising categories of various kinds. Our framework does not require distinctions among various kinds of complex knowledge structures, including categories, concepts, and schemas. We treat all of these as clusters of rules, as described in the preceding section. These may be formed either by "bottom-up" processes of covariation detection and revision of statistical parameters representing the distribution of properties or event likelihoods, or by "top-down" processes that we will describe at the end of this section and in the section on analogy.

Statistical Aspects of Category Formation

In chapter 6 we will discuss two important aspects of category formation. The first of these is the detection of the statistical aspects of property distributions over categories. We will show that people have a clear representation of these distributions and that they are formed in part on the basis of highly general rules about the nature of property distributions in general. Once formed, the implicit property distributions guide subsequent categorization decisions and subsequent generalizations about newly observed examples of the category.

The second important aspect of category formation that we will discuss in chapter 6 is the principle of focused sampling. When trying to learn the rule clusters that characterize a category or concept, people do not attend equally to all features in a complex array. Instead they focus on those features that are contained in rules that are proving usefully predictive (thus propagating useful shared components of rules, as described above). To the extent that features are associated statistically, this strategy can produce learning far more rapidly than an unfocused or random feature-sampling strategy could do. In such a "correlated feature" environment any initial focus could provide an entering wedge to learning the entire set of covariations.

Conceptual Combination

A complex form of rule generation at the cognitive level involves the integration of rule clusters of the sort that comprise "concepts" in the system PI. A concept is a data structure that explicitly clusters rules concerning a particular category. Thus the concept "chair" ties together various rules about chairs. Concepts can be formed in a bottom-up fashion by identifying multiple rules with similar conditions but varying actions. Here we will preview a more top-down mechanism by which new concepts can be formed from existing ones.

Conceptual combination is a pervasive feature of human language and thought, occurring in mundane contexts such as the utterance of adjective-noun pairs, but also playing an important role in scientific discovery, as described in chapter 11. Osherson and Smith (1981) offer many examples of conceptual combinations that are not adequately treated by simple syntactic mechanisms. They show that fuzzy set theory is inadequate to account for such combinations as "pet fish" and "striped apple". These examples show that complex representations and mechanisms are required to deal with cases where the combined concepts produce conflicting expectations: typical fish are not pets, and typical apples are not striped.

The formation of new concepts by directly combining old ones can be viewed as a sophisticated form of specialization, in which the "offspring" is an instance of two superordinates: a pet fish is both a pet and a fish. In all but the simplest cases, conceptual combination requires the resolution of conflicts between the features or rules attached to the concepts to be combined. In particular, default expectations often conflict. You probably expect a feminist to be politically active and a bank teller to be relatively apolitical, but what do you expect of a feminist bank teller? As we suggested in chapter 1, construction of such complex new structures is important for modeling novel situations. Combination of the concepts of feminist and bank teller should produce useful new rules about feminist bank tellers.

Combining two concepts requires the construction of a new concept that carries over some of the rules attached to the donors, but when and how is this done? Typically, combination is triggered when two highly active concepts have instances in common, but the rules attached to the concepts produce conflicting expectations about the instances. A new concept with new rules is then constructed in order to reconcile the expectations. One of the most important determinants of conflict resolution is the degree of variability characterizing each of the donor concepts with respect to the property in question. The less variable the donor is with respect to the property, the more it influences the offspring concept. In chapter 4 we will provide a more detailed discussion of conceptual combination as it is implemented in PI.

3.3.4 *Analogy*

Analogy, particularly in the guise of metaphor, is a subtle, powerful inductive process, often viewed as a mysterious fount of creativity. It imports experience to less familiar domains from other domains, to provide plausible hypotheses and plans. Because all of the types of mechanisms discussed thus far come to bear in the construction of analogies, it has a central place in our approach to induction. Consequently, we will devote the whole of chapter 10 to analogy. Here we want only to introduce the topic and indicate some of its connections with the discussion to this point.

We will argue that analogy can best be understood as a process for using a q-morphism in one domain to construct a q-morphism for another. As systems search for valid q-morphisms, they are guided primarily by their categorizations of both the target problem and potential donor or "source" problems. The primarily synchronic categorizations provide access to primarily diachronic rules underlying the solution in the source problem.

One of the major principles guiding categorizations is that they tend to be goal-centered. This pragmatic aspect of categorizations dictates that purely syntactic accounts of analogy are doomed to failure. Near-perfect syntactic matches often will not be detected if the characterization of the goal is not sufficiently similar to trigger an analogy. In contrast, goal characterizations that are sufficiently similar across donor and target may result in the detection and successful application of analogies that are relatively poor ones in a structural or syntactic sense.

Another consequence of categorization-guided analogy is that the detection of analogies will depend on the overlap of features between source and target. This means that feature matches that link remote problems may serve to trigger inappropriate analogies by virtue of their participation in shared categories. If the analogy is examined critically, this is not necessarily a problem, since the analogy ultimately may be rejected as the basis of action. On the other hand, when the system operates with real-time constraints or at a subcognitive level, such inappropriate analogies can be a source of error.

A final point here about analogies is that they are an important source of top-down category or schema construction. The construction of a novel analogy often results in the induction of a schema that provides an effective bridge across disparate domains.

3.4 Insertion of New Rules: Education

So far we have spoken about systems as if they had to go it alone, learning everything by the sweat of their brows or the hum of their central processors. Fortunately, that is not the case. New rules can be suggested to systems by external agents such as teachers and programmers. Our framework has a great deal to say about the effects of such instruction and the ways in which it both resembles and differs from knowledge acquired by induction.

The most important thing to say about inserted rules is that they will tend to act in some important aspects like induced rules. That is to say, they will enter into competition for the right to represent the environment along with the rest of the rules in the system's possession. This fact may seem obvious in terms of our framework, but in fact it is often forgotten by teachers, who frequently behave as if their charges were blank slates, upon whom they merely have to inscribe the new rules in order for them to carry the day under the appropriate conditions. We will show in chapter 7 how instruction in physics is often rather ineffective in influencing people's approaches to the mechanical problems they encounter in everyday life. This ineffectiveness is in our view best understood as the result of the inability of the new rules to compete effectively with old, well-established intuitive rules that are entrenched in the default hierarchy. As we will see, the problems of teaching social psychology are even more marked.

A second important aspect of inserted rules is that they will not even compete with older, induced rules if their application requires encodings that the system has not yet mastered. In chapter 8 we will show that people use particular abstract statistical rules only in domains for which they can readily encode the variability of events. In chapter 9 we will show that people can make no use of instruction in logical rules unless they also are shown how to encode events in terms that can make contact with the rules.

Finally, we will show that because people possess abstract, domain-independent inferential rules, it is possible to improve their ability to reason about a potentially limitless range of events by formal instruction in the nature of the abstract rules themselves. We will show in chapter 9 that people's ability to reason statistically about an extremely wide range of events is improved by purely formal, abstract instruction in statistics. We will argue that this is the case because people already possess intuitive versions of some statistical rules that they have induced by reasoning about uncertain events. Since they have intuitive versions of these rules, they also have means of encoding events in terms of them. Thus, abstract rule instruction is "carried through" to essentially the full range of events that people can already encode in the necessary way. It also follows from our analysis that people's ability to apply abstract rules could be improved by instruction in appropriate ways of encoding events. In chapter 7 we will present evidence that instruction is helpful in the case of empirical rules. In chapter 9 we will present evidence that this is also true of inferential rules.

3.5 Illustrations of Induction

We now return to Jennifer, who, you will recall from chapter 2, has just satisfied herself that the black animal in the middle distance is a cat, indicated in figure 3.3 by a message with a "confirmed" tag. Her goal of getting close to it is now given further importance. Also, quite automatically the rules that constitute her q-morphism for "cat" have been activated and have posted messages (figure 3.3). These include such default information as that it will be four-legged, sharp-clawed, and so on. Unfortunately for Jennifer, with her redoubled desire to get close, her cat q-morphism contains no indications of procedures she might use to achieve this goal. Further processing is required to search for a means of getting close.

The resulting search is illustrated in figure 3.4. Messages generated during the search are given a special tag ($[s]$ in figure 3.4) indicating "search". The messages generated by rules for which "cat" is a condition represent properties associated with cats, such as "round head" and "four-legged". These properties constitute simple categories that in turn activate rules that post messages corresponding to instances of the categories. Many shared properties converge on the category "dog", providing considerable support for rules for which "dog" matches the condition, causing such messages as "pet" to be posted. The q-morphism for "dog" provides a useful analogy, because a message (indicated by * in figure 3.4) generated by rules coupled to "dog", together with the goal message ("getting adjacent", and its possible subgoal "summon"), serves to match a rule that provides a potential solution ("If your goal is to summon X, and X is a certain kind of pet,

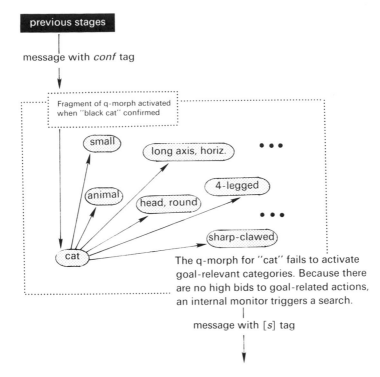

Figure 3.3
Search initiated by lack of goal-relevant categories.

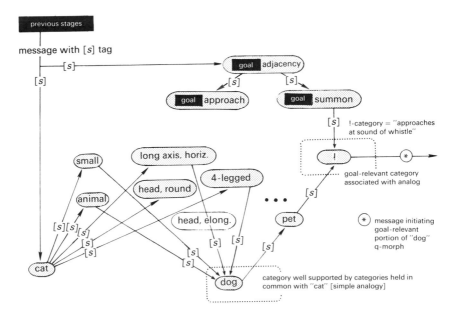

Figure 3.4
Goal-relevant category provided by simple analogy.

then whistle"). (The role of shared properties in finding useful analogies will be discussed more fully in chapter 10.)

The resulting analogical solution is depicted in more detail in figure 3.5. The category triggered by "dog", together with the goal, matches a rule specifying an effector action ("whistle"). (Compare the top portion of figure 3.5 with figure 3.1 (b).) To pursue the analogy, the initial category "cat" is tentatively assumed to satisfy the condition matched via "dog" (indicated by ! in figure 3.5). The system then enters a "lookahead" mode, in which generated messages are given a special "virtual" tag ([v] in figure 3.5) to suppress overt effector actions. Lookahead produces a match to rules that generate expectations, such as that if the cat is summoned it will approach and hence be adjacent.

Jennifer now has a hypothesis: The cat may come if I whistle. (Though older brothers are often annoying or worse, Jennifer's has his good points, among them the fact that he has taught her to whistle.) Jennifer accordingly whistles, in the expectation that the cat will approach. As indicated in figure 3.6, however, this attempt at solving her problem fails—the cat simply remains at a distance, grooming itself. The expectation that the cat will approach in response to the whistle fails to match the subsequent input from the environment. This predictive failure will serve as a triggering condition for the generation of new rules that will enter into competition with the extant rules. Figure 3.6 illustrates some of the new rules that may be generated. A new rule—(1) in figure 3.6—is inserted indicating that "cat" is a kind of thing that does not approach in response to a whistle. This rule is coupled to one—(2) in figure 3.6—that will inhibit whistling to summon such obstinate creatures. The new rules generated may include specializations of existing rules ("If X is a pet and a cat, it will not come when you whistle"), generalizations ("If X is a cat, then it won't come when you whistle"), and abductions ("If X is a cat, then it ignores whistling children").

In the next chapter we will describe in greater detail computational implementations of some of the procedures for rule modification that we have discussed.

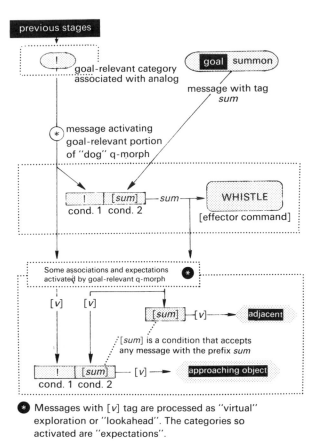

Figure 3.5
Action and expectations initiated by goal-relevant category.

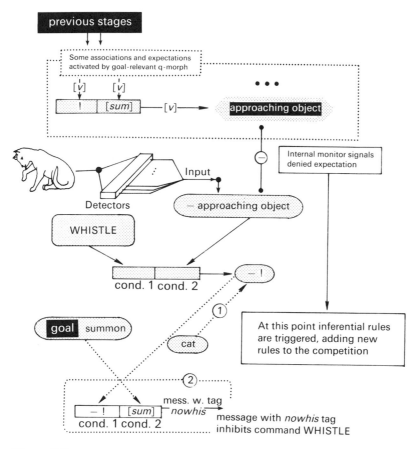

Figure 3.6
Q-morph revision caused by failed expectation.

Computational Implementations of Inductive Systems

In this chapter we will describe two examples of rule-based systems that can be characterized as learning by construction of mental models. One, the classifier systems of Holland (1986), operates with highly general learning mechanisms applied to a simple representational scheme. Many of the ideas about performance and learning presented in chapters 2 and 3 are generalizations of properties of classifier systems. The second system to be described, PI (Thagard and Holyoak 1985), operates with more constrained learning mechanisms that are applied to relatively complex representations in response to various triggering conditions. PI is evolving as an account of the generation of qualitative theories. Despite their differences, both systems exemplify such fundamental characteristics of our framework as parallel activity of rules, constraints on the generation of plausible new rules, and induction of default hierarchies.

It should be noted that this chapter is much more technical than those that precede or follow it, and readers who are unfamiliar with computational procedures may wish to read only selectively in it. An understanding of our treatment of the empirical phenomena in chapters 5–10 does not depend on appreciation of the details of our computational illustrations.

Computational implementation serves to demonstrate the coherence of a set of ideas about performance and learning. The framework we have outlined posits very complex processes of rule application and generation, but the efficacy of most of these processes has been tested in the two programs we will describe. Ideally, a full theory of induction would be implemented by a single processing system that carried out all the inductive operations deemed desirable. Unfortunately, much needs to be discovered before such a unified system will become possible. Our computational experiments have spanned the two levels mentioned in chapter 1, the cognitive and the subcognitive. Classifier systems employ simple but robust learning mechanisms not typically associated with conscious processes, while most of PI's learning mechanisms are close to those that humans might describe themselves as performing. The cognitive/subcognitive distinction applies to these systems only approximately, since classifier systems are capable of higher-order operations, such as planning, while PI includes some mechanisms that are not accessible to consciousness, such as conceptual combination. We must leave as a major long-term aim of a complete theory of induction the provision of an account of how learning at the subcognitive level is integrated with learning at the cognitive level.

4.1 Classifier Systems

4.1.1 Properties of Classifier Systems

Classifier systems are general-purpose programming systems that have many affinities to the rule-based (production system) approach to expert systems (see, for example, Davis and King 1977; Waterman and Hayes-Roth 1978). The most important properties of a classifier system are the following:

1) *Parallelism.* Large numbers of rules, called *classifiers*, can be active simultaneously. Problems of "scheduling" are avoided because the only action of an active classifier is to post a message to a message list—more active classifiers simply mean more messages. (The rules are called classifiers because they can be used to classify messages into general sets, but they are much more powerful than this name would indicate, providing both processing and recoding.) The system uses the rules as building blocks, activating many rules concurrently to summarize and act upon a situation.

2) *Message passing.* Classifiers, as is usual with production systems, consist of a *condition* part and an *action* part, but the conditions are all defined in terms of the set or class of messages that satisfy them. That is, a classifier becomes *active* when each of its conditions (there may be more than one in the condition part) is satisfied by the presence of an appropriate kind of message on the message list. The action part of the classifier then specifies a message to be posted to the message list on the next time-step. A classifier system can be viewed as a kind of office, with various individuals (the classifiers) processing selected memos (the messages) from a pool (the message list). To keep the definition of individual classifiers simple (which facilitates the generation of new classifiers, as we will see), all messages and conditions are standardized

as binary strings of a fixed length. All communication from and to the outside (input and output) is via messages, so that any given classifier system can be connected easily to an environment or to other classifier systems. Interactions with an environment are handled via input interfaces (often a set of property detectors) that generate messages, and output interfaces (message-controlled effectors) that react to messages.

3) *Lack of interpreters.* Because the interaction of classifiers is solely via messages and does not depend upon the ordering of the classifiers in some store, and because the satisfaction of conditions is determined by a simple matching operation, there is no need for high-level interpreters as part of the computational mechanism. Messages incorporating tags, along with conditions requiring the presence of those tags, can be used to couple classifiers, force predetermined execution sequences, and so on. In consequence, as we will see, classifier systems are highly modular and graceful: it is possible, usually, to add new candidate classifiers to a classifier system without causing global disruptions, and there are local syntactic operators that generate such candidates.

4.1.2 Definitions of the Basic Elements: Classifiers and Messages

The major technical hurdle in implementing a simple message-passing version of a production system is that of providing a simple way of defining conditions in terms of messages. Each condition must specify exactly the kind or class of messages that satisfies it. Formally, the condition specifies a subset of the set of all possible messages. Most large subsets can be defined only by an explicit listing, a requirement that would be fatal to the compact specification of classifiers. There is, however, one large and important class of subsets that *can* be specified compactly. If, for convenience of definition, we assume that the class of messages is recoded into the set of all binary strings of length k, then the subsets of interest can be specified by strings of length k over the three-letter alphabet $\{1, 0, \#\}$. The $\#$ symbol plays the role of a "don't care" element in the sense that, wherever a $\#$ occurs in the string specifying the subset, one can obtain a message belonging to the subset by substituting *either* a 1 or a 0 at that point. For example, the string $11...1\#$ specifies a subset consisting of exactly two messages, namely, the messages $\{11...11, 11...10\}$. Similarly, the string $1\#\#...\#$ specifies the subset consisting of all messages that start with a 1. For a formal definition see appendix 4A to this chapter.

This nonlinguistic representation facilitates the evaluation and generation of rules. In particular, it is easy to check whether a given message satisfies a condition. The condition and the message are matched position by position, and if the entries at all non-$\#$ positions are identical, then the message satisfies the condition. The notation is extended by allowing any string defining a condition C to be prefixed by a "$-$", with the intended interpretation that $-C$ is satisfied just in case *no* message satisfying C is present on the message list.

When the condition part of a classifier is satisfied, its action part specifies a message to be placed on the message list on the next time-step. The action part is also specified by a string of length k using the $\#$ symbol. Here, however, the $\#$ serves a different purpose. It plays the role of a "pass through" element: Wherever the $\#$ occurs in the action part, the corresponding bit in a message satisfying the condition is passed through into the outgoing message. For example, if the action part of the classifier has the form $11...1\#0\#$, and the message $00...010$ satisfies the classifier's condition, then the outgoing message will be $11...1000$.

Notationally, the conditions in the condition part of a classifier are separated by a "," and the action part is separated from the condition part by a "/". Thus the classifier $\mathbf{C}$ having conditions $C_1, C_2, ... C_r$ and action A is presented in the form

$C_1, C_2, \ldots C_r/A.$

A *basic classifier system* consists of a list of classifiers, $\{\mathbf{C}_1, \mathbf{C}_2, \ldots, \mathbf{C}_n\}$, a message list, an input interface, and an output interface. The *basic execution cycle* of this system proceeds as follows:

1) Place all messages from the input interface on the current message list.

2) Compare all messages on the current message list to all conditions of all classifiers and record all matches.

3) For each set of matches satisfying the condition part of some classifier, post the message specified by its action part to a new message list.

4) Replace the current message list with the new message list.

5) Process the message list through the output interface to produce the system's current output.

6) Return to step 1.

Basic classifier systems can be combined, by coupling their interfaces, to form larger systems simply called *classifier systems*. (Often the resulting classifier system can be converted back into a basic classifier system by the expedient of combining the message lists of the component systems into a single global message list; see the discussion of *tagging* in section 4.1.3.) A classifier system may be augmented by algorithms for planning, inference, and learning. A variety of such algorithms designed for classifier systems will be discussed in section 4.1.9.

In basic classifier systems the mechanism for activating rules is very simple: all matched rules are activated. For classifier systems with learning mechanisms it is desirable to make activation dependent on additional parameters. These include the *strength* of a classifier, which is a measure of its past success, and *support*, which is a measure of likely relevance to the current situation. In section 4.1.6 we will discuss the role of these parameters in selecting rules for activation.

4.1.3 Simple Examples

At this point we can introduce a small classifier system that will serve to illustrate both the interactions of classifiers and the effects of learning and induction upon such rule-based systems. It will be useful to think of the sets of rules examined in various parts of the example as fragments of a simple simulated organism or robot. The system has a vision field that provides it with information about its environment, and it is capable of motion through that environment. Its goal is to acquire certain kinds of objects in the environment ("targets") and avoid others ("dangers").

The system's input interface produces a message for each object in the vision field, as shown in figure 4.1. This message gives the values, produced by a set of *detectors*, for each of a variety of properties (such as whether the object is moving or not and whether it is large or small). The detectors and the values they produce will be defined as needed in the example. The system has three kinds of *effectors* that determine its actions in the environment. One effector controls the *vision vector*, a vector indicating the orientation of the center of the vision field. The vision vector can be rotated incrementally each timestep (V-LEFT or V-RIGHT, 15 degrees in one simulation). The system also has a *motion vector* that indicates its direction of motion, often independent of the direction of vision (as when the system is scanning while it moves). The second effector controls rotation of the motion vector (M-LEFT or M-RIGHT) in much the same fashion as the first effector controls the vision vector. The second effector may also align the motion vector with the vision vector, or set it in the opposite direction (ALIGN and OPPOSE, respectively), to facilitate

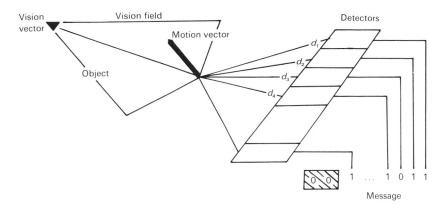

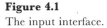

Figure 4.1
The input interface.

behaviors such as pursuit and flight. The third effector sets the rate of
motion in the indicated direction (FAST, CRUISE, SLOW, STOP).
The classifiers process the information produced by the detectors to
provide sequences of effector commands that enable the system to
achieve goals.

For the first part of the example let the system be supplied with the
following property detectors:

d_1 If the object is moving, the value of this detector is 1; otherwise, 0.

d_2, d_3 If the object is centered in the vision field, the value of this pair
of detectors is 0, 0; if the object is left of center, the value is 1, 0;
if the object is right of center, the value is 0, 1.

d_4 If the system is adjacent to the object, the value of this detector
is 1; otherwise, 0.

d_5 If the object is large, the value of this detector is 1; otherwise,
0.

d_6 If the object is striped, the value of this detector is 1; otherwise,
0.

In this example the detectors specify the rightmost 6 bits of messages
from the input interface, d_1 setting the rightmost bit, d_2 the next bit to
the left, and so on (see figure 4.1).

Example 1: A Simple Stimulus-Response Rule
Consider the following stimulus-response rule:

IF there is "prey" (*small, moving, nonstriped object*), centered in the vision field (*centered*), and not adjacent (*nonadjacent*),

THEN move toward the object (ALIGN) rapidly (FAST).

We can think of the system as an "insect eater" that seeks out small, moving objects unless they are striped (it does not seek out "wasps"). The condition part of the corresponding classifier attends to the specified detector values, using don't cares (#'s) elsewhere. It is also important that the classifier recognize that the message is generated by the input interface (rather than internally). To accomplish this, we assign each message a prefix or *tag* that identifies its origin—a 2-bit tag that takes the value 0, 0 for messages from the input interface will serve for present purposes. (Example 5 contains a discussion of the uses of tags.) Following the conventions of section 4.1.2, the classifier has the condition

$$00\#\#\#\#\#\#\#\#000001,$$

where the leftmost two loci specify the required tag, the #'s specify the loci (detectors) not attended to, and the rightmost six loci specify the required detector values, with $d_1 = 1 = moving$ being the rightmost locus, and so on. (This and other examples will use classifiers with 16-bit messages; realistic systems with more detectors will require longer messages.) When this condition is satisfied, the classifier sends an outgoing message, say

$$0100000000000000,$$

where the prefix 01 indicates that the message is *not* from the input interface. We can think of this message as being used directly to set effector conditions in the output interface. For convenience these *effector settings*, ALIGN and FAST in the present case, will be indicated in capital letters at the right end of the classifier specification. The complete specification, then, is

$$00\#\#\#\#\#\#\#\#000001/0100000000000000, \text{ ALIGN, FAST.}$$

Example 2: Rules Encoding Relations

A set of rules can detect a compound object defined by the relations between its parts. For example, the pair of rules below emit an identifying message when there is a moving T-shaped object in the vision field.

IF there is a centered object that is large, has a long axis, and is moving *along* the direction of that long axis,

THEN move the vision vector FORWARD (along the axis in the

direction of motion) and record the presence of a moving object of type *I*.

IF there was a centered object of type *I* observed on the previous time-step, and

IF there is currently a centered object in contact with *I* that is large, has a long axis, and is moving *crosswise* to the direction of that long axis,

THEN record the presence of a moving object of type T (blunt end forward).

The first of these rules is fired whenever the system "sees" an object moving in the same direction as its long axis. When this happens, the system scans forward to see if the object is preceded by an attached crosspiece. The two rules acting in concert detect a compound object defined by the relation between its parts (compare Winston's 1975 "arch"). Note that the pair of rules can be fooled; the moving "cross-piece" might be accidentally or temporarily in contact with the moving "*I*". As such, the rules constitute only a first approximation or default, to be improved by adding conditions or exception rules as experience accumulates. Note also the assumption of some sophistication in the input and output interfaces: an effector "subroutine" that moves the center of vision along the line of motion, a detector that detects the absence of a gap as the center of vision moves from one object to another, and beneath all a detector "subroutine" that picks out moving objects. Because we are interested in internal processes and induction, we will not go into further details about the interfaces; suffice it to say that reasonable approximations to such subroutines exist (see, for example, Jain 1981).

If we go back to our earlier fancy of the system as an insect eater, then the moving T-shaped objects can be thought of as "hawks" (not too far-fetched, because a "T" formed of two pieces of wood and moved over newly hatched chicks causes them to run for cover; Schleidt 1962).

To represent these rules as classifiers, we need two new detectors:

d_7 If the object is moving in the direction of its long axis, then the value of this detector is 1; otherwise, 0.

d_8 If the object is moving in the direction of its short axis, then the value of this detector is 1; otherwise, 0.

We also need a command for the effector subroutine that causes the vision vector to move up the long axis of an object in the direction of its motion; call it V-FORWARD. Finally, let the message 0100000000000001 signal the detection of the moving *I* and let the message 1000000000000010 signal the detection of the moving T-shaped object. The classifier implementing the first rule then has the form

00######01#1#110/0100000000000001, V-FORWARD.

The second rule must be contingent upon *both* the just-previous detection of the moving *I*, signaled by the message 0100000000000001, and the current presence of the crosspiece, signaled by a message from the environment starting with tag 00 and having the value 1 for detector d_8:

0100000000000001, 00######10#1#001/0100000000000010.

Example 3: Simple Memory

The following set of three rules keeps the system on alert status if there has been a moving object in the vision field recently. The duration of the alert is determined by a timer, called the alert timer, that is set by a message, say 0100000000000010, when the object appears.

IF there is a moving object in the vision field,

THEN set the alert timer and send an alert message.

IF the alert timer is not zero,

THEN send an alert message.

IF there is *no* moving object in the vision field and the alert timer is not zero,

THEN decrement the alert timer.

To translate these rules into classifiers, we need one effector, SET ALERT, that sets the alert timer, and another, DECREMENT ALERT, that decrements the timer. We also need a detector that determines whether or not the alert timer is zero:

d_9 If the alert timer is *not* zero, then the value of this detector is 1; otherwise, 0.

The classifiers implementing the three rules then have the form

00##############1/0100000000000011, SET ALERT,

00####1#########/0100000000000011,

00####1#########0/DECREMENT ALERT.

Note that the first two rules send the same message, in effect providing an OR of the two conditions, since satisfying either the first condition *or* the second will cause the message to appear on the message list. Note also that these rules check on an *internal* condition via the detector d_9, thus providing a system that is no longer driven solely by external stimuli.

Example 4: Building Blocks

To illustrate the possibility of combining several active rules to handle complex situations, we introduce the following three pairs of rules:

1) IF there is an alert and the moving object is near,
   THEN move at FAST in the direction of the motion vector.
   IF there is an alert and the moving object is far,
   THEN move at CRUISE in the direction of the motion vector.

2) IF there is an alert, and a small, nonstriped object in the vision field,
   THEN ALIGN the motion vector with the vision vector.
   IF there is an alert, and a large T-shaped object in the vision field,
   THEN OPPOSE the motion vector to the vision vector.

3) IF there is an alert, and a moving object in the vision field,
   THEN send a message that causes the vision effectors to CENTER the object.
   IF there is an alert, and *no* moving object in the vision field,
   THEN send a message that causes the vision effectors to SCAN.

Each of the rules in pair 3 sends a message that invokes additional rules. For example, "centering" can be accomplished by rules of the form

IF there is an object in the left vision field,

THEN execute V-LEFT.

IF there is an object in the right vision field,

THEN execute V-RIGHT,

realized by the pair of classifiers

$$00\#\#\#\#\#\#\#\#\#\#\#10\#/\text{V-LEFT},$$
$$00\#\#\#\#\#\#\#\#\#\#\#01\#/\text{V-RIGHT}.$$

Any combination of rules obtained by activating one rule from each of the three subsets 1, 2, and 3 yields a potentially useful behavior for the system. Accordingly, the rules can be combined to yield behavior in eight distinct situations; moreover, the system need encounter only two situations (involving disjoint sets of three rules) to test all six rules. The example can be extended easily to much larger numbers of subsets. The number of potentially useful combinations increases as an *exponent* of the number of subsets; that is, n subsets of 2 alternatives apiece yield 2^n distinct combinations of n simultaneously active rules. Once again, only 2 situations (appropriately chosen) need be encountered to provide testing for *all* the rules. Building the system's categories out of simple building blocks thus provides tremendous combinatorial advantages.

The implementation of the six rules as classifiers proceeds as in the earlier parts of the example; the requirement that the system be on alert status is met by using a condition that is satisfied by the alert message 0100000000000011. Thus the first rule becomes

$$0100000000000011,00\#\#\#\#\#\#\#\#\#\#\#\#\#1/\text{FAST},$$

where a new detector d_{10}, supplying values at the tenth position from the right in environmental messages, determines whether the object is far (value 1) or near (value 0). The other five rules are similarly implemented.

Example 5: Networks and Tagging

In each of the preceding chapters we have stressed the procedural importance of organizing knowledge into networks that constitute default hierarchies. In general, networks are built up in terms of *pointers* that couple the elements (nodes) of the network, so the basic problem is that of supplying classifier systems with the counterparts of pointers. In effect, we want to be able to couple classifiers so that activation of a classifier **C** in turn causes the activation of the classifiers to which it points. The passing of activation between coupled classifiers then acts much like Fahlman's (1979) marker-passing scheme, except that the classifier system is passing and processing messages. As in chapter 3, we will say a classifier $\mathbf{C_2}$ is *coupled* to a classifier $\mathbf{C_1}$ if some condition of $\mathbf{C_2}$ is satisfied by the message(s) generated by the action part of $\mathbf{C_1}$. Note that a classifier with very specific conditions (few #'s) will be coupled typically to only a few other classifiers, whereas a classifier with very general conditions (many #'s) will be coupled to many other classifiers. Looked at this way, classifiers with very specific conditions have few incoming "branches", whereas classifiers with very general conditions have many incoming "branches".

The simplest way to couple classifiers is by means of *tags*—bits incorporated in the condition part of a classifier that serve as a kind of identifier or address. For example, a condition of the form 1101##...# will accept any message with the prefix 1101. To send a message to this classifier, we need only prefix the message with the tag 1101. We have seen an example of this use of tags in example 4, where messages from the input interface are "addressed" only to classifiers that have conditions starting with the prefix 00. Because b bits yield 2^b distinct tags, and tags can be placed anywhere in a condition (the component bits need not even be contiguous), large numbers of conditions can be "addressed" uniquely at the cost of relatively few bits.

By using appropriate tags, one can define a classifier that attends to a specific *set* of classifiers. Consider, for example, a pair of classifiers $\mathbf{C}_1$ and $\mathbf{C}_2$ that send messages prefixed with 1101 and 1001, respectively. A classifier with the condition $1101\#\#...\#$ will attend only to $\mathbf{C}_1$, whereas a classifier with condition $1\#01\#\#...\#$ will attend to both $\mathbf{C}_1$ and $\mathbf{C}_2$. Using this approach in conjunction with pass-throughs ($\#$'s in the action parts) and recodings (where the prefix of the outgoing message differs from that of the satisfying message) provides great flexibility in defining the sets of classifiers to which a given classifier attends.

The most direct way of representing a network is to use one classifier for each pointer (arrow) in the network (though it is often possible to find clean representations using one classifier for each node in the network). As an illustration of this approach consider the network fragment in figure 4.2.

In the upper left corner of figure 4.2 there is a pointer from the MOVING node to the ALERT node. In marker-passing terms, the ALERT node acquires a marker when there is a MOVING object in the vision field. For the purposes of this example, we will assume that the conjunction of arrows at the TARGET node is just that, a requirement that all three nodes (ALERT, SMALL, and NOT STRIPED) be marked before TARGET is marked. Similarly, PURSUE will be marked only if both TARGET and NEAR are marked.

To transform this network into a set of classifiers, let us begin by assigning an identifying tag to each node. (The tags used in figure 4.2 are 5-bit prefixes.) The required couplings between the classifiers are then simple and can be achieved by coordinating the tags used in conditions with the tags on the messages to be passed. On this basis, assuming that the MOVING node is marked by the detector d_1, the arrow between MOVING and ALERT would be implemented by the classifier

$$00\#\#\#\#\#\#\#\#\#\#\#\#1/01001\#\#\#\#\#\#\#\#\#\#,$$

while the arrows leading from SMALL, NOT STRIPED, and ALERT to TARGET could be implemented by the single classifier

$$00\#\#\#\#\#\#\#\#00\#\#\#\#,01001\#\#\#\#\#\#\#\#\#\#$$
$$/10001\#\#\#\#\#\#\#\#\#\#.$$

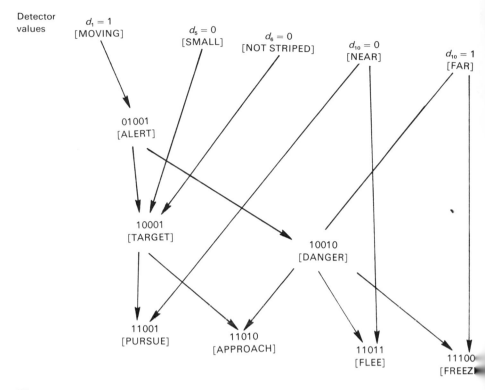

Figure 4.2
Fragment of a labeled network.

In turn, the arrows from NEAR and TARGET to PURSUE could be implemented by

$$0\#\#\#\#0\#\#\#\#\#\#\#\#\#,10001\#\#\#\#\#\#\#\#\#\#$$
$$/11001\#\#\#\#\#\#\#\#\#\#.$$

The remainder of the network would be implemented similarly.

Some comments are in order. First, the techniques for implementing Boolean connectives described in appendix 4A apply equally to arrows. For example, we could set conditions so that TARGET would be activated if *either* MOVING and SMALL or MOVING and NOT STRIPED were activated. Second, tags can be assigned in ways that provide direct information about the structure of the network. For example, in the network above, the first two bits of the tag indicate the level of the corresponding category (the number of arrows intervening between the category and the input from the environment). Finally, effector-oriented categories such as PURSUE would presumably call "subroutines" (sets of classifiers) that carry out the desired actions. For instance, the message from PURSUE would involve such operations as centering the object (see the classifiers in pair 3 of example 4), followed by rapid movement toward the object (see the classifier in example 1).

4.1.4 Rule Types in Relation to Classifier Systems

From the examples in the previous section we see that classifiers can be coupled to provide network-like interactions such as marker passing and message passing (compare Fahlman's NETL, 1979; and Hewitt's Actors, 1977). In particular, classifiers can be organized to represent mental models. Environmental messages cause the activation of a cluster of classifiers that provides the model wherein the system builds its responses to the situation. The tag on the outgoing message from a cluster can indicate the presence of some complex object, such as a "T" or an "arch", while the "pass through" bits carry incidental information, such as color and size, possibly relevant to further processing. When classifiers are used in this way to define categories, they constitute synchronic rules as defined in chapter 2. In addition, some classifiers serve the role of diachronic rules, furnishing expectations about future occurrences.

In addition to these two classes of empirical rules, classifiers can also be used to implement inferential rules. If the classifier system has *internal effectors*—message-sensitive operators for directly manipulating classifiers—then a classifier that sends messages to these effectors serves the role of an inferential rule. Because individual classifiers are simple and standardized, they are readily revised and recombined by such internal effectors. For example, consider a set of diachronic classifiers generating an expectation, together with a classifier that is activated if the expectation fails. The latter classifier can serve to trigger a set of classifiers that uses the internal effectors to provide specializations of the diachronic classifiers. (Normally these specializations would be added to the system as competitors for the original set.) This set of classifiers manipulating the internal effectors, along with the triggering classifier, would serve as an implementation of the specialization rule stated in chapter 2. Other inferential rules can be implemented through similar triggering mechanisms.

Inferential rules can be supplied to the system *ab initio*, or they may be generated by the system's operating principles. Classifier-system operating principles include the matching and message-passing mechanisms so far described, as well as two learning mechanisms to be described below: the *bucket brigade* algorithm and the *genetic* algorithm. The first of these provides the basis for competition between classifiers by apportioning credit to them on the basis of their past usefulness to the system; the second generates new classifiers by taking pieces of useful classifiers as building blocks. These two algorithms, working in concert, provide the basic learning mechanisms for the system, enabling it to construct goal-oriented models of its environment from its experience.

4.1.5 Rule Competition in Classifier Systems

Rule competition in classifier systems is implemented in terms of a *bidding* process, essentially as described in chapter 2, section 2.3.1, that determines which of the rules with matched conditions will be activated on a given processing cycle. The larger the bid made by a rule, the greater its probability of becoming active. Three parameters jointly determine the size of a rule's bid. Past usefulness is represented by a numerical parameter called *strength*. Relevance is a function of the *specificity* of the condition of the matched rule: the more detailed the rule's condition, the greater its specificity. By favoring more specific rules, the bidding process implements a default hierarchy in which specific exception rules tend to override more general default rules. Specificity can be determined in various ways but is particularly simple in classifier systems, since the specificity of a classifier's condition part can be measured by the number of non−$\#$'s therein: the more $\#$'s, the more general the condition.

A *support* parameter also enters into determining the bid. Let $\{\mathbf{C}^*\}$ be the set of active classifiers sending messages that satisfy conditions of classifier $\mathbf{C}$ at time t. Then the support $V(\mathbf{C}, t)$ for $\mathbf{C}$ is simply the sum of all the bids of the classifiers in $\{\mathbf{C}^*\}$,

$$V(\mathbf{C}, t) = \sum_{\mathbf{C} \in \{\mathbf{C}^*\}} B(\mathbf{C}, t - 1).$$

The bid made by $\mathbf{C}$, if *all* its conditions are satisfied, is then given by

$$B(\mathbf{C}, t) = bR(\mathbf{C}) S(\mathbf{C}, t) V(\mathbf{C}, t).$$

Here b is a constant, such as $1/8$, considerably less than 1; $R(\mathbf{C})$ is the specificity of $\mathbf{C}$, equal to the number of non−$\#$'s in the condition part of $\mathbf{C}$ divided by its length; $S(\mathbf{C}, t)$ is the strength of $\mathbf{C}$ at time t; and $V(\mathbf{C}, t)$ is the support of $\mathbf{C}$.

This formula indicates one way of evaluating the overall relevance of rules in terms of their strength and support. The size of the bid determines the probability that the classifier posts its message (specified by the action part) to the new message list. The use of probability in the selection step ensures that rules of lower strength sometimes get tested, thereby providing for the occasional testing of less-favored and

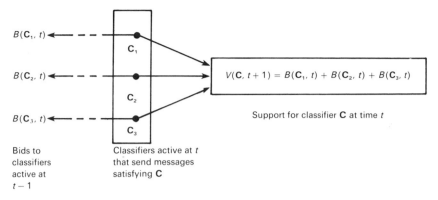

Figure 4.3
Bids change the strength of predecessors ("suppliers") and add support to
successors ("consumers").

newly generated lower-strength rules (see chapter 3). Note that a
classifier does not make a bid, regardless of the level of support, unless
all of its conditions are satisfied.

4.1.6 Strength Revision in Classifier Systems

Many of the learning mechanisms sketched in chapter 3 correspond
to specific operating principles that have been developed and tested
in the context of classifier systems. In current classifier systems the
bucket brigade algorithm (chapter 3, section 3.1.2) operates as follows. When a winning classifier **C** places its message on the message
list (under the competition described in section 4.1.5 above), it pays
for the privilege by having its strength $S(\mathbf{C}, t)$ reduced by the amount
of the bid $B(\mathbf{C}, t)$; that is,

$$S(\mathbf{C}, t + 1) = S(\mathbf{C}, t) - B(\mathbf{C}, t).$$

The classifiers $\{\mathbf{C}'\}$ sending messages matched by this winner (the
"suppliers") have their strengths increased by the amount of the bid.
In the simplest version it is shared equally among them:

$$S(\mathbf{C}', t + 1) = S(\mathbf{C}', t) + aB(\mathbf{C}, t)$$

where $a = 1/($number of members of $\{\mathbf{C}'\})$.

Bids now serve two purposes, as depicted in figure 4.3. In the
service of support, a bid moves *with* the flow of messages, adding to the
support of the consumers of those messages. The same bid, used to
revise the strength of a supplier, goes *against* the flow of messages,
serving as feedback.

4.1.7 Genetic Operators in Classifier Systems

As we argued in chapter 3, new rules can be generated by recombination only if the condition and action parts of rules can be decomposed into simple components that can be selected and combined easily. Hence the system must have a set of building blocks from which any rule can be constructed. The process of generating new rules then pivots on the use of experience to discover and exploit good building blocks. Candidate rules are generated by recombining good building blocks occurring in existing rules that are relevant to the triggering context. Classifier systems, by virtue of their simple representational scheme, allow the exploitation of powerful and general mechanisms for selecting good building blocks for new rules.

How is a cognitive system to rate the components from which its rules are constructed? The strength assigned to a rule provides an estimate of *its* usefulness to the system, but this does not give any direct estimate of the value of its components. There is, however, a simple way, and one quite effective for systems based on competition, to use this information to rate components: the rating of any component is taken to be the average of the strengths of the rules employing it. That is, a good building block is one that occurs in good rules. This is, of course, a crude estimate and one fraught with error in some cases. Nevertheless, the components so highlighted are plausible candidates for use in the construction of new rules, particularly if the system uses the estimates only to bias construction toward the use of such components.

At any given time t there will be several rules in the system employing any simple building block b. That is, the cognitive system has several *instances* of b. As suggested in the previous paragraph, we can assign value $v(b, t)$ to b at time t by averaging the strengths of its instances. For example, let the system contain rules $\mathbf{C}_1$ and $\mathbf{C}_2$ with strengths $S(\mathbf{C}_1, t) = 4$ and $S(\mathbf{C}_2, t) = 2$, respectively. If these are the only instances of b at time t, then we assign to the building block the value $v(b, t) = [S(\mathbf{C}_1, t) + S(\mathbf{C}_2, t)]/2 = 3$, the average of the strengths of the two instances. The general formula, when b occurs in each of $\{\mathbf{C}_1, \mathbf{C}_2, \ldots, \mathbf{C}_n\}$, is

$$v(b, t) = \sum_{j=1}^{n} S(\mathbf{C}_j, t)/n.$$

In classifier systems one can designate an important class of building blocks by simply specifying that certain letters from the alphabet $\{1, 0, \#\}$ must occur at certain positions in the condition and action parts of the strings defining the classifiers. (See appendix 4B for details.) We will call such building blocks *substring schemas*. Holland (1975) simply used the term "schema"; we use "substring schema" here to avoid confusion with the schema notion familiar in psychology. Under this interpretation a single rule can be an instance of an enormous number of building blocks: for a classifier condition of length k, the number of potential building blocks is 3^k. Accordingly, it is computationally infeasible to calculate and use the large set of averages $\{v(b, t)\}$ in reasonable amounts of time. The solution is to introduce recombination techniques, termed *genetic operators*, that accomplish this task implicitly by means of selective recombination of parts of rules (again, see appendix 4B). The main genetic operator we will discuss is *crossover*, which involves the recombination of two rules. Parts of each rule are combined to form a "hybrid" rule that is added to the system to compete with the other rules already there, including the "parent" rules. The offspring displace weak classifiers in the system. If the parent rules are of high strength, then the hybrid offspring is likely to inherit good building blocks from both parents.

Counterparts of this process of emphasis and recombination can be found at any level of abstraction, from the formation of neural cell assemblies (Hebb 1949) to the generation of complex concepts. It is vital to the understanding of genetic algorithms to know that even the simplest versions act much more subtly than "random search with preservation of the best," contrary to a common misreading of genetics as a process primarily driven by mutation.

Though genetic algorithms act subtly, the basic execution cycle is quite simple:

1) From the set of classifiers, select pairs according to strength—the stronger the classifier, the more likely its selection.

2) Apply genetic operators to the pairs, creating "offspring" classifiers. Chief among the genetic operators is crossover, which simply exchanges a randomly selected segment between the pairs (see figure 4.4). Note that crossover can be applied either to *both* the conditions and the actions of the parent rules (as in the generation of couplings, described below) or to only the conditions or only the actions.

3) Replace the weakest classifiers with the offspring.

This simple procedure can be proved to rate and exploit large numbers of building blocks using, implicitly, the averages $v(b, t)$. Surprisingly, more than M^3 building blocks will be usefully processed for every M classifiers processed by the algorithm, a phenomenon known as *implicit parallelism*. (See Holland 1975 for a proof and appendix 4B for an outline.) Genetic algorithms have been studied intensively by

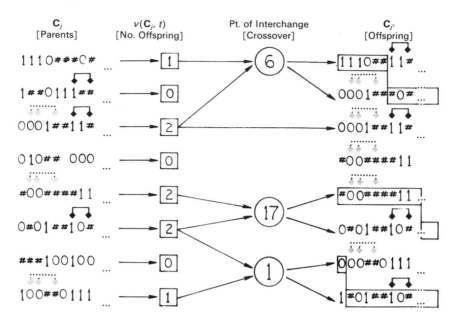

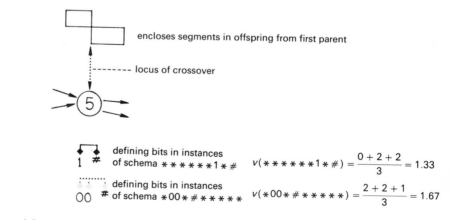

Figure 4.4
Illustration of the genetic algorithm.

analysis (Holland 1975; Bethke 1980) and simulation (for example, DeJong 1980; Smith 1980; Booker 1982; Goldberg 1983).

It is instructive to see how crossover can be used to produce couplings. Consider first a simple, direct procedure for coupling a pair of classifiers $\{C_1/M_1, C_2/M_2\}$: Simply replace condition C_2 in C_2/M_2 by the message specification M_1 from C_1/M_1, yielding a new classifier M_1/M_2. (Note that the #'s in M_1 are simply reinterpreted as "don't cares", yielding a valid condition from $\{1, 0, \#\}^k$.) Under this arrangement the message specified by M_2 will be emitted if either C_2/M_2 or M_1/M_2 is activated. But M_1/M_2 will be activated whenever C_1/M_1 is activated, providing the same effect as the direct activation of C_2/M_2 by C_1/M_1.

Now complicate this procedure somewhat by first crossing M_1 with C_2, as illustrated in figure 4.5. The "hybrids" H_1 and H_2 produced by the exchange of segments can be treated either as conditions or as message specifications, both being elements of $\{1, 0, \#\}^k$ (see appendix 4B). Adding the pair of classifiers $\{C_1/H_1, H_1/M_2\}$ or the pair $\{C_1/H_2, H_2/M_2\}$ to the system will produce the same coupling effect as the more direct procedure.

What advantage is there to adding the extra complication of crossover to the coupling procedure? The main advantage lies in the fact that the coupling is accomplished via a message specification distinct from M_1 and a condition distinct from C_2, yet with parts from both. This distinguishes activations produced by the new coupling rules from those produced by extant rules. There are serendipitous effects arising from the fact that the new action may "tap into" other conditions that share parts with it, and the new condition may respond to messages from other parts of the system because of shared parts. This would be intolerable if the new rules were other than plausible candidates or if the system were not graceful. As it is, crossover provides the system with a range of associations based on shared components (reminiscent of the role of overgeneralization in the formation of default hierarchies). Moreover, should the coupling prove to be important, the new rules substantially bias future possibilities under the genetic algorithm toward the patterns instantiated by the hybrids. The implicit parallelism of genetic algorithms assures a relatively rapid search of the patterns and combinations involved, leading to the generation of families of tags that produce useful couplings.

4.1.8 Generalization, Specialization, and Coupling

Classifier systems do not require any additional mechanisms for generalization and specialization. The genetic operators produce new

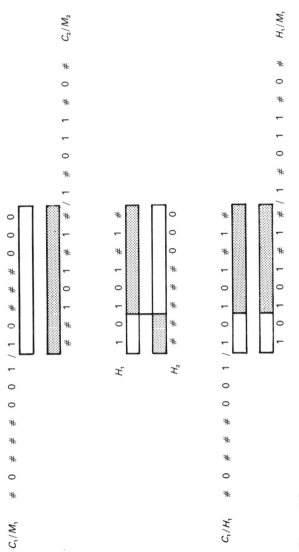

Figure 4.5
Coupling produced by crossing over.

rules that are generalized or specialized versions of existing rules. A more general rule is simply one that has had a 0 or 1 replaced by a don't-care #. This corresponds to the condition-simplifying generalization discussed in the last chapter. Conversely, replacement of a # by a 0 or 1 constitutes a specialization. Genetic operators will produce many such generalizations and specializations, with the useful ones preserved by the bucket brigade.

The essence of the problem of generating useful associations is, as before, the discovery of good building blocks. Tags serve as the building blocks from which associations are constructed. They can be used to "name" regions in a q-morphism and, used with synchronic rules, can associate regions in different q-morphisms. What tags, and pieces of tags, are useful? How are synchronic rules that contribute couplings to be rated? The technique is the same as with the rating of other building blocks: The rating of any tag is estimated by the average of the strengths of the rules using it. And, as before, we depend upon competition and operating principles, such as the bucket brigade and recombination, to refine this crude estimate. The result is the formation of coupled rule clusters embodying concepts useful in modeling.

The basic operating principles for coupling rules are triggered when strong (uncoupled or weakly coupled) rules are used together. Each time a strong rule is activated in the context of other strong rules, it tends to have offspring that are more tightly coupled to those rules. (Recall that a rule C_1 is tightly coupled to rule C_2 if C_2's condition is very specific with respect to the tag of messages sent by C_1.) This principle is both feasible and useful in systems where situations are "analyzed" by many simultaneously active rules, because rules that are active together are often mutually relevant. The mechanisms for apportionment of credit sort out which of these candidate couplings are in fact relevant to system goals. The generating procedures need only provide a reasonably restricted, plausible candidate set.

The more a rule becomes coupled to other rules, the more likely it is to be activated in varied contexts. If it survives under the bucket brigade, then its tags (and other components) are more likely to serve as building blocks for modeling goal-relevant parts of the environment. This, in turn, enhances the rule's role as an associator. As a common component of different concepts, it becomes a vehicle for the transfer of support and a dimension along which associated concepts (rule clusters) can be activated.

4.1.9 Applications of Classifier Systems

The earliest tests of genetic algorithms as rule generators for simplified classifier systems were reported in Holland and Reitman (1978). They demonstrated simple transfer of learning from problem to problem and showed that the genetic algorithm could provide order-of-magnitude speed-ups in learning over weight-changing techniques alone, even when the system's only task was to select appropriate rules from an initial repertoire that covered all possibilities. The results were encouraging enough to spark a variety of subsequent tests at several places. Smith (1980) completed a classifier system that competed against Waterman's (1970) poker-playing program (also a learning program) with overwhelming success. Wilson (1982) used a classifier system in a series of experiments aimed at TV camera–mechanical arm coordination. These experiments culminated in a successful demonstration of the segregation of classifiers, under the genetic algorithm, into sets corresponding to control routines. Booker (1982) has done an in-depth simulation study of classifier systems as models of the generation of cognitive maps based on experience.

The genetic algorithm is also useful outside the context of classifier systems. Robert Axelrod (1984) has been investigating the capabilities of the genetic algorithm for generating strategies for games such as Prisoner's Dilemma. In that game two prisoners must decide whether to cooperate with each other or to betray each other to the authorities. Axelrod ran a computer tournament in which strategies for playing Prisoner's Dilemma competed against each other. Surprisingly, the winner was one of the simplest strategies, called "Tit for Tat" because it requires performing whatever action—cooperation or betrayal—was most recently done by the opponent. Because the choice of actions is binary, strategies for this game have a natural representation in bit-strings, and Axelrod has been using the genetic algorithm to generate new strategies. The results are encouraging. The genetic algorithm has produced a strategy that outperformed Tit for Tat in a competition among a number of the best strategies from the computer tournament.

David Goldberg's (1983) use of the bucket brigade and genetic algorithms with a classifier system provides a particularly successful illustration of what can be accomplished within the framework we have been describing, and will be described in some detail. It is, to our knowledge, the first example of a system that, starting from a randomly generated set of rules, produces its own operational default hierarchy on the basis of experience.

Goldberg's system was designed to simulate the induction of the expert knowledge required to regulate gas-pipeline transmission. The system's objective is to meet demand at the end of a pipeline as economically as possible. This demand varies on an hourly basis and on a seasonal basis. Moreover, the pipeline may suffer transient leaks that upset the system's ability to deliver gas at appropriate pressures. The pipeline itself is a nonlinear system involving both storage and transmission, making it a fairly complex simulated environment.

At the beginning of each (hourly) time-step the input interface supplies a message summarizing the readings of a set of gauges and detectors in the environment: inflow, outflow, inlet pressure, outlet pressure, pressure change rate, season, time of day, time of year, and current temperature reading. It is important to note that none of these readings directly detects a leak; the system must induce the conditions under which a leak is present. The major control variable available to the system—the effector in its output interface—determines settings for pipeline inflow.

Payoff for the system is based upon the relation between the pressure delivered and the demand. The system also receives some payoff for successful leak detection and for appropriate action (for example, when the system acts to return the flow to an acceptable pressure when the pressure is out of acceptable range).

The classifier system that is coupled to this environment uses a message length of 16 bits, a message list that holds 5 messages, and a set of 60 classifiers. This is a *very* small system for such a complex problem. That it can accomplish so much bodes well for the theory underlying it. It is an interesting aside that the system was tested and run on a microcomputer with a 64K memory!

In a typical run there were 24 time-steps per day and the system achieved near-optimal (expert-level) performance in about 1,000 days of simulated experience (24,000 time-steps). The genetic algorithm was applied every 200 time-steps in order to give the bucket brigade time to summarize experience between changes in the rules. Thus a typical run involved approximately 120 generations under the genetic algorithm.

As we have emphasized, the system starts with a set of randomly generated classifiers. The bucket brigade algorithm strengthens the best rules in this set. They are typically overgeneral, incomplete, sometimes counterproductive rules. To give a concrete example (interpreted from the $\{1, 0, \#\}$ notation),

IF [input pressure is high, not rapidly increasing],

THEN [set the inflow control to a low value].

Such rules supply a starting point for the genetic algorithm and often serve (at least initially) as the top, most general level of the emerging default hierarchy. In the problem of leak detection, which is of most interest from the point of view of induction, the overgeneral rule retained in one case was

IF [anything (a condition with all #'s)],

THEN [send "no leak" message].

The genetic algorithm, acting by recombining parts of rules strengthened by the bucket brigade algorithm, eventually produced the rule

IF [input pressure low, output pressure low, rate of change of pressure very negative],

THEN [send "leak" message].

Both rules persisted in the system, the first indicating normal operation and serving as a default, the second serving to indicate an exceptional condition. When the conditions of both rules are satisfied, the second rule wins, if its strength is in the same range as that of the first rule, because of the higher bid based on its greater specificity. Note that the "profitability", and eventual strength, of the second rule depends upon its being coupled via its message to rules that take appropriate actions under leak upset and hence result in payoff under such conditions. Of course, these effector rules also must be discovered by the genetic algorithm. As the system gains experience, increasing specificity and correctness of the "leak indicator" rule and of the corresponding effector rules develop hand in hand. That is, parts of overgeneral, but better than random, rules are interchanged (crossed) to provide ever more specific, plausible refinements. Refinements that do indeed improve performance then serve under the genetic algorithm as the source of parts for still further refinements. The emergent default hierarchy, with its associated diachronic rules, is a consequence of this continual refinement of rules that improve performance.

4.2 PI

In earlier chapters we sketched how rules, organized into default hierarchies and operating in parallel, can constitute mental models. Classifier systems have provided a clear example of how to implement this computationally. We now describe another system, called PI for "processes of induction" (Thagard and Holyoak 1985), that also instantiates the framework we have sketched. Whereas classifier systems use genetic operators implicitly to carry out generalizations and specializations, PI has explicit algorithms for carrying out these kinds of induction, as well as abduction and concept formation.

PI is a program that performs several kinds of learning in the course of problem solving, including the development of simple qualitative scientific explanations. It also illustrates the use of various types of parallelism in solving ill-defined problems and in generating potential explanations for puzzling phenomena. We advise the reader that PI is still under development and so far has been tested only on the relatively simple examples discussed below.

Like classifier systems, PI uses rules to model relations in the environment. However, the rules are expressed as LISP structures, using a more linguistic representation than the classifier bit-strings encourage, and are explicitly organized into framelike data structures called *concepts*. PI solves problems by a process of rule firing and rule-directed spreading of activation of concepts. As problem solving progresses, working both from the starting conditions toward the goal and back from the goal to the starting conditions, several kinds of inductive inference are triggered in response to the currently active rules and concepts, as described below.

4.2.1 Rules and Concepts
In PI, conditions, actions, and messages are represented in LISP using a notation similar to that found in predicate calculus. For example, the effector rule

IF something is small, moving, and nonstriped, THEN pursue it

is expressed by a structure the condition of which is,

(SMALL (X) TRUE) (MOVING (X) TRUE) (STRIPED (X) FALSE)

and the action of which is,

(PURSUED (X) TRUE EFFECT).

Messages have the same structure as the components of conditions and actions; for instance, the information that Diane does not love Sam is expressed by

(LOVES (DIANE SAM) FALSE).

The goals and starting conditions of problems also have this structure.

There are losses and gains in using a richer representation than that found in classifier systems. The variable length of conditions and actions prohibits use of the simple but powerful algorithms for matching and combining classifiers. Moreover, the use of English predicates is potentially misleading, if one forgets that problem solving by animals (and probably a lot of it by humans) proceeds without benefit of linguistic representation. On the other hand, PI incorporates data structures that enable it to make several kinds of inductive inferences not easily made in elementary classifier systems. Also, PI constructs framelike declarative data structures that constitute a long-term memory; in classifier systems the long-term memory consists solely of rules and couplings between rules.

PI uses data structures termed concepts to organize both declarative information (equivalent to messages in long-term storage) and clusters of rules. Thus the concept DOG points to a set of rules about dogs, in addition to containing information about its superordinate ANIMAL and its instances (FIDO, ROVER). The rules attached to DOG include both synchronic rules such as "If X is a dog, then X is furry" and diachronic rules such as "If X is a dog and Y is a car, then X chases Y." Thus whereas rules are only implicitly organized in classifier systems by means of common tags in their conditions, rules are explicitly organized in PI by attachment to concepts. The factual knowledge against which the rules are matched is in the form of messages sent from active concepts to the central message list. Some messages describe instances of the concepts, so that when the concept DOG is active, the message that Fido is a dog—(DOG (FIDO) TRUE)—may be sent to the message list.

4.2.2 *The Processing Cycle*

The methods for generating and evaluating rules in PI differ from those in classifier systems. In addition, the attachment of rules to concepts makes possible a complex processing mechanism that carries out a kind of spreading activation of concepts and rules. PI is like a typical rule-based system in that processing is primarily determined by the firing of condition-action rules. But whereas most rule-based systems consider all rules for firing, PI considers only rules that have been activated through attachment to active concepts. Moreover, the "facts" against which the rules are matched are messages sent from active concepts to the central message list. Activation spreads through the system by the following cycle:

1) Active concepts make their associated rules and messages available for matching. Initially, the active concepts are those mentioned in the starting conditions and goals of the given problem.

2) The *conditions* of active rules are matched against the active messages and a predetermined number selected for firing; criteria for rule

evaluation include strength, support, and contribution to satisfaction of goals and subgoals.

3) The *actions* of active rules are matched against the goals to be accomplished. A successful match of a rule's action means that it can accomplish the goal if its conditions are met. For example, the rule "IF X is at a restaurant, THEN X can eat" will enable you to accomplish the goal of eating if you are at a restaurant. If the conditions are met, then the goal is accomplished; and if all goals are accomplished, then the problem is solved. Otherwise, the unmet conditions are established as *subgoals* to be accomplished in the next cycle. Concepts mentioned in those conditions are activated.

4) The actions of the selected rules are carried out: either new factual information is added to memory by storing lists of instances with relevant concepts, or, if the action is an effector, an operation is carried out.

5) The concepts mentioned in the actions of the fired rules become active.

6) Concepts not used on this time-step have their degree of activation decremented, and ones that drop below a certain threshold become inactive, along with their attached rules.

7) Return to 1.

For example, if the message that Fido is a dog matches the rule that "IF X is a dog, THEN X is furry," then the information that Fido is an instance of FURRY is stored with that concept, which becomes active. Then the other instances of FURRY generate active messages, and the rules attached to that concept become available for firing.

The decision whether a rule should be among those fired is determined by three factors: the strength of the rule, its degree of support, and its contribution toward the satisfaction of goals and subgoals. The fact that a rule would satisfy a goal is not sufficient reason to fire it, since there might be other better rules capable of satisfying a goal. As in classifier systems, strength is a measure of the past usefulness of the rule. Also as in classifier systems, support is a measure of the apparent relevance of the rule to the current situation; but in PI support is determined by the degree of activation of the concepts to which the rule is attached. The more active the concept, the more support for the rule; and if the rule is attached to more than one active concept, it accrues support from each. In turn, if a concept is used in the action of more than one fired rule, its degree of activation is incremented by both. Notice that the spreading activation of concepts in PI is directed by its problem-solving activity, working forward with concepts activated by firing rules and backward by concepts activated through subgoal formation. The directed kind of spreading activation that occurs in PI contrasts with the more automatic spreading activation of Anderson's (1983) ACT* model (see chapter 2).

4.2.3 Problem Solving

The central function of PI is problem solving, in which context various kinds of learning take place. Since at any time only the active subset of all the rules is available for firing, the problem situation is constantly being redefined, just as we suggested in our earlier discussions of problem solving. A successful solution depends not simply on means-ends analysis but also on activating the appropriate rules by spreading activation. Initially, the concepts mentioned in the initial conditions and goals of the problem are active, and activation spreads until the goal state has been achieved or failure is acknowledged. Objects involved in the problem are recategorized by synchronic rules in order to activate relevant diachronic rules. The search for problem solutions thus requires more than the application of operators to reduce the distance to a goal. Useful operators become available only through recategorization of the objects involved, so that PI is searching through the space of concepts for useful categories at the same time that it searches through the space of operators.

In order to simulate planning, effector rules (which in a real system would produce effects on the environment) do not result in overt actions. Rather, the system begins a *projection*, a kind of simulated action leading to possible future states. While a projection is under way, all inferred information is marked as only projected to be true. If the projected operation leads to a successful solution of a problem, then the rule that initiated the projection is rewarded by having its strength increased. Conversely, if a rule produces an unsuccessful projection—one that eventually contradicts the desired goal or other constraints—then the rule is punished by having its strength decreased, and the projection is stopped.

In firing rules, PI proceeds by forward chaining, the procedural analog of *modus ponens*, in which the system infers from IF p THEN q and p to q. Many rule-based systems work by backward chaining, from the goal back through subgoals to the starting conditions. Effective human problem solving involves search in both directions, which PI simulates by spreading activation of concepts back from the goals and by positing subgoals, while firing rules forward from the starting conditions.

In chapter 1 we described the use of modeling to solve the problem of how to use a piece of paper to support a cup above a table. We will now illustrate how PI operates, using simplified versions of the concepts relevant to this problem.

Initially, the only active concepts are the ones concerning the starting and goal conditions: CUP, PAPER, SUPPORT. Stored with these concepts is the factual information that object A is a cup and object B is a piece of paper. The goal is to have B support A. The rules for the attached concepts then become active; among these are rules indicating that paper can be rolled, paper can be folded, and cups typically weigh around six ounces. A more complete simulation would contain additional rules specifying other actions that can be done with paper, such as crumpling and writing. What actions are performed is determined by which rules have their conditions matched and, in the case of incompatible actions, which rules have the greatest strength. At the beginning of its run PI attaches more strength to the rule for folding paper than for rolling it, since folding is assumed to be more frequently useful. Hence, rules are fired that lead to the projection that paper has been folded, as well as to the inference that cup A weighs six ounces. Activation of the concept FOLDED makes available a rule that specifies what weight a folded paper can support. Subsequent inferences lead to a conclusion that the weight that folded paper can support is less than the weight of the cup, so the projection fails. The rule for folding accordingly has its strength decreased, and a new projection is started based on rolling.

Meanwhile, activation is also spreading backward from the goal concepts. Rules concerning what it takes for one object to support another are used to set subgoals. Rules stating that folded paper will support objects of certain weights and that paper cylinders will support objects of greater weights lead to activation of the concepts FOLDED and CYLINDER. Since folding fails to support enough weight, the rule that has the effect of rolling the paper into a cylinder is fired. Proceeding forward from this effect produces a solution to the problem, so the rule for rolling paper is rewarded with increased strength. Learning has taken place: the next time the system is faced with the problem, it will try the rule for rolling paper before wasting its efforts on the now weaker rule for folding.

This improved performance is guaranteed not only by the refinement of existing rules through strength revision but also by the generation of new rules. The rule for rolling started a projection that led to accomplishment of the goal, so success triggers the production of a new rule that says, "If you have a piece of paper AND your goal is to support something, then roll the piece of paper." This can be thought of both as a specialization of the previous rule about rolling paper and as a generalization about how to accomplish the goal of supporting things. This rule enables PI to improve its problem solving on future trials, since rolling is then immediately preferred over folding. This effect could be increased further by using the failure of folding to produce the exception rule: "If you have a piece of paper AND your goal is to support something, then do not fold the paper."

This simulation of course falls well short of capturing the complexity of how humans might solve the problem, because they operate with a wealth of possibly useful and possibly misleading information that the program does not have. Adding many more rules and concepts to PI would produce a much slower and less direct solution to the cup and paper problem, and it is entirely possible that dead ends would prevent a solution. PI's mechanisms of directed spreading activation and rule competition, however, should help to constrain search so that increasing the size of the knowledge base makes problem solving more difficult but not impossible.

The example discussed is also inadequate in that it does not bring out the extent to which recategorization is important in problem solving. A fuller example would include rules that lead paper to be classified under such headings as "foldable", "rollable", and "burnable". Each classification would make available many different rules, concerning for example the many different ways in which paper can be folded. Clearly, the shift from conceptualizing paper as foldable to conceptualizing it as rollable is important to making progress with the problem of supporting a cup. PI's bidirectional spreading activation, from starting conditions to goals by rule firing and from goals to starting conditions by subgoaling, would lead to focusing on the valuable category of "rollable" and consideration of rules about various kinds of rolling.

It should now be clear how well suited PI is to the generation of mental models. Parallel processing derives from the simultaneous activation of concepts, rules, and messages, and from the firing of more than one rule per time-step. The system is computationally efficient because only plausibly relevant rules—those attached to active concepts—are likely to be considered on a processing cycle. Similarly, the only factual information that needs to be matched against the conditions of active rules consists of messages derived from active concepts. A great deal of knowledge may be simultaneously active, but the active knowledge will be drawn from only a small subset of the truly vast numbers of concepts and rules stored in the conceptual network of a realistic cognitive system.

The system is modular in the sense that concepts and rules that work well together tend to be simultaneously active. But the system also encourages various types of potentially beneficial cross-fertilization of knowledge. Two messages that were never previously coactive may each be activated independently and then turn out to jointly match the conjunctive condition of a rule. A rule activated by one concept may be triggered by a message attached to another. And as noted earlier, multiple sources of support may aggregate to increase the activation level of a concept and thereby activate its attached rules in a novel context.

Multiple sources of evidence can play an important role in classification. A set of synchronic rules can each suggest a conclusion only to a small degree, but with a decisive accumulated effect. For example, PI is given the three rules,

If X is small, it is a cat.
If X is black, it is a cat.
If X has a tail, it is a cat.

Each of these is clearly a very weak rule. But if the active messages include the information that an object is small and black and has a tail, the conclusion that it is a cat will begin to become more plausible. Since all three rules are fired in parallel, the accumulation of evidence takes place on a single time-step.

Synchronic connections are captured in PI, not only by synchronic rules as in classifier systems but also by explicit pointers between concepts. Thus in addition to the rule that "IF X is a robin, THEN X is a bird," the concept of a robin contains the information that the superordinate of ROBIN is BIRD. Such directly available information about superordinates and subordinates is typical of frame systems and semantic networks, and we include it to facilitate the complex kinds of inductive inference described in the next three sections. The interconcept pointers constitute an explicit default hierarchy, which is also implicit in the various rules in the system.

Diachronic rules provide the basis for projections, which are a main function of mental models. They provide the system with expectations about contingent possibilities for future situations, which serve several functions. As in the cup and paper problem, projections are essential to planning problem solutions. Since a projection from the current situation can itself be treated as if it were the current situation, further projections can be derived from it, providing the system with the capacity to perform "lookahead"—a diachronic search through the space of potentially reachable future states. Similarly, the backward spread of activation by means of subgoal formation involves a kind of projection in the other direction, making available to the system concepts and rules that may afford potential solutions.

Problem solving in PI provides occasions for the triggering of many of the inductive mechanisms described in chapter 3. Next we will describe the various kinds of inductive inference that are triggered in PI in the course of its problem-solving process. PI monitors the currently active messages, concepts, and rules and at appropriate times triggers subroutines for generalization, specialization, abduction, and conceptual combination.

4.2.4 Generalization and Specialization

In earlier chapters we stressed the importance of various mechanisms for generating the rules that constitute mental models and the need to constrain these mechanisms pragmatically. In PI, constraint is provided by the triggering conditions that monitor the current state of problem-solving activity. Induction occurs only in the context of problem solving.

Consider generalization from examples. A realistic cognitive system in a particular situation will have before it an enormous range of potential sources of generalization, but most of the results would be trivial with respect to the goals of the system. PI's triggering conditions for instance-based generalization ensure that only generalizations of some relevance to the system will be made. First, active messages produced during problem solving must state that two or more objects are instances of the same two concepts; and second, the two instantiated concepts must each have a high degree of activation. Noticing a number of objects that are both swans and white will not be sufficient to prompt a generalization, unless the concepts of SWAN and WHITE have been rendered highly active by previous rule firings. Hence generalization is pragmatically constrained to what is important to the system at the time. It is not necessary to select from the huge space of all the generalizations that the system might be able to make, since only a small subset will be triggered by the current state of the system.

Generalizations are triggered in this way, but the formation of new rules requires additional processing to ensure that a generalization of the form "If X is A then X is B" is warranted by the evidence. First, PI checks the instances of A and B stored with the relevant concepts to make sure that it is not aware of things that are A but *not* B. If the check turns up no counterexamples, it determines whether generalization is warranted by considering both the number of instances of A that are B and the *variability* of A's with respect to B's. A detailed discussion of variability and its role in generalization must wait until chapter 8.

In proofs in logic and mathematics, generalization often occurs without a consideration of the number of instances or variability. This is because the examples generalized from are chosen arbitrarily, as in geometry, where a proof might begin, "Consider an arbitrary triangle T." PI keeps track of such arbitrary variables and uses them for generalizations that proceed without concerns of warrant; one such generalization plays a role in the simulation of the discovery of the wave theory of sound described in chapter 11.

Generalization is not limited to rules with simple one-place predicates such as "swan" and "white". Much knowledge requires predicates that express relations among more than one object, such as "X loves Y" or "X gives Y to Z", and generalization should be able to produce rules with predicates of this complexity. PI is able to generalize from the examples

(LOVES (JOHN MARY)) (LIKES (MARY JOHN))
(LOVES (ALICE FRED)) (LIKES (FRED ALICE))

to the conclusion

If (LOVES (X Y)) then (LIKES (Y X)),

that is, If X loves Y, then Y at least likes X.

PI can also perform a kind of condition-simplifying generalization of the sort described in chapter 3. If two rules with the same actions and with conditions differing in only one clause are simultaneously active, then a new rule is produced that drops the clause that differed. For example, from

If X is a McDonald's hamburger, it is greasy,
If X is a Burger King hamburger, it is greasy,

it constructs the new, simplified rule:

If X is a hamburger, it is greasy.

This kind of generalization, however, seems excessively syntactic. It would be desirable for condition-simplifying generalization to take into account the number of kinds of hamburgers as well as background knowledge about variability, just as in instance-based generalization.

PI's generalizations from examples occur only after a check for counterexamples has been made. *Specialization* can be triggered by such checks. If counterexamples to an already existing strong rule arise, through inferences that have been made or new information from the environment, then it is appropriate to consider specializing the existing rule. If PI has generalized the strong rule

If X is a dog, then it is friendly,

then finding a counterexample of a mean dog will trigger construction of an exception rule based on unusualness. PI uses synchronic relations to determine what is unusual about the example that contradicted the existing rule. For example, if the mean dog is a Doberman and all the stored examples of friendly dogs were not Dobermans, then PI specializes:

If X is a dog and not a Doberman, then it is friendly.

Moreover, PI also checks stored examples to see what is unusual about the example in the sense that it *lacks* a property that all the friendly dogs have, such as being small. This results in the specialized rule

If X is a dog and small, then it is friendly.

The result is a complex of rules having the desirable properties of a default hierarchy described in chapter 2. Thus PI can start with simple examples, use instance-based generalization to produce rules, then generate more complex rules when new examples trigger specialization.

4.2.5 Abduction
Abduction, as described in chapter 3, involves the generation of hypotheses in order to find potential explanations of puzzling phenomena. Explanation can be thought of as a kind of problem solving. In PI, requests for explanations are recast as other kinds of problems to be solved. If what is to be explained is a fact such as Fred's being late, then that fact is set as a goal to be reached by the system. If, on the other hand, what is to be explained is a general rule such as that people caught in traffic tend to be late, then a problem is set up with starting conditions consisting of a description of an arbitrary person X caught in traffic and a goal to be derived stating that X is late. An explanation is found when the corresponding problem is solved. Abduction is triggered only when the problem to be solved is one involving explanation.

Search for explanatory hypotheses is constrained by the currently active messages and rules. If the fact to be explained is why Reggie is ill behaved, then the availability of the rule that children with learning disabilities are ill behaved might give rise to the abduction that Reggie has a learning disability. Such hypotheses are clearly risky and tentative, which is how they are treated by PI. If all that is available is the already established fact that Reggie has a learning disability, then the system (or the parent) might conjecture that this is the cause of his ill behavior, hypothesizing the general rule that children with learning disabilities tend to be ill behaved. Such rules will be treated as highly provisional, subject to rejection or strengthening in the face of additional instances, using the mechanisms for assessing instance-based generalizations. Notice that abduction in PI is not simply the derivation of a general rule to account for a set of data but rather is highly constrained by the explanatory context, which includes the goals to be reached as part of achieving an explanation and the current state of spreading activation of concepts and rules.

Abduction to a particular fact is very much like subgoaling. Given the rule "If A then B" and the goal B, PI sets A as a subgoal to be reached. Similarly, if B is to be explained, A will be hypothesized by abduction. Not surprisingly, there is evidence that people sometimes confuse these two processes, forming causal theories not on the basis of what the theories explain but on the basis of how the theories would further their ends (Kunda 1985).

Normatively, hypotheses should be subject to several kinds of evaluation. First, we want to ensure that a hypothesis is not incompatible with other knowledge. If a projection started from an abduction leads to a violation of some constraint on the problem to be solved, then PI terminates the projection and abandons the hypothesis. Second, we want the hypothesis to explain as much as possible. PI accomplishes multiple abductions by increasing its confidence in a hypothesis with each additional fact explained. For example, given the rules

If X is a murderer, then X was at the scene of the crime,
If X is a murderer, then X has a weapon,
If X is a murderer, then X is nervous,

and the messages that Smith is nervous, has a weapon, and was at the scene of the crime, PI multiply abduces in parallel that Smith is a murderer. Third, we want the evaluation of hypotheses to be comparative, ensuring that a hypothesis is a better explanation than its alternatives. This occurs implicitly in PI, as the confidence in one hypothesis surpasses that of its competitors. For a discussion of a form of inference to the *best* explanatory hypothesis rich enough to apply to scientific theories, see chapter 11.

The murder example is abduction to a fact, using already existing rules. Chapter 3 outlined another kind of abduction, to explanatory rules. In PI such abductions are triggered by the same conditions as instance-based generalization, but the warranting process is different. Instead of considering number of instances and variability, PI constructs a very tentative rule if it, together with some active message, would furnish a desired explanation.

4.2.6 Concept Formation

PI can thus construct new rules by generalization, specialization, and abduction. But what of concepts, the frame-like structures that cluster rules into useful packages and play an important role in spreading activation? PI currently contains two mechanisms for learning concepts.

The first answers the question of how and when new concepts can be formed. The *when* is as important as the *how*, since pragmatically a system must not clutter up its knowledge base with irrelevant concepts. We clearly do not want to have a concept corresponding to just any set of properties: we may have an instance of someone who is a Canadian philosopher who writes AI programs and plays softball, but that cluster of properties is unlikely to be of much general application. The triggering conditions for concept generation must be sufficiently constrained to restrict the number of concepts to those potentially useful to the system.

PI triggers concept generation only when simultaneously active rules indicate that a cluster of properties has predictive value. For example, the concept of a Yuppy will be formed if the following rules are simultaneously active:

IF X is young, urban, professional, then X drinks Perrier.
If X is young, urban, professional, then X eats quiche.

These two rules indicate that the cluster of properties "young, urban, professional" has potential general application, so a new concept, YOUNG-URBAN-PROFESSIONAL, is generated. As the result of this generation, new rules are formed about the new concept, stating that Yuppies drink Perrier and eat quiche. Once a new concept has been formed, instances of it can trigger generalizations that otherwise would not have been made.

Thus bottom-up concept formation does not have to do an extensive search for possible new concepts. In accord with our general framework, concept formation is severely constrained by pragmatic concerns and triggering conditions. Pragmatically, only particular problem-solving contexts will lead to the formation and simultaneous activation of rules such as those about young urban professionals, so that sets of features will rarely get merged into new concepts.

Of course, this is not the only possible kind of bottom-up concept formation consistent with our pragmatic framework. A more sophisticated sort would be based on more than just the conditions of rules, taking into account background knowledge about variability in order to decide whether a new concept was needed. The importance of variability in bottom-up concept formation is discussed in chapter 6.

When such concepts have arisen, more complex concepts can be formed by the top-down mechanisms of conceptual combination described in chapter 3. Thagard (1984) described how conceptual combination can be performed by reconciling slots in frames. PI uses essentially the same mechanisms of reconciliation, adapted to apply to rules rather than slots. The rules attached to concepts in PI have several properties in common with frame slots, so the translation is straightforward. Slots in frames have *slot-names*; for example, the frame for SWAN has a slot named COLOR containing the value WHITE. Similarly, in PI the rule attached to the concept of swan that states, "If something is a swan, then it is white," is marked as concerning color. This property of a rule is called its *topic*. Topics can be generated from the synchronic relations of the properties in rules: the system can determine that the topic of "If something is a swan, then it is white" is color, since it knows that white is a kind of color.

Slots in frames can contain various kinds of values, including default and range values (Winston and Horn 1981). Another useful kind is an *actual* value, which unlike a default value may not be overridden. Similarly, rules can be assigned a *status* as expressing either actual or default values. In the rule "If X is a triangle, then X has three sides" the value of having three sides is actual rather than a default. Most rules, however, will express only defaults, since generalization normally generates only default values.

To combine two concepts, PI proceeds as follows. First, the expectations produced by the rules attached to the two concepts are compared. If no topic with conflicting values is found, as in a mundane combination such as "red apple", no further processing is required. If a conflict is found, however, this triggers the generation of a new concept to represent the combination. In essence, the system assumes that a contradiction signals a potentially interesting concept that requires more elaborate processing to be understood in a consistent manner.

PI builds up a new structure by the following steps. First, a new concept is built, named after the two donor concepts; for example,

the combination of FEMINIST and BANK TELLER is called
FEMINIST–BANK TELLER. Both donor concepts are listed as superordinates of the new concept, and its list of instances is the intersection of the lists of the donor concepts. Second, rules that do not pose
reconciliation problems are simply left attached to the "parent" concepts and are inherited as defaults for the new offspring.

A more complex process is required to construct a new rule when
two rules from the donor concepts have the same topic but generate
different expectations. The basic principle for conflict resolution is
that further evidence is marshaled to decide which of the competing
expectations is more firmly established. PI reconciles conflicts by considering a number of different cases. The most straightforward occurs
when one rule has a default status while the other has an actual status:
we clearly want to give the actual value priority over the default.
Several such cases have been described by Osherson and Smith (1981;
Smith and Osherson 1984), in arguments showing that conceptual
combination is not well captured by mechanisms of fuzzy set theory.
For example, our expectations about something characterized as a
"striped apple" is no simple linear amalgam of STRIPED and
APPLE. PI creates the concept of STRIPED-APPLE by noticing that
the "striped" property attached to the concept STRIPED has actual
status, whereas the competing rule attached to APPLE, "If X is an
apple, then X is solid red," is only a default. The resulting rule, "If X
is a striped apple, then X is striped," explains why people consider an
object that is a striped apple as more "typical" of the new concept
than of either of the donor concepts.

Most rule conflicts will not be so easily reconciled. If the message
list describes instances of the donor concepts that suggest a resolution,
then a new rule can be formed in a fairly bottom-up manner. For
example, suppose you are forming the concept of a Canadian violinist,
with the conflicting expectations that Canadians are rugged, lumber-
jack types and that violinists are refined. In such a situation PI con-
sults instances of concepts with properties of the relevant type. If it has
some examples of Canadian violinists, it uses their properties to resolve the conflict. Thus if the instances of Canadian violinists are all
refined, then the new rule attached to the concept CANADIAN-
VIOLINIST will express this expectation.

A more top-down mechanism can proceed without any instances.
In combining the concepts of "feminist" and "bank teller", PI encounters conflicting expectations about how political a feminist bank
teller will be. One natural way of reconciling the conflict is to notice
that feminists are much less *variable* in their political views than are

Table 4.1
FEMINIST

Concept:	Feminist
Degree of activation:	1.0
Superordinates:	Person
Instances:	Gloria Steinem, Betty Friedan, Marilyn French
Rules:	R1 FEMINIST

	Topic:	Gender
	Status:	Default
	Condition:	If X is a feminist
	Action:	Then X is a woman
	R2 FEMINIST	
	Topic:	Employment
	Status:	Default
	Condition:	If X is a feminist
	Action:	Then X is a professional
	R3 FEMINIST	
	Topic:	Political activity
	Status:	Default
	Condition:	If X is a feminist
	Action:	Then X is politically active

bank tellers, so that we would expect feminist bank tellers to have the political attitudes of feminists rather than those expected much less reliably of bank tellers. To assess variability, PI uses much the same mechanism as that which plays a crucial role in generalization, to be described in greater detail in chapter 8.

Tables 4.1–4.3 give a fuller picture of the structure of concepts in PI, showing how the concept of a feminist bank teller can result from two donor concepts. Obviously, many additional rules could be included. Notice that no rule need be attached to FEMINIST–BANK TELLER on the topic of gender, since there is no conflict between the rules on that topic in the donor concepts. The new concept takes on the nonprofessional rating of bank teller, since that was an actual value for bankteller. But in political activity feminist bank tellers are rated to be more like feminists, who are more invariably politically active.

The simple mechanisms so far described will not always suffice to reconcile conflicting rules. In keeping with our pragmatic framework, it is often then best for the system to construct such rules as will help it to accomplish its goals. Rule reconciliation can therefore be abductive, generating just those rules that furnish desired explanations. In

Table 4.2
BANK TELLER

Concept:	Bank teller
Degree of activation:	1.0
Superordinates:	Employee
Instances:	
Rules:	R4 BANK TELLER

	Topic:	Gender
	Status:	Default
	Condition:	If X is a bank teller
	Action:	Then X is a woman

R5 BANK TELLER

	Topic:	Employment
	Status:	Actual
	Condition:	If X is a bank teller
	Action:	Then X is not a professional

R6 BANK TELLER

	Topic:	Political activity
	Status:	Default
	Condition:	If X is a bank teller
	Action:	Then X is apolitical

Table 4.3
FEMINIST–BANK TELLER

Concept:	Feminist–bank teller
Degree of activation:	1.0
Superordinates:	Feminist, bankteller
Instances:	
Rules:	R7 FEMINIST–BANK TELLER

	Topic:	Employment
	Status:	Actual
	Condition:	If X is a feminist–bank teller
	Action:	Then X is not a professional

R8 FEMINIST–BANK TELLER

	Topic:	Political activity
	Status:	Default
	Condition:	If X is a feminist–bank teller
	Action:	Then X is politically active

chapter 11 we will see that this kind of "problem-driven" conceptual combination is often important in scientific discovery.

If conceptual combination were unconstrained, the system would quickly become cluttered with uninteresting new concepts. PI constrains conceptual combination first by attempting combination only when there are simultaneously active concepts with common instances, and second by forming a new combined concept only when reconciliation of conflicting expectations is required. In most mundane cases such as "brown cow", "red apple", and "feminist professional" no permanent combined concept will be formed, so the system avoids useless clutter.

We have described PI's mechanisms for generalization, specialization, abduction, and concept formation independently, in applications that were designed to test their operations in isolation. Chapter 11 provides an integrated illustration of the operations of PI, in which several mechanisms play a role in simulating the discovery of the wave theory of sound. All the examples so far run have been small, none involving more than 30 concepts and rules. Further experiments must be conducted to determine how well PI will scale up to capture aspects of problem solving and learning in richer situations. Because PI tightly constrains both spreading activation and induction as part of the process of problem solving, there are grounds for optimism that scaling up will be possible.

4.3 Inductive Adequacy

In chapter 1 we proposed a principle of inductive adequacy that imposed on computational systems for performance and learning the following constraint: The basic knowledge structures of the system should be derivable by the system's own inductive principles. Few artificial intelligence systems can satisfy this constraint; most expert systems, for example, depend entirely on having rules written by their programmers. But we see it as an important constraint, necessary to avoid brittleness and the use of arbitrary internal symbols with no pragmatic significance.

Classifier systems clearly satisfy this principle. The only knowledge structures are rules, and the simple fixed-length bit-string representation ensures that any possible rule usable in a given system could be generated by the genetic operators. Thus we saw in section 4.1.9 how Goldberg's (1983) system, starting with randomly generated rules, was able to produce a large set of useful rules.

The principle of inductive adequacy is much harder to satisfy for a system such as PI, with conditions and actions of arbitrary length, n-place predicates, and complex concepts. Still, PI goes a long way toward meeting it. Like classifier systems, PI operates in a simulated environment that can send messages into the system in an analog of observation. These messages can then trigger generalizations to produce rules, which can lead in turn to the production of more complex rules through specializations. Multiple rules with similar conditions can then lead to the formation of new concepts, as in the Yuppy example above, and concepts still farther removed from observation can be formed by conceptual combination. More work is required, however, to ensure that the triggering conditions and inference mechanisms suffice to generate absolutely any rule or concept that might operate in the system. For example, there are currently no mechanisms for generating concepts representing n-place relations.

In the next chapter we will employ only a small number of the inductive mechanisms described in chapters 3 and 4 to explain the learning of simple diachronic rules. As we proceed through the remaining chapters, we will add back progressively more of these mechanisms as we deal with increasingly complicated phenomena..

Appendix 4A Some Formal Aspects of Classifier Systems

Formally, we specify a condition (subset of messages) by a string

$$s_1 s_2 \ldots s_j \ldots s_k, \quad \text{where } s_j \in \{1, 0, \#\}.$$

Then the k-bit message

$$m_1 m_2 \ldots m_j \ldots m_k, \quad \text{where } m_j \in \{1, 0\},$$

belongs to the specified subset just in case

(1) $m_j = s_j$, when $s_j = 1$ or $s_j = 0$,
(2) m_j is *either* 1 or 0 when $s_j = \#$.

The condition is *satisfied* by any message that meets this requirement. We define an action (message specification) by a string

$$a_1 a_2 \ldots a_j \ldots a_k, \quad \text{where } a_j \in \{1, 0, \#\}.$$

If

$$m_1 m_2 \ldots m_j \ldots m_k, \quad \text{where } m_j \in \{1, 0\},$$

is a message satisfying the condition of a classifier with the given action, then at position j of the outgoing message the value is

(1) a_j, if $a_j = 1$ or 0,
(2) m_j, if $a_j = \#$.

If a classifier has more than one condition, then the message satisfying the *first* condition is used to determine the pass-through bits.

Despite the fact that only certain subsets of the set of all messages can be defined using this notation, combinations of classifiers can be used to implement conditions over arbitrary subsets in much the same way that AND, OR, and NOT can be combined to yield arbitrary Boolean functions in logic. Once this is established, it is not difficult to show that classifier systems are computationally complete, that is, capable in principle of executing any program in a general-purpose language. An AND-condition is expressed by a single multicondition classifier such as $M_1, M_2/M$, for M is only added to the message list if *both M_1 and M_2* are on the list. Similarly, the *pair* of classifiers M_1/M and M_2/M express an OR-condition, for M is added to the message list if *either M_1 or M_2* is on the list. NOT, of course, is expressed by a classifier with the condition $-M$. As an illustration, consider the Boolean expression

$$(M_1 \text{ AND } M_2) \text{ OR } ((\text{NOT } M_3) \text{ AND } M_4).$$

This is expressed by the following set of classifiers, with the message M appearing if and only if the Boolean expression is satisfied.

$$M_1, M_2/M$$
$$- M_3/M_6$$
$$M_6, M_4/M$$

The judicious use of #'s and recodings often substantially reduces the number of classifiers required when the Boolean expressions are complex.

Appendix 4B Formal Aspects of Genetic Algorithms in Classifier Systems

Understanding genetic algorithms requires a careful definition of the notion of a substring schema as a building block. To start, recall that a condition (or an action) for a classifier is defined by a string of letters $s_1 s_2 \ldots s_j \ldots s_k$ of length k over the 3-letter alphabet $\{1, 0, \#\}$. It is reasonable to look upon these strings as built up from the component letters $\{1, 0, \#\}$. Possible combinations of component letters that can be used as building blocks can be defined with the help of a (new) "don't care" symbol, $*$. To define a given substring schema, we specify the letters at the positions of interest, filling out the rest of the string with the "don't care", $*$. (The procedure mimics that for defining conditions, but at a different level of description.) Thus, $*0\#\#1**\ldots*$ focuses attention on the combination $0\#\#1$ at positions 2 through 5. Equivalently, $*0\#\#1**\ldots*$ specifies a *set* of conditions, the set of all conditions that can be defined by using the combination $0\#\#1$ at positions 2 through 5. Any condition that has $0\#\#1$ at the given positions is an *instance* of substring schema $*0\#\#1**\ldots*$.

The set of all substring schemas (all combinations that can be used as building blocks) is just the set $\{1, 0, \#, *\}^k$ of all strings of length k over the alphabet $\{1, 0, \#, *\}$. (Note that a substring schema defines a subset of the set of all possible conditions, whereas each condition defines a subset of the set of all possible messages.)

A classifier system, at any given time t, often has many classifiers that contain a given component or substring schema s; that is, it has many instances of s. Following the suggestion in section 4.1.7, we can assign a value $v(s, t)$ to s at time t by averaging the strengths of its instances. For example, let the system contain classifier $\mathbf{C}_1$, with condition $10\#\#110\ldots0$ and strength $v(\mathbf{C}_1, t) = 4$, and classifier $\mathbf{C}_2$, with condition $00\#\#011\ldots1$ and strength $v(\mathbf{C}_2, t) = 2$. If these are the only instances of substring schema $s = *0\#\#1**\ldots*$ at time t, then we assign to the substring schema the value $v(s, t) = [v(\mathbf{C}_1, t) +$

$v(\mathbf{C}_2, t)]/2 = 3$, the average of the strengths of the two instances. The general formula is

$v(s, t) = \Sigma_{\mathbf{C} \text{ an instance of } s} v(\mathbf{C}, t)/[\text{no. of instances of } s]$.

Consider now a system with M classifiers that uses the observed averages $\{v(s, t)\}$ to guide the construction of new classifiers from substring schemas. Let $v(t)$ be the average strength of all rules at time t. Then substring schema s is above-average if $v(s, t)/v(t) > 1$, and vice versa. Let $M(s, t)$ be the number of instances of substring schema s in the system at time t, and let $M(s, t + T)$ be the number of instances of s after the M original rules have been replaced by M new rules (the equivalent of obtaining M new samples). The simplest heuristic for using the information $v(s, t)/v(t)$ would be to require that the number of instances of s increase (or decrease) at time $t + T$ according to that ratio,

$$M(s, t + T) = c[v(s, t)/v(t)]M(s, t),$$

where c is an arbitrary constant. That is, the use of building blocks is biased according to the ratio $v(s, t)/v(t)$.

Explicit calculation of the ratings required by the above heuristic would be computationally intractable. A single condition (or action) is an instance of 2^k substring schemas. (This is easily shown by noting that a given condition is an instance of *every* substring schema obtained by substituting an $*$ for one or more letters in the definition of the condition.) In a system of M single-condition classifiers there is enough information to calculate averages for somewhere between 2^k and $M2^k$ substring schemas. Even for very simple classifiers and a small system, $k = 32$ and $M = 1,000$, this is an enormous number, $M2^k$ = almost 2 million trillion.

Genetic operators accomplish implicitly what cannot be carried out explicitly. By combining substring schemas carried by high-strength classifier "parents", genetic algorithms construct "hybrid offspring" classifiers that, typically, are instances of a large number of good substring schemas. To see this, we must specify exactly the steps by which a genetic algorithm generates new classifiers.

Assume the algorithm acts on a set $B(t)$ of M strings $\{\mathbf{C}_1, \mathbf{C}_2, \dots \mathbf{C}_M\}$ over the alphabet $\{1, 0, \#\}$ with assigned strengths $S(\mathbf{C}_j, t)$.

1) Compute the average strength $v(t)$ of the strings in $B(t)$, and assign the normalized value $S(\mathbf{C}_j, t)/v(t)$ to each string $\mathbf{C}_j$ in $B(t)$.

2) Assign each string in $B(t)$ a probability proportional to its normal-

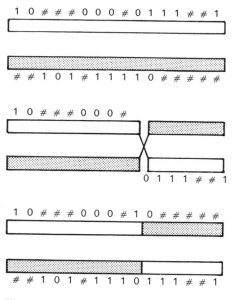

Figure 4.6
Crossing over.

ized value. Then, select n pairs of strings, $n \ll M$, from $B(t)$, using this probability distribution, and make copies of them.

3) Apply *crossover* (and, possibly, other genetic operators) to each copied pair, forming $2n$ new strings. Crossover is applied to a pair of strings as follows: Select at random a position i, $1 < i < k$, and then exchange the segments to the left of position i in the two strings (see figure 4.6).

4) Replace the $2n$ lowest-strength strings in $B(t)$ with the $2n$ strings newly generated in step 3.

5) Set t to $t + 1$ in preparation for the next use of the algorithm.

As an operating principle the algorithm will be invoked repeatedly, either periodically or under the control of triggering conditions, producing successive "generations" of new classifiers. In more sophisticated versions of the algorithm, the selection of pairs for combination may be biased toward classifiers active at the time crossover occurs. Also, step 4 may be modified to prevent "overcrowding" of $B(t)$ with strings of one kind; details are in Bethke (1980) and DeJong (1980). The other genetic operators, such as *mutation* and *inversion*, have lesser roles in this use of the algorithm, mainly providing "insurance" (see Holland 1975, chapter 6, sections 2, 3, 4 for details).

To see how this procedure implicitly biases the use of substring

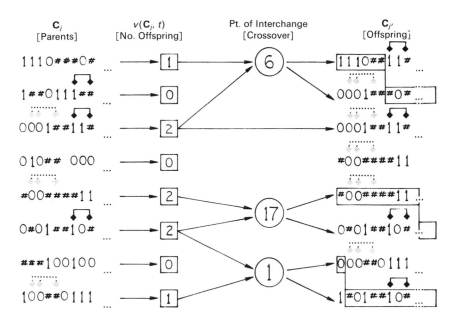

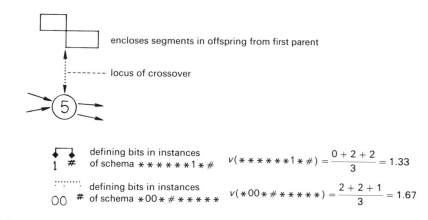

Figure 4.7
Illustration of the genetic algorithm.

schemas according to the ratio $v(s, t)/v(t)$, it is helpful to divide the algorithm's action into two phases, as illustrated in figure 4.7. Phase 1 consists of steps 1 and 2; phase 2 consists of steps 3 and 4.

First consider what would happen if phase 1 were iterated, without the execution of phase 2 but with the replacement of strings in $B(t)$. In particular, let phase 1 be iterated $M/2n$ times (assuming for convenience that M is a multiple of $2n$). Under $M/2n$ repetitions of phase 1, each instance **C** of a given substring schema s can be expected to produce $v(\mathbf{C}, t)/v(t)$ "offspring" copies. The total number of instances of substring schema s after the action of phase 1 is just the sum of the copies of the individual instances. Dividing this total by the original number of instances, $M(s, t)$, gives the average rate of increase and is just $v(s, t)/v(t)$, as required by the explicit heuristic described above. This is true of every substring schema with instances in $B(t)$.

Given that phase 1 provides just the emphasis for each substring schema required by the heuristic, why is phase 2 necessary? Phase 2 is required because phase 1 introduces no new strings (samples) into $B(t)$; it merely introduces copies of strings already there. Phase 1 provides emphasis but no new trials. The genetic operators, applied in phase 2, obviously modify strings. It can be proved (see theorem 6.2.3 of Holland 1975) that the genetic operators of step 3 leave the emphasis provided by phase 1 largely undisturbed, while providing new instances of the various substring schemas in $B(t)$ in accord with that emphasis. Thus, phase 1 combined with phase 2 provides, implicitly, just the sampling scheme suggested by the heuristic.

Conditioning and Covariation Detection

With this chapter we begin a treatment of a variety of empirical issues in terms of our framework, considering first the most basic sort of induction question—the generation and learning of simple diachronic rules. We will apply some of our concepts to phenomena arising in studies of animal conditioning, an area often tacitly treated as the last refuge of behaviorist psychology. Although cognitive psychology recently has had a substantial impact on work in conditioning, the cognitive approach is far from universally accepted. Often cognitive theories of conditioning have been left vague, which contributes to their lack of impact on behaviorists. Most cognitive psychologists, for their part, pay little attention to animal research. Although most work on machine learning has emphasized higher-level forms of learning, recent interest in connectionism has led to a few explorations of conditioning (Sutton and Barto 1981; Granger and Schlimmer 1985).

Our excursion into the realm of the behaviorists is prompted by the fact that conditioning studies provide clear illustrations of the generation and testing of simple empirical rules. As we cross the frontier, we leave a great deal of our framework behind us. Left unused for the moment are such aspects of the framework as complex inferential rules, mechanisms for generating abstract concepts, and rules for constructing analogies. We will be traveling light, carrying with us only the essential elements of an adaptive default hierarchy— primarily generalization and specialization mechanisms, together with strength revision procedures based on the testing of predictions and a single inferential rule, namely, the "unusualness rule".

These tools will be the only ones necessary for dealing with some extremely important findings that were generated by latter-day behaviorists after the cognitive revolution was already in full swing. These findings destroyed once and for all the simple associationist perspective of behaviorism, which held that the only conditions necessary for learning to take place were the association of stimuli coupled with the "stamping in" of the association by virtue of positive or negative reinforcement. That perspective has been shown to be quite mistaken. Whether learning takes place or not has to do with confirmed or disconfirmed expectations about the environment, not simply with positive or negative reinforcement; and it has to do with covariation detection that leads to improved statistical prediction, rather than with association in the sense of mere co-occurrence.

5.1 Adaptive Default Hierarchies and Conditioning

In a typical classical conditioning experiment, a rat might be trained to press a lever to get food. After the rat has been pressing the lever to get the food for a good many sessions, it suddenly hears a tone that lasts for thirty seconds. The rat typically turns toward the tone briefly but continues business as usual, pressing and eating. Just as the tone stops, however, a shock is delivered to the rat's feet through the grid floor on which it is standing. As this sequence of events repeats itself, the rat begins to show signs of fear of the tone. It stops eating and pressing the lever, stands up on its hind legs to explore ("Is there any way to get out of this joint?"), and engages in nervous grooming behavior. The rat is displaying a conditioned emotional response. The tone signals shock and the rat exhibits fear in response to the tone.

Let us see how we can account for the simple learning behavior exhibited in such experiments in terms of some of the concepts introduced in chapters 2 and 3. (The theory presented here has been developed by Holyoak, Koh, and Nisbett, 1986. They also present a classifier-based simulation of some of the experimental paradigms discussed here.) Our account focuses on classical conditioning, in which an environmental event signals some other event such as food reward or punishment. However, our framework can also be applied to instrumental conditioning, in which the organism's own behavior produces the circumstances that generate reward or avoid punishment.

We can explain elementary processes of conditioning by drawing on just two operating principles from the framework: (1) an unusual input event or the failure of a strong extant rule triggers the creation of new rules by the recombination of rules and messages active at the time; and (2) feedback regarding success or failure modifies rule strengths via an apportionment-of-credit algorithm.

Generally, very simple stimulus-response rules can be used. The condition part need only attend to messages from the environment (stimuli), and the action part can specify some overt action (effector setting). For example, if we have a *hungry* (H) rat in a standard conditioning *box* (B), and it has learned to *press* (P) a bar to obtain food, the corresponding rule would have the form

$$B, H \rightarrow P. \tag{1}$$

It is important to understand that this rule only serves to abbreviate the salient features of what must be a complex process at a more detailed level of description.

To pursue the example a bit further, let us consider the effect of a *shock* (S) to the rat while it is in the box. We can think of the rat as having a very general rule that, under the impetus of pain, causes it to cease any current activity in an attempt to escape. In the context of bar pressing in the box, the shock should *interrupt the bar pressing* ($\bar{P}$). Under the first principle cited above, shock, as an unusual and important occurrence, should trigger the formation of an exception rule:

$$B, H, S \rightarrow \bar{P}. \tag{2}$$

At the same time a modified default rule can be formed:

$$B, H, \bar{S} \rightarrow P. \tag{1a}$$

Rule (2) will now compete with rule (1) when shock occurs. Although rule (2) will ultimately prevail in this competition, the action specified by rule (1) (pressing) will be preserved as a default in a more restricted context by rule (1a).

We can extend the example to classical conditioning by considering the case where the shock is consistently preceded by a *tone* (T). Once again the unusualness criterion is satisfied and a further refinement is triggered:

$$B, H, T \rightarrow \bar{P}. \tag{3}$$

(We are ignoring several details here. Rule (3) can be viewed as an abbreviated version of a coupled rule sequence, in which a rule that uses tone to predict shock serves to activate rule (2).)

It might also happen that the experimenter has arranged the environmental contingencies so that the rat sometimes receives shock in the absence of the tone or any other unusual signal. In that case the rat will eventually form a rule that is simply based on the relatively constant background conditions, such as

$$B, H \rightarrow \bar{P}. \tag{4}$$

Note that rule (4) directly contradicts rule (1) and is more general than rule (3). Both of these relations are competitive: whenever rule (1) is correct, rule (4) will be in error, and vice versa; and whenever rule (3) is correct, rule (4) will be as well, possibly rendering rule (3) redundant.

The second principle drawn from the framework is adjustment of rule strength under an apportionment-of-credit scheme. Rules producing responses that are appropriate are strengthened, while rules producing inappropriate responses are weakened. For example, when the rat executes rule (1) and food is forthcoming in the absence of shock, the resulting payoff (reduction of hunger) strengthens the rule. On the other hand, execution of (1) in the presence of shock causes bar pressing at a time when the payoff of a bit of food is far outweighed by the effects of the shock. The rule's strength is accordingly reduced in this context. (It has paid out a bid far larger than the amount it receives from the environment; we can even think of the environment as presenting it with a debit or negative payoff.) We will also assume, as suggested in chapter 3, that when multiple rules make the same correct prediction, the attendant reward will be divided among the successful rules in relation to their prior strength. In Holyoak, Koh, and Nisbett's simulation the highest bidding rule in a redundant set, such as rules (3) and (4), will receive all the reward (a subcognitive version of "Them that has, gets"). Redundant rules thus compete for a limited "niche" in the environmental reward structure.

In brief, these simple principles provide for the emergence of an adaptive default hierarchy, wherein new rules, often specializations, are inserted under the prompting of the unusualness heuristic. All rules, new and old, compete for the right to determine action when the environment presents stimuli satisfying their conditions. As we will soon see, this view of conditioning implies that mere association of a stimulus with a reinforcing event is not always sufficient to produce conditioning. The stimulus and the reinforcing response will indeed be linked to form a new rule, but that new rule must compete with extant rules. Conditioning (control of behavior by the new rule) results only when the new rule is, on the average, more effective than its competitors in evoking appropriate responses in the context in which it applies.

We are now ready to treat some important conditioning experiments that have confounded behaviorist interpretations. In fact, rules (1)–(4) are sufficient for a treatment of Rescorla's (1968) experiments, with which we will begin.

5.2. Rule Generation and Testing in Classical Conditioning

5.2.1 Statistical Covariation and Rule Learning

Rescorla's (1968) experiments involve just the situation cited in the example above. A hungry rat was placed in a box with a bar that

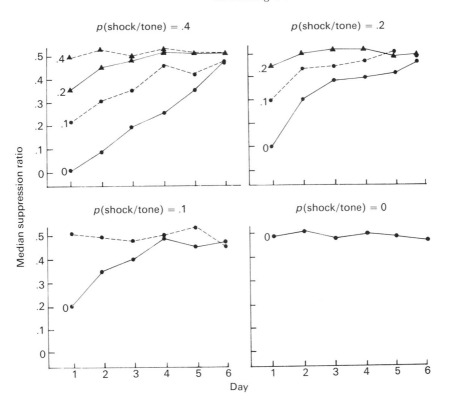

Figure 5.1a

Median suppression ratio for each group over six extinction test sessions. Within each panel all groups had the same probability of the shock during the tone; the parameter in each panel is the probability of the shock in the absence of the tone. From Rescorla (1968).

could be pressed to obtain food. At various times a brief electric shock was administered to the rat's feet, resulting in an immediate suppression of any bar pressing. Rescorla divided his rats into two groups. For one group, shock was always presented, and only presented, during 2-minute periods in which a tone sounded. For the other group, shocks occurred during the intervals in which the tone was absent, as well as while the tone sounded. After a *training* period, in which the rats were repeatedly subjected to the regime of their group, both groups underwent a set of *extinction* trials in which shock was no longer presented at all. Figure 5.1a shows changes in bar pressing during the extinction sessions. The changes are presented in terms of a *suppression ratio* calculated by dividing the bar pressing during a 2-minute tone period by the sum of the bar pressing during the tone period plus the immediately preceding 2-minute quiet period. With this measure, complete suppression would be indicated by a ratio of 0, while no suppression would be indicated by a ratio of .5. In the first case the rat is not pressing the bar at all during the tone period (it "expects" shock when there is a tone), whereas in the second case the rat is pressing the bar as often when it is quiet as when there is a tone (it does not use tone as a "predictor").

In standard terminology, the shock in Rescorla's experiments serves as an *unconditioned stimulus* (US) for which ceasing to press the bar is the *unconditioned response* (UR). The tone, a previously neutral stimulus, serves as a *conditioned stimulus* (CS), and the suppression of bar pressing in the presence of tone becomes the *conditioned response* (CR). Initial behaviorist accounts of conditioning focused on frequency of association between US and CS as the basis of conditioning. However, a research program conducted primarily by Leo Kamin, Robert Rescorla, and Allan Wagner in the late 1960s and early 1970s showed that association is not a sufficient basis. These researchers demonstrated that for conditioning to occur, the CS must *predict*, in a statistical sense, the occurrence of the US. The Rescorla (1968) experiment just described is a typical experiment of this genre. The investigator pairs the CS with the US equally often in two different experimental conditions, but in one condition the US is completely contingent upon the occurrences of the CS, while in the other it is completely independent of the CS. Such experiments show that relative contingency, not mere frequency of pairings, is essential for conditioning.

The detailed results of the Rescorla (1968) experiment, drawn from figure 5.1a, are as follows. Each panel of figure 5.1a shows suppression ratios under a different contingency between the tone and the shock during learning trials. The top left panel shows the results when there was a .4 probability of the shock in the presence of the tone (p(shock/tone) = .4); the top right panel gives the results for a .2 probability; the bottom left corresponds to a .1 probability; and the bottom right corresponds to a 0 probability. The parameter associated with each curve in a given panel (0, .1, .2, or .4) is the probability of the shock in the *absence* of the tone: p(shock/no tone). Thus, in the upper left panel the top curve shows the degree of suppression when the probability of the shock was the same—.4—both in the presence of the tone and in its absence. The bottom curve in the same panel shows the degree of suppression when the probability of shock was .4 in the presence of the tone and 0 in its absence.

As the data in the upper left panel of figure 5.1a indicate, suppression was complete at the beginning of the extinction trials, when the tone predicted shock with high probability and the absence of the tone predicted absence of shock with certainty [.4, 0]. Suppression was nil when the presence of the tone predicted shock with high probability but so did its absence [.4, .4]. Suppression was intermediate when the absence of the tone was sometimes associated with shock [.4, .2 and .4, .1]. Comparable results, but with less initial suppression, were obtained when the tone predicted the shock with probability .2 or .1. In particular, note that the top line in each panel is approximately flat at a suppression ratio of .5, indicating that suppression was always nil when the probability of shock did not differ during learning as a function of whether or not the tone was presented. Thus, sheer number of pairings was irrelevant to the degree of conditioning obtained. The key variable is clearly degree of predictability in a statistical sense.

These results are readily explained in terms of rules (1)–(4) from the previous section. Consider the panel in the upper left corner of figure 5.1a (probability of shock given tone is .4), and consider the curve with parameter .2 (probability of shock given no tone is .2). During training, rule (3), $B, H, T \rightarrow \bar{P}$, will be correct on 40 percent of its activations during the tone period because shock occurs only 40 percent of the time, and only then is it appropriate to cease bar pressing. Similarly, rule (4), $B, H \rightarrow \bar{P}$, will be correct 20 percent of the time when tone is absent and 40 percent of the time when tone is present, or 30 percent overall (assuming tone intervals and silent intervals have equal durations). Because rule (3) is more likely to be correct when its conditions are matched than rule (4) is when its conditions are matched, rule (3) will become stronger than rule (4). Rule (4) will receive some reward when rule (3) does not apply (when no tone occurs), however, so both rules will remain in the system.

During a tone interval rule (1) will compete with both rules (3) and (4) in their attempt to set the effectors, the former urging bar pressing and the latter urging cessation. In this circumstance only one of the rules can win the competition on a given trial. Rules (1) and (4) conflict when tone is absent, so that again only one can be a winner on a given trial.

Because competition between rules is probabilistic, no rule in a conflicting set will win all the time. The ratio of wins for the rule (or rules) calling for a particular effector action will, however, be proportional to its strength relative to the strengths of competing rules that call for the alternative effector action. Clearly, rule (1) is less likely to win when it competes with both rules (3) and (4) (that is, when a tone is present) than when it competes against the weaker rule (4) alone (when the tone is absent). Thus there will be less bar pressing during the tone interval than during the absence of tone. In other words, at the beginning of the extinction trials the suppression ratio should be considerably less than .5 in the case of the curve with parameter .2. This is indeed the case in figure 5.1a.

As extinction proceeds, neither rule (3) nor rule (4) is ever correct (because there are no shocks). Each steadily loses strength with the consequence that rule (1) wins ever more frequently. Ultimately, rule (1) wins almost all the time in both intervals, with the consequence that bar pressing approaches equal frequency in the two intervals and the suppression ratio goes to .5. Again, this is what figure 5.1a shows.

Contrast this with the case where the parameter of the curve is .4, indicating that shock is as likely in the absence of tone as in its presence. In this situation rule (3) is completely redundant with rule (4) and hence must compete for the same niche in the system. Rule (4) will always receive the full reward when it is the sole correct rule in intervals in which shock occurs in the absence of tone, whereas rule (3) must always compete with rule (4) for reward for its successes during tone intervals. Assuming the stronger rule in a redundant set tends to receive greater reward, it follows that rule (4) will become progressively stronger than rule (3), so that eventually rule (4) will receive all the reward for success during tone as well as no-tone intervals, driving the redundant rule (3) out of the system. Accordingly, by the end of training rule (1) will be competing with rule (4) alone in both types of intervals, so that bar-pressing frequencies will be the same and the suppression ratio will be .5 at the beginning of the extinction trials. Once again, figure 5.1a shows this to be the case.

The same line of argument can be used to explain each of the parametrized curves in each of the panels of figure 5.1a. Figure 5.1b presents the results of a computer simulation by Holyoak, Koh, and Nisbett (1986), using slightly different parameters from those in figure 5.1a. It may be seen that the simulation results are qualitatively similar to those obtained by Rescorla. The essential result, supporting the explanation based upon our framework, is that statistical predictability, rather than sheer number of pairings, is the key variable in these experiments.

A major implication of our account is that during training animals should show an initial degree of suppression in response to the tone during the period in which rule (3), $B, H, T \rightarrow \bar{P}$, is generated and remains in competition for a time, even if the tone does not actually predict shock. The reason for this is that the unusualness inferential rule should often generate the specialized rule even if it will later be discredited as redundant by the strength-revision procedure. This

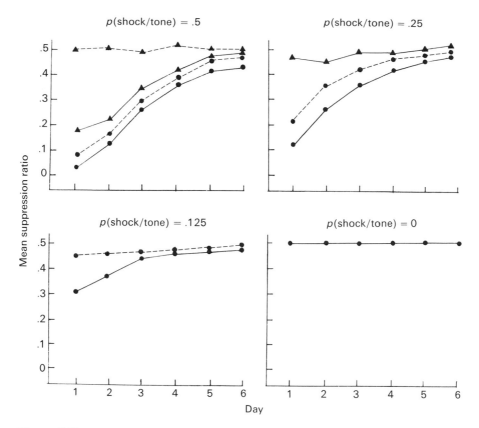

Figure 5.1b
Predictions from the computer simulation of Holyoak, Koh, and Nisbett (1986) for conditions similar to those used in the study that produced the curves in figure 5.1a. The data plotted are median suppression ratios based on ten simulated rats in each condition.

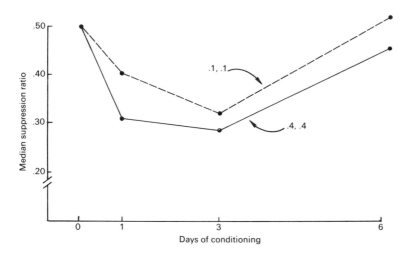

Figure 5.2

Median suppression ratio after different durations of exposure to either [.4, .4] or [.1, .1] uncorrelated procedures. Data are taken from a single nonreinforced testing session. From Rescorla (1972).

prediction is supported by data reported by Rescorla (1972). He examined the suppression ratio during initial training on the uncorrelated procedures of [.4p(shock/tone), .4p(shock/no tone)] and [.1, .1]. For all animals each conditioning session contained twelve 2-minute tone CSs and involved the presentation of a shock. For half the animals the shock rate was .1 per 2-minute interval; for the other half it was .4 per 2-minute interval. In all cases shocks were programmed to occur independently of the CSs. Within each shock rate, one third of the animals received, respectively, one, three, or six conditioning sessions prior to testing. An additional group of rats received no conditioning. Figure 5.2 presents suppression ratios for separate test sessions in which four 2-minute tones were introduced into a bar-pressing situation in which shock was never presented.

The evidence indicates that at least some rats initially entertain rule (3). Rats that had received no shocks show no suppression in response to the tone. There is initial conditioning to the tone, however, after the first session of 12 random tone occurrences and several uncorrelated shock occurrences. At this point the unusualness heuristic sometimes will have generated rule (3), $B, H, T \rightarrow \bar{P}$. Approximately the same degree of conditioning is seen after three sessions. By the sixth session, however, rule (3) appears vanquished; there is no suppression to the tone at all. Thus the unusualness rule, "unexpected events signal other unexpected events," generated a rule that was then tested and ultimately found to be redundant. Such results support the most basic distinction that our framework makes between mechanisms for induction, namely, rule generation and rule refinement, even for organisms with intellectual capacities considerably more limited than those of humans.

5.2.2 Predictability, Redundancy, and Conditioning

Several other experiments establish that other factors in addition to mere statistical covariation govern predictability and consequently determine the degree of conditioning. One of these is a simple but important phenomenon called "blocking". Consider two groups of rats, both of which are exposed to a compound stimulus, that is, to A and X presented simultaneously. The compound is invariably followed by shock. Suppose that for one group of rats A has been presented previously, always followed by shock, while X has never been presented. The second group of rats has never been presented with either A or X. Note that for the first group the occurrence of A has a history of predicting shock and hence suppressing bar pressing via the rule $B, H, A \rightarrow \bar{P}$. The presence of X adds nothing to predictability. Since the initial rule suffices to predict the occurrence of shock, the rule $B, H, X \rightarrow \bar{P}$ need never be considered and there should be no conditioning to X despite the repeated association of X and S.

This is indeed what occurs. If A has a prior history of predicting S, it completely blocks conditioning to X. This result follows naturally from our theory, since if a strong successful rule has already been established to predict some event, a basic triggering condition for forming a new rule—failure of prediction—will never be met. In contrast, the result is the very opposite of what would be expected on the basis of standard behaviorist notions about "secondary reinforcement". These notions rested on the simple idea that the properties of any given conditioned stimulus can be expected to "rub off" onto any additional stimuli that are associated with it, so that X would become a conditioned stimulus simply by virtue of its pairing with A.

Our account also correctly predicts that blocking will be incomplete, and therefore some conditioning of X will occur, if conditioning of A is less than asymptotic at the beginning of compound training, or if A is a substantially less salient stimulus than X, or if A is familiar (hence no longer unusual) prior to introduction of shock. If a strong rule has not already been established, a predictive failure may occur and additional rules will have an opportunity to be formed. If there are two correlated cues, A and X, the system might eventually form up to three rules: $B, H, A \rightarrow \bar{P}$, $B, H, X \rightarrow \bar{P}$, and $B, H, A, X \rightarrow \bar{P}$. Note that the two former rules are generalizations of the third. Since all these rules will be matched on the same occasions (given that A and X invariably co-occur) and hence are redundant, they will compete with each other for reward. Depending on the initial strength of the rules and statistical fluctuations in bidding, multiple rules may coexist for an extended period or one rule may succeed in driving out the others. Such variation in blocking effects has been modeled in the simulation by Holyoak, Koh, and Nisbett.

An experiment by Wagner, Logan, Haberlandt, and Price (1968) makes another important point about predictability and redundancy, one that favors a prediction-based view over traditional notions of secondary reinforcement. They showed that when a given stimulus X is paired 50 percent of the time with an unconditioned stimulus such as shock, the degree of conditioning that occurs to X is to a substantial extent a function of the degree to which X serves to predict uniquely the occurrence of the shock. These investigators presented X simultaneously with stimulus Y half of the time and with stimulus Z half of the time. For group 1 the compound XY was always reinforced with the shock and the compound XZ was never reinforced, while for group 2 the compound XY was reinforced 50 percent of the time and so was the compound XZ. It may readily be seen that for group 1 the stimulus X was entirely unhelpful as a predictor of the shock. It was present on half the occasions of reinforcement, but another stimulus, Y, was present on 100 percent of the occasions and thus was a much better predictor. For group 2, on the other hand, Y was no better predictor than X (nor was Z). Thus we would expect more conditioning to X in group 2 than in group 1, which was in fact the result obtained.

In terms of our theory, in both group 1 and group 2 the unusualness inferential rule will generate several empirical rules that will then compete with one another. These would likely include the rules $B, H, Y \rightarrow \bar{P}$, $B, H, Z \rightarrow \bar{P}$, and $B, H, X \rightarrow \bar{P}$. In group 1, the first rule was always confirmed, the second rule was never confirmed, and the third rule was confirmed half as often as the first. Moreover, the occasions of confirmation were arranged so that the third rule was always redundant with the first rule, and hence the third rule would not always be rewarded for its successful predictions. As a result, the operation of the strength-revision procedures would favor the first rule over the third in the competition. In group 2, by contrast, all three rules were confirmed half the time, so that no one rule was favored to drive out any of the others.

5.2.3 Secondary Reinforcement versus Signaling

We have yet to arrive at the coup de grâce for the traditional perspective on conditioning. Several experiments, including some we have discussed, establish that when a new stimulus is associated with a CS signaler such as a tone, this does not result automatically in the new stimulus taking on the properties of the CS. But other experiments go further and show that under some conditions the new stimulus can take on properties *opposite* to those of the established CS. In general, a new stimulus can have "excitatory" (that is, US-like) effects, no effects, or even "inhibitory" effects (that is, effects that counter those of the US), depending on the expectations generated by the pattern of association within a given time period. The experiments that make these points also show that "conditioning" effects can be extremely rapid—occurring virtually full-blown in one or two trials—so that one is pressed toward an inferential account of the data as opposed to the incremental, trial-and-error, "stamping-in" account of the sort more traditional in learning theory, including recent connectionist proposals (see, for example, Sutton and Barto 1981).

An experiment by Rescorla (1972) establishes the point that a given stimulus may serve initially as an excitatory agent and then as an inhibitor. On the first two days of conditioning, rats were presented with four 10-second flashing lights (L), each of which ended with a 1/2-second shock. At this point the rule $B, H, L \rightarrow \bar{P}$ should be established. For the next 15 days the rats received one trial with the 10-second flashing light ending in shock and three trials with a 40-second tone (T), the last 10 seconds of which were accompanied by the light. The second kind of trial was never accompanied by shock. This procedure establishes tone as a signal of nonshock, which can be captured by generation of the exception rule $B, H, L, T \rightarrow P$ (that is, a rule indicating that in the presence of tone as well as light it is safe to press the bar). However, the unusualness rule plus the pairing of the tone with the light—a known signaler of shock, and hence an event with acquired importance—should also initially generate the rule $B, H, T \rightarrow \bar{P}$ (or an equivalent sequence of coupled rules), which initially will make the tone an excitatory stimulus. Although the resulting expectation of shock will never be confirmed, and hence will fail in competition with the valid rule $B, H, L, T \rightarrow \bar{P}$, the fact that the former rule was generated would be established by a demonstration of initial suppression in the presence of the tone.

As may be seen in figure 5.3, initial suppression, indicating an initial excitatory effect, was indeed found, followed by a period of

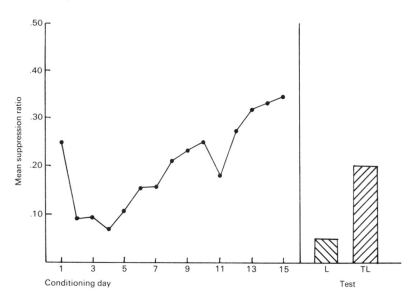

Figure 5.3
The panel to the left shows suppression to the tone (X) over the course of an
$AX - A +$ procedure in which X precedes A on the compound trials. The right-
hand panel shows suppression to the light (L) when presented alone and when
preceded by the tone (TL) on a test session administered after day 15. From
Rescorla (1972).

increasing inhibition. Figure 5.3 also shows the remarkable speed of
the initial suppression effect. The average suppression ratio on the
very first three trials (on the first day) was .23. By the second day the
rule $B, H, T \rightarrow \bar{P}$ is apparently well established as a hypothesis: the
suppression ratio on the second day is lower than on the first. This rule
sequence hangs around for several sessions before the apportionment-
of-credit procedures noticeably weaken it.

Eventually, however, the erroneous rule will lose strength, and the
tone will become an *inhibitory* stimulus. This is clearly established by
data presented in the far right portion of figure 5.3. These data show
that the valid rule $B, H, L, T \rightarrow P$ (formed by specialization to protect
the strong default rule $B, H, L \rightarrow \bar{P}$, which fails when a tone is present)
has by now emerged as the victor in the competition. At the end of the
15 conditioning trials depicted on the left in figure 5.3, the rats were
given a series of three test sessions during which the light was presented alone on two trials and presented along with the tone on four
other trials. It is clear that there is much greater suppression to the
light alone than to the light-plus-tone compound. Indeed, the suppression to the light alone is nearly asymptotic. This is as it should be,

given that the light in the absence of the tone continued to signal shock over the entire training period, sustaining a modified version of the original rule, $B, H, L, \bar{T} \rightarrow \bar{P}$. This default rule was protected from strength reduction when the tone was presented (in which case its condition would not be matched), and the exception rule $B, H, L, T \rightarrow P$ was selected instead on trials when the tone occurred.

An experiment by Kamin (1969) makes similar but even more dramatic points. He trained rats for 16 trials to associate white noise (N) with shock. He then created two different groups. Group LN received eight trials of a compound, simultaneous light-plus-noise stimulus that was never reinforced by shock, followed by four trials of the original noise stimulus that was again nonreinforced. Group N simply received 12 standard extinction trials, during which the noise was presented but never with shock. All animals received four trials per day.

Before presenting the results, let us analyze our expectations based on our predictions regarding rule generation and subsequent competition. Group N is of course expected to show just the customary gradual extinction as the rule $B, H, N \rightarrow \bar{P}$ dies a slow death due to nonreinforcement. In contrast, group LN, via the unusualness heuristic, should on the initial extinction trial generate a new specialized rule, $B, H, N, L \rightarrow P$. Consequently, this group might be expected to show some inhibition of suppression even on the very first trial. Furthermore, the new rule will of course be confirmed, and so the animal should show rapid inhibition—faster than group N, which has no cue to suggest that the initial learning situation has now changed.

What should happen when, after the first eight trials, the noise alone is presented? For group N, nothing interesting. This is merely a continuation of the slow competition between the rule $B, H, N \rightarrow \bar{P}$ and its original competitor rule (1), $B, H \rightarrow P$. For group LN, however, we expect a reversion to substantial suppression effects, because for them the modified default rule $B, H, N, \bar{L} \rightarrow \bar{P}$ has never yet failed. This default will have been protected by the highly successful exception rule $B, H, N, L \rightarrow P$.

Figure 5.4 presents the results. The results for group N, presented with the noise alone, may be seen at the bottom of figure 5.4. These animals showed the customary slow extinction process. The results for group LN are utterly different. The very first trial shows a substantially reduced suppression effect. The next trial—the first that confirms the new exception rule, $B, H, N, L \rightarrow P$—shows a further reduced suppression effect. By the fourth experience of the nonreinforced compound, the suppression ratio has become asymptotic.

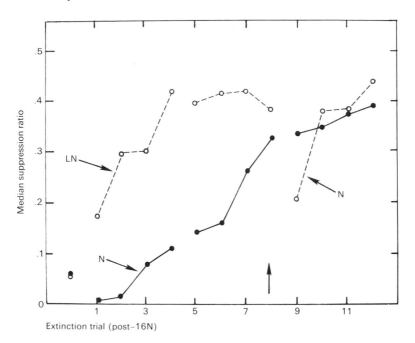

Figure 5.4
Extinction of suppression, by trial, following conditioning to noise. The groups were extinguished either to noise alone or to the compound. The arrow in the abscissa indicates point at which group extinguished to compound is switched to noise alone. From Kamin (1969).

Then, four trials after that, the single stimulus N is introduced. For group N this is by now business as usual, but for group LN it is an event not encountered since the original conditioning trials, during which N alone was always accompanied by shock. Accordingly, group LN rats show considerable suppression on the very first presentation of N alone.

5.2.4 Comparison with Behaviorist Accounts
It should be noted that the original investigators never provided a full theoretical account of the findings we have just reviewed. Wagner and Kamin spoke of "expectancy", "attention", "priming of short-term memory representations of the US", and "cue validity", but a unified account did not emerge from these theoretical constructs. Rescorla preferred to eschew such cognitivist constructs altogether: "Indeed, the puzzle of this kind of experiment for an informational description is how a stimulus can undergo such dramatic changes in value despite the fact that its prediction of the US remains unchanged.... Continu-

ing to follow the intuition that information is important in conditioning does not seem likely to be helpful" (Rescorla 1972, p. 42).

Rescorla and Wagner (1972) provided the major treatment of this set of results, and it remains the standard account in the conditioning literature. They offered a simple linear model to deal with the full range of results we have just reviewed. Two of the principles underlying the model were adapted from Hull's (1943) theory and from the basic Bush and Mosteller (1955) linear model of conditioning. The first of these was that the amount of conditioning that can occur on any given trial is limited by the amount of conditioning that is still possible. Early on, when a great deal of conditioning is still possible, the incremental effect of a reinforced trial will be large; but later, when conditioning is near its asymptote, the possible increase is small. The second principle was that the amount of conditioning that can occur on any given trial, as well as the total that can ultimately occur, is limited by the magnitude of the US. A weak US can only sustain small increments on each trial and can never produce very great associative strength with any given CS.

The Rescorla and Wagner contribution was to add a third principle, namely, that the associative strength of a given stimulus is limited not only by the associative strength that a particular stimulus already has but also by the associative strengths that any other concurrent stimuli may already have. The amount of conditioning to a stimulus A is limited by the amount of conditioning that has occurred to some other stimulus X that is present. These three principles are usually expressed in the following simple equation. If we consider the amount of conditioning that may occur to the stimulus A on a given trial, and denote this ΔV_A, then the equation states that

$$\Delta V_A = B(\lambda - V_A - V_X),$$

where B is a constant that determines how fast conditioning can occur, and λ denotes the limit of conditioning that can be supported by the US. V_A and V_X represent the conditioning already accrued to the stimulus A and to any other incidental stimuli X.

The Rescorla and Wagner version is capable of accounting for some, but not all, of the results we have reviewed. The limits of their approach can be characterized quite simply—their equation is generally able to account for phenomena that primarily depend on strength revision but is generally unable to account for phenomena that depend on rule generation. Our adaptive default-hierarchy theory differs from the Rescorla and Wagner account and variants of it in postulating the role of the unusualness heuristic in rule generation and in the induction of exception rules that subsequently protect useful but overly general default rules from the strength reduction to which they would otherwise be subject.

In showing the inadequacy of the Rescorla and Wagner account for certain phenomena, it will be useful to begin with the Kamin (1969) experiment with which we concluded our review. In that experiment animals were first taught that a noise was a signal for shock. Then some of the animals were presented with a compound stimulus consisting of the noise plus a light. It will be recalled that on the very first trial in which the light was presented in conjunction with the noise CS, the animals showed less suppression than on the previous trial, in which the noise had been presented by itself. There is no way that the Rescorla and Wagner account can handle such a phenomenon (as they themselves admit, 1972, p. 79) except by positing that the effect of any given new stimulus, in a situation in which the animal is "at risk" for receiving the US, is inhibitory. In fact, however, the effect of new stimuli in such situations is generally excitatory.

In contrast, our rule-based account provides a satisfactory explanation for the circumstances that will result in an immediate inhibitory effect of the light. The animal had previously learned the rule $B, H, N \rightarrow \bar{P}$. Given that a trial in the Kamin (1969) experiment spanned a fairly long interval (several minutes), this period would correspond to several cycles of matching and firing rules. Since no shock was presented on the first trial in which the light occurred along with the tone, the strong rule $B, H, N \rightarrow \bar{P}$ would repeatedly fail. Accordingly, the triggering conditions for the unusualness rule for specialization (a prior unusual event followed by failure of a strong rule) would be met, producing the new exception rule $B, H, N, L \rightarrow P$. By the end of the very first light-plus-tone trial, then, some rats would have generated an exception rule that would be competing with the original rule $B, H, N \rightarrow \bar{P}$, producing some inhibition of suppression. Thus our account indicates that the introduction of a new stimulus can sometimes be inhibitory, so long as its introduction causes the formation of a new rule suggesting that the conditions predicting the US are not in effect—that is, suggests a new specialization of an extant rule.

A second major problem with the Rescorla and Wagner account is that it predicts that conditioned inhibitors should be extinguishable by presenting them alone, in the absence either of the US or of excitatory CSs. If a stimulus X is paired with a stimulus A that has been conditioned to a US, and the compound is nonreinforced, X will become an inhibitor, as in the Kamin experiment above. Then, as Zimmer-Hart and Rescorla (1974) put it, "Assuming that nonreinforcement supports a zero asymptote . . . a simple nonreinforcement of a previously established inhibitor should produce a change. If V_X is negative, then the quantity $(0 - V_X)$ is positive and consequently V_X should be incremented toward zero when it is separately nonreinforced. That is, the theory predicts that repeated nonreinforced presentation of an inhibitor should attenuate that inhibition" (pp. 837–838).

In contrast, our account leads to the expectation that nonreinforcement of an inhibitor should, if anything, make it more of an inhibitor. Assume that a light has been established as an inhibitor because it has been paired with a tone previously established to be a signaler of shock and the compound has then been nonreinforced. The animal will have formed the rule $B, H, T, L \rightarrow P$, but as noted earlier it might also have formed a rule that is a generalization of that one, such as $B, H, L \rightarrow P$. When light is subsequently presented alone but nȯt reinforced (that is, no shock occurs), the animal learns nothing about the consequences specifically of a light-tone combination, but it should learn something about the occurrence of a light, namely, that it indeed predicts non-occurrence of shock. Then, when a light-tone combination subsequently recurs, there should be a match for both the rule $B, H, T, L \rightarrow P$ and the rule $B, H, L \rightarrow P$. The latter rule, which may have been strengthened, will elicit bar pressing. Consequently, instead of a reduction in inhibition, an increase in inhibition might be obtained.

The results obtained by Zimmer-Hart and Rescorla (1974) are entirely consistent with these suppositions. When they attempted to extinguish the inhibitory effect of the light by presenting it alone after the tone-light combination was at asymptotic levels of inhibition, they were unsuccessful. In one experiment, instead of introducing light-alone trials after asymptotic levels of inhibition had been established, they instead merely trained for the tone-shock pairing and then instituted either alternating tone-light and light-alone trials (both always nonreinforced) or just tone-light trials (nonreinforced). This experiment produced the result our account predicts—namely, *increased* inhibition for the former group during early trials before the $B, H, T, L \rightarrow P$ rule achieved asymptotic levels of inhibition.

There is a third major respect in which the Rescorla and Wagner account is deficient. As Sutton and Barto (1981) note, the application of the Rescorla and Wagner equation requires the prediction of a strictly negatively accelerated acquisition curve. The consensus, however, is that this curve is initially positively accelerating (Mackintosh 1974). The basic distinction our rule-based approach makes between rule generation and strength revision allows us to accommodate an initial positive acceleration in the learning curve. If the initial strength of a new rule is relatively low, whereas the reward provided for subsequent correct predictions is relatively high, then the strength increase on the trial on which the rule is formed (from 0 to the initial strength value) may be less than the increase on the next trial (from the initial value to the level produced by the first reward). The result will be an initial positive acceleration in strength, followed by negative acceleration toward the asymptote. This set of conditions is particularly likely to be met when there is no highly salient or unusual cue in the environment (so that any rule will initially be set at low strength) and reward for success is high (as when the US is a painful electric shock). The experiments that have found initial positive acceleration in the learning curve seem to have satisfied these conditions.

Finally, it should be noted that more recent connectionist accounts have not avoided the difficulties encountered by the Rescorla and Wagner theory. Indeed, Sutton and Barto (1981) explicitly acknowledge that their account shares the shortcomings of the Rescorla and Wagner approach.

5.3 Rule-Based Approach to Instrumental Conditioning

The experiments we have reviewed to this point used a so-called "classical" conditioning paradigm, in which the central aspect of learning is an association between two stimuli, the CS and the US, where the latter leads to a preexisting response, the UR. Another major paradigm, largely associated with Skinner and his followers, is "operant" or "instrumental" conditioning, in which the central aspect of learning is an association between a behavior and goal attainment, as when a pigeon learns to peck a key to receive food. Although the division between classical and operant conditioning figures prominently in textbook discussions of conditioning, there is considerable overlap between the two with respect to learning mechanisms (Schwartz 1978). For example, effects of statistical covariation of the sort described above are also obtained in the operant paradigm. In this section we will sketch the ways in which our adaptive default-hierarchy theory can be extended to instrumental conditioning paradigms.

5.3.1 *Acquisition and Extinction of Behavioral Sequences*

The literature on instrumental conditioning is especially relevant to understanding the acquisition and extinction of *sequences* of goal-directed behaviors. The bucket brigade algorithm is well suited to accounting for the learning of such rule sequences. Let us first consider the acquisition of a chain of behaviors. As we saw in chapter 3, the bucket brigade passes strength *backward* from the rule that is directly strengthened by goal attainment to earlier, stage-setting rules. Although stated in more cognitive terms, this aspect of the bucket brigade is quite similar to Hull's (1932) "goal-gradient" hypothesis. Like Hull, we would predict that rats learning a route through a maze to find food will tend to learn the final turn to the goal box first, then the next-to-last turn, and so on backward to the start of the maze. Although the data are complicated by other covarying factors, this prediction is generally confirmed (see Kimble 1961 for a review). The evidence is much clearer with the Skinnerian "chaining" procedure. For example, if one wishes to train a rat to pick up a marble from the experimenter's hand, deposit it in a hole, pull on a string that drops from the ceiling of the cage at that point, and then press a lever, all to receive a pellet of food, then the behavioral chain must be built up gradually in backward order (Millenson 1967).

Our framework, by virtue of the bucket brigade algorithm, also provides an account of major phenomena associated with the extinction of behavioral sequences. A basic generalization from results in the operant paradigm is that if a chain of behaviors is broken at some point and reinforcement is withheld, all components *up to* the point of disruption are weakened, whereas components subsequent to that point are preserved (Skinner 1938). Suppose, for example, that after the rat learns the sequence described above, conditions are altered so that depositing the marble in the hole no longer makes the string available. The rat will repeat the opening sequence (picking up the marble and inserting it in the hole) a few times and then cease responding. If the string is then again dropped down within reach, however, the rat will quickly pull it and press the lever, demonstrating that the later steps in the sequence have not been extinguished. From our perspective, this pattern is to be expected because the rules triggering the behaviors subsequent to the break in the chain will not have had their conditions satisfied during the extinction period and therefore will have simply remained unused, rather than being weakened as the result of nonreinforcement.

Our conception of rule competition yields other points of agreement with Hull's theory in addition to the goal-gradient hypothesis. For example, the notion that rules calling for alternative behaviors can coexist but compete is reminiscent of Hull's (1934) "habit-family hierarchy". Thus, if a particular behavior in a learned sequence is blocked, another will have an opportunity to replace it (for example, if the shortest route through a maze is blocked, the rat will use a longer known route as a detour).

5.3.2 *Hierarchical Relations among Rules*

On the other hand, our perspective departs from the theories of Hull and Skinner in very basic ways. For example, we emphasize that a rule system typically forms a hierarchical structure. Low-level rules specifying individual effector actions ("If the goal is to perform the maze-running routine, and a white corridor is to the left, and a black corridor is to the right, then enter the right corridor") can be supported by higher-level rules ("If the goal is to obtain food, and there is food in the goal box, then set the subgoal of performing the maze-running routine"). Unlike Hull's theory, in which action sequences were definable only in terms of sequential couplings of effector actions, our framework can accommodate evidence that actions are often organized hierarchically (Lashley 1951).

The hierarchical structure of procedures allows us to account for a phenomenon known as "latent extinction", which is troublesome for strictly behaviorist accounts. In a typical demonstration, rats are first trained to run a maze to reach food in a goal box. Some of the animals are then simply placed in the goal box several times when it is empty, whereas the others are placed elsewhere. Finally, all the animals undergo regular extinction training, receiving no reward for reaching the goal box. The rats that had been previously exposed to the empty goal box cease running to it much more quickly (see Kimble 1961).

In terms of our view of rule learning, at least two factors operate to encourage latent extinction. First, exposure to the empty box will directly weaken the final rules in the sequence (approach to the food tray). Accordingly, the process of weakening the strength of earlier-acting rules will proceed more rapidly once the regular extinction trials begin. Second, a possibility obvious to all but old-fashioned behaviorists is that the rats placed in the empty goal box will conclude that food is no longer available there! In our view, the entire maze-running routine depends on a high-level rule such as "If the goal is to obtain food, and there is food in the goal box, then set the subgoal of performing the maze-running routine." So if the rat learns there is no food to be had in the goal box, the goal of getting there will not be set and the maze-running sequence simply will not be initiated. As a result, the rat will show extinction of the sequence on the very first trial after the latent-extinction experience, before the early components in the behavior chain have ever been executed unsuccessfully. Nonhierarchical descriptions of behavioral sequences, whether of the Hull or of the Skinner variety, fail to provide a mechanism for such rapid extinction.

5.3.3 Prediction-Based Latent Learning

As the example above illustrates, a fundamental distinction between our framework and behaviorist accounts is that we assume learning depends most directly on confirmations and disconfirmations of predictions, rather than on the provision of overt reinforcement per se. We thus follow in the early cognitivist tradition of Tolman (1932, 1948, 1959). In addition to accounting for latent extinction, our framework can readily accommodate evidence for "latent learning" (Blodgett 1929; Tolman and Honzik 1930; for a review see Thistlethwaite 1951), another phenomenon that created difficulty for the Hullian approach. In a typical demonstration of latent learning, rats in an experimental group are permitted to freely explore a maze in the absence of any overt reinforcement such as food. At a later time food is introduced. Compared to a control group that did not receive any prior opportunity to explore the maze, the experimental group will learn to run the maze more quickly once the food is introduced.

Such results demonstrate that rats tend to learn the layout of their environment even in the absence of overt reinforcement, with the result that they are better prepared to learn a specific route once food is introduced. Our view implies that an organism will learn simply by generating and testing predictor rules that successfully model the environment, thus increasing its ability to generate accurate expectations. Learning, we would argue, is less a matter of drive reduction than of surprise reduction.

5.4 The Pragmatics of Covariation Detection

In subsequent chapters we will apply our framework of adaptive default hierarchies to a wide range of phenomena that at first may seem far removed from animal conditioning. Nonetheless, we will argue that there is substantial overlap in many of the inductive mechanisms that operate across all these domains. In the remainder of this chapter we will prepare the way for these extensions by highlighting some very general principles that determine the degree to which cognitive systems are able to form rules that capture covariations in their environment.

Since rats are such fine detectors of covariation, even under the ecologically unnatural stimulus conditions presented in psychology experiments, it might seem inevitable that people, with their superior intelligence, would be able to detect most of the relevant covariations in their own natural environments. Certainly the syntactic faith of the behaviorists led them to assume that what was true for rats in a laboratory with artificial stimuli would hold true elsewhere both for rats and for humans. In fact, however, there are three major respects in which the animal experiments differ from more ecologically common circumstances. Each of these differences is crucial for the covariation-detection capacities of both animals and humans. And each of the differences represents factors that are well understood in terms of our pragmatic framework. One set of differences has to do with the motives and goals of the organism, a second has to do with the organism's prior experience with the *type* of rule to be learned (reflected in knowledge available via higher levels in the default hierarchy), and the third has to do with the codability of events and event relations that must be incorporated into the rule to be learned.

5.4.1 *Motivational Factors*

Associations are likely to be learned if they involve properties that are important by virtue of their relevance to the goals of the organism. In experiments such as those we have been describing, the goal relevance of such environmental properties as food and shock is altogether obvious. Indeed, the intensity of the motive states in such experiments may come as a surprise to those who are only casually familiar with animal learning experiments. Rats typically are starved down to 80 percent of their initial body weight to ensure their complete attention when it comes time to teach them about behaviors that will provide them with food. Shock levels are set at a sufficient intensity to cause paralysis and great rippling jerks of the body. One may rest assured that animals so treated will be scanning their environment for clues that might predict subsequent occurrences. Motivational factors in typical conditioning studies thus are designed to encourage covariation detection by ensuring that attention will be directed to the environmental facts that are to be associated by rules.

To our knowledge, no one has explored the conditionability of rats at the lower ranges of motivational states. (Though investigators did thoroughly examine the question of whether rats unmotivated by hunger or thirst will learn about the spatial layout of mazes. As we have seen, they will.) It would be interesting to examine covariation-detection tasks posing differing degrees of learning difficulty to see at what motivational levels they would cease to be learned.

5.4.2 *Prior Experience with the Rule Type to Be Learned*

The behaviorists' faith in the syntactical universality of the laws of learning led them to the view that, as Watson (1924) himself claimed, "We can take any stimulus calling out a standard reaction and substitute another stimulus for it" (p. 24). Nothing, as it turned out, could be farther from the case. As Seligman (1970) put it half a century later, animals are very differently *prepared*, by virtue of past experience and perhaps genetic wiring as well, to make different kinds of associations. An animal that gets sick after eating a distinctive food will avoid that food ever after, even if the illness occurs twelve hours after the food was eaten (Garcia, McGowan, Ervin, and Koelling 1968; Garcia, McGowan, and Green 1972). Cats that readily learn to escape from a puzzle box by pulling strings or pressing levers learn only with great difficulty to escape by licking or scratching themselves, and this is the case despite the fact that the "operant level" of the latter responses is much higher than that of the former. Pigeons will die of starvation before they discover that *not* pecking at a lighted key, rather than pecking, will get them food reinforcements. (See Seligman 1970 for a review of such phenomena.) The natural ecology of cats has of course redundantly taught them that itches, not hungers, are to be relieved by scratching. Similarly, a lifetime of experience has taught the pigeon that pecking, not not-pecking, yields food.

Until very recently, behaviorists were insulated from discovering these extreme preparedness effects because they examined *arbitrary* stimulus associations, such as the association between light and shock or between lever pressing and delivery of a food pellet. Arbitrary associations, in Seligman's terms, are just those for which the organism is neither prepared nor counterprepared. Associations for which the organism is prepared may be learned on a few trials or even on one trial. Associations for which the organism is counterprepared may never be learned. And, it should be borne in mind, arbitrary associations are likely to be learned only when the stimuli in question are clearly goal-relevant. Evidence to be reviewed in chapter 6 (Chapman and Chapman 1967, 1969) indicates that human covariation detection is also heavily influenced by the degree of preparedness to see certain associations.

5.4.3 Codability of Events and Event Relations

Just as the perception of covariation can be distorted by the degree to which prior rules interrelate the critical properties, so it can be clouded by the opacity of events or of relations between events. Some events and event relations are easier to "see" than others, and the easier they are to see the more accurate covariation detection is likely to be. We may distinguish several types of "codability" that are likely to be important to covariation detection.

Clarity and Salience of Events

The to-be-conditioned stimuli used in animal learning studies are generally quite distinctive and noticeable. The tones and lights are sufficiently intense that they would not be confused with background conditions. When animals are required to distinguish among stimuli, the experimenters typically make this easy for them by presenting the stimuli in different modalities—for example, a light will be super-imposed on a tone, rather than a tone of 750 Hz being superimposed on one of 1,500 Hz.

To be sure, many of the most important associations that humans have to learn are composed of just such clear and salient stimuli; but many others, especially in the social realm, are not. Many physical stimuli, as well as most social stimuli, require substantial coding. For example, suppose one wishes to evaluate the truth of the proposition that red-headed people are hot-tempered. Learning such a rule requires coding particular people as having red, auburn, sandy, or brown hair, and requires coding particular behaviors as being expressive of a hot temper or as being justifiably heated responses to provocation. The implication of this is that covariation detection should be most accurate for those social stimuli that are most codable. There is substantial evidence for this proposition, which we will present in chapter 7.

Stimulus Contiguity

Another critical codability factor is the temporal relations among stimuli. In most conditioning experiments, stimuli are presented simultaneously, or at least with no more than a one- to two-second delay between them. Indeed, temporal contiguity is normally absolutely crucial: delays much beyond a few seconds between CS and US, or between an "operant" (instrumental behavior) and reinforcement, typically result in no conditioning at all. This must be borne in mind when one considers the difficulty that people are likely to encounter in learning most relations of importance to them. Especially in the social domain, such short delays between an action and knowledge of its consequences may be the exception. Only if the person is engaged in some activity that serves to maintain an active representation of the action over the time until its consequences are encoded, or if prior rules cause the consequences to reactivate a representation of the action, will there be any possibility of "bridging" to an association.

Invariance of Association

Stimulus linkages, especially during the initial learning periods of conditioning, are typically invariant. (The experiments by Rescorla 1968, 1972 provide some exceptions.) If the CS appears, it is invariably followed by the US; if a to-be-conditioned operant occurs, it is invariably followed by the reinforcement. This factor alone is enough to make one hesitate before assuming that the rule-learning powers of the white rat in the laboratory can be extrapolated to those of either rats or humans outside the laboratory. Many if not most behaviors of importance to people have variable payoffs. For example, careful preparation of lectures sometimes results in clear presentations that are appreciated, and sometimes in dry and stilted performances. A soft answer sometimes turneth away wrath and sometimes seems to have the effect of pouring oil on the fire.

Remarkably, there have been few studies, either of humans or of animals, that allow us to gain a clear idea of the capacity to detect less-than-invariant associations. There is a literature on people's ability to read correlations from 2 × 2 contingency tables, but this is of little relevance to their ability to detect covariation among the events that make up such summary tables. One of the exceptions is a series of studies by Jennings, Amabile, and Ross (1982). These investigators found that when people were presented with pairs of arbitrarily related stimuli—for example, number pairs, or pairs consisting of a musical note and a letter of the alphabet—they were unable to detect correlations below around .3 and were not very good at detecting correlations in the range .3 to .6. If these observations were to extend to less barren stimuli, they would suggest that people's covariation detection capacities are very poor indeed. Work to be discussed in chapter 7 suggests, however, that such a conclusion would be too pessimistic.

The considerations that we have just reviewed should make it clear that work on conditioning has for the most part presented us with a one-sided portrait. Animals have been studied under conditions in which stimuli were clear and motivationally relevant, the animals were not counterprepared to learn the relevant associations, and the associations were usually quite strong in a statistical sense. But rats and humans live in a world in which the motivational relevance of stimuli may not be so evident, the nature of the stimuli may not even be clear, the relevant associations are ones that they are often counter- prepared to learn, and the associations may be weak in a statistical sense. Small wonder we don't learn everything we ought.

In the next chapter we will examine people's ability to detect multi- ple, and synchronic, associations between events. This ability is funda- mental to human categorization and, as we will see, provides further illustrations of the operation of adaptive default hierarchies.

6

Category Formation

In the previous chapter we noted that people demonstrate only modest ability to detect imperfect covariations between aspects of the environment. Yet at the same time people clearly are quite proficient at dividing the world into categories, a task in which covariation detection plays a central role. People can learn to distinguish between cows and horses, between saddle horses and draft horses, between Belgians and Percherons. Such discriminations are based on detecting multiple covariations among the properties that serve to define the categories.

We want to address three central questions concerning categories. The first concerns their use: What are categories for? The second concerns their formation: How are categories built up from experience? The third concerns what initiates their formation: What triggers the initiation of a new category? In discussing these questions, we will emphasize the representation of categories as rule clusters, the importance of considerations of variability, and the pragmatic significance of triggering conditions.

6.1 Categorization and Induction

6.1.1 Functions of Categorization
The most obvious function of categorization is to classify and organize instances. But in our view the classificatory function is in fact derivative of the more fundamental function of generating goal-relevant inferences. This conclusion follows from our assumption that categories are best defined as clusters of interrelated rules and that rules are in turn the product of goal-directed inductive mechanisms.

The inferential utility of categories is particularly evident for concepts that represent "natural kinds"—the categories that almost inevitably emerge from everyday experience, such as giraffes and

Figure 6.1
An example of a triad used by Gelman and Markman (1983).

rocks. In philosophy, Quine (1969) emphasized the central role that natural categories of this sort play in the generation of inferences. To know that an instance is a member of a natural category is to have an entry point into an elaborate default hierarchy that provides a wealth of expectations about the instance. Moreover, such inferences can involve not only the salient perceptual properties by which individuals are typically classified (the giraffe's long neck, for instance) but also less readily observable properties (such as the giraffe's inner biological structure).

A study by Gelman and Markman (1983) demonstrates that children as young as four years old rely heavily on categories to direct their inferences, even when category membership is pitted against perceptual similarity. In a typical experiment children were presented with a triad of pictures such as those in figure 6.1. For this example, the experimenter would first tell the child, "This bird gives its baby mashed-up food" (pointing to the flamingo) and "This bat gives its baby milk" (pointing to the bat). Then the child was asked, "Does this bird (indicating the black bird) give its baby mashed-up food or milk?" Even though the critical instance was always more similar perceptually to the out-of-category instance (here, the bat), about 85 percent of the children selected the answer corresponding to that associated with the initial category member (here, that the new bird would feed its babies mashed-up food). In contrast, control subjects who were asked the question without seeing any comparison examples responded at the chance level, with about 50 percent selecting each of the two possible alternatives.

In another experiment Gelman and Markman found that some of their young subjects were able to discriminate between properties for which category membership is a reliable guide for inferences (for example, feeding behavior) and properties for which category membership is not such a reliable guide (for example, weight). Children were told, in one study, that a pictured tropical fish weighs 20 pounds and that a dolphin weighs 100 pounds, and then were asked to judge the weight of another pictured fish—a shark that looked like the dolphin. Some (but not all) of the four-year-olds gave the answer consistent with the perceptually similar out-of-category instance, rather than being guided by the dissimilar category instance.

The results of the Gelman and Markman studies demonstrate the inferential role that natural categories can play, and also indicate that inferential rules based on default hierarchies operate at a very early age. Perhaps most important, almost all their subjects consistently allowed category membership to direct their inferences for properties of a kind known to be relatively invariant for categories of the given type (for example, feeding behavior tends to be invariant for bird species), while many subjects behaved quite differently for properties of a kind known to be variable (for example, weight tends to vary across fish species). This is evidence for one of our major contentions, namely, that representations of the statistical incidence of properties across categories serve to direct inferences and generalizations. In section 6.2 we will discuss how such variability information can be learned, and in chapter 8 we will have more to say about the role of variability in the assessment of potential generalizations from newly observed objects or from newly observed properties of familiar objects.

6.1.2 The Structure of Natural Categories
The inferential utility of natural categories, as well as the mechanisms by which they may be learned, can be better understood in the light of what is known about their psychological structure. We will discuss first the organization of instances that belong to a common immediately superordinate category and then the organization of categories at successively higher levels of abstraction in a default hierarchy.

Prototypes and Typicality

The view that categories are invariably defined by a set of necessary and sufficient conditions for membership has by now been thoroughly discredited (for a review see Smith and Medin 1981). Largely as a result of the philosophical analyses of Wittgenstein (1958), the cross-linguistic studies of Berlin and Kay (1969), and the psychological research of Rosch (1973), the current consensus on natural categories is that they have clear "best examples" or "prototypes" but relatively vague boundary conditions. The exemplars of natural categories tend to fall on a rough continuum from prototypical instances to unclear borderline cases.

Three major lines of research support this conclusion (see Glass and Holyoak 1986, chap. 5). First, people reliably rate some category instances as more "typical" than others (Rips, Shoben, and Smith 1973; Rosch 1973). Second, when people are asked to list instances of a category, they reliably generate some instances both earlier and more frequently than others (Battig and Montague 1969). The items that are produced most readily tend to be just those that people consider most typical of the category (Rosch 1973). And third, both of the above measures (typicality ratings and frequency of production) predict the speed with which people classify instances as members of a category. For example, people can verify the truth of the sentence "A robin is a bird" more quickly than they can verify "A goose is a bird" (Glass, Holyoak, and O'Dell 1974; Rips, Shoben, and Smith 1973; Rosch 1973). Such results suggest that natural perceptual categories are organized in terms of "prototypes", or representations of central tendency.

Degrees of prototypicality can be readily interpreted in terms of the organization of a default hierarchy. The mental model of an individual object will constitute a q-morphism based on rules derived from a variety of superordinate concepts plus any individuating information that is available. Typical instances will be those for which the default rules attached to the relevant superordinate category tend to hold, whereas atypical instances will tend to match exception rules. The default rules attached to the concept "bird" (such as "If X is a bird, then X can fly") will generally hold for robins; penguins, however, will match various overriding exception rules (such as "If X is a bird with small wings and a large body, then X cannot fly").

One implication of our view is that it is not necessary to assume that an explicit category prototype, in the sense of an ideal example constructed by averaging presented instances, is either necessary or sufficient to represent all that is induced about category structure. Rather, as we will elaborate below, more general knowledge of property distributions is abstracted and represented by rule clusters. Such knowledge enables a concept corresponding to a prototype to be constructed if needed to perform some task. In other situations, when a prototype is not directly required, it may not exist except in the implicit sense of an amalgamation of default assumptions. We may speculate that the existence of a salient example embodying all or most of the default values may result in the "precipitation" of a prototype concept where otherwise there might be none. In section 6.2 we will describe evidence indicating that people learn a great deal more about category structure than simply information about central tendencies or mental pictures of prototypes.

Pragmatics and Levels of Category Abstraction
In addition to emphasizing that there are degrees of typicality across instances of a category, Rosch and her colleagues have argued that there are important differences among categories at different levels of abstraction. Rosch, Mervis, Gray, Johnson, and Boyes-Braem (1976) hypothesized that there is a "basic level" at which it is natural to divide the world into alternative categories. This level maximizes the perceptual and functional similarities among instances of the same category while it maximizes the differences between instances of different categories. The notion of basic levels is based on two related assumptions: "that (1) in the perceived world, information-rich bundles of perceptual and functional attributes occur that form natural discontinuities, and that (2) basic cuts in categorization are made at these discontinuities" (Rosch 1978, p. 31). These properties define natural categories in a sense similar to that of Quine (1969). For example, consider the hierarchical sequence "kitchen chair", "chair", and "furniture". "Furniture" is a relatively abstract category with few invariant or nearly invariant properties. In contrast, "chair" has a considerable number of such properties, which serve to distinguish instances of "chair" from alternative categories, such as "table". "Kitchen chair" also has many properties, but these are largely shared with similar alternatives, such as "living-room chair". In this example "chair" appears to be the basic level of categorization. Rosch and her colleagues found that several categorization tasks can be performed most readily at the basic level. For example, people classified pictures most quickly into the basic-level category rather than the subordinate or superordinate.

Given our emphasis on rule clusters as category representations, we find the hypothesis that basic-level categories are characterized by distinctive clusters of co-occuring properties to be attractive. Furthermore, as we will argue in section 6.3.2, there is evidence that the mechanisms of category induction favor the acquisition of categories with properties organized in such a manner. Nonetheless, the notion of a basic level is somewhat less fundamental in our framework than in Rosch's view. Because categorization takes place in the context of problem solving and generation of predictions, the search for useful categorizations will focus on categories at the level of abstraction at which a pragmatically acceptable solution plan emerges. From our perspective, then, it is natural to consider the "basic" level to be that which most often affords a satisfactory plan of action. Since this level of categorization will tend to be dominant in making decisions about how to respond to the instance, we will refer to it as the *dominant* level in the default hierarchy.

In many cases it is likely that the basic level posited by Rosch will correspond to the dominant level in our sense. In dealing with a piece of furniture, for example, it is typically important to know whether or not one should sit on it. Accordingly, the object must be classified at the level of "chair" versus "table" rather than solely at the superordinate level of "furniture". Moreover, in most circumstances the "chair" concept provides satisfactory default rules regardless of the subordinate type involved. The natural clustering of properties in the environment ensures that a single level of the default hierarchy will generally prove most important to planning.

On the other hand, because it varies with the goals of the cognitive system, the dominant level of category abstraction will be less rigid than the Roschian concept of a basic level seems to imply. A furniture maker is likely to focus on concepts corresponding to very specific types of chairs, for example, blond oak reproduction Windsor rockers with rush seats—although even for a furniture maker the "chair" concept serves as the default level when he is simply looking for something to sit on. In general, the dominant level should vary with the problem context. The pragmatic view of the natural level of categorization was expressed by Roger Brown (1958) in a paper entitled "How Shall a Thing Be Called?" A particular coin is likely to be called a dime in a grocery store because for purposes of economic exchange all dimes are alike, and different from pennies and quarters. A coin collector, however, may use a much more specific level of categorization.

Our conception of the determinants of the dominant level of classification predicts that atypical instances, for which default rules often do not apply, will be most readily classified not at Rosch's basic level but at the subordinate level at which relevant exception rules are mainly defined. For example, whereas a picture of a typical "bird" instance such as a robin will be classified as a bird more quickly than as a robin, as Rosch and colleagues observed, a different pattern would be expected for a picture of an atypical bird such as a penguin. Since in this case the lower exception level would be dominant, we would expect people to classify the atypical instance as a penguin more quickly than as a bird. In fact, recent studies have confirmed that pictures of atypical instances are categorized more rapidly at the subordinate than at the "basic" level (Jolicoeur, Gluck, and Kosslyn 1984). In general, our approach leads to the expectation that people's use of categorical default hierarchies will prove more flexible and responsive to context than Rosch's view suggests.

6.2 *Induction of Distributional Knowledge*

We have argued throughout this book that induction critically depends on the ability to accommodate variability in the environment. For example, a system must be able to learn partially predictive rules even if some irreducible amount of "error variance" cannot be accounted for. The mechanism of support summation used to make categorization decisions, sketched in chapter 2, is designed to exploit knowledge of the variability of property values with respect to alternative categories.

There are good reasons to suppose that information about variability will be useful. The dispersion of category members over their dimensions of variation is not simply error variance in its usual sense; rather, it is itself a property of the environment. A statistician would not wish to classify objects into categories given knowledge only of central tendencies if there were overlap among the properties of the category alternatives. The statistician would require some estimate of the dispersion of the dimensions defining each category before classification could be justified. A new object would then be classified as an A or a B as a function both of its average distance from the central tendency of each of the dimensions underlying category A and category B, and of the dispersion of each of the dimensions around their central tendencies. In addition, knowledge of the dispersion of A and B would be used to decide whether a novel instance is so unlikely to belong to *either* known category that a new category concept should be formed to accommodate it.

Standards

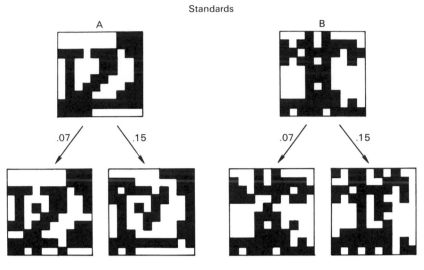

Figure 6.2
Examples of random distortions. From Fried and Holyoak (1984).

6.2.1 Knowledge of Variability

The utility of storing and employing some index of dispersion is so manifest that it scarcely seems possible that organisms would fail to do so. In fact, the early studies of Posner and Keele (1968, 1970) demonstrated that subjects abstracted knowledge of the variability of categories as well as knowledge of central tendencies. These investigators found that although artificial categories exemplified by relatively variable instances were more difficult to learn, subjects were subsequently more likely to classify highly distorted novel patterns into a category if the training instances had been relatively variable. In a statistical sense this was a normatively correct decision, since a category based on a relatively broad distribution of examples is more likely to generate a highly distorted instance than is a category based on a narrow distribution.

Research by Fried and Holyoak (1984) provides more detailed evidence of variability learning. They presented their subjects with patterns like those shown in figure 6.2, produced by randomly distorting a standard pattern of light and dark squares on a grid. The numbers .07 and .15 refer to the proportion of squares altered to make a new pattern from the standard.

Fried and Holyoak told their subjects that they were about to view a series of geometric patterns designed by two artists, named Smith and Wilson, and that they would have to distinguish the work of

Smith from that of Wilson. The two standards shown in figure 6.2 were used to generate patterns for all the subjects, but each subject saw a different random sample of distortions, and no subject saw the standard. The patterns that the subjects saw were produced by distorting the standard either by 7-percent changes on the average or by 15-percent changes. The distributions around the average distortions were binomial approximations to the normal. Thus for one group of subjects the variability of the instances around the central tendency was relatively low, whereas for the other group of subjects the variability was relatively high.

Subjects were shown patterns until they responded correctly for 10 trials in a row or reached a maximum of 200 patterns. After completion of the learning phase, all subjects received an additional 100 transfer trials, without error correction of any kind. They were told that the patterns would include new Wilsons and new Smiths, but also an unspecified number of designs by other people. In fact, there were no true "others"; all the patterns presented during the transfer phase were actually derived from the two original standards. The patterns presented on the transfer test were derived using four distortion probabilities, .10, .20, .30, and .40. The transfer patterns thus included instances at higher levels of distortion than occurred during learning, even in the high-variability learning conditions.

As would be expected, it was more difficult for the subjects in the high-variability condition to learn the patterns than for those in the low-variability condition. It took significantly more trials for the former subjects to reach the learning criterion. During the subsequent transfer phase, however, subjects in the high-variability condition were more accurate in classifying new instances, because they were significantly less likely to assign an instance to the "other" category. Thus they were more accepting of outlying instances because their representations of category variability allowed for the possibility of highly distorted exemplars.

Fried and Holyoak next demonstrated that subjects assign a new exemplar to a given category on the basis of its *likelihood* of having been generated by the category, given the latter's central tendency and dispersion, rather than on the perceptual *distance* of the exemplar from the prototype for the category. Subjects were shown patterns from one low-variability category and one high-variability category: the "Smith" patterns were produced by a random distortion probability centering on .07, and the "Wilson" patterns by a random distortion probability centering on .15. In the transfer phase, the subjects were shown new works by Smith and Wilson and were forced to assign each pattern to one category or the other. The transfer set consisted of a total of 100 patterns, half derived from each standard, with equal numbers generated at distortion probabilities of .15, .25, .30, and .35. The composition of the set made it possible to test whether the subjects were simply assigning patterns to categories on the basis of the distance of the pattern from the prototype for the category, or were instead responding to the likelihood that the pattern could have been generated from the category, given its central tendency and dispersion. The results indicated that the latter was clearly the case. For those patterns that were equally far from the prototype for Smith and that for Wilson, subjects were substantially more likely to assign the pattern to Wilson, the high-variability category (which was in fact more likely to have generated it).

6.2.2 Rule-Based Representations of Distributions

In chapter 2 we argued that the conditional probability of a category, given the observation of certain property values for an instance, can be represented implicitly by the strengths of a set of rules. Such rules have the general form "If $P_i = V_j$ for instance X, then X is a member of category C_k, " where V_j is the value of property P_i (for example, "If an animal has size = ⟨medium large⟩, then it is a dog"). The higher the conditional probability of the category given the specified property value, the more often the rule will yield a correct classification decision, and hence the greater the strength that will tend to accrue to it under the apportionment-of-credit mechanisms described in chapter 3. To a first approximation, the distribution of a property P_i over a set of categories C_k can thus be represented by a set of $n \times m$ rules with their attendant strengths, where n is the number of discriminable values of P_i and m is the number of alternative categories.

In order to classify an instance, as we saw in chapter 2, all the rules with matched conditions will compete to activate messages representing the alternative categories. Support for each category will sum, and if the categories are mutually exclusive, the category messages will in turn trigger inhibitory rules that reduce the support of competitors. The outcome, if the observed property values in fact favor one category over the others, is that the "winning" alternative eventually will acquire sufficient support to effectively suppress its competitors, activating the rules that ultimately generate an overt response.

This process is sufficient to account for results such as those of Fried and Holyoak (1984), which indicate that people use variability information to classify novel instances. If the training instances for a category C_k are highly variable with respect to a property P_i, then rules in which the value of V_j is extreme, and which provide evidence for C_k, will acquire more strength than they would if the training instances were less variable. As a result, a novel instance with an extreme value of V_j will provide more evidence for C_k (reflected in a higher support level) in the former case.

Our view of classification also accounts for other factors known to influence categorization decisions. For example, the greater the overlap in the property values of the instances of alternative categories, and the more alternative categories there are, the more difficult it is to classify instances (Homa and Vosburgh 1976). Both category overlap and number of categories will contribute directly to the degree of competition between alternative possible categorizations of instances. Increased overlap will result in the rules referring to any particular property value providing relatively equal support for different categories. An increased number of categories will require more rules to be learned, and also, at least initially, will cause rules referring to any particular property value to send support to more categories (hence providing less selective support to any one). In addition, it should be clear that the mechanisms of strength revision described in chapter 3 will lead to more accurate classification performance with increasing numbers of training instances. Categories defined by broad distributions will be learned relatively slowly (Posner and Keele 1968) because relatively difficult discriminations will be more dependent on accurate tuning of the strength values associated with the categorization rules (that is, strength values better calibrated to the relevant conditional probabilities).

The inductive mechanisms for rule generation will interact with those for strength revision to determine the actual set of rules eventually used to perform categorizations. The "first approximation" mentioned above for representing property distributions assumed that a rule would be defined for each possible pairing of a property value and a category. This approximation is at once too restrictive and too profligate in specifying an adequate set of rules. It is too restrictive because it will often be the case that better rules can be defined using conjunctions of properties as their conditions ("If an animal has size = ⟨medium large⟩ and color = ⟨brown⟩, then it is a dog"). Conjunctive rules, by virtue of their greater specificity, will have a greater chance of winning in the bidding competition; and if the conjuncts are individually predictive of the supported category and uncorrelated with each other, a conjunctive rule is more likely to be correct and hence will acquire greater strength than any individual rule in the corresponding set of rules with single conditions.

Conjunctive rules will be most favored when the predictiveness of the individual properties is not independent. Suppose, for example, that use of alcohol indicates a person has a slight health risk and use of sleeping pills indicates a slight health risk, but use of both alcohol and sleeping pills indicates a major health risk. In this case the conjunctive rule "If a person uses alcohol and sleeping pills, then that person is a high-risk individual" would acquire much greater strength than either of the two possible rules with single conditions. There is experimental evidence that people are in fact sensitive to correlations among properties that predict category membership. Medin, Altom, Edelson, and Freko (1982) presented subjects with cases indicating symptoms associated with hypothetical diseases. In some cases two symptoms were correlated, so that whenever one was associated with the disease, the other was as well. Subjects were more likely to classify novel cases as exhibiting the disease if their symptom pattern preserved the correlations observed in the training examples.

Although conjunctive rules will often be generated and used in categorization, many possible rules (with both single and multiple conditions) will either never be generated or eventually be discarded after losing strength. Rules that have features in their conditions that do not distinguish among the categories will fail to contribute to correct decisions and will consequently lose strength. The triggering conditions for creating rules with conjunctive conditions will be biased in favor of conjoining properties that are individually predictive (see section 6.3.2 below). Furthermore, the inferential rules and operating principles will tend to generate new rules mainly if errors of classification are being made. Consequently, if early in learning some salient property or properties provide rules that distinguish very well among the alternative categories, there will be little or no inductive pressure to generate new rules. (This is comparable to the "blocking" principle in diachronic rule learning discussed in chapter 5). In contrast, difficult discriminations will force the generation and testing of larger rule sets, using less salient properties to form conditions (compare the account of perceptual learning proposed by Gibson and Gibson 1955).

Decisions between mutually exclusive categories are guided by inhibitory rules that translate evidence in favor of any particular alternative into evidence *against* its competitors. The generation of inhibitory rules will be triggered in response to conflicts between the actions indicated by simultaneous categorizations of an object. For example, to view an animal as both a dog and a pet may actually be useful, since the two categorizations provide complementary information on which to base expectations (the animal may be expected to like both chewing bones and being petted). In contrast, categorizing the animal as both a dog and a wolf would be problematic, since rules suggesting the incompatible reactions of approach and flight would be supported. Such a conflict is a triggering condition for the generation of inhibitory rules linking "dog" and "wolf", thereby forcing earlier resolution of the conflict and avoiding the triggering of incompatible rules. Thus, while coexistence of alternative categorizations of an input is the system's tacit default, occasions of error and conflict provide triggers for the induction of inhibitory rules that render specific categories mutually exclusive.

6.2.3 *Theory-Guided Induction of Distributions*
So far we have emphasized "bottom-up" procedures for category induction. Many categories of importance to humans, however, arise at least in part as the result of more top-down processes that construct rule clusters on the basis of prior knowledge. A major top-down mechanism is direct instruction by a teacher. Instruction is often used to impart concepts that have "technical" as opposed to folk definitions (Glass and Holyoak 1975). For example, our everyday concept of "mammal" is likely to center on typical furry four-legged animals. The technical biological definition, which involves such properties as bearing live young and warm-bloodedness, is likely to be a product of formal instruction. The two concepts may coexist, so that we know that a whale is technically a mammal despite its evident atypicality. We will discuss learning by instruction in chapters 7 and 9.

The account of category induction provided so far might suggest that the induction of category distributions proceeds in a steady progression from a more or less random initial set of rules to a set that veridically matches the observed distribution of instances over property values. On the contrary, it is natural within our framework to suppose that the initial set of rules will not be generated in any random fashion but rather will be guided by inferential rules embodying prior theories about the nature of the category to be learned (compare Murphy and Medin 1985). This is a manifestation of the concept of "preparedness" for conditioning, discussed in chapter 5. Whether induction is speeded up or retarded will depend on the validity of the relevant prior theories held by the cognitive system.

Distortions Caused by Misleading Theories
The earliest and still the most systematic and elegant work on the topic of theory-driven induction is by Loren and Jean Chapman (1967, 1969; Chapman 1967). These investigators were clinical psy-

chologists puzzled by the failure of their fellow clinicians to heed the literature showing that so-called projective tests, such as the Rorschach ink-blot test and the Draw-a-Person test, have little validity. That is, "signs" seen or drawn by clients only rarely have much predictability for symptoms or other client characteristics. Such valid associations as do exist, moreover, tend not to have "face validity"; that is, the associations seem implausible in terms of one's prior theories. For example, though many clinicians were wont to report that their male homosexual clients tended to see male and female genitals in Rorschach ink blots, as well as human figures ambiguous as to sex, men dressed in women's clothing, and so on, none of these presumed associations is supported by the empirical research. On the other hand, some associations do exist between homosexuality and certain test signs. For example, homosexuals tend to report seeing monsters on one card and a figure that is part animal and part human on another card.

The Chapmans (1969) polled several dozen practicing clinicians who indicated that they had analyzed the Rorschach protocols of a number of homosexual men, asking them to report which Rorschach signs were most commonly associated with a homosexual orientation. The five most commonly listed signs were all sexual-content signs having substantial face validity but no empirical validity. Only two of the clinicians reported one of the empirically valid signs. The Chapmans next asked a large number of lay subjects to rate the tendency of homosexuality to "call to mind" each of the valid and invalid signs. The tendency of homosexuality to call to mind each of the invalid but plausible signs was "moderately strong", while its tendency to evoke the two valid but implausible signs was "very slight".

In the next phase of the research, lay subjects were exposed to a set of purported clinical data. The materials were a series of Rorschach cards allegedly responded to by homosexual clients or by clients with other characteristics, such as depression. The client characteristics were listed on one part of each card, and the client's alleged response to the card on another part. The latter were either the valid homosexual signs, the invalid (but face-valid) sexual-content signs, or neutral signs such as geographic or food signs. The series was constructed so that there was no relationship whatever between the symptoms and the response categories presented. The naive observers were given one minute to examine each of thirty cards that were presented. After that, the subjects were asked to indicate which responses had been more characteristic of the homosexual clients.

The naive lay subjects reported seeing the same pattern of correlations that the clinicians had reported in summarizing their experiences with actual clients. That is, invalid signs were reported to have been very common for the homosexual clients, while neither the valid signs nor the neutral signs were reported to have been associated with homosexuality. The Chapmans concluded that their subjects' reports of association (as well as those of the clinicians) had been produced almost entirely by the similarity between homosexuality and the particular verbal responses.

In our terms, the synchronic associative rules linking homosexuality with sexual signs are extremely influential in determining perception of an association. The data available both to practicing clinicians and to subjects must compete with strong default assumptions about what goes with what in the world. This would not be a serious problem if people's covariation-detection capacities were limitlessly precise, but they are not. The slippage introduced by imperfect abilities allows for substantial intrusion from other internal cognitive sources.

Just how massive this intrusion can be was shown by a variation of the Chapmans' basic design. They manipulated the degree of covariation between valid signs and the homosexuality characteristic, while holding constant the degree of covariation between symptoms and both the invalid and the neutral signs. In all conditions, all symptoms were associated 50 percent of the time with each of several invalid and neutral signs. In one condition, homosexuality was also associated 50 percent of the time with the valid signs. For the other conditions, homosexuality was associated with one of the two valid signs 67 percent, 83 percent, or 100 percent of the time. The results showed that the naive observers, like the clinicians, failed to recognize the presence of true covariation. Of course, nothing in the subjects' prior experience would tend to lend any support to the notion of an association between such a characteristic as homosexuality and the tendency to see monsters or figures that are ambiguously human versus animal. Indeed, from our perspective it is hard to imagine how two such features could ever become candidates for association in a rule under anything approximating the noisy data conditions of everyday life or clinical practice. In order for such a connection to become a candidate rule, the covarying properties would need to be linked by some overarching causal theory or strong semantic association.

It is important to note that it was not literally impossible for subjects to respond to actual data configurations within the Chapmans' experimental paradigm. They found that if all of the invalid signs were deleted from the series, then subjects could be at least somewhat sensitive to the true covariation of the valid signs with homosexuality.

For example, when the misleading invalid signs were deleted, more subjects reported that the valid signs were associated with homosexuality when the covariation held 83 percent of the time than when it held 50 percent of the time. Furthermore, in a study (1967) using Draw-a-Person instead of Rorschach materials, they found that when they built in massive *negative* covariations between symptoms and illusory covariates, the reported covariation, though still perceived as positive, was at least reduced in magnitude.

What the Chapmans' work shows is that even under data-presentation circumstances where the "noise level" is probably below that normally experienced in everyday life, the covariation that is perceived can be more nearly a function of the prior rules relating the properties than of the actual statistical association present in the data. These are very dramatic errors. But they would seem to be the other side of the induction coin for systems that do not bother to examine every possible association. Peirce's statistician from space would see no associations that weren't there. On the other hand, the alien would never get around to detecting very many of the associations that are most important for survival. It is only those types of covariation consistent with prior rules that are likely to emerge as candidates for examination in the light of the data. What the Chapmans' work most clearly shows is that people sometimes have flawed procedures for checking the presence of covariation, accepting a hypothesis as sustained if there are positive instances and paying too little attention to the disconfirming nature of negative instances. What the work does *not* show is any inherent flaw in people's tendency to be guided by prior expectations about what kind of associations are likely to exist in the world. Covariation detection, and hence categorization, are heavily dependent on the initial mental model constructed on the basis of prior knowledge.

In general, the effect of prior beliefs will be most pronounced when covariation detection is difficult owing to the various factors discussed in the previous chapter, such as lack of clarity and of temporal contiguity between examples. Differences in learning conditions likely underlie the distinctive connotations of the terms "prototype" and "stereotype". Whereas prototypes connote relatively veridical representations of typical category instances, social stereotypes connote error and bias.

These differences in what is learned can be readily understood when we consider differences involving the circumstances of acquisition (Holyoak and Gordon 1984). In studies of perceptual category learning, subjects typically view several examples of the category, presented for a reasonable duration under clear exposure conditions. The distinguishing properties of the category are concrete, and they are available simultaneously. That is, all of the visible properties of a bird, for instance, are present at the same time, so that their associations to one another may be learned simultaneously. When, as is often the case, different examples of a perceptual category can be examined at the same time, or at least in close succession, there may be particularly rapid learning of the category and its subcategories. Most people, for example, experience something close to a revelation when attending their first well-designed wine tasting.

Social categories are often acquired under conditions strikingly different from those characterizing the learning of perceptual categories. First, many stereotypes are not induced from observations of instances at all, but rather are learned by instruction (or hearsay). Even if instances are observed, the occasions for induction may be widely separated in time. Furthermore, inferences about behavioral dispositions form the core of many social categories. To be accurate, such inferences require many observations. But in fact they often are made on the basis of few, intermittent, and unrepresentative observations. In general, then, it will be much more difficult to induce accurate diachronic rules describing people's dispositions than to induce synchronic rules relating clear, temporally and spatially contiguous perceptual properties. Since most social categories are defined largely in terms of difficult-to-detect diachronic rules, they will be more error prone than perceptual categories. Stereotypes will be preserved when dubious prior beliefs override limited observations. It is this, rather than any putatively greater error variance for social events, that governs our relative ignorance about the social world.

On the other hand, as we will demonstrate in the next chapter, there is plenty of error in people's conceptions of the physical world as well. Some of the errors people make in their understanding of physical events are of the same type and stem from the same sources as their errors about social events.

Biases Introduced by Expectations about Distributions

The influence of prior expectations on induction is not limited to semantically meaningful categories that are highly familiar, as in the case of those investigated by the Chapmans. There is evidence that category induction is also guided by much more abstract expectations regarding the form of the distribution of examples. Fried and Holyoak (1984) have proposed that people may expect instances of categories to form unimodal and approximately symmetric distributions over continuous properties, such as size. Accordingly, a few initial observations might be used to estimate the modal property values associated with a category and to form some rough notion of the expected range. An initial set of rules with property values as conditions could then be established, with the initial strengths of the rules declining monotonically as a function of the distance between the specified property value and the hypothesized mode.

Such a theory-driven procedure for initiating the set of rules for predicting category membership would be far better than random if the category distribution in fact had the anticipated form. The cost, of course, is that learning would be greatly impaired if the distribution was actually very different. For example, suppose the instances in a category actually formed a bimodal distribution (for example, either brightly colored or achromatic, but seldom moderately colored). If the initial set of rules were formed on the basis of an expectation of a central mode, the learner's early classification decisions would be not simply random but actually opposite to veridical. The learner would at first be most confident that moderately colored instances belonged to the category, when in fact such instances would be the least probable members.

This prediction was tested by Flannagan, Fried, and Holyoak (1986). In one experiment Flannagan and colleagues showed subjects what they called "Blockist paintings", which were computer-generated patterns of rectangles varying along just three dimensions—height of an outside frame, width of an upper horizontal rectangle, and height of a lower vertical rectangle. For some subjects these dimensions were distributed approximately normally across category instances, forming a unimodal symmetric distribution; for others the dimensions were distributed in an opposite, bimodal "U" fashion.

The ability of subjects to learn the actual distribution of the dimensions was massively dependent on distribution type. Subjects readily learned to classify a pattern as belonging to a particular category (that is, as a painting by "Vango" versus some other of the "Blockists") if its dimensions were distributed normally. The probability of assigning such patterns to a given category was greatest near the dimension's actual center and fell off in proportions dictated by the shape of the normal curve. In contrast, subjects given instances generated by U-shaped distributions of dimensions were much less successful in tracking the actual frequencies of the dimension values in their assignments to categories. Indeed, after 20 trials these subjects made their classifications as if they believed the dimension distributions were actually unimodal. Even after 150 trials subjects failed to distribute their responses in the same fashion as the actual dimension distributions. Instead their classifications were distributed in an essentially flat fashion across the dimensions. After observing 600 exemplars, however, subjects had successfully overcome their apparent assumption of unimodality and veridically favored instances with extreme dimension values as likely category members.

This experiment, and other evidence reported by Flannagan and colleagues, indicates that people have a heavy bias in favor of assuming that the dimensions of perceptual categories are distributed unimodally. People are almost surely well served by this bias, since most perceptual categories probably in fact form unimodal distributions. In chapter 8 we will present evidence that similar principles are involved in people's induction of distributions of social phenomena.

6.2.4 Comparison with Alternative Accounts of Categorization

Since a great deal of theoretical work in psychology has been directed toward developing schemes for representing category distributions, it may be useful to briefly compare our approach with other accounts. (For a thorough review of alternative classes of theories, see Smith and Medin 1981.) Recent accounts of categorization can be divided into three classes. *Parametric* models attempt to summarize the information in the training instances in terms of a relatively small number of statistical parameters. The earliest such accounts were prototype models assuming that categories were represented by the arithmetic average of the property values associated with their instances (Posner and Keele 1968; Reed 1972). More recently, Fried and Holyoak (1984) proposed that variances (a statistical parameter representing dispersion) are also explicitly learned. *Feature-frequency* models assume that learners accumulate counts of the frequencies with which various property values or combinations of property values are associated with each of the alternative categories (Hayes-Roth and Hayes-Roth 1977; Neumann 1977; Reitman and Bower 1973). *Instance* accounts assume that learners simply encode representations of instances of alternative categories; the learner classifies a novel instance by retrieving stored instances, comparing them to the novel input, and assigning the latter to the category associated with the instances most similar to it (Medin and Schaffer 1978).

Our proposal, with rules referring to property values, and strengths that reflect the probability of the specified category given the property values in the condition of each rule, is in the feature-frequency tradition, although it shares some assumptions of parametric accounts and instance accounts. Purely parametric accounts have had difficulty accounting for people's sensitivity to relational information, such as correlated properties (see section 6.2.2), as well as their ability to learn (albeit with some difficulty) categories with unusual distributional forms. Instance theories have difficulty accounting for evidence showing that the presentation of instances with common property values in temporally contiguous clusters facilitates induction (Elio and Anderson 1981). Contiguity of similar instances would be expected to foster the formation of more general rules (by the intersection of conditions); yet if only instance-level information is used in categorization, it is unclear why presentation order should be important. Instance models also have difficulty explaining why classification decisions can be systematically nonveridical, as observed in the early stages of exposure to bimodal distributions (Flannagan, Fried, and Holyoak 1986). In our view, instance storage may nonetheless play an auxiliary role in induction by enabling stored declarative representations of instances to be retrieved later and used to generate rules. Such a process might resemble the simple type of analogy use described in chapter 3.

The greatest difficulty for feature-frequency accounts is to constrain the potentially enormous number of property value combinations about which frequency information might be accumulated. For example, the account proposed by Hayes-Roth and Hayes-Roth (1977) assumed that the power set of feature combinations (that is, the set of all subsets) is tabulated. Our proposal, through restrictions on the conditions for rule generation and through mechanisms for strength revision, suggests how constraints can be imposed. For example, rules with conjunctive conditions will tend to be formed when simpler rules fail to accurately predict category membership; erroneous and redundant rules will be weeded out by prediction-based strength revision of the sort described in the model of conditioning presented in the previous chapter. Our model is in some ways similar to the rule-based model of Anderson, Kline, and Beasley (1979). It differs from their account in several important respects, however, including the introduction of support summation, inhibitory rules, and inferential rules for forming initial assumptions about properties in accord with prior expectations about the form of the distribution to be learned. Our account, by incorporating constraints that reduce the computational burden to a level that seems feasible, renders a feature-frequency approach more plausible than it would otherwise be. Distributional properties of categories are represented implicitly by clusters of rules, and stored instances play an auxiliary role in categorization by means of an analogy mechanism.

6.3 Learning Complex Synchronic Associations

In experiments such as those performed by Flannagan, Fried, and Holyoak (1985), subjects were able to learn the distribution of category properties by observing objects that they understood to be instances of categories. But people sometimes learn about the structures of complex categories from observations of instances even when they are not told that the items form a category (Reber and Allen 1978; Reber, Kassin, Lewis, and Cantor 1980). Our framework accommodates such learning by assuming that people generate rules linking properties observed to co-occur in the instances ("If $P_1 = V_a$, then $P_2 = V_b$"; for example, "If size is small, then color is dark"). When subsequently asked to determine whether novel instances belong to the same category, those instances that trigger firing of the induced property-to-property rules will tend to be accepted.

6.3.1 Prediction-Based Internal Feedback

The above case, in which a single category is learned by observation of instances, provides a simple illustration of the way in which rule-generated internal feedback can provide information to guide induction. Similar sorts of internal feedback can be used to perform more complex inductive tasks in the absence of overt feedback. For example, people sometimes can learn to discriminate instances of two complex categories after seeing unlabeled instances of each category randomly intermixed (Evans 1967). Fried and Holyoak (1984) demonstrated that people often can induce category distributions in the complete absence of external feedback regarding their success or failure in making classifications. In some of the learning conditions subjects saw randomly ordered mixtures of instances drawn from two categories and were never told the category membership of any individual instance. Nonetheless, later transfer performance revealed that these subjects, like others who had been given feedback during learning, had acquired representations of the central tendencies and variability of the categories.

In fact, category learning can take place with even less external guidance than was provided in the above experiments, in which subjects were told at least that there were two categories to be learned. In a further experiment Fried and Holyoak found that subjects were able to learn categories without feedback even when they did not know the number of categories to be learned or (yet more remarkably) when they did not even know there were categories to be learned at all. In the latter condition subjects were simply told to watch the patterns carefully, and only afterward were informed that they had seen instances of two categories and would now have to categorize further novel examples.

This type of learning clearly depends on people's ability to make use of some form of internal feedback. Let us examine in more detail how such feedback might be generated and used.

6.3.2 Learning Clustered Regularities

Because we maintain that categories are represented by clusters of rules organized into q-morphisms, our framework suggests that an inductive system should be particularly adapted to find *groups* of regularities. Once one regularity has been identified, we would expect that the formation of related regularities will be facilitated, since the components of the already formed rule will provide promising candidates for the formation of related rules.

This capacity is important for inductive systems, since it is rare that a property relevant to our goals is encountered in pristine isolation. Instead we are confronted with a torrent of information hiding a few associated regularities in a plethora of irrelevancies. Billman (1983) has highlighted three characteristics that attend learning problems of this prevalent kind: (1) the features and cues far exceed the system's ability to attend to them; (2) external feedback about the specific relevance of features and cues is minimal; (3) cues are generally only partially valid, and regularities are marred by exceptions. Although Billman concentrated on language acquisition, her characterization encompasses an important and pervasive class of induction problems of which language is only one example. It might be claimed, in fact, that most of the central problems in induction satisfy Billman's description. We should note, however, that the characterization in general holds much more for synchronic category learning than for diachronic rule learning. "Bird" is a much more complex kind of entity, representing far more relationships among features, than is the event sequence *tone → shock*.

How can a system take advantage of clustered regularities to deal with the types of complexity characteristic of category learning? Billman has proposed a learning mechanism that facilitates the acquisition of rules based on interrelated properties. We will first describe her proposal and the evidence in favor of it, and then suggest how the proposal can be interpreted within our framework.

Billman proposed that in a complex learning environment of the sort described above, in which not all properties of inputs can be encoded, learners will use what they are finding to be predictive to guide subsequent encoding. The learner, faced with the need to selectively encode only a subset of the properties of the environment, tends to encode those that are already involved in useful regularities. Billman called this *focused sampling*, since the learner's sample of possible observations of the environment will be biased through focusing on those properties already proved useful.

The focused-sampling hypothesis makes an important prediction regarding the acquisition of groups of interrelated rules. Suppose the environment is such that when property 1 has value a ($P_1 = V_a$), then property 2 has value b. This regularity can be described by the following rule:

Rule 1: If $(P_1 = V_a)$, then $(P_2 = V_b)$.

Suppose we now compare two conditions, one in which the above regularity is the only one that involves properties 1 and 2, and another in which these properties are involved in additional regularities involving property 3, such as those expressed by the following rules:

Rule 2: If $(P_1 = V_a)$, then $(P_3 = V_c)$.

Rule 3: If $(P_2 = V_b)$, then $(P_3 = V_c)$.

The focused-sampling hypothesis predicts that rule 1 will be learned more readily in the latter condition, in which it forms part of a group of regularities, than when it is an isolated regularity. In the grouped condition it is possible that rules 2 and/or 3 (or their converses) will be formed and strengthened because of their successful predictions. If the probability of using properties to form new rules increases when they are already participating in other successful rules, such focused sampling will increase the probability of forming and testing rule 1 in the grouped condition relative to the condition in which it is an isolated regularity.

Billman tested the above prediction of the focused-sampling hypothesis in experiments involving induction of syntactic categories in an artificial language. As Billman emphasized, syntax acquisition is a task that fully meets her description of complex inductive tasks. A child learning language must acquire synchronic rules representing the hierarchical structure of word classes (as, proper noun, noun, noun phrase) and diachronic rules representing grammatical sequences (to generate a noun phrase, one can generate a determiner followed by an adjective followed by a noun). Adults typically provide the child with sample utterances that occasionally contain errors, and they do not clearly inform the child as to which utterances are grammatical. The sheer complexity of language, coupled with the paucity of external guidance provided to the learner, has motivated heavily nativist accounts of the acquisition of syntax. In contrast, Billman's approach and that of a few others (Anderson 1983; Maratsos and Chalkley 1980) has been to investigate mechanisms for exploiting partial regularities in the data provided to the learner.

Billman tested the prediction about ease of learning grouped regularities in a series of experiments in which subjects attempted to learn an artificial language, "Neptunese". Subjects were not given any instruction in the language, which had properties quite unlike those of English. Rather, they were simply told to learn Neptunese by watching "spaceship maneuvers" displayed on a computer-controlled video monitor. The animated display was accompanied by a four-word "sentence" describing the depicted event (a spaceship of a particular shape striking another, for instance, while a third remained passively positioned nearby; see figure 6.3).

Billman constructed several versions of the artificial language, which differed in the degree of grouping of certain properties. The regularities of interest involved the organization of nouns into three classes, roughly analogous to a noun declension in a natural language. The system was based on three properties: (1) the shape of objects referred to by nouns, (2) the vowel in the noun's stem, and (3) the vowel in its ending. In the clustered condition all three of these properties were mutually predictive; for instance, a particular type of shape, such as elongated "spaceships", would be associated with a particular stem vowel in the corresponding noun. Subjects in three isolated conditions were exposed to alternative variants of the language in which just one of the three possible regularities was present.

After the learning session, subjects in all conditions received a battery of tests to diagnose whether or not they had learned particular aspects of the language. It would not have been sufficient simply to have subjects judge whether sentence-picture pairs were correct, since of course there would be more possible cues in the clustered condition than in the isolated conditions: in the former case the detection of a violation of any one of the three regularities would be sufficient to reveal an error. To provide an appropriate test, Billman presented her subjects with displays in which parts were omitted so that only one regularity was available. For example, the picture might be omitted so that the property of object shape was not provided and only the relationship between the stem and ending vowels could be assessed. Billman found that subjects were significantly better able to learn the individual regularities related to noun categories if they formed part of a cluster. This result was obtained both when each relationship

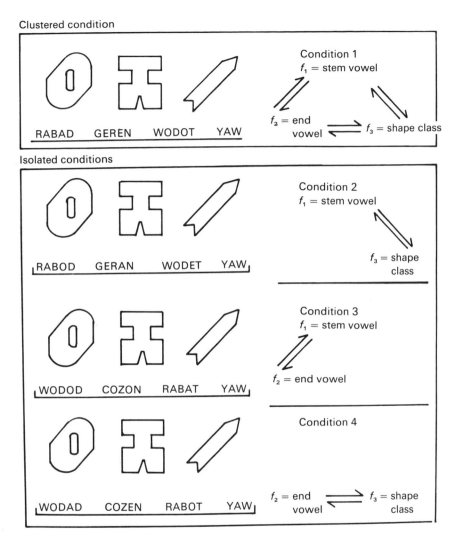

Figure 6.3

Examples of stimuli used in the clustered and isolated conditions. From Billman (1983).

between two properties was entirely regular and when exceptions were introduced. Thus, multiple, interrelated associations are learned more readily than single associations, both when the associations are deterministic and invariant and when they are merely probabilistic.

The superior learning of a rule that formed part of a cluster is particularly noteworthy because there were of course more rules to be learned in the clustered condition. Consequently, one might have supposed that any particular rule would receive less attention than if it were the only regularity. Billman's results, in contrast, clearly support the assumption that human mechanisms for induction are designed to facilitate the acquisition of such interrelated groups. It can be easier to learn many things at once than to learn a single isolated regularity.

Let us examine more closely how Billman's results fit within our framework. In general, our emphasis on the clustering of rules in categories and the coupling of rules in sequences leads us to expect that grouping of rules will be important. Billman's focused-sampling account has learners focusing attention on properties that are proving predictive, and we have described several mechanisms that will have this result. In our framework, predictive properties are those in the conditions of strong rules. Once a system has succeeded in encoding an important property in a rule and enhancing its strength through successful prediction, that property will be much more easily available for subsequent rule formation. One successful episode of encoding and rule generation will facilitate subsequent rule generation using the diagnostic property. Both classifier systems and PI have the desirable property of using components of existing strong rules for the generation of new rules. In classifier systems the genetic operators favor strong rules, employing their substrings in the creation of new rules. In PI, concepts that are used in strong rules are more likely to play a role in subsequent rule generation, since triggering conditions take into account their enhanced degree of activation. Hence we should expect focused sampling to result from the use of elements found to be predictively useful in the past as building blocks for new rules. Once one rule has been formed, related rules will be easier to form because much of the encoding work has already been done.

We will have more to say about the induction of categories, particularly in the context of analogical problem solving and theory construction, in chapters 10 and 11. In the next chapter we will describe the relationship between default hierarchies and covariation detection in the complex, naturalistic contexts of the physical and social world.

7

Modeling the Physical and Social Worlds

We have made the case that the rat's understanding of the limited world inside a shock box is well captured by our framework: rules, organized in a default hierarchy, compete with one another for the right to represent the situation and to predict its successor situations; winning rules that generate accurate predictions are more likely to be favored for representing subsequent situations. We have argued, further, that rule clusters that are habitually activated together become associated in categories. The rule clusters comprising categories serve to represent variability in the objects they describe by the strength with which they indicate that an object will have a given property. Variability is also represented by differences in the dominant level of the default hierarchy. Objects that seem prototypical of a super-ordinate category will be dealt with at that high level. Objects that seem less prototypical will be dealt with at some lower level of the hierarchy.

In this chapter we will argue that the same machinery of rule competition and default hierarchies can be seen at work in many aspects of people's understanding of the physical and social worlds. Specifically, we will maintain the following:

1) People model the physical and social worlds using empirical rules organized into default hierarchies.

2) People have a preference for using rules at the lowest, most specific hierarchical level; they customarily use rules at higher, more general levels only when no more specific rule provides an answer at a satisfactory level of confidence.

3) The rules that people use to model the physical world and those that they use to model the social world can be shown to be erroneous in many important respects. This is due in part to limitations on the encoding mechanisms that people use for understanding the world—

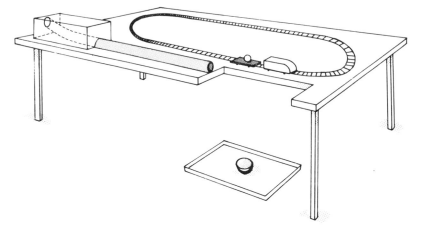

Figure 7.1
Device for examining intuitive beliefs about motion. From Kaiser, Proffitt, and McCloskey (1986).

limitations that are primarily perceptual in the case of the physical world and primarily conceptual in the case of the social world. In addition, fundamentally inadequate default hierarchies may be preserved in the face of apparently disconfirmatory evidence by the persistent generation of exception rules.

4) Education should not be thought of as replacing the rules that people use for understanding the world but rather as introducing new rules that enter into competition with the old ones. People reliably distort the new rules in the direction of the old ones, or ignore them altogether except in the highly specific domains in which they were taught.

7.1 Modeling the Physical World

7.1.1 Default Hierarchies of Intuitive Physical Rules
Imagine the physical setup shown in figure 7.1 (from an experiment by Kaiser, Proffitt, and McCloskey 1986). At the left end of a table a ball is released into a tube. The ball falls out of the tube at the notch in the table. Where does it land? Or, the model engine starts moving at the left end of the table and a lever pushes a ball off the side of the flat car just at the notch in the table. Where does the ball land? Preschool children think that in both cases the ball will fall straight down. When asked to place the cup where they think the ball will land, children place it directly under the left end of the notch on the table. College

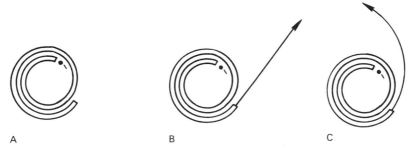

Figure 7.2
Device for examining intuitive beliefs about the persistence of curved motion. From Kaiser, McCloskey, and Proffitt (1986).

students almost universally recognize that the ball will continue its forward motion when released from the tube. Thirty-five percent of college students, however, believe that the ball will fall straight down when released from the train. Moreover, *most* college students believe that if they were to walk along carrying a ball and then drop it, the ball would land directly under the point in the air where it was released (McCloskey 1983).

Now imagine that a ball is injected with some force into the tube in figure 7.2 at the point indicated by the arrow in A. What trajectory will it follow on exit, that indicated in B or that indicated in C? If your answer is the straight trajectory in B, you voted with a bare majority of college students studied by Kaiser, McCloskey, and Proffitt (1986). Fully 40 percent of their subjects preferred the curved trajectory in C—as did the great majority of elementary-school children studied.

What accounts for subjects' errors in these problems? What accounts for the correct answers made by some subjects, especially the older ones? Research over the past decade on "intuitive physics", conducted by McCloskey, Siegler, and Kaiser, among others, has yielded some very interesting generalizations.

First, it seems clear that the intuitive physics even of adults is not Newtonian at base. It is better characterized as Aristotelian, or perhaps as medieval. The central concept of intuitive physics is that of *impetus*. Intuitive physics holds that when an object is set in motion, for example by someone's pushing it or throwing it, an impetus is imparted to it that serves to keep it moving for some time after it was in contact with the mover. The impetus dissipates steadily, however, and the object correspondingly slows to a stop. As one college student put it in justifying his preference for the curved motion in figure 7.2, "The momentum from the curve of the tube gives the ball the arc. The force that the ball picks up from the tube eventually dissipates and it will follow a normal straight line" (Kaiser, McCloskey, and Proffitt 1986). This reasoning accords with the best scientific thought of the fourteenth century: "A mover in moving a body impresses on it a certain impetus, a certain power capable of moving this body in the direction in which the mover set it going, whether upwards, downwards, sideways or in a circle.... It is by this impetus that the stone is moved after the thrower ceases to move it" (Buridan, cited in Kaiser, McCloskey, and Proffitt 1986).

This erroneous physical theory is not prewired, nor does it simply develop automatically in infancy. Rather, it is a laborious accomplishment of the older child, who must *learn* to make the error of predicting a curvilinear trajectory from a curved tube. Preschool children predominantly believe that the ball will take a straight path when released from the tube, perhaps because this is the simplest answer or perhaps because they are reporting accurately from memories of similar events. Third- and fourth-grade children overwhelmingly prefer the curved trajectory. These children have begun to generalize from their experience in the physical world and have abstracted certain principles, including a principle of the *path persistence* of motion, which leads them to expect that objects will continue the path (and the manner of motion) that they have been following unless interrupted in it. This is of course a useful general principle as far as it goes, but it is overgeneralized by children of this age. And some adults never subsequently circumscribe the generalization sufficiently.

Such rule-produced errors, resulting in curvilinear developmental trends, are well known in the field of language development. For example, Brown (1973) has reported that a few months after children begin to use the regular past tense form in English, namely *-ed*, they begin to make errors on irregular past tense forms that they previously used correctly—they begin to say "goed" and "breaked" where previously they said "went" and "broke".

Thus the older child has a well-developed hierarchy of rules that can be invoked if the problem does not produce a simple match to some other problem. These rules are often effective, but their overly general nature means that they sometimes will be erroneously applied. It is important to note that the general rules enter into competition with more specific rules, and at least in familiar domains for which specific rules of high strength exist, the specific rules often will be preferred. For example, older subjects will not make the error of assuming that water will come out of the end of the tube with a curvilinear trajectory, even when they do assume that a ball or a stream of sand will do so (Kaiser, Jonides, and Alexander 1986). This is because most people have direct experience with water coming out of a garden hose and thus have a specific rule for that specific event. They therefore need not resort to overly general rules about impetus.

7.1.2 The Origins of Erroneous Beliefs about the Physical World

Certain basic rules of intuitive physics have been distinguished by Champagne, Klopfer, and Anderson (1980, p. 1077): (1) a force, when applied to an object, will produce motion; (2) under the influence of a constant force, objects move with constant velocity; (3) the magnitude of the velocity is proportional to the magnitude of the force, and hence any acceleration is due to increasing forces; (4) in the absence of forces, objects are either at rest or, if they are moving (because they stored up momentum while previous forces were acting), they are slowing down (and consuming their stored momentum). Why do such incorrect rules about the nature of the physical world arise? Clearly nature does not punish their holders severely. Partly this is because impetus theory as a set of propositions is a better q-morphism for the world we live in than for the idealized world Galileo and Newton had in mind. Objects that operate under constant conditions of friction do indeed often behave as if they possessed an impetus subject to gradual diminishment. On the other hand, it should be clear that the rules of intuitive physics do not necessarily provide a perfect q-morphism of the everyday physical world. There are many anecdotes attesting the treachery of intuitive physical rules. One of our favorites concerns World War I bombardiers dropping hand-held bombs (McCloskey and Kaiser 1984). The pre-Newtonians among them, needless to say, habitually overshot their targets.

Another important reason that errors arise and fail to be corrected lies in the *encoding capacities* of human observers. The human visual apparatus is just not very good at recognizing acceleration, the physical concept that lies at the heart of Newtonian physics. In contrast, people are quite good at gauging velocity, which plays the central role in intuitive physics.

It is of course possible to push the question back and ask why the human sensory apparatus is so poor at judging acceleration. We might speculate that acceleration is simply not that important to recognize. It is far more important to realize that a sabertoothed tiger is running toward one with a particular velocity than to recognize that it is accelerating or decelerating. To be sure, subsequent judgments about *relative* velocity—one's own versus the tiger's—are important, but acceleration per se is much less so.

Indeed, there is evidence that it is precisely people's attention to relative motion rather than to absolute motion that is responsible for many of their failures when dealing with physical events. People seem to believe that a ball dropped by a moving person falls straight down because in the past when they have observed such events they have been attentive to the motion of the object *relative* to the motion of the person who drops it (McCloskey 1983). And of course the relative motion of the object is in fact straight down. Thus the rules that people learn are dependent upon their encoding capacities—and incapacities.

Encoding can be influenced not merely by perceptual capacities but by attentional factors as well. Siegler (1983a) found that five-year-old children were generally not good at balance-beam problems that eight-year-olds usually could solve. The younger children understood that the weight on each side of the fulcrum was important, but they seemed to have no rule about the distance of the weight from the fulcrum. Siegler found that even those eight-year-old children who did not have a distance rule could induce it fairly quickly if given feedback about the accuracy of their guesses about the movement of the balance beam under various weight and distance conditions. Five-year-olds, however, tended not to learn from such feedback. Siegler reasoned that that was because they were for the most part not even paying attention to the distance factor and thus could not be expected to encode it in such a way that it could become the basis for a rule.

To test his theory, Siegler gave both five-year-olds and eight-year-olds practice in attending to the distance of weights from the fulcrum. The children were simply required to count the weights on each side of the fulcrum and to count the number of pegs away from the center that each weight was. Three days later they were given the same feedback that had improved the performance of previously untrained eight-year-olds but not the performance of previously untrained five-year-olds. Now the trained five-year-olds learned—and almost as well as the trained eight-year-olds. Thus the study indicates that most of the older children were initially attending to the distance dimension and hence either had formed a rule incorporating it or were quite ready to do so under the proper feedback conditions. The younger children were not even attending to the factor; hence it could not be encoded and could not become a candidate for rule status.

Encoding deficiencies can contribute to the maintenance of a sub-optimal rule system in several related ways. First, if a property of the input is not encoded at all, as in the case of distance for untrained five-year-olds, that property will simply not be available for formation of a rule. Second, if a property is encoded with little accuracy, as in the case of the acceleration of moving objects, feedback that would disconfirm erroneous rules will not be available. Finally, if an erroneous general rule is clearly violated only in a small number of specific domains, as in the case of the rule of path persistence for motion, then domain-specific exception rules may allow the erroneous rule to be maintained as a default. The exception rules will effectively protect the erroneous rule from the consequences of its predictive failures.

7.2 Modeling the Social World

The notion of a default hierarchy of rules seems especially well suited to an understanding of people's construal of the social world. In our view, one's understanding of a social situation or of another person is best regarded as a q-morphism, with predictions about the situation or person being made at the lowest level in the hierarchy for which one has adequate experience to allow confidence. For example, imagine three-year-old Jennifer at a wedding for the first time. The "dress-up" clothes and the novel location (church, hall, or garden), together with the air of specialness, will convey to her that distinctive manners are probably appropriate. The distinctive-manners default is to exhibit quiet but attentive behavior. (At least it seems to be for other people's children!) The child is therefore likely to err in the direction of overly staid conduct. Subsequent events will teach the child, however, that the specialness of a wedding does not dictate as much sobriety as docs the specialness of otherwise similar occasions. The second time around she is likely to be less tentative and more ebullient.

One's understanding of another person can similarly be regarded as a q-morphism. For any person whom we know, some predictions can be generated by virtue of knowing the person's past behavior in the same situation or a similar one. The accuracy of such predictions will depend largely on the accuracy of people's perceptions of covariations among social behaviors. Let us examine the evidence regarding the determinants of covariation detection in the social world.

7.2.1 Detection of Covariations in the Social World

The clear implication of the analysis of covariation detection presented in chapter 5 is that, for events in the noisy world of social happenings, preparedness to perceive certain associations should be the major determinant of perceived covariation *except* where events are clear enough not to impose a severe burden on coding capacity. Under the latter circumstances we might expect substantial accuracy about covariation.

In order to test this proposition, Kunda and Nisbett (1986) examined subjects' perceptions of the covariation between two sorts of events that differ substantially in codability. One type of event was social behavior such as friendliness and honesty. Such events are manifestly difficult to code reliably, both for laypeople and for social scientists. Even the question of the appropriate *unit* to code is problematic. Should friendliness be measured in smiles per minute, "good vibrations" per encounter, or what? Given that one has the appropriate unit to code, there still remains a serious problem of clarity of the code to be applied. Was John being friendly to you just now, or was he being ingratiating, or was he simply responding in kind to your pleasant overtures? Is telling on a schoolmate an act of honesty or of dishonesty?

Events such as these contrast with events for which society has managed to find clear units and codes. This second category includes athletic contests and academic performance. Many events of interest at a basketball game can be readily unitized and coded—for example, baskets per game, baskets per minute or per contact with the ball, number of free throws, percent of free throws made. The same is true for performance on spelling or arithmetic tests. This is not to say that *someone*—for instance, a referee or an English teacher—may not be confronted with coding problems; just that, once coded, the events are far clearer than others in the social domain. Thus it should be substantially easier for people to be accurate about the degree of covariation that exists for athletic and academic events than for other kinds of social events.

Kunda and Nisbett tested these possibilities by asking people to indicate the probability that a person observed on one occasion to be higher on some social dimension than another person (for example, to be more friendly or to score more basketball points) would also be observed to be higher on another occasion. This simple estimate of contingent probability can be converted by a simple formula into an estimate of Spearman's r and compared to objective indicators of the relevant correlations. The investigators also asked their subjects to indicate the probability that a person observed on 20 occasions to be higher on average on some social dimension than another person would also be observed on the next 20 occasions to be higher on average. Because of the "aggregation principle" in statistics, a version

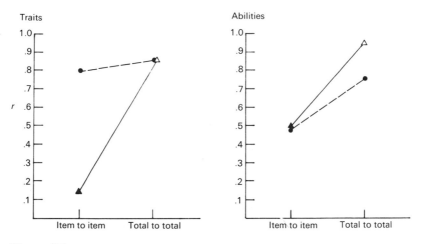

Figure 7.3
Estimates of correlation (dashed lines) and actual correlations (solid lines) at two
levels of aggregation for traits and for abilities. From Kunda and Nisbett (1986).

of the law of large numbers that holds that highly reliable observations are more likely to be repeated than less reliable ones, the latter
correlations should be higher than the comparable correlations based
on one observation.

As the data in figure 7.3 indicate, subjects were indeed substantially
less accurate in their perception of the correlation between social trait-
related behaviors such as friendliness and honesty than in their perception of the correlation between ability-related behaviors such as
sports and academic accomplishments. Actual correlations for single
observations of social behaviors as coded by social scientists run in the
vicinity of .10–.20. Yet subjects guessed contingent probabilities for
these events that correspond to correlations of nearly .80! The actual
correlations between aggregates of such events are far higher, but
subjects had no recognition of this fact. They believed there is little
difference between the correlation for single events and the correlation for aggregates of 20 events.

The picture is quite different for estimates of correlations between
ability-related events. Subjects were quite accurate in their judgment
that the averages of any two single events are correlated about .50.
Similarly, they were able to detect the fact that the correlation between aggregates of 20 such events is substantially higher than between single events.

The fact that people overestimate the stability of social behavior has
long been known to social psychologists (see, for example, Heider

1958; Jones and Davis 1965; Jones and Nisbett 1972; Nisbett and Ross 1980; Ross 1977). We believe that our framework is useful for understanding the phenomenon. People are of course prepared to believe that social behavior is consistent: friendly behavior is very similar to friendly behavior, or at any rate it is when described at that level of abstraction. People's inability to clearly code social behavior leaves them at the mercy of these prior judgments: poorly coded data will not suffice to overturn a theory. In the case of abilities, however, the greater codability of events enables people to detect the true levels of covariation much more accurately, and they are not so inclined to overestimate consistency.

People's overestimation of the consistency of social behavior encourages them to operate at too low a level in their default hierarchies when attempting to make predictions about social behavior. The corollary of assuming great consistency within individuals is assuming much more diversity across individuals than actually exists. This encourages people to model events at the level of "Joe", even when there is little diagnostic information available about Joe, rather than modeling events at the level of "college students" or perhaps even at the level of "people". The causes and consequences of this tendency will be discussed more fully in section 7.2.3 below.

7.2.2 *Default Hierarchies of Intuitive Social Rules*
Unless we know a person intimately, there are bound to be some situations for which we have little or no relevant data. For these we must resort to default values, or generalizations we have about similar people in the same or similar situations—other computer scientists we have known, or other academics, or perhaps just other women. In effect, we jump to a higher level in the default hierarchy. This necessarily means that we are dependent upon the accuracy of stereotypes we have about various classes of people. The role of such stereotypes, as against individuating information, in guiding judgments about other people is examined next.

Stereotypes versus Specific-Level Evidence
Reasoning about other people by reference to group stereotypes is a practice much frowned upon. On the other hand, it is clear that in the absence of reliable information about the past behavior of an individual, the default values we have for people of that person's *kind* are the preferred, indeed often the only, basis for making a prediction about the person. Although the general presumption is that people are inclined to take the lazy way out and to base their judgments

about others on default values at relatively high levels of a default hierarchy, there is a mounting body of evidence suggesting that the opposite is true. Work by Locksley and Borgida and their colleagues (Borgida, Locksley, and Brekke 1981; Locksley, Borgida, Brekke, and Hepburn 1980; Locksley, Hepburn, and Ortiz 1982), together with work by Nisbett and Zukier and their colleagues (Nisbett, Zukier, and Lemley 1981; Zukier 1982; Zukier and Jennings 1984), suggests that people's behavior is actually nonnormative in the opposite direction from that generally assumed. People seem to override defaults at the category level in favor of quite weak information at the level of the specific object itself.

Locksley and colleagues (1980) asked their subjects to rate the assertiveness of targets who were described in one of three ways: (1) the name only was given, so that there was information about nothing but the gender category of the target; (2) the name was given plus a brief, one-paragraph description of the person's behavior on a particular occasion, written in such a way as to convey no information about assertiveness; or (3) the name was given plus a one-paragraph description of the person's behavior suggesting that the person had behaved in an assertive way on a particular occasion. An example of the latter sort of paragraph is given below.

The other day Nancy was in a class in which she wanted to make several points about the readings being discussed. But another student was dominating the class discussion so thoroughly that she had to abruptly interrupt this student in order to break into the discussion and express her own views. (Locksley et al. 1980, p. 827)

When subjects knew only the sex of the target or when they knew only the sex plus some piece of irrelevant information, they rated male targets as being more likely to be assertive than female targets. If they had a piece of information that was diagnostic of assertiveness, however, they did not rate a male target as being any more likely to be assertive in general than a female target characterized by the same information. Thus the category default values exerted no effect in the presence even of a small amount of individuating information.

In a companion study Locksley and her colleagues presented subjects with more ecologically typical information. They asked the subjects to read alleged transcripts of telephone conversations in which the target described three different incidents. In one condition the target's behavior was in all three cases assertive. In the other condition the target's behavior was in all three cases passive. For example, in both conditions the target was harassed by a seedy character while shopping downtown for a jacket. In the assertive condition the target forcefully told the seedy character to go away, while in the passive condition the target just ignored the seedy character until he finally drifted off. The nature of the behavior had a massive effect on how assertive the target was presumed to be, as well as on the number of masculine traits in general that were attributed to the target. Targets believed to be male, however, were rated as no more assertive and as possessing no more masculine traits than targets believed to be female. Thus, in both studies category default values were not passed along to the target, given that even a small amount of individuating information was presented to subjects.

Locksley and her colleagues (1982) obtained similar results for a very different pair of categories—"night people" and "day people". They found, first of all, that there are fairly strong stereotypical assumptions about the two kinds of people (at least for the New York University students who served as subjects). Night people are presumed likely to be unpredictable, rebellious, unconventional, and depressed. Day people are presumed likely to be responsible, dependable, healthy, and self-controlled. Locksley and her colleagues had subjects rate eight targets for these various traits. One set of subjects knew only that the target was a day person or a night person. A second set of subjects received that category information plus some additional information in a brief vignette that was weakly suggestive of one of the four traits mentioned above as characteristic of day people or night people. These subjects received vignettes like the following, in which the target was first identified either as a day person or as a night person. The trait that subjects were asked to make a judgment about from the vignette was self-control.

Gene W. has an IQ of 118 and does fairly well in his college classes. His mother works as a nurse and his father is a lawyer in the town where Gene grew up. Gene has a couple of friends in college, one of whom went to the same high school as he did. (Locksley et al. 1982, p. 29)

A third group of subjects was given the category information plus additional information that was strongly suggestive of one of the four traits presumed to be characteristic of day people or night people. These subjects received vignettes like the following, for which the subjects were asked to rate the target's unpredictability.

Last year Lou A. had planned for months to spend his winter vacation skiing in Colorado. At the last minute he abruptly decided to go to Mexico instead.

He wound up staying a lot longer than he expected and got into trouble with his boss. (Locksley et al. 1982, p. 29)

For the first group of subjects, given information only about the social category of the target, category information had a pronounced effect on ratings of the likelihood that the target had the trait they were asked to judge. Targets identified as night people were judged to be 46 percent more likely to have the stereotypical night-people traits on the average. But subjects given individuating information—even weakly diagnostic individuating information—ignored the social category information in making their judgments, rating night people and day people as equally likely to have the trait.

The preference for individuating evidence over inferences based on stereotypes can be readily understood in terms of default hierarchies that constitute one's mental model of a person. Rules based on more specific information will tend to dominate in competition with rules based on general categories. The domination of specific rules over general ones is especially likely if the latter do not have high strength values, as may often be the case for questionable generalizations based on stereotypes.

The Dilution Effect

The findings described above are very reminiscent of Kahneman and Tversky's (1973) work showing that people are inclined to set aside base-rate information about target cases when given individuating information about them. In a typical Kahneman-Tversky study subjects are told that an investigator has assembled a group of psychological profiles of professional people, both engineers and lawyers. The group consists of 100 people, 70 of whom are engineers and 30 of whom are lawyers (or 30 and 70, respectively). Then a thumbnail sketch of an individual, sampled at random, is presented to the subject, and the subject is asked to guess whether the target is an engineer or a lawyer. The individuating information in the sketch is either strongly suggestive of an engineer (or lawyer), weakly suggestive, or uninformative.

Regardless of what kind of information is presented, subjects pay virtually no attention to the base rate in guessing the profession of the target. That is to say, if a particular individual sounds rather like a lawyer from the sketch, subjects guess that he is a lawyer with essentially the same probability when they know he is a member of a mostly-engineer group as when they know he is a member of a mostly-lawyer group. Normatively, this is quite inappropriate, since the group-membership information (that is, the base rate) ought to be combined with the individual-level information in some Bayesian fashion to produce a probability estimate that the target is a lawyer.

The fact that the base rate is ignored even when the individuating information is useless (for example, the target is "ambitious" or "well-liked") suggests that the preference for specific-level evidence is so great that the base rate or high-level default information is not even retrieved once the subject tries to make a prediction on the basis of the specific information. Instead, it seems likely that the subject tries to use each successive piece of individual-level information to make a prediction; but none is suggestive of profession; finally the subject despairs and asserts the odds to be 50–50!

We may make the equation between the Locksley-Borgida studies and the Kahneman-Tversky studies if we are willing to assume that a social stereotype is a kind of categorical base rate ("Most night people have property X"). Conversely, we may think of a Kahneman-Tversky type of base rate as a very weak category stereotype ("Most of the people in the group are engineers"). A set of findings by Nisbett, Zukier, and Lemley (1981) suggests that this equation is legitimate, and that category membership may be set aside in favor of useless individuating information in the same way that more pallid base rates are.

In a typical study Nisbett and colleagues asked pretest subjects to rate the utility of a large number of items of information about college students for predicting the amount of electric shock that would be taken by the students if they were in an experiment in which they were asked to tolerate as much shock as possible. From these items the investigators selected a number that were believed by the pretest subjects to be essentially useless, for example, "Catholic", "from Detroit", "3.1 grade point average". They also selected a number of items describing category memberships that the pretest subjects believed to be quite usefully predictive, for example, "engineering major", "music major". Some subjects then were given only the presumably diagnostic information about category membership and asked to make a prediction about the amount of shock taken by the target. Other subjects were given the "diagnostic" category membership plus from eight to ten items of useless information and then asked to make predictions.

In one study subjects predicted that an engineering student would take much more shock than a music major. Subjects given the additional information that the engineering major was a Catholic sophomore from Detroit with a 3.1 grade point average, et cetera, predicted that the engineering major would take very little more shock than a music major about whom they had similar nondiagnostic information. It did not matter whether the nondiagnostic information was presented in written form or whether it was presented in the context of a videotaped interview. Similarly, subjects were asked to predict how many movies would be attended over the course of a term by an engineering student and by a music major. Subjects thought the music major would go to many more movies than the engineering major— unless the information was accompanied by nondiagnostic information in a videotaped interview. The results of both studies are presented in figure 7.4 (which gives data for the shock study based on stereotypes about premedical students versus English majors). In studies using other sorts of material, it was found that as few as two items of nondiagnostic information were sufficient to significantly "dilute" the implications of information considered to be diagnostic.

These studies show that even useless information about an individual serves to distract people from using information about group membership that they believe to be relevant to the required judgment. In terms of our approach, it seems that nondiagnostic information is used to activate rules that enter into competition with rules based on diagnostic information. Because the nondiagnostic rules will add equal support for each of the alternatives, the *relative* support for the preferred alternative (that is, the ratio of its support to that of its competitors) will be reduced. Nondiagnostic information will therefore produce judgments that the instance will be "average" on the variable, creating a dilution effect.

The Preference for Specific-Level Evidence

In general, it appears that individuating information, whether diagnostic or nondiagnostic, has substantial power to override default assumptions based on category membership. Do these results, based on admittedly rather sterile laboratory materials, fly in the face of common sense about the importance of stereotypes, especially pejorative stereotypes, in everyday life? Well, yes and no. Although the received opinion of laypeople and social scientists alike on this matter is that stereotypes are of overwhelming importance in social life, some real-world data are quite consistent with the laboratory evidence. As Locksley, Hepburn, and Ortiz (1982) note, the evidence indicates that job discrimination on the grounds of race and sex is much more marked for entry-level jobs than for jobs requiring high-level skills. For the latter sort of jobs, of course, there normally would be much more individuating information available about the candidates than

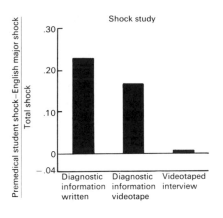

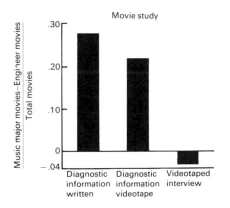

Figure 7.4
Differential predictions of shock tolerance and of movie attendance as a function of means of presentation of diagnostic information and presence of nondiagnostic information. From Nisbett, Zukier, and Lemley (1981).

for the former. Similarly, although clinicians have sex-stereotyped beliefs about the distributions of psychologically healthy and unhealthy traits—believing, for example, that women are more prone to anxiety and hysteria (Broverman, Vogel, Broverman, Clarkson, and Rosenkrantz 1972)—several studies have shown that when clinicians are presented with information about the specific client in addition to information about sex, the sex stereotypes exert little or no effect on judgments (Abramowitz and Dokecki 1977; Stricker 1977).

Thus the mere fact that social stereotypes can be very important to judgment does not contradict our assertion that social-category default values are typically suppressed in the face of individuating evidence. The work just reviewed simply suggests that the effects of stereotypes may be limited to situations in which individuating information is not available or can be avoided. (At least one study, however, by Bodenhausen and Wyer, 1985, does show a powerful effect of social stereotypes even in the face of substantial specific-level information.)

Despite our optimistic conclusion that social stereotypes are often easily suppressed, it should be noted that the inferential tendencies of subjects in the studies just discussed are quite nonnormative. The correct judgmental procedure to follow would be to blend the implications of all diagnostic information, whether category-based or individually based, in some essentially Bayesian fashion, and to ignore nondiagnostic information. It is premature to speculate about how much judgmental damage is done by the nonnormative suppression of defaults, but it should be noted that the practice shades imperceptibly into the normatively appropriate one of ignoring category defaults in favor of actual values for objects. For example, the default expectation for the color of a cow is brown or black; nonetheless, if we encounter a green cow, then green it is. (See the discussion of conceptual combination in chapters 3 and 4.)

One reason that people may be heavily influenced by individuating information is that we all know individuals (for example, close friends) with distinctive behaviors that are best predicted by knowledge of the individual rather than by knowledge of the categories to which the individual belongs. Because highly specific rules are required to predict the behavior of many individuals, the general inferential strategy of seeking specific rules for particular people will be strengthened. There clearly are potentially beneficial aspects of such a strategy. If one knows a person quite well, or if the behavior in question can be accurately predicted from a small sample of behavior, then the strategy of searching for and using specific-level evidence will be effective. In addition, even when these criteria do not hold, specific-level evidence can serve as the basis for generating hypotheses about the person, to be tested in the crucible of experience.

But the errors that can be produced by a focus on specific-level information also should be highlighted. Experience with objects known to be variable will not readily serve to overturn an erroneous hypothesis. Thus, incorrect specific-level rules may be retained indefinitely in the face of evidence that is recognized as disconfirmatory in character but, quite correctly, is not regarded as definitive by itself. Similarly, the very existence of multitudinous specific-level hypotheses, many of which operate as exceptions to higher-level rules, will serve to protect erroneous stereotypes from disconfirmation. Some of my best friends are . . . .

7.2.3 *The Fundamental Attribution Error*
The work we have just reported indicates that people's judgmental strategies in the social domain, like their empircal rules in the physical domain, are defective. As we suggested above, people probably prefer individuating information about social objects because they believe social behavior to be more predictable at the level of the individual than it actually is. Ross (1977) has labeled this belief, and the related preference for explaining social behavior in terms of the dispositions of the actor rather than the character of the situation confronting the actor, the "fundamental attribution error".

A substantial amount of evidence supports the assertion that people overestimate the stability of an individual's behavior across situations and underestimate the contribution of the situation. For example, Jones and Harris (1967) asked college student subjects to read essays advocating or opposing the legalization of marijuana or Castro's leadership of Cuba. Subjects inferred that the author held the view espoused in the essay even when it was made clear that the substance of the essay had been dictated by a political science instructor, debate coach, or psychology experimenter. The overwhelming situational constraints, in other words, were discounted by observers in favor of a tendency to assume that the views were congruent with the dispositions of the author. Similarly, Kunda and Nisbett (1986) found that people substantially overestimate the predictability of future behavior from an interview. In general, a one-hour interview is nearly useless for predicting almost any kind of behavior that society expects it to predict—job success, undergraduate, graduate, and professional school success, and recidivism of criminals and mental patients. Yet people believe that interviews have substantial predictive power.

As we saw in section 7.2.1, difficulty in covariation detection for social behavior can certainly produce errors in estimating the degree of stability for an individual. But this does not tell us why people habitually *overestimate* the degree of stability of social behavior rather than simply producing large unsystematic errors. Our view is that the overestimation is related to another encoding problem that people have. People tend not to recognize fully the role played by situational factors in producing behavior. Psychologists have long argued that situational factors, especially as seen from the perspective of the actor, are relatively difficult to discern. Behavior, asserted Heider in his classic treatment of the fundamental attribution error, "has such salient properties that it tends to engulf the field rather than be confined to its proper position as a local stimulus whose interpretation requires the additional data of a surrounding field—the situation in social perception" (1958, p. 54). In other words, the actor's behavior is so vivid against the "ground" of its situational context that it is attended to and subsequently encoded at the expense of the very situational factors that elicited it. As a consequence of the slighting of situational factors, observers simply have no choice but to look to the actor for the cause of the actor's behavior. Presumed dispositions of the actor then present themselves as the inferred cause.

One interesting implication of the hypothesis that encoding drives the production of rule candidates is that one should have a very different set of rules for predicting and explaining one's own behavior than for predicting and explaining the behavior of others. The situational factors that drive and constrain one's own behavior are far more salient than the same factors for others. In addition, one's own behavior is apt to be less salient, certainly less salient in a literal perceptual sense, than the behavior of others: our eyes are not well placed to observe our own behavior. We would therefore expect that people would be more inclined to explain their behavior in situational terms, and less inclined to explain it in dispositional terms, than would observers of the same behavior (Jones and Nisbett 1972). This result has been obtained in many contexts. For example, Nisbett, Caputo, Legant, and Marecek (1973) asked each of a group of male college students to explain either why he had chosen his college major or why he dated the person he did, and asked each to answer the same question about his best friend. Subjects explained their own choices in terms of the object ("Chemistry is a high-paying field"; "She's a very warm person") and explained their friends' choices in terms of their friends' dispositions ("He was always good at math"; "He's kind of dependent and needs a take-charge kind of woman"). An amusing consequence of perennially perceiving oneself as responding to situations and others as behaving in accordance with their dispositions is that individuals report themselves as having fewer personality traits than others (Nisbett et al. 1973).

The tendency to see dispositions in the object at the expense of influences from the environment, it should be noted, is not limited to the modeling of social events. The social psychologist Kurt Lewin was well aware of the broad outlines of intuitive physics, forty years in advance of any formal research on the topic. He was also quite cognizant of some important continuities between the errors of intuitive physics and those of intuitive psychology. Of the fundamental attribution error in the perception of physical objects, he wrote, "The kind and direction of the physical vectors in Aristotelian dynamics are completely determined in advance by the nature of the object concerned. In modern physics, on the contrary, the existence of a physical vector always depends upon the mutual relations of several physical facts, especially upon the relation of the object to its environment" (1935, p. 28). In other words, in ancient (and modern intuitive) physics the behavior of objects is understood almost exclusively in terms of the object itself: A stone sinks when placed in water because it has the property of "gravity"; a piece of wood floats because it has the property of "levity". Lewin noted the similar, and conceptually related, impoverishment of understanding of social objects. As for physical objects, it is often their properties alone, rather than their properties in conjunction with states of the environment, that are seen to produce their behavior.

7.3 Educating the Intuitive Scientist

One of the chief implications of the present framework is that education in the fields of physics and psychology does not much resemble writing on a blank slate. Instead, we must expect that the facts of physics or psychology taught by professors will simply enter as new rules in competition with old ones. The available evidence, which we will now review, amply supports this view.

7.3.1 Teaching Physics

Many investigators have found recently that formal instruction in physics does not necessarily have a pronounced impact on students' answers to the kinds of problems we presented in the first section. For some problems the effects of a physics course are substantial (though rarely sufficient to guarantee that none of the educated will make mistakes on problems on which substantial numbers of the uneducated make errors). For other problems, perhaps the majority studied to date, the effects of a physics course are detectable statistically but are not massive. For still other problems there are no detectable effects of a physics course (Clement 1982a; Champagne, Klopfer, and Anderson 1980; McCloskey 1983).

There is substantial evidence that the new rules do not merely compete with the old, but rather that the old rules are themselves modified by the new ones. Kuhn (1977) has reported the difficulty the scientific community had in responding to the new concept of acceleration. Even after Galileo's demonstrations of the paradoxes entailed by viewing acceleration and average velocity as identical, many scientists continued to conflate the two notions. The problem is compounded when dealing with "naive physicists", that is, laypeople. Champagne and her colleagues have described the extreme plasticity of the naive view:

Their preinstructional belief system has a loose structure, displays little inter-connectedness, and lacks an overlying formalism. In consequence, the belief system is highly flexible and can accommodate new information locally without producing any conflict with other parts of the system. In this way, the system can "learn" without a major reconceptualization. In any case, the system remains fundamentally Aristotelian. (1980, p. 1078)

Some of their physics student subjects had learned that objects accelerate in free fall.

One might think that this piece of knowledge is a sufficient contradiction of the Aristotelian belief to engender a major disruption of the system. Instead, we found that students rationalized the acceleration by hypothesizing that the force of gravity increases closer to the ground. (p. 1078)

In this example the students were simply modifying their preexisting default hierarchy rather than forming one that was fundamentally different. In fact, this kind of tension between a conservative strategy of modifying an existing theory and the revolutionary strategy of substituting a fundamentally different view recapitulates the course of scientific development (see chapter 11).

7.3.2 Teaching Social Psychology
If physicists have so little effect on their undergraduate charges, pity the poor social psychologist, who lacks both the prestige and the virtually infallible demonstrations of the physicist but who also must

face students who hold firm yet erroneous preconceptions about the subject domain.

Take what is perhaps the most impressive demonstration of the power of the situation in the entire field of psychology—the Milgram (1963) experiment on obedience. The ordinary citizens who were subjects in that experiment were requested to deliver a series of steadily increasing electric shocks to an experimental confederate who was confined in an adjacent room and who was allegedly attempting to learn a list of words. When the trappings of scientific authority are present (white lab coat for the experimenter, and so on) and when the experimenter keeps up intense pressure on the subject to continue to administer shocks ("The experiment requires that you continue"; "You *must* go on"), most subjects continued delivering increasing shocks even after the confederate ceased responding to the learning trials, then banged on the wall in response to each shock, and finally ceased reacting in any way to the shock.

The customary classroom explanation of the Milgram study holds that the remarkable compliance rate is entirely due to situational demands, inasmuch as the experimenter's absence, or even a less firmly insistent stance on his part, ensures that most subjects promptly cease delivering shocks. Despite this, students prefer dispositional explanations, inferring that Milgram's subjects were unusually cruel people or, if one blocks this inference by pointing out that Milgram's subject population was a reliable cross-section, that all people, not only Milgram's subjects, are cruel.

Safer (1980) demonstrated the pervasiveness of dispositional explanations by showing students a film of the Milgram experiment that emphasizes the extent to which it was the situational constraints that compelled obedience. Despite this emphasis, subjects subsequently greatly overestimated the amount of shock that would be administered when the situational constraints were absent.

Another study provides a striking example of the power of seemingly slight situational factors to produce dramatic differences in behavior. Darley and Batson (1973) asked theological seminary students to walk across campus to deliver a sermon. Some students were in a hurry because they had been told that they were already late and that an audience was waiting. Others were not in a hurry. All subjects passed an apparent "victim" moaning for help in a doorway. Only 10 percent of the subjects who were in a hurry helped the victim, whereas 63 percent of the subjects who were not in a hurry did so. In contrast, an individual-difference measure, having to do with the nature of the subject's religious orientation (an emphasis on personal salvation versus a desire to help others), did not predict behavior. The latter variable is, however, just the sort of dispositional factor that subjects think is an important basis of individual differences in behavior.

In order to show how difficult it is to teach students about the power of situational factors and the weakness of dispositional factors, Pietromonaco and Nisbett (1982) asked subjects to make predictions about two helping situations that were similar to the one confronting the Darley and Batson subjects. Some subjects had read about the Darley and Batson study before they made their predictions, and others had not. Reading the study had very little effect on the subjects' predictions. They still thought the majority of target cases would help even though they were in an extreme hurry. Reading about the study had even less effect on subjects' predictions about individual differences. Subjects who had read about the study were just as convinced that the nature of the target's religious orientation would have a big impact on the probability that he would help as subjects who had not read about the study.

Nor does more intensive education seem to have much effect on students' adherence to a preference for dispositional interpretations of behavior. Lehman and Nisbett (1986) examined the effects of four years of undergraduate training in the social sciences versus four years of training in the physical sciences or humanities on students' causal explanations for events that could be given either a primarily dispositional or a primarily situational interpretation. For example, subjects were asked to indicate whether they thought a school administrator who was known to be a disciplinarian at school would be likely to be a particularly harsh disciplinarian for his own children, and they were asked whether riots in prison were best understood in terms of prison conditions or in terms of the character of the prisoners. Social science majors did not differ from either physical science majors or humanities majors in their degree of preference for dispositional over situational explanations.

7.3.3 Implications for Instruction

What is an educator to do? Investigators who share our view of knowledge as rules in competition have argued that there must essentially be reeducation for those disciplines where students arrive with strong prior belief systems. (Note that not all disciplines are likely to have as serious a problem as physics and social psychology do in this regard. Students probably do not come into chemistry or botany classes with the same strong intuitions they have for physics and mechanics, and they probably do not come into sensory or developmental psychology classes with intuitions as strong as those they have for personality and social psychology.)

Siegler (1983a, 1983b) has already demonstrated that what students learn is a function of what they already know. Students with appropriate encoding capacities will learn a given rule; those without will not. He has also shown that students who already possess a given rule may benefit either more or less from instruction than those who do not have the rule. Sometimes knowledge of a given rule is a prerequisite for advancing to a better one. On the other hand, students who have a given rule that has already proved generally workable will not necessarily abandon it on the authority of the instructor. Thus it will sometimes be the case that less cognitively mature students will actually learn more from instruction than more mature students. It is necessary, therefore, to have a good idea of the belief system of the student, at least for those fields where belief modification rather than passive learning is the true nature of the educational task at hand.

Champagne and her colleagues have argued that students will benefit from making their intuitive belief systems explicit.

We propose that instruction in classical mechanics can be improved by continuously encouraging the students to reject an Aristotelian system of beliefs and to adopt a Newtonian paradigm. The main strategy of this approach, which acknowledges the pre-existing belief system of the students, is to compare and contrast the two paradigms. When both have been fully articulated and the benefits and weaknesses of each have been discussed, students will understand the motivation for choosing the Newtonian formulation. It could be argued that the proposed approach is inefficient since it involves the teaching of the Aristotelian system, only to have the students later reject it. How much more elegant and frugal it is to just teach the Newtonian paradigm directly! This argument, however, ignores the fact that the customary and elegant approach has repeatedly shown itself to be ineffective. (1980, p. 1078)

Siegler, McCloskey, and others have noted that education in the fields where students have strong prior intuitions should incorporate much more in the way of demonstrations designed to defeat those intuitions and to highlight the utility of the new rules. We feel that the same strategy is, if anything, even more essential for social psychology than for physics. People's ability to generate new rules to explain exceptions to their prior beliefs is even more breathtaking for social events than for physical ones. What is needed is demonstrations where students are required to make predictions about the likely outcomes of events, then to articulate the bases of their predictions, then to explore the possibility that other rules might exist that would do a better job of prediction. If they fail to induce the preferred rules, these can be suggested by the instructor. This can be followed by a new iteration where predictions based on the two rules can be explicitly compared.

It should be noted that the influence of prior knowledge need not always be pernicious, as in the examples we have discussed here. In chapter 9 we will examine pragmatic training strategies that use specific, approximately correct, prior knowledge as the base on which to build abstract inferential rules for inductive and deductive inference. But first, in the next chapter, we will show how people use intuitive versions of rules for statistical inference in reasoning about everyday life events.

Generalization and Knowledge of Variability

In the preceding several chapters we have dealt with various forms of the central inductive problem of identifying constancies in the environment. We have discussed simple forms of covariation detection, then moved on to more complex covariation-detection tasks underlying the induction of categories, and finally described the relationship between the structure of default hierarchies and inferences about the physical and social worlds. In this chapter we will examine both the empirical knowledge and the inferential rules involved in a major mechanism for the identification of constancies: instance-based generalization of the sort described in chapter 4. Such generalization requires an assessment of the role of variability information; in addition, it involves sophisticated inferential rules of the sort we will discuss further in chapter 9.

Since Aristotle, generalization has been the paradigmatic form of inductive inference. He and many subsequent logicians discussed the structure and legitimacy of inferences from the knowledge that some observed instances of a kind A have a property B to the conclusion that all A have the property B. Some philosophers, such as Hume and Popper, have questioned whether such inferences are ever warranted, but most have attempted to solve the narrower problem of determining under what circumstances the inference can be justified.

In the past several decades in philosophy of science, the problem has been conceived in terms of the conditions under which observed instances can be said to *confirm* the generalization that all A are B. As we described in chapter 1, attempts to characterize confirmation syntactically have encountered intractable problems. Relatively little progress has been made on the problems of specifying syntactically just when, and just how much, a generalization can be confirmed by its instances. Even less has been learned about the conditions under which a generalization might be accepted as true.

This chapter breaks from such remote, abstract discussions of generalization in several important respects. Our approach is procedural, pragmatic, and psychological. It is procedural in that we are interested in more than static logical characterizations of the relation between a generalization and its instances. We want to describe the computational processes that can lead a computer or an organism to add a generalization to its store of knowledge. These processes must be more goal-directed and context-sensitive than the generalization algorithms that have been discussed in most work in AI. Our approach is pragmatic, saying close attention to the environmental conditions under which generalization might be appropriate for an organism or other inductive system. Finally, we tie our discussions closely to psychological examinations of how people actually make generalizations.

8.1 The Pragmatics of Generalization

8.1.1 The Scope of Generalization

Instance-based generalization is a mechanism for adding new rules to existing concepts. In dealing with this topic our emphasis will be on inferential procedures that evaluate possible generalizations to assess whether they merit incorporation in the rule system. Most generalizations are made about abstract categories, but we are also interested in generalizations about individuals. Whereas generalizations about categories introduce variables ranging over objects—"If X is a dog, then X barks"—generalizations about individuals usually introduce variables ranging over times or situations—"If you insult Fred at any time t, he will punch you". The simple generalization about an individual produces the expectation that a property observed in an object is a constant, stable one. Most of the time this is taken for granted; for example, we expect that a particular swan, once observed to be white, will continue to be white. But some properties of some objects are not necessarily presumed to be stable. This is especially the case when the objects are people and the properties are behavioral. No one expects that a child observed to be solemn in church is generally solemn. On the other hand, some behavioral properties usually are taken to be general. Which behaviors are usually assumed to be general has been a central question for social psychologists.

8.1.2 How to Generalize?

Our major concern in this chapter is with a central epistemological problem: What are the factors that contribute most to the inferability of a potentially useful generalization? To put it more simply, *how* should we generalize? How should we determine that we have enough instances of a generalization to warrant its acceptance? Mill (1843/ 1974, p. 314) noticed that the required number of instances is not constant. He asked, "Why is a single instance, in some cases, sufficient for a complete induction, while in others myriads of concurring instances, without a single exception known or presumed, go such a very little way towards establishing a universal proposition?"

On the basis of psychological research on generalization in people, which we will describe below, we see two major components to evaluating the acceptability of a generalization that every F is G (or in a probabilistic case, that many Fs are G). The first is the obvious one that has occupied the attention of most inductive logicians: The number of instances of F that have been found to be G. The second is more complex, because it concerns the background knowledge possessed by the organism about the statistical properties of the populations about which it is concerned to generalize. If the Fs and Gs are kinds of things known to be highly invariant and little subject to random fluctuation, then generalization from few instances will be legitimate. Conversely, if such things are subject to high variability or randomness, then generalization should take place only given many confirming instances. We will provide numerous examples of the relevance of variability and randomness below. (We take for granted a third component, namely, checking for possible counterexamples of things that are F but not G; see the discussion of generalization in PI in chapter 4.)

To estimate the variability of events, it is necessary to establish, at least tacitly, the reference class for the events, that is, what *kind* of events they are. More generally, as Thagard and Nisbett (1982) put it, "our confidence in inferring a generalization 'All F are G' depends on background knowledge about how *variable* Fs tend to be with respect to Gs. This knowledge is based on F being a kind of K_1, G being a kind of K_2, and on the variability of things of kind K_1 with respect to things of kind K_2" (p. 380). When people believe that the kind of object in question is highly variable with respect to the kind of property in question, they infer little or nothing from the observation that several examples of a subkind have a given property. On the other hand, if they believe that a given kind of object is invariant with respect to a given kind of property, or nearly so, then even a single example may serve to establish a confident generalization.

Notice that this account of generalization emphasizes the crucial role played by the selection of what statisticians call a *reference class*, the most appropriate category of events to use for purposes of assessing the variability of the kind of events in question. It follows that the organization of the relevant default hierarchy will have a direct impact on generalization.

In the program PI described in chapter 4, instance-based generalization makes use of default hierarchies furnished by framelike concepts. Each concept has slots for subordinates and superordinates. Variability calculations can be made at any level. In the course of problem solving, generalization is triggered when there are active messages indicating that a single instance belongs to multiple highly active concepts. For example, an object that is both a shreeble (the new kind of bird first mentioned in chapter 1) and blue will trigger an attempt to generalize that all shreebles are blue. PI retrieves from the concepts SHREEBLE and BLUE the number of common instances and makes sure that there are no shreebles that are not blue. The superordinate slots in those concepts indicate that shreebles are birds and that blue is a color. So PI calculates the variability of birds with respect to color by checking the various colors of the subordinates of bird: robin, parrot, and so on. This calculation tells us how variable we should expect shreebles to be with respect to color, and is taken into account along with the number of blue shreebles in deciding whether to construct the generalized rule that all shreebles are blue.

Thus the organization of concepts into default hierarchies is crucial to making the variability judgment, which is just as important to generalization as is the number of instances. A more sophisticated program would not take the superordinate kinds as given but would search through the default hierarchy for the most relevant reference class. In the shreeble case we might get a more accurate expectation of variability by considering *tropical* birds or birds of the Pacific. At the end of this chapter we turn to the question of what this search might look like for a human confronted with a realistic problem. (See Salmon 1967 for a discussion of the problem of finding the best reference class.)

8.1.3 Paradoxes of Confirmation Theory

Our pragmatic approach to generalization has implications for long-standing philosophical issues. For several decades philosophical discussions of generalization have largely concerned the question of *confirmation*. A general hypothesis is confirmed when instances of it are observed to be true; for example, finding a black raven confirms the hypothesis that all ravens are black. Confirmation theory has been concerned primarily with giving a formal account of when a hypothesis "All *F* are *G*", represented in predicate calculus by a formula such as

$(x)\ (Fx \rightarrow Gx)$, is confirmed by its instances (see, for example, Hempel 1965).

This program has proved to be far more difficult than anyone could have anticipated, and most of the research of the past decades has concerned ways of getting around various paradoxes that complicate the syntactic approach. What is usually called "Hempel's paradox" or the "raven paradox" concerns the following problem. The hypothesis that all ravens are black is logically equivalent to the hypothesis that all non-black things are non-ravens. On the standard account that a hypothesis $(x)\ (Fx \rightarrow Gx)$ is confirmed by its instances such as Fa and Ga, it would seem that a white shoe confirms the hypothesis that all non-black things are non-ravens. But intuitively, a white shoe does not seem to confirm the logically equivalent statement that all ravens are black.

Our approach to generalization justifies this intuition. The hypotheses that all ravens are black and that all non-black things are non-ravens are pragmatically very different, despite their formal equivalence. Thus we should not expect the two propositions to be inferable in the same way. The inferability of generalizations is in part a function of rich background knowledge about the kinds of things and properties involved. We have knowledge of the variability of the superordinate concepts for "raven" and "black" that enables us to evaluate the degree of confirmation of the hypothesis that all ravens are black. "Non-black" and "non-raven" do not have meaningful superordinates, so it is difficult even to begin to make variability judgments. Our background knowledge enables us to see a black raven as a significant confirmation of the generalization that all ravens are black, since we know a lot about the variability of birds with respect to color. We can hardly get started, however, with the non-concepts of non-black and non-raven. The only likely judgment of variability would be that it is indefinitely high, so that a single observation of a non-black non-raven confers scarcely any confirmation on the generalization.

A similar pragmatic resolution is available for Goodman's "grue" paradox, described in chapter 1. The problem, it will be recalled, is to specify why we consider "All emeralds are green" to be better confirmed by a green emerald than is "All emeralds are grue", where something is grue if it is green before a future time t and blue thereafter. From a syntactic point of view, no solution is available. It is irrelevant that "grue" seems to be defined in terms of "green" and "blue", since we could turn around and define "green" in terms of "grue" and "bleen", where something is bleen if it is blue before t and green after; something is green if it is grue before t and bleen after.

In any pragmatically reasonable inference task, however, the grue problem will never arise. Concepts such as "grue", which are of no significance to the goals of the learner, will never be generated and hence will not form part of the default hierarchy that is employed in making generalizations. As we pointed out in our discussion of category induction, the concepts that an organism possesses are created, stored, and maintained because they incorporate rules that are useful in accomplishing the organism's goals. Perhaps in a different world concepts like "grue" *would* become useful (for example, if the laws of optics were known to change at time t). But generalization need not take into account hypothetical possibilities such as "grue". Generalization, like other sorts of inference in a processing system, must proceed from the knowledge that the system already has. Abstract concerns about "grue" derive solely from preoccupation with the unattainable goal of giving a purely syntactic account of confirmation.

Goodman himself tried to develop a pragmatic account of generalization using the concepts of "projectibility" and "entrenchment". He said that hypotheses concerning green things are more projectible than hypotheses concerning grue things, because the concept green is entrenched while the concept grue is not. But he provided little analysis of what constitutes entrenchment besides previous use. In our framework the entrenchment of a concept depends on its place in a default hierarchy. Once so placed, a concept's superordinates and subordinates can be accessed, making possible calculations of variability crucial to generalization. We know nothing about what kinds of things are grue. So just as variability considerations yield more confidence in "All ravens are black" than in "All non-black things are non-ravens", they also yield more confidence in "All emeralds are green" than in "All emeralds are grue".

8.1.4 Assessing the Role of Chance

For generalizations about many kinds of events, assumptions about the role of chance in producing the events in question are important. If the individual recognizes no possibility that chance might influence which properties of an object happen to be observed, or what behaviors happen to be exhibited by a person, then a strong dispositional inference is likely to be made. (A dispositional inference is a diachronic rule that specifies that a given state of the object or organism is generally associated with a given "next state".) On the other hand, if the individual recognizes that chance can play a role in determining what occurs or what is observed, then generalizations will be less strong.

One way of construing people's recognitions of the possible role played by chance is to assume that they can see, for some events, the analogy between the mechanism producing the events or the mechanism determining which events are observed, and the operation of a "chance setup". People in our culture learn at a very early age to recognize a chance setup and to reason about such setups using rules that are fundamentally statistical. This is shown by the work of Piaget and Inhelder (1951/1975). They presented children of various ages with randomizing devices of various kinds and asked the children to predict or explain the behavior of such devices. For example, they showed children a wheel with colored wedges and a pointer that could be spun so as to land on any of the wedges. Very young children (under age seven) were quite willing both to predict where the pointer would land and to "explain" why it had landed on a given wedge. Older children recognized that such predictions and explanations are silly and that the behavior of the device has to be regarded as due to the operation of chance. This recognition in turn is due to the children's correct analysis of the causal factors at work. Their appreciation of these factors makes them recognize that any particular outcome for the device can neither be predicted nor explained.

The children also come to recognize that some inferences about the behavior of the device are permitted, however, and that the proper rules for generating these inferences are statistical in nature. Older children (age eight or more) realize, for example, that the pointer has more chances of hitting a given color the more times it is spun—a simple application of the law of large numbers. Similarly, for devices with unequal chances for all possible outcomes, children come to use the base rate for the outcomes when making predictions. That is, they predict that outcomes are likely in proportion to their chances for occurrence as determined by examination of the physical setup or by observation of the actual frequency of occurrence of the events.

In sum, an inductive system must select candidates for generalization based on what general conclusions are likely to contribute to future problem-solving behavior. Then it must decide whether the number of positive instances and the degree of assessed variability and assessed randomness warrant the potentially useful generalization. These decisions, if they are to result in correct generalizations, require accurate representations of the variability in the environment and the role of chance, as well as the application of complex inferential rules related to the statistician's law of large numbers.

8.2 Variability and Generalization

In the previous section our discussion of generalization was primarily normative; that is, most of our assertions amounted to prescriptions for how to generalize correctly. Do people actually generalize in accordance with these prescriptions? We will now examine the empirical evidence.

First, we will see how people deal with variability information. A basic question is whether people in fact encode information about the variability of properties. In chapter 6 we described evidence that people are adept at learning the distributional properties of perceptual categories, at least if the distributions are unimodal in form. It is less obvious, however, that people can construct veridical representations of the variability of distributions in the social domain. As we pointed out in chapter 7, there are many reasons why social properties are difficult to induce. The coding of social variables poses many potential problems, and people may hold mistaken theories about the nature of social distributions, causing them to imagine larger or smaller differences between individuals than actually exist. For example, they might believe that bimodal distributions ("our kind" and "not our kind") are the rule for social variables, which would result in overestimation of variability.

8.2.1 Knowledge of Social Distributions

Nisbett and Kunda (1985, study 1) examined the accuracy of people's perceptions of various social distributions. They asked a large number of University of Michigan undergraduates about their behavior and attitudes along a number of dimensions. The behavioral questions probed such information as how often subjects had trouble getting to sleep, went to concerts, came late to class, went to movies, got angry, and felt blue. Each question was answered on a 10-point scale labeled "never", "once a year", . . . , "4–6 times a week", "daily". Attitudes were assessed regarding abortion, defense spending, taking hard drugs, the university president's conduct in office, and so on. Answers were made on 10-point scales ranging from "very strongly approve" to "very strongly disapprove". The investigators' basis for selection of the particular dimensions employed was haphazard, within the constraint that they tried to maximize the chances of obtaining both bimodal distributions (for example, by examining political attitudes with a substantial left-right component) and "J" distributions (ones with peaks near to one end or the other of the scale), as well as unimodal symmetric distributions. This made it possible to examine subjects' accuracy both about relatively normal distributions and about non-normal distributions of various kinds.

A set of subjects was asked to make estimates about these data: "We would like you to estimate the pattern of 100 University of Michigan students' responses to each of the items. How many students out of the 100 fell in each of the 10 response categories?" Each of these latter subjects thus produced a number of histograms, one for each behavior and attitude we examined.

It is possible to ask several interesting questions about the accuracy of these latter subjects' estimates. We can examine how accurately they perceived the mean, variance, and distribution shapes of each of the dimensions. (It should be noted that the data reported below differ slightly from those reported by Nisbett and Kunda, because they reported on the results of 5-point as well as 10-point attitudinal scales.)

Central Tendencies of Distributions

Subjects' perceptions of the means of both behavioral and attitudinal dimensions were fairly accurate on the whole. The average absolute error of judgments about the means of behavioral distributions was only 1.19 on the 10-point scale. Since actual means ranged from 2.66 to 5.95, subjects' accuracy was not due to limits on the range of possible error. The average correlation between a given subject's estimates of the means of the 17 behavioral dimensions and the actual means of the dimensions was .42. There was a very systematic, though not large, bias toward overestimating behavior of almost all kinds, from getting angry to going to concerts.

Subjects were somewhat more accurate about the means of attitudinal distributions. The average subject's estimate of the mean was only .89 away from the actual mean. (Actual means ranged from 2.91 to 6.14.) The average correlation between a given subject's estimate of the means of the eight attitudinal distributions and the actual means of the dimensions was .66. There was no systematic bias in estimates of the mean.

Dispersion and Distribution Shape

Subjects' estimates about dispersion were also fairly accurate, despite a bias toward overestimating dispersion. On average, subjects overestimated the standard deviation of both attitudinal and behavioral distributions by 10–12 percent. (That is, the average standard deviation calculated from subjects' histograms was off by this amount.) The average correlation between a given subject's estimate of the

Table 8.1
Percent of subjects who estimated each type of distribution shape, for each type of actual distribution shape (from Nisbett and Kunda 1985)

Actual distribution shape	Estimated distribution shape			
	J Left	J Right	Unimodal	Bimodal
J Left	32	2	43	23
J Right	1	34	42	23
Unimodal	12	3	66	19
Bimodal	9	6	51	34

standard deviations of behavioral distributions and their actual standard deviations was .47. For attitudinal distributions the correlation was .25.

Subjects' estimates of distribution shapes were still more impressive. Despite the fact the many of the distributions were J-shaped and some were bimodal, subjects were fairly accurate in their judgments. All distributions, both actual and estimated, were categorized by the investigators (using a set of somewhat arbitrary criteria) as being either J-left (that is, central tendency on the left of the scale), J-right, bimodal, or unimodal symmetric. Table 8.1 shows the cross-tabulation of estimated and actual distribution types. It may be seen that most distributions, despite the investigators' best efforts to the contrary, were in fact unimodal symmetric. For such distributions the subjects' guesses were overwhelmingly accurate. For non-normal distributions the subjects' guesses always favored a unimodal symmetric distribution, with the actual distribution shape coming in a strong second in every case.

These data indicate (1) very high accuracy in guessing distribution shapes and (2) a bias in favor of conceiving distributions as unimodal symmetric. Subjects probably would be well served by this bias when making guesses about social distributions, since it is not likely that as high a proportion of actual social distributions are non-normal as in the present set. The results of Nisbett and Kunda concerning social perceptions thus converge with those of Flannagan, Fried, and Holyoak (1986), who found that people tend to assume that perceptual categories will be unimodally distributed (see chapter 6).

Implications for Inductive Processes
The results of the Nisbett and Kunda study are important because they indicate that erroneous inductive reasoning about social vari-

ables is not due to false beliefs about social distributions, or at any rate to an inability to construct reasonably accurate social distributions when confronted with that task. Rather, such errors are likely due to a failure to access or construct such distributions in the context of solving inductive problems that logically require their use.

The results also pose an intriguing puzzle. How do people manage to be so accurate in constructing social distributions? The most obvious mechanisms seem quite incapable of producing such accuracy. The simplest strategy that one might imagine would be simply to guess that everyone has the same value as the subject's own, or one very near it, on every distribution. This strategy would of course produce extremely high accuracy on estimated means when averaged over a large number of subjects. Subjects do not follow such a simplistic strategy, however. It would produce estimates of dispersion that are extremely low, whereas the estimated dispersion is in fact greater than the actual dispersion.

Another strategy might be simply to try to recall as many actual values for acquaintances on a given dimension as possible, and then to construct a distribution of 100 cases by generalizing from the density of the recalled distribution. It seems entirely possible that the subjects constructed some of their estimated distributions in this way—the distribution of lateness to class, for example, or even of a somewhat less public behavior such as frequency of getting angry at someone. On the other hand, many of the behaviors and attitudes seem to be too private to allow for the generation of very accurate distributions by generalization from actual recalled cases. These include the number of hours per night of sleep and the frequency of feeling blue.

The construction of such distributions is probably not achieved by exclusively bottom-up techniques. In addition to memories of actual cases and knowledge about the specific item at hand, subjects undoubtedly have theories about the kind of item in question and about social behavior and attitudes in general. For example, although subjects might have little first-hand knowledge about the actual attitudes of many of their fellow students toward increasing defense spending, they might view this question as the kind of issue heavily saturated with right-left ideological significance and might have reasonably accurate estimates of the percent of the student population occupying each of various locations on this continuum. And, at the most general level, people seem to have tacit beliefs about the likely distribution shapes for social dimensions, just as they do for physical dimensions. Given knowledge about one's own position, reasonably accurate memory for a few cases, and a good guess about the shape of the underlying distributions, one could generate quite accurate estimates of the mean and standard deviation of the distribution.

8.2.2 Variability Assessment and Propensity to Generalize

Given that empirical studies have established that people are able to assess the degree of variability quite accurately for many properties, we can proceed to consider evidence that such variability information is in fact used in generalizing. A number of studies on the statistical aspects of generalization were conducted by Nisbett, Krantz, Jepson, and Kunda (1983). Some of these studies show the importance of assumptions about the variability of the reference class, some show the importance of recognition of a chance setup, and some reflect the importance of both factors. The first of these studies, described below, shows the influence of assumptions about variability.

Subjects were first given information about several novel kinds of objects and then asked for their generalizations about the objects:

Imagine that you are an explorer who has landed on a little-known island in the Southeastern Pacific. You encounter several new animals, people, and objects. You observe the properties of your "samples" and you need to make guesses about how common these properties would be in other animals, people, or objects of the same type.

Suppose you encounter a new bird, the shreeble. It is blue in color. What percent of all shreebles on the island do you expect to be blue?

Why did you guess this percent?

Subjects were also told that the shreeble was found to nest in a eucalyptus tree and were asked what percent of all shreebles they expected to nest in eucalyptus trees. The subjects then were told to imagine that they had encountered a member of the "Barratos" tribe. He was brown in color, and obese. The subjects were asked what percent of all male Barratos they expected to be brown and what percent they expected to be obese. Finally, they were told that they had encountered a sample of a rare element called "floridium". It was found to conduct electricity and to burn with a green flame when stretched out to a filament and heated to a very high temperature. The subjects were asked what percent of all floridium they expected to conduct electricity and to burn with a green flame.

There were two other experimental conditions. In one, subjects were told that three samples of each object were encountered. In the other, subjects were told that twenty samples of each object were encountered.

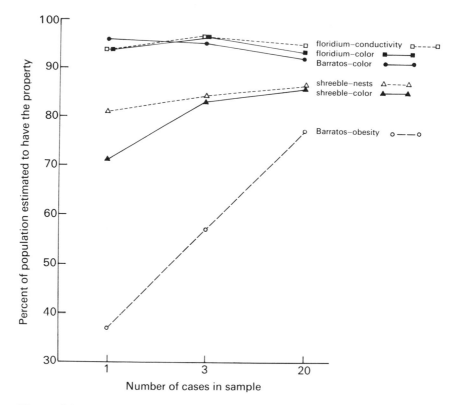

Figure 8.1

Percentage of each population estimated to have the sample property as a function of number of cases in the sample. From Nisbett, Krantz, Jepson, and Kunda (1983).

The reasons subjects gave for proposing their estimates were coded as to their content. There were three basic sorts of answers: (a) references to the homogeneity of the kind of object with respect to the kind of property; (b) references to the heterogeneity or variability of the kind of object with respect to the kind of property, attributed to the existence of subkinds having different properties (for instance, male vs. female), or to some causal mechanism producing different properties (such as a genetic mistake), or to purely statistical variability ("where birds nest is sometimes just a matter of chance"); and (c) other sorts of answers, which were mostly mere tautologies or other non-answers.

The results were quite clear-cut. Figure 8.1 presents the subjects' estimates of the percentage of objects of each kind that they expected to have the attribute found in the sample. It may be seen that the subjects expected that essentially all floridium would have the properties of conductivity and of burning with a green flame. They also expected that essentially all Barratos would be brown. These expectations held regardless of the number of cases in the sample. In contrast, subjects did not expect all shreebles to be blue or to nest in eucalyptus trees, even if twenty shreebles had been observed. The subjects expected an even smaller percentage of obese Barratos than of blue shreebles or shreebles nesting in eucalyptus trees, and their beliefs about the percentage of obese Barratos were highly dependent on the number of cases in the sample.

The subjects' beliefs about the variability of the objects in question with respect to the properties in question clearly determined this pattern of responses. Subjects reported believing that the properties of elements are invariant across samples and that isolated tribespeople are homogeneous with respect to color. They believed that bird types are only sometimes homogeneous with respect to color and preferred nesting location; and they believed that even isolated human groups are quite heterogeneous with respect to body weight. *Within* each point of the graph, individual differences in estimates of percentages were dependent on individual differences in beliefs about variability. The subjects who estimated higher percentages were those who thought the kind of object was not highly variable with respect to the kind of property.

For this simple kind of generalization, then, it is clear that people are capable of tempering the strength of their conclusions about kinds of objects according to the degree of homogeneity they expect. At one extreme, a quite strong generalization may be formed on the basis of a single case, if homogeneity is presumed. At the other extreme, where great heterogeneity is presumed, even a fairly large number of cases will not result in a strong generalization.

8.2.3 *Recognition of Degree of Variability*

Sometimes the variability of a class of objects is not as immediately salient as it apparently was in the above experiment. If variability is underestimated, people will be inclined to generalize too strongly from the available evidence. Similarly, if people do not recognize the role of chance factors in producing their observations, they are also likely to generalize too strongly.

Cueing the Variability of Events
A study by Nisbett, Krantz, Jepson, and Kunda (1983) provides an example of overgeneralization that seems to be produced by failures

both in recognizing the variability of an event and in recognizing chance factors. The study also shows that it is possible to affect the statistical modeling of events by cues presented in the problem context. The cue that was manipulated was intended to call subjects' attention to both the heterogeneity of the events in question and the chance aspect of event sampling.

The investigators asked one group of subjects to read a description of a choice facing a high-school senior, David L. David had decided to go to one of two colleges that were essentially equivalent in prestige, cost, and distance from his home. He had several friends at each school. The friends were quite similar to him in terms of background and interests. His friends at College A were in general very pleased on both academic and social grounds, while his friends at College B were mostly dissatisfied on both grounds. Initially David had thought he would go to A, but he decided to visit both campuses for a day. Subjects in the "no cue" condition read the following account of his visit:

He did not like what he saw at A: Several people whom he met seemed cold and unpleasant; a professor he met with briefly seemed abrupt and uninterested in him; and he did not like the "feel" of the campus. He did like what he saw at B: Several of the people he met seemed like vital, enthusiastic, pleasant people; he met with two different professors who took a personal interest in him; and he came away with a very pleasant feeling about the campus.

A second group of subjects read the identical story, except that the possibilities for an erroneous impression were highlighted by having David draw up a list of all the things that might be seen on the two campuses and then selecting randomly from among them for his actual schedule. The following paragraph was added to the "cued" version:

He proceeded systematically to draw up a long list, for both colleges, of all the classes which might interest him and all the places and activities on campus that he wanted to see. From each list, he randomly selected several classes and activities to visit, and several spots to look at (by blindly dropping a pencil on each list of alternatives and seeing where the point landed).

Subjects were then asked to indicate which college they thought David should go to and to justify their answer. These justifications were coded with respect to whether they showed any recognition of the statistical questions involved—either the dubiousness of David's impressions, due to the relative paucity of the evidence he obtained, or the superiority of his friends' testimony because of their greater experience.

Most subjects in the uncued, control condition—74 percent— thought David should go to the school his own sample of events favored, rather than to the school his friends preferred. When the cue as to the diversity of events that might be sampled was present, how- ever, the percent dropped to 56. Subjects in the cued condition were also more likely to refer to statistical considerations having to do with the adequacy of the sample of events that could be obtained on a single day's visit. Fifty-six percent of the subjects in the cued condition raised statistical issues in their open-ended answers, whereas only 35 percent of the subjects in the uncued condition did.

It should be noted that these effects were in no way due to a belief on the part of cued subjects that the sampling procedure in the cued version was a poor one. On the contrary, subjects who were shown both sampling procedures believed that the generation of a list, with random sampling from it, was superior as a technique of collect- ing evidence to the haphazard manner of collecting evidence pre- sented in the uncued version. This means that subjects are placed in the untenable position of believing that the superior technique of col- lecting information generates evidence that should be given less weight than the evidence generated by the inferior technique! This paradox arises from the fact that the superior method of generating informa- tion also includes a tipoff both as to the extreme variability of events that might be sampled on a college campus and as to the role played by chance in determining which of these events is sampled. When the variability of events and the role played by chance in producing the sample are made clear, the observation produced by a single day's sample seems inadequate and is viewed as likely to be misleading.

Variability Assessment and Stereotyping
One way of understanding the social-psychological phenomenon of stereotyping is in terms of erroneous assessment of variability. A set of people who are labeled as belonging to a given group is presumed to be more homogeneous than is in fact the case. Quattrone and Jones (1980) have pointed to the inductive consequences of this kind of error. They argue, "An observer's tendency to generalize from the behavior of a specific group member to the group as a whole is pro- portional to the observer's perception of the group's homogeneity" (p. 141).

Since people are more familiar with the members of groups to which they belong, they will recognize "the group's general variability, the extent to which its members ... differ from one another when viewed over all dimensions" (p. 141). Since people are less familiar with outgroups, they are at liberty to assume that their members are relatively uniform. Thus people may generalize more readily from observations of the behavior of outgroup members than from observations of the behavior of ingroup members.

To test this hypothesis, Quattrone and Jones showed Princeton and Rutgers undergraduates videotapes of male students who were allegedly serving as participants in psychology experiments. These students had been asked to make choices such as waiting for a few minutes by themselves versus waiting in the company of others, or listening to rock music versus listening to classical music. Half the subjects at each campus believed they were viewing Princeton men, and half believed they were viewing Rutgers men. After seeing the choice of one participant, subjects were asked to predict what the 100 participants in the study did. Quattrone and Jones found greater generalization from the participants' behavior to outgroup members than to ingroup members. For example, Princeton subjects generalized more strongly about the behavior of the Rutgers population after observing the choice of the "Rutgers" participant than they did about the Princeton population after observing the choice of the "Princeton" participant.

It thus seems that one consequence of stereotyping, due to the assumption that outgroup variability is low, is that people learn more than they should from information about the characteristics of any given outgroup member. But the reverse also seems possible. We may exaggerate the variability of ingroup members. If so, we might generalize too little from knowledge of a sample of ingroup members on some dimension about which we had little previous information.

Such an exaggeration of ingroup variability seems particularly likely in the case of one's own university. People are probably inclined to regard their own university populations as being immensely variable, since diverse examples of many different subgroups are likely to be salient—foreign students, athletes, "brains", bohemians, and so on. In fact, of course, the populations even of "multiversities" are not infinitely heterogeneous. They are composed primarily of bright young middle-class people of fairly restricted geographic and ethnic background. It seems possible, therefore, that if subjects in the Quattrone and Jones experiment had been required to contemplate the "central tendencies" of their own university populations before they had been asked to observe the choices of participants, they might have been less reluctant to generalize about students from their own universities.

Such an exercise would have required them to model the population variability more reflectively and thus to discover more homogeneity than casual consideration normally would produce.

In order to test this notion, Nisbett, Krantz, Jepson, and Kunda (1983) employed the procedure of Quattrone and Jones. It was followed almost exactly, except that the subjects, all of whom were University of Michigan students, were told the videotapes were either of University of Michigan or of Ohio State University students, and half the subjects were exposed to a "central tendency" manipulation before viewing the videotapes. This manipulation consisted of asking subjects first to list "what you would guess to be the ten most common majors at the University of Michigan or at Ohio State University" and next to list the five most common ethnic-group backgrounds and religious backgrounds at that university. This manipulation was expected to influence the subjects' subsequent tacit assessment of the variability of the university population and thus to affect their generalizations from the behavior they subsequently observed on the videotapes.

The videotapes were introduced as having been made during psychology experiments conducted at the University of Michigan (U of M) or at Ohio State University (OSU). In each of the three tapes a male participant was asked to choose between one of two different behaviors. In the first scenario a target person had to choose between waiting alone and waiting with other subjects while an experimenter fixed a machine. In the second the choice was between listening to classical music and listening to rock music during an experiment on auditory sensitivity. In the third the choice was between solving mathematical problems and solving verbal problems during an experiment on the effects of noise on intellectual performance. Half the subjects in each condition saw the participants in the three scenarios make one set of decisions and the other half saw the complementary set. Thus subjects in Set A saw the target persons choose (1) to wait alone, (2) to listen to classical music, and (3) to solve mathematical problems. Subjects in Set B saw targets make the opposite choice in each case.

The primary dependent variable of interest was subjects' generalizations—that is, their estimates of how many out of 100 participants in each of the three experiments chose each of the two options. Figure 8.2 presents subjects' generalizations about the U of M and OSU populations for control subjects and for subjects exposed to the cueing manipulation. ("Generalization" was operationally defined as the difference between population estimates for subjects presented with

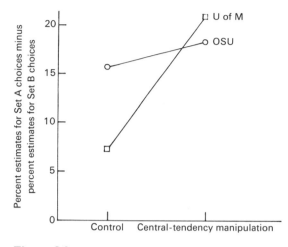

Figure 8.2

Generalization from sample to population as a function of campus population and central-tendency manipulation. (U of M = University of Michigan; OSU = Ohio State University.) From Nisbett, Krantz, Jepson, and Kunda (1983).

Set A choices versus those presented with Set B choices. The higher this index is, the more a group of subjects was influenced by the behavior of the particular target they observed.) It may be seen that the Quattrone and Jones "ingroup/outgroup" finding was replicated. Control groups exposed to "OSU" participants generalized more about the entire population than subjects exposed to "U of M" participants. It may also be seen that the cueing manipulation was effective. Subjects exposed to it generalized more from their observations than subjects who were not. The effect was essentially limited to the "U of M" group, which is not surprising given that the U of M subjects would of course be better able to assess the distribution of people on their own campus than on another with which they were not familiar.

These findings indicate that inductive generalizations are mediated by tacit assessments of population distributions. People generalize less about populations with which they are familiar, presumably because they are very much aware of the variability of such populations. On the other hand, people can be encouraged to think about central tendencies of populations, and this apparently makes it more likely that they will model the population as being sufficiently homogeneous that at least a moderate degree of generalization is permissible. More generally, the research makes it clear that pragmatic factors, having to do with problem goals and problem contexts, can be expected to have a substantial impact on the way people model the distribution of events and the role of chance in producing the events. These factors thus will have a major impact on the way people generalize.

8.3 The Impact of Prior Knowledge on Generalization

The evidence we have reviewed indicates that people's assessments of variability, and hence their propensity to generalize, depend on their prior knowledge and experience. Let us consider some implications of this conclusion.

8.3.1 Domain Specificity of Inferential Rules

One important implication is that people would be expected to reason quite differently about events in different domains. In domains in which event variability and the random aspects of event production are relatively easy to assess, people would be expected to reason more statistically—to generalize less strongly from extreme events, to be less inclined toward causal explanations when outcomes are different on superficially similar occasions, and so on. In domains in which assessment of the above factors is more difficult, people would be expected to reason less statistically.

In general, events that fit the former description are those that are highly codable in the sense discussed in chapters 5 and 7. In the social domain this would include athletic events, academic performance, and many kinds of occupational achievements in which performance is indicated by uniform units and clear codes. Events that fit the latter description include those that are normally assessed only by global, subjective judgments, such as social behavior of a kind usually presumed to be produced by traits such as friendliness, honesty, and so on. For such behavior, unitization and coding are not sufficiently uniform to permit comparisons across people and occasions.

In order to test whether people normally reason more statistically about objective, easy-to-code events than about subjective, hard-to-code events, Jepson, Krantz, and Nisbett (1983) presented subjects with both types of problems. In some problems the behavior in question was an achievement or some other outcome that could be assessed by clear objective means. In other problems the behavior was either a social one or a choice between objects, where the properties of the objects were assessable only by subjective means. The two types of problems may be described as (1) "objective" problems, that is, problems in which the target behavior or attribute is assessable by objective means that should facilitate the identification of statistical factors such as variability and randomness; and (2) "subjective" problems, that is, problems in which the target behavior or attribute is assessable only by subjective means, as when one judges another person's friendliness or makes a choice between two colleges. The investigators found that subjects were much more likely to use the law of large numbers and simple versions of the regression principle when reasoning about the objective attribute problems than when reasoning about the subjective attribute problems. (See also Fong, Krantz, and Nisbett 1986.)

The evidence is thus consistent with the view that inductive reasoning strategies may be quite different across different content domains for reasons that are well understood in terms of people's ability to model events in such a way that the relevance of statistical heuristics is clear. Inductive reasoning will often be guided by inferential rules that embody statistical principles when people are thinking about domains where the target properties are easily evaluated with respect to their variability and the role played by chance in producing them. Statistical principles will be used less often in domains that are hard to model with respect to these factors.

8.3.2 Expertise and Inferential Skill

Perhaps the most obvious source of differences in knowledge that would be expected to affect generalization is the degree of expertise in the relevant domain. Experts—people who are highly knowledgeable about events in a given domain—could be expected to assess the statistical aspects of events differently from nonexperts. Experts should be more aware of the degree of variability of events in the domain and should be more cognizant of the role played by chance in the production of such events. As a consequence of these differences in their relevant mental models, experts could be expected to generalize differently from nonexperts when presented with certain kinds of information. In a domain characterized by variable events with some degree of randomness in their production, experts should be inclined to generalize less strongly than nonexperts from a given small amount of data. In addition, experts should be disinclined to engage in causal explanations for discrepancies between the character of events on one occasion and the character of events on another similar occasion, since such discrepancies are anticipated on the basis of their model for events in the domain.

These predictions were tested by Nisbett, Krantz, Jepson, and Kunda (1983), who examined the possibility that expertise would facilitate recognition of a statistical "regression" effect. Subjects were presented with a problem in which an extreme result was obtained in a small sample of events. When a larger sample of events was examined, the overall level was observed to be less extreme than in the sample. Experts could be expected to avoid generalizing too strongly on the basis of the small sample. They would then find nothing to explain when the less extreme level was found in the larger sample. In contrast, nonexperts could be expected to generalize more strongly from the small sample of events and thus would be confronted with the need to provide a causal explanation for the discrepant level in the larger sample.

The two domains examined were sports and acting. The problem was virtually the same in both domains, except for slight wording changes. The full text of the sports version of the problem is presented below.

Harold is the coach for a high school football team. One of his jobs is selecting new members of the varsity team. He says the following of his experience: "Every year we add 10–20 younger boys to the team on the basis of their performance at the tryout practice. Usually the staff and I are extremely excited about the potential of two or three of these kids—one who throws several brilliant passes or another who kicks several field goals from a remarkable distance. Unfortunately, most of these kids turn out to be only somewhat better than the rest." Why do you suppose that the coach usually has to revise downward his opinion of players that he originally thought were brilliant?

The acting version of the problem was almost identical, except that it was about "Susan, the director of a student repertory company," who gets excited about "a young woman with great stage presence or a young man who gives a brilliant reading."

Subjects were asked which of the following explanations they preferred for the fact that the coach/director usually had to revise downward his/her opinion of the brilliant performers. The second alternative is the statistical one, suggesting that the explanation is simply that the tryout performances were uncharacteristically good for the "brilliant" performers.

1. Harold was probably mistaken in his initial opinion. In his eagerness to find new talent, he exaggerates the brilliance of the performances he sees at the tryout.

2. The brilliant performances at tryout are not typical of those boys' general abilities. They probably just made some plays at the tryout that were much better than usual for them.

3. Boys who did so well at tryout probably could coast through the season on

their talent alone and don't put out the effort necessary to transform talent into consistently excellent performance.

4. The boys who did so well at tryout may find that their teammates are jealous. They may slack off so as not to arouse envy.

5. The boys who did so well at tryout are likely to be students with other interests. These interests would deflect them from putting all their energies into football.

The wording was altered very slightly for the acting version: "boys" became "actors" and "tryout" became "audition".

Experience in sports was assessed by asking the subjects whether they had played any organized team sports in high school or college. Those who had were defined as experienced. Experience in acting was defined as having had "more than a bit part" in a play in high school or college.

Expertise had a marked effect on preferences for explanations of the discrepancy. Of subjects with athletic experience, 56 percent preferred the statistical explanation for the football version of the problem; of those without experience, only 35 percent preferred the statistical explanation. Of subjects with acting experience, 59 percent preferred the statistical explanation for the acting version; of those without experience, only 29 percent preferred the statistical explanation. These results indicate that expertise in a content domain can have a major impact on inferential practices. In the next chapter we will examine the effect of expertise in inference itself. We will examine the possibility that expertise in statistics and formal logic will improve everyday reasoning.

8.3.3 Default Hierarchies, Generalization, and Explanation

We are now in a position to be explicit about some very important relationships that govern the process of generalization. The relationships are among the concepts of *default hierarchies* of categories, the *empirical rules* that correspond to one's beliefs about the causal structure of some domain of events, and the *statistical properties* of the observed events.

Not only is the degree of generalization from an event governed by one's beliefs about the variability of that kind of event, but the categorization of events is itself a highly variable and fluid process. A given event may be categorized in many different ways in a given problem context. The event will be represented at many different levels in the q-morphic default hierarchy in which it is embedded. In addition, the dominant or basic level of categorization may be expected to change from time to time.

There are two primary implications of these considerations. The first is that generalizations from a given event may have effects at a number of levels of the default hierarchy. Thus the observation of a large number of shreebles that are blue can be expected not only to create a strong generalization that shreebles are blue, but also to affect higher-order expectations about the variability of Pacific island shore birds with respect to color and about the variability of birds in general with respect to color, perhaps even about animals in general with respect to properties in general. The subsequent observation of a green shreeble will similarly have effects on generalizations and variability estimates at relevant levels of the default hierarchy.

The second major implication is that the currently dominant level of categorization in the default hierarchy will affect what generalizations are made, and even whether any generalizations are made at all. Whether shreebles are presumed to be universally blue on the basis of twenty shreebles observed to be blue is a function of how they are categorized, since knowing that shreebles are birds is essential to the calculation of the relevant background variability. The expert may be expected to have a different dominant reference category from the novice and thus to generalize differently.

A third point to emphasize is that statistical issues are relevant not only to background variability but also to the triggering conditions for generalization. Events that seem within the normal level of variability for their reference class may not be noticed at all and hence may produce no generalizations. Events that seem outside the range of previously observed variation may command attention and demand both explanation and further generalizations.

To illustrate these interrelationships, we return to our example of Reggie, recently turned four years old, who has been acting up lately. The first thing to note is that his acting up must exceed some kind of threshold to be noticed at all. If Reggie often acts up and the recent episode is merely a minor increment, it may not be perceived as a change in the general state. A second thing to note is that one's causal theories influence one's recognition of statistical abnormalities. Suppose that just after one of Reggie's incidents of acting up, he happens to sneeze. This event is likely to trigger the formation of the hypothesis that Reggie has a cold, along with a search for other corroborating evidence that he has a cold. The search may turn up the fact that although there is no other physical evidence, there does seem to be some behavioral evidence in the form of his acting up lately. Thus confidence in the hypothesis that Reggie has a cold increases as more facts are noticed that it explains. This is an instance of multiple abduction, as discussed in chapters 3 and 4.

Suppose, on the other hand, that one spontaneously notices that Reggie has been acting up an awful lot more than usual lately. This is likely to trigger a search for an explanation for this event, requiring categorization of Reggie at a level in the default hierarchy furnishing a rule that would predict his behavior. A good place to look, given one's knowledge about kids and behavior, is Reggie's health. If one recalls a few sniffles during the day and fatigue over the last few days, Reggie is categorized as a sick kid and the search for an explanation is likely to be over.

Or suppose many possibilities for an explanation exist. Suppose Reggie has seemed a bit under the weather lately, *and* his nursery school teacher volunteered a few weeks ago that he has begun to seem bored with the routine there, *and* Reggie was told just last week about the imminent arrival of a new sibling. Which of these categories— sick, bored, or jealous—is likely to predominate is a function of the strength of belief in various causal theories about human behavior as well as the sheer salience of the various relevant facts. It is possible to supercede them all, interestingly, by the introduction of a new category. In this case, exposing the worried parent to the concept of "the fearsome fours" (the age-four parallel to "the terrible twos") may override all other categorizations and any need for further explanation. (There is of course still the question "Why are four-year-olds fearsome?" But this is the province of psychology, not routine parenthood.)

The picture of generalization and explanation is complicated still further by the existence of rules at a still higher level of generality. These are the inferential rules that govern inductive and deductive reasoning. We have touched on one class of these rules, related to the law of large numbers, in this chapter. It is now time to examine in detail their nature and their role in inference.

Learning Inferential Rules

In the last chapter we described how people use the law of large numbers and knowledge about variability in making generalizations. While modeling the world, they make observations that trigger the application of inductive inferential rules. As we noted in chapter 2, the function of inferential rules is not to model the environment directly but to generate empirical rules, adding these to the permanent base of general knowledge.

We hope to show in this chapter that statistical rule systems are not the only abstract inferential schemas that people possess, but that such schemas are common. As it happens, our belief that inferential rule systems exist is controversial. No one doubts, of course, that scientists, statisticians, and logicians possess such rules and can use them for analyzing formal propositions and for reasoning about scientific data. But some theorists hold that people do not use abstract inferential rules when reasoning about ordinary events but instead make inferences exclusively by means of domain-specific empirical rules. We wish to show that these theorists are mistaken and that laypeople do in fact possess inferential rules and use them for thinking about everyday events.

A second, related goal is to show that such inferential rules, in addition to being induced by people in the course of ordinary daily existence, can be taught. And at least some of them can be taught by purely abstract means, that is, by giving information about the rules themselves rather than by showing how they can be used to reason about particular concrete problems. Finally, we will suggest that inferential rules of the sort beloved by the logician, that is, the rules of formal logic, are not an important part of the layperson's repertoire and cannot readily be taught by purely abstract means. Instead, the rule systems that people actually use are what we call *pragmatic reasoning schemas*, that is, rule systems that are highly generalized and abstracted but nonetheless defined with respect to classes of goals and types of relationships, rather than being purely syntactic. Pragmatic reasoning schemas, unlike the rules of formal logic, can be easily taught in such a way that they are accessible for solving ordinary, everyday life problems.

9.1 Teaching Statistical Rules

Although we did not emphasize it, there were two different lines of evidence in the last chapter that indicated that subjects were solving problems using abstract statistical rules rather than more domain-specific empirical rules tied to particular types of events. The first is that when subjects were asked to justify their statistically correct answers, they often simply appealed to abstract statistical principles. Indeed, Piaget and Inhelder (1951/1975) found that subjects as young as ten could supply generalized statistical justifications for particular inferences about the behavior of randomizing devices. Second, the cues that were shown to increase the likelihood of statistical reasoning are just the ones that would be expected to do so if subjects were using domain-independent statistical rules. These included manipulations of the salience of the central tendencies of distributions versus the dispersion of distributions, and manipulations of the apparent role of chance in producing the events in question. It is less ad hoc to say that people have generalized rules about uncertainty and apply them whenever they can code the uncertainty of the events in question than it is to say that subjects' rules for each empirical domain examined include rules that merely mimic the operation of statistical rules.

But we believe we have more solid evidence that people actually possess statistical rules in a highly abstract form and can apply them to ordinary events. This is the fact that the teaching of statistical rules in an abstract way, as it is normally done in statistics courses, for example, has an effect on the way people reason about problems in everyday life. Research by Fong, Krantz, and Nisbett (1986) shows that the teaching of statistics affects the way people think about every-day problems far removed from the content of the typical statistics course. This work indicates that (a) purely abstract forms of statistical training affect reasoning about concrete events, and (b) even when statistical rules are learned in particular content domains they may be abstracted from those domains to a very great degree, sufficient to allow their application to quite different domains.

9.1.1 The Effects of Statistics Courses

In a series of studies Fong and colleagues (1986) examined four groups of subjects differing widely in statistical training. The subjects were college students who either had or had not had statistical training in an elementary course, graduate students who had had one or more semesters of training, and Ph.D.-level scientists who had had several years of training. Subjects were presented with one of a pair of problems about meal quality in restaurants. In each a protagonist experienced a truly outstanding meal on the first visit to a restaurant but was disappointed on repeat visits. The subjects were asked to explain, in writing, why this might have happened. The explanation was classified as "statistical" if it suggested that meal quality on any single visit might not be a reliable indicator of the restaurant's overall quality (for example, "Very few restaurants have only excellent meals; odds are she was just lucky the first time"). Nonstatistical answers assumed that the initial good experience was a reliable indicator that the restaurant was truly outstanding, and attributed the later disappointment to a definite cause, such as a permanent or temporary change in the restaurant (for example, "Maybe the chef quit") or a change in the protagonist's expectation or mood. Explanations that were statistical were coded as to whether they merely referred vaguely to chance factors or whether they also articulated the notion that a single visit may be regarded as a small sample and hence as unreliable. Explanations thus were coded as falling into one of three categories: (1) nonstatistical, (2) poor statistical, and (3) good statistical. The frequencies in each of these categories were used to define two dependent variables: *frequency* of statistical answers, defined as the proportion of responses in categories 2 and 3, and *quality* of statistical answers, defined as the proportion of category 2 and 3 answers that were category 3.

It should be noted that the presence of nonstatistical statements in an answer did not by itself cause the answer to be coded as nonstatistical. On the contrary, answers were coded as statistical if there was any statistical statement at all. In order to be coded as a good statistical answer, however, the statistical portion had to contain a lucid conceptualization of the sample notion *and* express a preference for that over any nonstatistical answers that were offered. The consequence of this coding scheme is that the frequency measure is free of normative commitments: it simply expresses the proportion of subjects who made a statistical observation. The quality measure, on the other hand, reflects the investigators' views about the correct approach to the question.

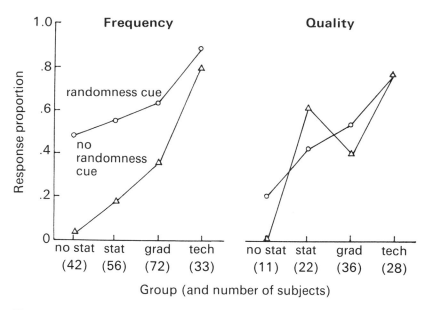

Figure 9.1
Frequency and quality of statistical answers to restaurant problem as a function of presence versus absence of probabilistic cue and level of statistical training (no stat = college students with no statistics; stat = college students with one or more statistics courses; grad = graduate students in psychology, most of whom had had two or more courses in statistics and methodology; tech = technical staff at a research laboratory). From Fong, Krantz, and Nisbett (1986).

The two versions of the restaurant problem differed. A probabilistic-cue version included a random mechanism for selection from the menu: the protagonist did not know how to read a Japanese menu and selected a meal by blindly dropping a pencil on the menu and observing where the point lay. The other version had no such cue. Within each group tested, half the subjects received the cue and half did not.

The effects of training on both dependent measures were dramatic, as may be seen in figure 9.1. College students without statistical training almost never gave an answer that was at all statistical unless the problem contained the probabilistic cue, in which case about half the answers were statistical. In contrast, more than 80 percent of the answers of Ph.D.-level scientists were statistical, whether or not there was a cue about randomness. The quality of the statistical answers also depended on the level of training. Only 10 percent of the statistical answers by untrained college students were rated as good, whereas almost 80 percent of the statistical answers by Ph.D.-level scientists were rated as good.

Although the presence of the randomness cue was very important in determining whether less-trained subjects would give statistical answers, it did not affect the quality of the statistical answers for subjects at any level of training. Apparently cues about randomness can trigger the use of statistical rules, but they do not necessarily produce good statistical answers. Such cues can only trigger rules at whatever level of sophistication the subject happens to possess.

Statistical training also influences inductive reasoning outside the classroom and laboratory. Fong and colleagues conducted a telephone "survey of opinions about sports". The subjects were males who were enrolled in an introductory statistics course and who admitted to being at least somewhat knowledgeable about sports. Some subjects were randomly selected and "surveyed" during the first two weeks of the term they were enrolled in statistics, the others at or near the end of the term. In addition to filler questions on NCAA rules and NBA salaries, subjects were asked questions for which a statistical approach was relevant, as in the example below.

In general, the major league baseball player who wins Rookie of the Year does not perform as well in his second year. This is clear in major league baseball in the past ten years. In the American League, 8 rookies of the year have done worse in their second year; only 2 have done better. In the National League, the rookie of the year has done worse the second year 9 times out of 10. Why do you suppose the rookie of the year tends not to do as well his second year?

Most subjects answered this question in a purely nonstatistical way, invoking causal notions such as "too much press attention" and "slacking off". Some subjects answered the question statistically ("There are bound to be some rookies who have an exceptional season; it may not be due to any great talent advantage that one guy has over some of the others—he just got a particularly good year"). The statistics course markedly increased the percentage of statistical answers and also increased the quality of statistical answers to this question and to two of four others that were asked.

9.1.2 Abstract Rule Training and Concrete Example Training

It could be argued that statistics courses do not constitute fully abstract rule training, inasmuch as students are taught how to apply the rules to specific, concrete problems. To the degree that that is done, students may emerge not with fully abstract rules that can be applied across essentially the full range of problems for which a statistical approach is relevant, but with empirical rules for many domains that have a statistical flavor. In our view this is implausible, because most statistics courses with which we are familiar spend very little time teaching the use of the rules on content domains beyond IQ tests, agricultural plots, gambling devices, and so on.

But it is simple to rule out the possibility that subjects are learning merely domain-specific rules. This was done by Fong, Krantz, and Nisbett (1986), who taught subjects about the law of large numbers in brief, fully abstract training sessions. The subjects were given one or both of two training packages. One covered formal aspects of the law of large numbers, and the other presented examples showing how to use the law of large numbers as a heuristic device in modeling problems. The abstract rule training consisted of definitions of population and sample distributions, a statement of the law of large numbers, and urn-problem illustrations showing that a population distribution is estimated more accurately, on the average, from larger samples. The examples training consisted of three problems (in the general style of the restaurant problem and similar to the subsequent test problems), each followed by a written solution that used the law of large numbers and emphasized the analogy between amount of evidence and size of sample.

There were four major conditions: a control group given no instruction, and three experimental groups—one given abstract rule training only, one given examples training only, and one given both types of training. The subjects were adults and high school students. The test consisted of fifteen problems. Five of these had clear probabilistic cues in the form of a randomizing device, five dealt with objective attributes such as abilities or achievements, and five dealt with subjective judgments, such as are involved in the restaurant problem or the "college choice" problem described in chapter 8.

Training effects were marked for all three problem types, for both the frequency of statistical answers and the quality of statistical answers. Both abstract rule training and examples training produced very substantial effects. It may be seen in figure 9.2 that abstract training and examples training were about equally effective, and the combination of the two was substantially more effective than either alone.

A particularly important finding for present concerns is that examples training showed no domain-specificity effects. In the study just described, examples training was provided on objective-attribute problems only, yet these problems showed no more improvement due

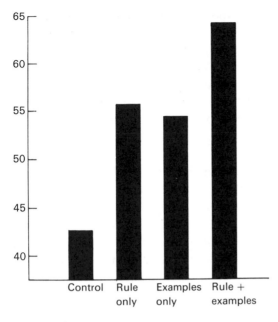

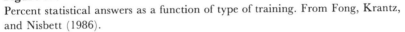

Figure 9.2
Percent statistical answers as a function of type of training. From Fong, Krantz,
and Nisbett (1986).

to training than did either probabilistic-cue problems or subjective-
judgment problems. More important, in a companion study the investigators manipulated the type of problem on which training
took place. Type of problem on which subjects were trained had no
effect on performance. Subjects trained on subjective problems,
for example, did no better on subjective problems than did subjects
trained on either probabilistic or objective problems, and subjects
trained on probabilistic-cue problems did no better on probabilistic-
cue problems than did subjects trained on objective or subjective
problems. These findings suggest that learning based on specific problem types is abstracted to a degree sufficient for use on widely different problem types.

The evidence thus indicates that statistical solutions to problems
can be made more likely and their quality improved by purely
abstract training as well as by training in how to model example
problems in terms of the rules. In addition, training in a given domain generalizes to a very great degree. We interpret these results
as indicating that people already possess some statistical rules in an
abstract form. Purely abstract manipulations of the rules help people
to solve problems because they already have substantial experience

in solving problems by means of more primitive versions of them. Improvements in the rules thus can be "passed along" without further training in interpreting events in terms of the rules. Similarly, training in the use of the rules in a given domain produces improvements in a wide variety of other domains because people already possess rudimentary abstract versions of the rules and can readily generalize from the solutions applied to particular problems to improved versions of the rules in their abstract form.

9.1.3. Higher Education and Inductive Inferential Rules

One implication of the work of Fong and his colleagues is that different types of higher education ought to differ substantially in the degree to which they increase people's ability to reason using particular types of inductive rules. At one extreme are the social sciences, notably psychology, where the graduate curriculum contains a very heavy dose of formal inductive rules, in the form of statistics and methodology courses. At another extreme are various "hard science" fields such as chemistry and electrical engineering, which have little need to emphasize inferential rules for dealing with uncertainty, and nonscientific fields, such as law and the humanities.

A field such as medicine forms an interesting contrast. While training in medicine does not emphasize purely formal inductive rule training in the same way that social science training does, the pragmatic content of medicine is inherently probabilistic. It deals with uncertain events, and thus training in it might be expected to convey some appreciation of inductive rules.

Lehman, Lempert, and Nisbett (1986) examined the effects of graduate training in various fields on the use of inductive rules—both statistical rules of the kind examined in chapter 8 and in the studies just reported, and methodological rules such as rules for appropriate control groups and rules for recognizing various artifacts in correlational studies. Subjects were tested over two very broad content domains. Some of the problems involved inductive reasoning about scientific studies (both natural science studies and social science studies) and some concerned everyday life. An example of a "methodological" problem with everyday-life content is one that asked whether the police chief of Indianapolis should be fired on the basis of the increased crime rate observed during his tenure. A correct answer required recognizing that a decision should await comparison with appropriate "controls", for example, crime rates in other Midwestern cities during the same time period. The subjects were graduate students in psychology, chemistry, law, and medicine at the University of

Michigan. They were tested either at the beginning of their first year of study or at the beginning of their third.

The effects of the various types of graduate education were markedly different. The most dramatic effect was for the influence of psychology training. It had a strong effect on reasoning about material both with scientific content and with everyday-life content. Medical training had a weaker but still significant effect on both. Neither chemistry nor law training produced any improvement in reasoning about either type of problem.

The results of the Lehman, Lempert, and Nisbett study indicate that formal education can have an effect on the way people reason about uncertain events in everyday life. The results suggest that to do so, however, a discipline must either teach about inductive rules in a formal way or illustrate their use in the context of reasoning pragmatically about everyday-life content.

9.1.4 Domain Specificity and Encoding

The studies just discussed help to demonstrate that people have abstract statistical rules that can be applied to a wide range of events, but they do not help us to understand the extreme domain specificity of statistical rules discussed in chapter 8. Indeed, the studies tend to deepen the mystery of domain specificity. The studies by Fong and colleagues showed no domain specificity of training results, and those by Lehman and colleagues suggest that training in the fields both of psychology and of medicine transfers to a very wide range of everyday events.

Fong and Nisbett (1986) reasoned that no domain specificity was found in their initial training studies because the domains employed were extremely broad and diverse, encompassing essentially all problems referring to events that could be described as "objectively codable abilities and achievements", "subjective judgments about the properties of a social object", and so on. They conjectured that if subjects were shown how to model problems in narrower content domains there might be some domain specificity of training effects, at least if the training effects were examined after a delay, when subjects would no longer have the training problems fresh in their memories for purposes of analogizing and generalizing their solutions to the target domain.

In order to examine this possibility, Fong and Nisbett (1986) gave subjects example problems either in the domain of sports or in the domain of mental ability testing, showing them how to solve the problems using the law of large numbers. They then tested subjects in

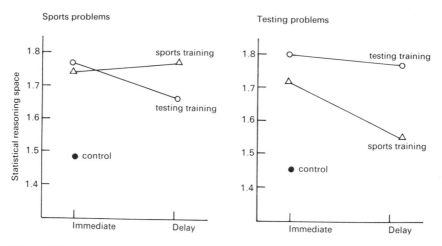

Figure 9.3
Statistical reasoning as a function of domain of testing, domain of training, and immediate versus delayed testing. From Fong and Nisbett (1986).

both domains. But for some subjects testing took place immediately after the training, while for others testing took place two weeks later. It was anticipated that showing subjects how to encode the events and relationships in a given domain in terms of the law of large numbers would confer a lasting ability to do so. When subjects were tested immediately on some other domain, they should be able to make substantial use of the training because they should be able to see the analogy between how to code events in the training domain and how to code events in the other domain. When subjects were tested after a substantial delay, however, they could not be expected to have sufficient memory of the training problems to be able to reason from them by analogy to the new domain. Thus there should be a significant reduction in the generalization of training to the new domain after a delay.

These anticipations were largely borne out, as may be seen in figure 9.3. For both sports problems and ability testing problems, there was no domain specificity of training effects immediately. Training on sports problems produced just as much improvement on ability problems as did training on ability problems, and vice versa. After a delay, however, matters were quite different. There was very substantial domain specificity, such that subjects trained on a different domain from that on which they were tested performed at a lower level than subjects trained on the same domain as that on which they were tested. Remarkably, there was no loss of training effects for subjects who were tested on the same domain on which they were trained. We have no ready explanation for the fact that there was no forgetting at all for this group, but it clearly suggests that encoding training can be extremely effective. Once subjects are taught in a brief training session how to think about the events in a given domain in terms of the law of large numbers, they may fully retain that ability, at least when the context is also reinstated, for a very substantial period of time.

The main results seem quite clear. They establish that there is no logical incompatibility between the extreme domain specificity of statistical reasoning reported in chapter 8 and the extreme lack of domain specificity of training effects. People are able to fully generalize the lessons of training to new domains so long as those lessons are fresh in memory. Once the lessons are no longer fresh, people cannot be expected to retain them in very great strength except in the domains in which they were taught.

We must add one more, broader caveat to the generally quite optimistic set of results we have been discussing. The law of large numbers is actually a very large and diverse set of rules, some of them nonintuitive or even counterintuitive, and it is applicable not merely to the kinds of relatively simple problems in the studies we have just reviewed, but to far more difficult prblems as well. In addition, there are many other fundamental statistical principles that have relevance to everyday events, some of which are also complex or counterintuitive. Thus the literature shows that even people who are highly trained in statistics are sometimes no more likely than laypeople to apply particular statistical rules to particular problems (Kahneman, Slovic, and Tversky 1982; Kunda and Nisbett 1986; Tversky and Kahneman 1971, 1983). Just which rules are most natural for people, which are most easily taught, and what are the best teaching techniques, are intriguing questions for the future.

9.2 Teaching Logical Rules

Do rules of deductive logic have the same properties as statistical rules? That is, do people possess logical rules in the same abstract form that they possess statistical rules, and are logical rules readily accessible for making inferences about everyday problems? In short, how do ordinary people reason about problems that the logician can solve by applying formal syntactic rules? One answer, since Aristotle, has been that ordinary people themselves use formal syntactic rules. According to both philosophers and psychologists (including Piaget and his followers) who are sympathetic to the syntactic view, these deductive rules are either known *a priori* or induced by everyone in the course of normal development because of their manifest utility in problem solving.

We will review evidence for an alternative view, based on the proposal that everyday reasoning typically relies on sets of inferential rules that constitute pragmatic reasoning schemas (Cheng and Holyoak 1985; Cheng, Holyoak, Nisbett, and Oliver 1986). First, however, we will critically examine earlier proposals.

9.2.1 Problems with the Syntactic View

It has always been known, of course, that people make errors when attempting to reason logically, but this fact usually has not been regarded as fatal to the syntactic view. Errors are often presumed to reflect vagaries in the interpretation of the material from which one reasons, including changes such as the addition or omission of premises (Henle 1962). For example, it has been pointed out that different conversational contexts invite different pragmatic assumptions (Fillenbaum 1975, 1976; Geis and Zwicky 1971). The sentence "If you mow the lawn, I'll give you five dollars," for instance, clearly invites the inference "If you don't mow the lawn, I won't give you five dollars." Such an inference, although fallacious according to formal logic (it is functionally equivalent to the fallacy of Denying the Antecedent), is actually pragmatically valid within its context.

There is abundant evidence for such invited pragmatic inferences, but interpretive mistakes of that kind cannot account for typical patterns of errors produced by college students in a variety of deductive reasoning problems employing *arbitrary* symbols and relations. (See Evans 1982 for a review.) The best known of these problems is Wason's (1966) selection task. In this task subjects are informed that they will be shown cards that have numbers on one side and letters on the other, and are given a rule such as "If a card has an *A* on one side, then it has a 4 on the other." Subjects are then presented with four cards, which might show an *A*, a *B*, a 4, and a 7, and are asked to indicate all and only those cards that must be turned over to determine whether or not the rule holds. The correct answer in this example is to turn over the cards showing *A* and 7. More generally, the rule used in such problems is a conditional, "if p then q", and the relevant cases are p (because if p is the case it must be established that q is also the case) and *not-q* (because if it is not the case that q then it must be established that it is also not the case that p). When college students are presented with such problems in an abstract form, it is usually found that fewer than ten percent of them can produce the correct answer.

Each of the four alternatives in the selection task corresponds to the minor premise in one of the four possible inference patterns (two valid and two invalid) for the conditional. Selection of p corresponds to the minor premise in the valid rule of *modus ponens*:

If p then q

p
_____

Therefore, q.

Selection of *not-q* corresponds to the valid rule *modus tollens*:

If p then q

not-q
_____

Therefore, *not-p*.

Selection of *not-p* corresponds to the fallacy of Denying the Antecedent:

If p then q

not-p
_____

Therefore, *not-q*.

Selection of q corresponds to the fallacy of Affirming the Consequent:

If p then q

q
_____

Therefore, p.

From a logical perspective it might seem that subjects in these experiments mistakenly interpret the rule as a biconditional (that is, p *if and only if* q), which requires that all four cards be turned over. In fact, however, this error is rare. Instead, most subjects select patterns that are irreconcilable with any logical interpretation, choosing, for example, A and 4 (that is, p and q). One of the errors in such an answer is omission of the card showing 7, indicating a failure to see the equivalence of a conditional statement and its contrapositive (that is, "If a card does not have a 4 on one side, then it does not have an A on the other"). Other errors include the fallacies of Affirming the Consequent (which corresponds to insistence on examining 4, which is unnecessary because the rule does not specify anything about the obverse of cards with a 4 on one side) and Denying the Antecedent (which corresponds to insistence on examining B, which also is unnecessary because the rule does not specify anything about cards that do not have an A on one side). Such errors suggest that typical college students do commit fallacies due to errors in the deductive process itself, at least with abstract materials.

9.2.2 Abstract Rules versus Specific Knowledge

Other research, however, has shown that subjects can solve problems that are formally identical to the selection task if they are presented in "realistic", "thematic" contexts. Johnson-Laird, Legrenzi, and Legrenzi (1972), for example, took advantage of a now-defunct British postal rule requiring that sealed envelopes have more postage than unsealed envelopes. They asked their subjects to pretend that they were postal workers sorting letters and had to determine whether rules such as "If a letter is sealed, then it has a 5*d*. stamp on it" were violated. The problem was cast in the frame of a standard Wason selection task. The percentage of correct responses for this version was 81, whereas only 15 percent of the responses given by the same subjects to the "card" version were correct.

In contrast, younger subjects in more recent studies, unfamiliar with the old postal rule, turn out to perform no better on the envelope version of the task than they do on the card version (Griggs and Cox 1982; Golding 1981). This pattern of results has suggested to some that the source of facilitation in the experiment by Johnson-Laird and colleagues was prior experience with a rule, particularly prior experience with counterexamples. It has been argued that subjects familiar with the postal rule do well because the falsifying instance— a sealed but understamped letter—would be available immediately through the subjects' prior experience. Several theorists have generalized this interpretation, suggesting that people typically do not reason using the rules of formal logic at all, but instead rely on memory of specific experiences or content-specific empirical rules (D'Andrade 1982; Griggs and Cox 1982; Manktelow and Evans 1979; Reich and Ruth 1982). This is a position of extreme domain specificity, which holds that subjects do not possess general and abstract inferential rules at all, but instead possess only rules covering specific, concrete content domains and an ability to check for counterexamples in those domains to ensure that the rule obtains.

The syntactic view has not been abandoned by all theorists, however (Braine 1978; Braine, Reiser, and Rumain 1984; Rips 1983). Braine (1978), for example, has proposed that there is a *natural* logic, different in its content from standard logic, but computationally complete and "mappable" onto a valid logical rule system. Natural logic is different from standard logic in that the connectives capture essential syntactic and semantic properties of the corresponding English words. Particular rules present in most standard logics—for example, *modus tollens*—are simply not represented in natural logic.

Work by Braine and his colleagues (1984) shows that people who have not been tutored in logic can indeed solve purely arbitrary problems with great accuracy. For example, subjects can solve problems of the following form:

If there's a D or a J, then there's not a Q

There is a D

Is there a Q?

According to Braine and his colleagues, subjects solve this problem by means of sequential application of their inference schemas P7 and P3 (out of a total of 16 schemas):

P7   IF p_1 OR ... p_n THEN q

p_i
_____

q

P3 p;
        False that p
        _____
        INCOMPATIBLE

The fact that people are quite accurate in solving problems like those presented by Braine, Reiser, and Rumain poses problems for positions at the empirical extreme. Subjects cannot be plausibly held to have empirical rules, or memories for counterexamples, for problems involving Ds and Qs.

A quite different approach, which can be viewed as an attempt to merge the extreme positions represented by specific knowledge and abstract syntactic rules, has been taken by Johnson-Laird (1982, 1983). He has proposed that people possess a set of procedures for modeling the relations in deductive reasoning problems so as to reach conclusions about possible states of affairs given the current model of relations among elements. In Johnson-Laird's theory, mental models are constructed using both general linguistic strategies for interpreting logical terms such as quantifiers, and specific knowledge retrieved from memory. The modeling procedures themselves are general and domain-independent.

9.2.3 Pragmatic Reasoning Schemas

The approach advocated by Cheng and her colleagues is based on a type of knowledge structure qualitatively different from those postulated by other theories of logical reasoning. This approach assumes that people often reason using neither formal syntactic rules nor memories of specific experiences, but rather pragmatic reasoning schemas, which are knowledge structures at an intermediate level of abstraction. Pragmatic reasoning schemas are highly abstract rule systems, inasmuch as they potentially apply to a wide range of content domains. Unlike syntactic rules, however, they are constrained by particular inferential goals and event relationships of certain broad types. Although pragmatic reasoning schemas are related to Johnson-Laird's (1983) concepts of mental models, some important differences are evident. For example, whereas Johnson-Laird focuses on limitations in working-memory capacity as an explanation of reasoning errors, the schema approach explains errors (as defined by the dictates of formal logic) in terms of the ease of mapping concrete situations into pragmatic schemas, as well as the degree to which the evoked schemas generate inferences that in fact conform to standard logic.

Cheng and Holyoak (1985) obtained several empirical findings that speak strongly for the existence of reasoning schemas. In one experiment using the selection paradigm, they compared the effect of direct experience to the effect of simply adding a rationale to rules that might otherwise seem arbitrary. Groups of subjects in Hong Kong and in Michigan were presented with both the envelope problem described earlier and another problem having to do with rule following. In the latter problem passengers at an airport were required to show a form, and it was necessary to check whether the rule "If the form says 'ENTERING' on one side, then the other side includes cholera among the list of diseases" was violated by each of four different cases corresponding to p, q, not-p, and not-q.

There was no reason to expect subjects in either location to have experience with the cholera rule. But because a version of the envelope rule had been in effect in Hong Kong until shortly before the experiment, subjects in Hong Kong were expected to have relevant specific experience to draw on. In addition, half the subjects in each location received brief rationales for the two rules. The stated rationale for the postal rule was that a sealed envelope defined first-class mail, for which the post office wished to receive more revenue; the rationale for the cholera rule was that the form listed diseases for which the passenger had been inoculated, and that a cholera inoculation was required to protect the entering passengers from the disease. It was anticipated that in both cases the rationale would trigger a "permission schema", or set of rules having to do with circumstances under which action Y is required if action X is to be permitted (for example, higher postage must be paid if a letter is to be mailed first class).

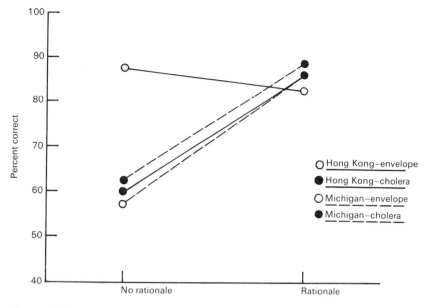

Figure 9.4

Percentage of subjects who solved the selection task correctly in each condition as a function of provision of a rationale. From Cheng and Holyoak (1985).

The results of the experiment are depicted in figure 9.4. As expected, in the absence of a stated rationale only the Hong Kong subjects given the envelope problem performed particularly well. All groups, however, performed very well when an appropriate rationale was provided. For subjects lacking experience with a rule, the solution rate went from about 60 percent without the rationale to about 90 percent with the rationale.

This benefit conveyed by provision of a rationale is inexplicable according to either the domain-specificity view or the syntactic view. Except for the Hong Kong subjects given the envelope problem, subjects had no experience with the specific content in question and hence no memory for counterexamples to the rule. Thus improvement due to the rationale cannot be attributed to processes advocated by proponents of the domain-specificity view. On the other hand, improvement cannot be plausibly attributed to manipulation of the formal properties of the problems either, since the added rationale did not affect the logical structure of the problems.

These results are understandable, however, in terms of pragmatic reasoning schemas. The rules attached to such schemas are not abstract syntactic rules, but general rules or heuristics for solving problems of rather broad types. The schemas summarize habitually encountered relations among events of various kinds and rules for solving problems involving pragmatically important types of relations. Examples of pragmatic reasoning schemas include schemas for various types of regulations, such as "permissions", of which both the postal rule and the cholera rule are instances. Provision of a rationale for an otherwise arbitrary rule facilitated subjects' performance by supplying a cue that elicited a relevant reasoning schema for evaluating permissions.

The permission schema is particularly useful in performing the selection task because the rules that comprise it map well onto the rules of the logical conditional. The core of the permission schema is a rule of the form "If one is to do X" (for instance, buy liquor), "then one must satisfy precondition Y" (be over 21), together with an implicit or explicit justification for the regulation. Since satisfying precondition Y generally does not dictate doing X, the biconditional assumption is ruled out in this context. Moreover, the concept of permission stresses that one will not be allowed to do X if one violates precondition Y. Consequently, the contrapositive, "If one does not satisfy precondition Y, then one cannot do X," seems to be part of the permission schema, rather than derived by some indirect means such as the general logical rule of contraposition that states the equivalence of "If *p* then *q*" and "If *not-q* then *not-p*". Since an analysis of a problem in terms of a permission schema should dictate the same choices as would the conditional in formal logic, invocation of such a schema should especially facilitate performance on problems of the selection type.

In contrast, an arbitrary rule, being unrelated to typical life experiences, does not evoke any reasoning schemas. Subjects confronted with such a rule would therefore have to draw upon their knowledge of abstract reasoning principles to arrive at a correct solution. Only a small percentage of college students apparently knows the logical conditional well enough to use *modus tollens*. Instead, some might draw on some nonlogical strategy such as "matching" (that is, selecting the terms mentioned in the rule regardless of whether or not they are negated), as observed by Reich and Ruth (1982) and Manktelow and Evans (1979), among others.

Cheng and Holyoak (1985) obtained further evidence for the facilitative effect of a permission schema by presenting subjects with a selection problem based on an abstract description of a permission situation: "If one is to take action A, then one must first satisfy precondition P." Subjects were also given the arbitrary card problem. About 60 percent of the subjects solved the abstract permission problem correctly when it was presented first, versus only about 20 percent who correctly solved the card version of the selection problem when it was presented first. The fact that a purely abstract description of a permission situation produces facilitation supports the schema hypothesis over the hypothesis that domain-specific knowledge is necessary to obtain high levels of performance.

9.2.4 *Purely Formal versus Pragmatically Based Training*

A series of training studies by Cheng, Holyoak, Nisbett, and Oliver (1986) provides additional evidence differentiating the syntactic and pragmatic views. If people do not naturally reason using purely formal operations that are analogous to those of standard logic, and hence do not know how to map the terms in the abstract rules onto concrete cases, then it should be difficult or impossible to teach them effectively by purely abstract means. That is, it should be difficult to teach the rules in such a way that they actually are used in problems other than those that are presented during logic training. (It has long been known, of course, that teaching logic results in learning logic defined as manipulating the exact sorts of symbols presented in logic classes.) If, on the other hand, people typically do reason using purely abstract logical rules, then direct training in manipulating such rules according to standard logic might improve people's ability to reason in accord with logical requirements, just as purely abstract instruction in statistical rules has been shown to have substantial effects on people's ability to reason in accord with statistical principles (Fong, Krantz, and Nisbett 1986).

Cheng and her colleagues argued that the pattern of results for training in the logic of the conditional would not be comparable to that found by Fong, Krantz, and Nisbett for training in the law of large numbers, because the full logic of the conditional has no counterpart in natural reasoning processes. They predicted instead that abstract training in logic would by itself have little or no impact on people's ability to reason about the Wason selection task, whether the task was presented in arbitrary form or in a form intended to evoke pragmatic reasoning schemas. They anticipated, however, that training in abstract logic would facilitate performance if it were coupled with training on how to model selection problems in terms that would facilitate the application of the conditional. Learning an abstract rule of logic and learning how to apply it to a particular type of problem may be separate requisites for correctly solving a reasoning problem by means of formal logic. If so, and if people typically do not naturally possess either requisite, then effective training for most people will require training both on the rule itself and on techniques for applying it. Only a small minority, who either are able to induce the relevant abstract rule from specific instances of it or are especially adept in applying newly learned rules, would benefit from training on either component alone.

Abstract Rule Training and Concrete Example Training
The first experiment by Cheng and colleagues was designed to assess the influence of a permission schema on performance in the selection task, as well as the usefulness of various training procedures based on abstract logic and/or examples of selection problems. Subjects who received abstract training read a seven-page booklet consisting of an exposition of conditional statements, followed by an inference exercise. The exposition consisted of an explanation of the equivalence between a conditional statement and its contrapositive, as well as an explanation of the two common fallacies of Affirming the Consequent and Denying the Antecedent. The contrapositive was explained in part by the use of a truth table, in part by Venn diagrams that used concentric circles to show the relations between a conditional statement and its contrapositive, and in part by an illustrative conditional statement, which expressed a realistic causal relation. Similarly, the fallacies were explained in part by diagrams and in part by alternative possible causes related to the illustrative statement.

Subjects who received examples training were requested to attempt to solve two selection problems. Neither problem bore any obvious surface similarities to the later test problems. Feedback was given about the subjects' success, and they were shown how to set up and solve the problem in terms dictated by the logic of the conditional. The correct answer for each example was explained in terms specific to the particular problem. Rule-plus-examples training consisted of the materials for the abstract condition followed by those for the examples condition. The only further addition was that for these subjects the explanation of the correct answer for each example was couched in terms of the abstract rules they had just learned.

The subjects were given a test that presented two types of problems involving a conditional rule—problems expressing an arbitrary relation and problems expressing a permission situation. (Other types of problems were also included, but these will not be discussed here.) Each problem took the form of a brief scenario, within which were embedded a conditional rule, a question asking the subject to determine the correctness of the rule, and a list of the four possible cases (p, *not-p*, q, and *not-q*) from which the subject was to select.

Two measures of performance were analyzed for each task—whether the subject made the correct selection (*p* and *not-q*) and whether the subject made any of the four possible kinds of errors. The four kinds of errors in the selection task were failing to select *p*, failing to select *not-q*, selecting *q*, and selecting *not-p*. These errors correspond respectively to errors on *modus ponens*, *modus tollens*, Affirming the Consequent, and Denying the Antecedent.

As expected, performance was much more accurate for the permission problems than for the arbitrary problems (66 percent versus 19 percent correct). Permission problems produced fewer errors of all four types than did arbitrary problems. It is particularly noteworthy that the permission problems yielded more accurate performance even for the choice of *p*, which corresponds to *modus ponens*, perhaps the most plausible of all the syntactic inference rules that Braine (1978) posited as components of natural logic.

A comparison of the two permission problems provided a test of the domain-specificity hypothesis, which claims that only rules with which subjects have prior familiarity will yield good performance. One of the two rules was a "drinking age" rule ("If a customer is drinking an alcoholic beverage, then he or she must be over 21"), which was presumably quite familiar to the college subjects. The other rule was a version of the "cholera rule", which was presumably less familiar. Although the percentage of subjects making a correct selection was marginally higher for the more familiar rule (71 percent versus 61 percent), even the relatively unfamiliar rule produced a much lower error rate than did either arbitrary problem. Thus subjects were able to reason in accord with standard logic even for a relatively unfamiliar rule if it evoked a permission schema. These results indicate that while specific experiences may play a role in reasoning, they cannot possibly provide a full account of reasoning performance.

The impact of the various training conditions, collapsed over type of selection problem, is indicated by the data in table 9.1. Abstract training coupled with examples training significantly decreased the frequencies of three types of errors—failure to select *p*, failure to select *not-q*, and erroneous selection of *q*. The frequency of correct selections increased from 25 percent for the control condition to 61 percent for the group given abstract training plus examples. Neither abstract training nor examples training alone decreased error frequencies significantly. This pattern suggests that knowledge of abstract rules of logic and the ability to apply them are two separate skills and that college students typically have not yet acquired either of them.

Table 9.1
Performance as a function of training condition (after Cheng, Holyoak, Nisbett, and Oliver 1986)

Training condition	Percent correct	Percent errors of each type			
		p	*not-q*	*q*	*not-p*
Abstract plus examples	61	5	27	28	8
Abstract only	35	14	48	33	7
Examples only	38	10	45	37	12
Control	25	18	51	44	14

Because the confidence intervals for pairwise differences between means were quite wide, however, the null hypothesis that neither abstract training nor examples training alone yielded any benefit cannot be accepted with confidence on the basis of this experiment alone.

The Effects of a Logic Course
The results of the above experiment indicated that training in standard logic, when coupled with training on examples of selection problems, leads to improved performance on subsequent selection problems. In contrast, logic training without such examples failed to significantly improve performance. An obvious possibility is that the experimental "microcourse" on the logic of the conditional was simply too minimal to convey much benefit. To assess this possibility, Cheng and colleagues (1986) performed a second experiment that examined the impact of a much broader and more prolonged abstract training condition, namely a one-semester undergraduate course in standard logic.

Two introductory logic courses, one at the Ann Arbor campus of the University of Michigan and one at the branch campus at Dearborn, provided subjects. Both courses covered topics in propositional logic, including *modus ponens, modus tollens*, Affirming the Consequent, and Denying the Antecedent, and the distinction between the conditional and the biconditional. In both courses the treatment of the valid and invalid inference patterns was primarily formal. While meaningful conditional sentences were introduced in lectures to illustrate the inference rules and fallacies, the emphasis was on formal logical analyses (truth-table analyses and construction of proofs). Neither course provided any exposure to the selection task or other psychological research on deductive reasoning.

A pretest was given in the first week of class before any discussion of the conditional had taken place; a post-test was given in the final week of the semester. To generate matched test materials, the selection problems used in the previous experiment were divided into two matched sets.

The results provided little comfort for the notion that formal instruction in logic is sufficient to improve reasoning performance as measured by the selection task. No significant improvement was obtained in the percentage of problems solved correctly; the mean improvement was a bare 3 percent. Indeed, the only apparent influence of a one-semester logic course was a small (10 percent) decrease in the tendency to make the error corresponding to Affirming the Consequent (that is, selecting the q alternative).

Training Based on a Pragmatic Schema

The ineffectiveness of abstract instruction in formal logic supports our contention that formal syntactic rules are not the vehicle for everyday reasoning. If this role is in fact played by pragmatic reasoning schemas, it should be possible to develop an effective training method that focuses on the elaboration of preexisting schemas. To test this possibility, Cheng and colleagues (1986) performed a further experiment in which one group of college students was given training about *obligations*. Obligations are a type of regulation closely related to permissions. As the instructions pointed out, "Obligations can often be stated in an 'If ... then' form. For example, the following regulation specifies an obligation: 'If a student is a psychology major, then the student must take an introductory psychology course.' More generally, if we call the initial situation I and the action C, an obligation has the form 'If I arises, then C must be done.'"

The obligation instructions went on to describe four rules related to the fulfillment of obligations. The rule for checking p, for example, was explained to subjects as follows: "If I occurs, then it is obligatory to do C. Clearly, if I arises, then failure to take the required action would constitute a violation of the obligation. To use our example, if a student is a psychology major, then that student must take an introductory psychology course." The four rules discussed were directly related to the rules governing the formal conditional: rule 1 is analogous to *modus ponens*, rule 2 rejects Denying the Antecedent, rule 3 rejects Affirming the Consequent, and rule 4 is analogous to *modus tollens*. The instructions were of a highly procedural nature, focusing on the conditions under which an obligation may or may not be violated. Except for the use of the single example about the psycho-

Table 9.2
Percent correct as a function of problem type and training condition (after Cheng, Holyoak, Nisbett, and Oliver 1986).

	Training condition			
Problem type	Control	Contingency	Obligation	$\bar{X}$
Arbitrary	27	45	55	42
Obligation	64	66	92	74
$\bar{X}$	46	55	73	

logy major, obligations were described only in abstract terms. No examples of selection problems were provided (unlike the "examples" conditions of the training study described earlier).

Other subjects were given training on the same checking procedures that obligation schema subjects were. They were shown how to reason about "contingencies" using precisely the same example about psychology majors. The training never made mention, however, of the notion of situations in which obligation arises, or indeed of any semantic interpretation at all.

Subjects who received instruction, as well as control subjects, were given a series of selection problems. Some of the problems contained conditional rules that could readily be interpreted as obligations, whereas others were relatively arbitrary.

The results are presented in table 9.2. It may be seen that, as usual, untrained control subjects solved more schema-interpretable problems than arbitrary problems. Even though both training packages presented the same formal checking procedures, the schema-based obligation training was more effective than the syntactic contingency training. Indeed, the nonsignificant trend was for the obligation training to be more effective even for the arbitrary problems. It is important to note that the syntactic contingency training had no effect at all on subjects' solutions to the semantically meaningful problems. This bolsters our view that pragmatic reasoning schemas are dominant wherever a semantic interpretation can be applied. Even when subjects have just been shown the exact checking procedures to be applied, they do not use them for the semantically meaningful problems. In our view, this is because a semantic interpretation will always lead to a search for reasoning schemas rather than for syntactic rules.

It should be noted that the obligation instruction used in this experiment forms an important contrast to the teaching of new empirical rules for physics and social psychology discussed in chapter 7.

Whereas instruction in the latter case competes with rules the student already possesses, instruction in pragmatic reasoning schemas builds upon and supports prior knowledge. In our view, instruction in purely syntactic rule systems lies between the two extremes in that it neither competes with nor builds upon preexisting knowledge. On the other hand, because it is an alien type of rule system for understanding actual events in the world, it also will not add to the individual's effective repertoire of pragmatic rules.

9.3 Induction, Deduction, and Default Hierarchies

The results just reviewed provide support for the view that people typically reason using knowledge structures at a level intermediate between the extreme localism implied by the domain-specificity view and the ultra-generality implied by the formal view. Subjects reasoned in closer accord with standard logic when thinking about problems intended to evoke regulation schemas (permissions and obligations) than when thinking about purely arbitrary elements and relations. These results on problem types are incompatible with the domain-specificity view because experience with the precise rules referred to in the regulation problems was not necessary for successful performance. The results are incompatible with the formal view because all problem types were stated in syntactically equivalent forms. The results from the training studies are also incompatible with the formal view. An entire course in standard logic had no effect on the avoidance of error (save for a slight reduction in the fallacy of Affirming the Consequent). A brief training session, of a type shown to produce substantial effects on people's ability to reason in accord with the law of large numbers (Fong, Krantz, and Nisbett 1985), had no significant effect on subjects' ability to use *modus ponens* or *modus tollens* or to avoid the error of Affirming the Consequent or Denying the Antecedent. This was not simply because the training was inherently useless: when it was combined with examples training, subjects were able to make substantial use of the abstract training.

The near-total ineffectiveness of purely abstract training in logic contrasts starkly with the ready ease with which people seem able to apply a naturally acquired pragmatic reasoning schema. For example, after one semester's training in standard logic, students solved only 11 percent of the arbitrary problems correctly, whereas the same students solved 62 percent of the permission problems correctly before receiving any formal training. The generality of the benefit apparently conveyed by evocation of a permission schema is also striking.

The permission problems yielded significantly fewer errors of all types, including not only the common error of failing to select *not-q* (equivalent to *modus tollens*) but also the much less frequent error of failing to select *p* (equivalent to *modus ponens*).

In contrast to the benefit conveyed by the evocation of a permission schema, a course in logic produced no significant reduction in either of these errors. The failure to reduce the frequency of errors for *modus ponens* cannot be attributed to a floor effect, since evocation of the permission schema did reduce the frequency of errors for the *p* alternative. This failure of abstract training to facilitate the use of *modus ponens* suggests that even this rule may not be a general rule of logic for at least a substantial fraction of subjects. Evidence that *modus ponens* can be overridden by a matching strategy (Manktelow and Evans 1979; Reich and Ruth 1982) also supports this hypothesis. If *modus ponens* is not a robust rule of natural logic, as our results suggest, it is difficult to imagine any formal deductive rule that is universally held and widely used for the solution of problems with meaningful content.

The primacy of pragmatic reasoning schemas received further support from the final training study performed by Cheng and colleagues (1986), which demonstrated that brief instruction about the pragmatics of obligations greatly improved performance both on selection problems involving clear obligations and on problems involving relatively arbitrary rules. Instructional methods based on appropriate preexisting pragmatic knowledge appear to be far more effective than those based directly on syntactic rules.

9.3.1 A Default Hierarchy of Deductive Rules

The results we have reviewed speak strongly for the existence of pragmatic schemas at an intermediate level of abstraction, since the findings are inexplicable according to either the domain-specificity view or the formal view. Nonetheless, the findings need not be interpreted as evidence against the very possibility of the two extreme modes of reasoning. It is conceivable that these three modes coexist within a population and even within an individual. In fact, the results are consistent with this interpretation.

First, as in other reasoning studies, most of the subjects' inferences were in accordance with *modus ponens*, whereas very few were in accordance with *modus tollens*. Although *modus ponens* may not be universal, the results do not exclude the possibility that many people may in fact reason with this formal rule—or even that all people may use it under particularly favorable circumstances. The same individuals who use *ponens* as a formal rule may use a rule corresponding to *tollens* only within the context of certain intermediate-level schemas.

Second, familiarity with a rule may in itself sometimes facilitate performance, as suggested by the marginal difference in selection performance between the two permission problems used in the first experiment by Cheng and colleagues (1986). The presumably more familiar drinking-age rule yielded slightly better performance than did the cholera-inoculation rule. Familiarity may facilitate indirectly by evoking an appropriate schema more reliably, or it may do so more directly by providing relevant specific knowledge, as hypothesized by proponents of the domain-specificity view.

If multiple levels of concepts relevant to reasoning coexist, within a population as well as within an individual, how are the levels related to each other and what determines the level of abstraction attained? Our pragmatic approach to induction suggests a possible answer. As we have emphasized throughout, the process of induction from experience across many different domains results in a default hierarchy of rules. Rules are used to make predictions about regularities in environmental inputs to the cognitive system. Successive levels in the default hierarchy are related in that the more abstract level comprises a set of default categories and rules, relative to which the more specific level comprises a set of exception categories and rules. The default rules are generally predictive and are consequently followed in most circumstances, except when they are overridden by more specific exception rules.

Basic inductive processes, such as generalization and specialization, are applied to environmental inputs to produce a default hierarchy that has predictive utility in achieving the learner's problem-directed goals. If induction proceeds in a bottom-up, experience-driven manner, then successively more abstract concepts and associated rule schemas will be formed by generalization on the basis of constancies observed in inputs. Increasingly abstract default levels will emerge as long as concepts capturing significant regularities with predictive utility can be formed.

Let us consider how induction might proceed in the domains relevant to conditional logic. At the most specific level, experience with particular contingencies between events (such as the relationship between touching a stove and feeling pain, or between a request for assistance and help from a parent) will accrue to the learner. The concepts and rules induced in the process of dealing with specific contingency situations will be of the kind assumed by the domain-specificity hypothesis. At this point the person will be able to reason effectively in familar situations and in those highly similar to them, but not elsewhere.

As experience with a range of contingency situations accrues, people will, through the operation of generalization mechanisms, induce a more abstract set of default concepts and rules. Many important subtypes of contingency situations will emerge, involving such concepts as causation, regulation, and set inclusion. This is the level at which pragmatic reasoning schemas emerge. Each schema will consist of a cluster of rules for dealing with a particular type of contingency situation. Because the concepts at this level are quite abstract, rules for dealing with situation types as general as "deterministic causation", for example, will be applicable to novel situations with little superficial resemblance to those from which the concepts were originally induced.

Kelley's (1972, 1973) *causal schemas*, it should be noted, are excellent examples of the kind of constructs we wish to include under the rubric of pragmatic reasoning schemas. Kelley proposed that people have very general rules for dealing with causality that are attached to particular kinds of causal relationships. People have, for example, a schema for reasoning about relationships that they take to involve a single determining cause, that is, those in which only a single cause can produce the effect and if present it invariably does so. They also have a schema for reasoning about multiple-cause, probabilistic relationships, namely, those in which many factors can produce the effect but the presence of any one of the factors does not entail certainty that the effect will occur. These causal schemas exist at a purely abstract level, independent of any content domain.

Eventually, constancies across various types of reasoning schemas may, through the same inductive mechanisms, produce yet more abstract concepts and rules at the level of a natural formal logic. The results we have reviewed suggest that this level of abstraction in conditional reasoning is seldom attained; and at any rate, rules at that level are probably only rarely applied to semantically meaningful material.

9.3.2 *Why Formal Deductive Rules Are Difficult to Induce*

In view of our negative conclusion regarding the prevalence of a natural logic based on syntactic rules, an obvious question arises: Why are such rules so difficult to induce? Or at least, why are they seldom used for reasoning about real events? Logicians through the centuries have assumed the existence, and the everyday use, of a natural repertoire of purely abstract logical rules, as have psychologists such as

Piaget. We contend that although Piaget was right in believing that people develop and heavily use a schema corresponding to the inductive rule system embodied in the law of large numbers, he was wrong in believing that they make much use of formal operations of deductive logic.

The reason for the difficulty in inducing rules for deductive logic appears to be that too few reliable, useful constancies in deductive rules hold at such abstract levels. In particular, the material conditional— the abstract formal conditional taught in elementary logic courses —has limited pragmatic value. The various pragmatic reasoning schemas differ from each other in many important ways. For example, in a causal statement of the form "If ⟨cause⟩, then ⟨effect⟩," the cause temporally precedes the effect. In the corresponding form of a permission statement, "If ⟨action⟩, then ⟨permission required⟩," the action typically *follows* the necessary permission. The individuating aspects of pragmatic reasoning schemas are far more important to successful problem solving than their commonalities. In order for the conditional to be employed in assessing causal claims, for example, extensive interpretation of problems in terms of causal direction, number of possible causes, certainty of effects given causes, and so on, is required. For most lay purposes the formal conditional therefore may not be an economical default rule.

Of the various syntactic rules associated with the formal conditional, virtually none have general utility. The formally valid contrapositive transformation cannot by itself solve many pragmatic problems that are expressible in its terms, because substantial interpretation concerning causality and other matters is required before it can be applied. Moreover, the "fallacies" of Denying the Antecedent and Affirming the Consequent often lead to pragmatically useful inferences in many contexts (Fillenbaum 1975, 1976; Geis and Zwicky 1971). For example, abduction of a hypothesis A to explain B using the rule "If A then B" is formally equivalent to the deductive fallacy of Affirming the Consequent but can be an inductively important form of inference.

Not only is contraposition lacking in positive utility, in some important cases it actually fails. Lewis (1973) points out that contraposition fails for counterfactual conditionals, in which the antecedent is known to be false. For example, it may be true that if the power hadn't failed, dinner would have been on time; but it does not follow that if dinner had not been on time, then the power would have failed (Ginsberg 1985). Our ability to determine the truth of counterfactual conditionals depends on special knowledge about causality in the world, of the sort that pragmatic reasoning schemas can encapsulate. It thus seems that only *modus ponens* constitutes a plausibly pragmatic abstract rule of inference, although the results of Cheng and colleagues (1986) suggest that even *modus ponens* may not be available as a fully abstract rule for purposes of everyday reasoning. It may be that rather than inducing an isolated abstract rule, many people maintain a more specific rule analogous to *modus ponens* within each of a number of pragmatic reasoning schemas.

In contrast to people's apparent failure to induce some abstract deductive rules, we have seen evidence that they do induce some abstract *inductive* rules, such as simple versions of the law of large numbers. This difference has a ready explanation within the present framework. Unlike deductive rules such as *modus tollens*, the law of large numbers is an excellent default rule (or set of rules) that does not require extensive domain-specific interpretation in order to be made applicable. Given (codable) uncertainty, the rule system in its totality has potential relevance. Consequently, everyday learning conditions will be favorable to induction of the law of large numbers at the highest level of generality and abstraction.

We are led, then, to the surprising possibility that the mechanisms of induction may result in the induction of various abstract inductive rules, but not certain abstract deductive rules, for the good reason that many abstract inductive rules are more obviously useful than some of their deductive counterparts in formal logic.

9.4 Implications for Education

It is interesting to relate the present findings to the old debate at the turn of the century about faculty psychology. The defense offered for the classical education consisting of Latin, mathematics, and memorization was that pursuit of these disciplines caused the mental faculties to improve. They served, in effect, to exercise the muscles of the mind. The consequence was a smarter person, with better faculties, just as the consequence of physical exercise is a stronger person, with bigger muscles. This view was derided by early psychologists, who argued that there is little transfer of training across tasks unless they share a large proportion of identical elements.

One set of results that we have presented constitutes an important counterweight to the generally correct view of those early psychologists. Training in statistics has a demonstrable effect on the way people reason about a vast range of events in everyday life. Thus formal training of that particular type of rule system does indeed make people smarter in a pragmatic sense. (At least it does if one shares our view that statistical considerations are normally helpful.)

Another set of results we have presented constitutes a reaffirmation of the early psychologists' critique of faculty psychology. Teaching people formal logic does not seem to make them smarter in the sense of increasing the scope of problems to which they can apply the material conditional. Our interpretation of the results also gives a firmer foundation to the critique: Rule systems that are foreign to the rules governing everyday pragmatic reasoning cannot readily be made to influence such reasoning. There are plenty of justifications for teaching formal logic to special groups such as philosophy students and computer programmers, but we should not expect much of an impact on reasoning in everyday life.

Another aspect of the experimental results suggests an important respect in which education does improve logic in everyday life. This work gives support to the view that various pragmatic reasoning schemas can be taught, and that unlike the teaching of logic and some types of empirical rules, such instruction may amount to "swimming downstream" educationally. Teaching causal schemas and methodological principles, such as the need for control conditions and the need to accommodate the vagaries of correlational evidence, is the sort of thing that formal education probably does rather well.

Our analysis of these results also suggests several respects in which education could be improved. Perhaps the most fundamental suggestion is that one should have a clear idea about the nature of the rule system that one is teaching. Is it one that is "graceful" in the sense that it is likely to build upon, rather than be irrelevant to or even compete with, rule systems that the student already possesses? If the rule system is graceful in that sense, then probably one can expect improvements in it to be carried through to reasoning in everyday life. If the rule system is alien, as we believe most purely syntactic systems to be, then the justification for teaching the system has to be on grounds other than pragmatic reasoning improvements. In addition, there is probably little point in trying to dress up education in such rules in the clothing of everyday-life examples, as many teachers of logic try to do. Formal logic is probably just going to be a rule system that cannot be made to have much impact on pragmatic reasoning.

A second implication is that the effects of education in those rules that do have ready impact on everyday reasoning could probably be much enhanced by just the kind of dressing up that has little impact in logic courses. Statistics and methodology courses might be made to have substantially greater impact on everyday reasoning if teachers were to take the trouble to teach their students how to reason about various kinds of everyday domains using the rules. Although it has been shown that abstract training can be effective in itself, it has also been shown that its effectiveness can be enhanced by—indeed its effectiveness often may depend on—teaching students how to model particular events in terms of the rule system. Statistics and methodology courses have an important place in the liberal arts curriculum quite independent of any utility they have for scientific reasoning. The teachers of those courses ought to capitalize on the new-found justification for their role by thinking of inventive ways to extend the scope of the rules they teach.

Most of the new teaching techniques would make use of analogies between scientific problems and everyday problems, and show that a given rule holds for similar reasons in both cases. It is to the topic of analogy, and how it can best be employed in transferring knowledge from one domain to another, that we now turn.

Analogy

Of all the inductive mechanisms discussed in chapter 3, perhaps the most intriguing is analogy. In its more complex forms analogy is a device for integrating diverse knowledge sources to model a novel situation. This chapter will present a comprehensive account of the role of analogy in problem solving, placing it within our general framework. We will argue that analogy must be understood pragmatically rather than purely syntactically, and that both finding and using analogies depend on appropriate use of synchronic and diachronic rules.

In the case of problem solving, analogy is used to generate new rules applicable to a novel target problem by transferring knowledge from a source domain that is better understood. The usefulness of an analogy depends on the recognition and exploitation of some significant similarity between the target and the source. The key questions regarding analogy turn on how "significant similarity" can in fact be recognized. The impact of an analogy is often to make two concepts seem more similar than they did previously, by selectively highlighting abstract properties that they share.

Consider, for example, the analogy between an argument and a building, one of many systematic metaphors of English explored by Lakoff and Johnson (1980). A variety of metaphorical expressions flow from this analogy, such as, "The foundation of the argument was carefully laid," "The argument collapsed under its own weight," and "Her argument needs to be buttressed with facts." We readily understand such expressions because the underlying analogy allows rules relevant to the source domain ("If a building has a stable foundation, then it will withstand storms") to be transformed into rules relevant to the target domain ("If an argument has a firm logical basis, then it will withstand efforts to discredit it").

As Lakoff and Johnson point out, our conception of what an argument can be like is molded by other analogies besides that of building, such as a path and a combat analogy. These multiple source domains can contribute to a single expression ("His tortuous argument was finally demolished by a multipronged assault"). Note that in this example the various source analogs pick out different aspects of the argument being described: its course of development (a "tortuous" path), its status as a constructed object (a building to stand or fall), and its nature as a type of social interaction (combat, in the form of a "multipronged assault"). The various sources thus complement rather than contradict one another. As we will see in chapter 11, scientific theories too can be developed in part by the integration of multiple analogical sources.

It is not the case, of course, that speakers of English will need to perform elaborate analogical reasoning on every occasion that an argument is said to have been "demolished" in order to understand what the speaker means. Such once-metaphorical expressions have long since led to the development of a more abstract notion of what kinds of things can be "built", "embellished", "destroyed", and so on. Such action terms can now be readily applied to examples of abstract objects, such as arguments, ideas, hopes, and so on. In chapters 3 and 6 we discussed the role of analogy as a device for performing categorization in the absence of immediately applicable rules. As we will demonstrate in this chapter, a natural side effect of analogy use is the generation of more abstract categories, or schemas, that specify the abstract properties that are shared by the individual analogs.

Much more could be said about the relationship between analogy and literary uses of metaphor (Gentner 1982; Holyoak 1982; Miller 1979). In keeping with the theme dominant throughout this book, however, our discussion in this chapter will emphasize the role of analogy in problem solving. In terms of our framework, analogy is a top-down mechanism for constructing mental models. The basic theoretical concepts introduced in chapter 2, such as q-morphisms and default hierarchies, can be directly applied to develop a theoretical treatment of analogy.

Analogy differs from other generative mechanisms in that it is less directly focused on the current problem situation. To solve a problem by analogy, one must attend to information other than the problem at hand. This gives rise to two related puzzles. First, how can a relevant source analog be found efficiently? The target problem typically will be related in some way or another to an enormous range of knowledge, most of which will be entirely unhelpful in generating a solution. Second, once a relevant analog is identified, what determines which of the properties of the source will be used to develop a model of the target situation? Especially when the source and the target are highly dissimilar on a surface level (as are buildings and arguments, for example), only a small subset of knowledge about the source can be transferred to the target. We will address both of these questions as our discussion proceeds. Let us begin by analyzing the structure of analogy.

10.1 The Structure of Analogy

Analogies can be found between entities with differing degrees of initial similarity. For example, it is common for students learning such activities as geometry theorem proving and computer programming to use initial examples as analogical models for solving subsequent problems (Anderson, Greeno, Kline, and Neves 1981; Pirolli and Anderson 1985). In such cases at least the possibility of an analogy will be suggested by the high degree of overall similarity between the analogs, and usually also by their temporal and spatial contiguity. (Anecdotally, students seem much less likely to use an analogy if the analogs appear in separate chapters of their textbook.)

Of course, useful analogies can sometimes be found between concepts that are superficially very different. We will term such cases *interdomain* analogies. An interdomain analogy is based on the perception of abstract, systematic, and pragmatically important similarities embedded among the more obvious surface differences. As Hofstadter (1984) has observed, "deep" analogies can be found within a single domain as well as between domains. An analogy seems deep when it forces a reanalysis of the analogs, and generation of new and more general rules, rather than simply providing an occasion for applying rules already learned to a new example. A deep analogy requires the generation of new categories. Intradomain analogies can certainly have this character, as Hofstadter illustrates by the use of deceptively simple analogies between alphabetic sequences (see section 10.1.3). Novel interdomain analogies are especially likely to seem deep because the analogs lack any surface similarities, so that reanalysis is required to find any useful similarity at all. As we will see in chapter 11, interdomain analogies play an important role in the generation and initial justification of scientific hypotheses.

10.1.1 An Example: The Convergence Analogy
To make our discussion concrete, it will be useful to look closely at an example of an analogy between remote domains. Gick and Holyoak

Table 10.1   Possible initial model for radiation problem

Goal description:	Use rays to destroy tumor.
Object description:	Tumor is in patient's stomach.
	Doctor has rays.
	High-intensity rays can destroy both tumor and healthy tissue.
	Low-intensity rays can destroy neither tumor nor healthy tissue.
Operators:	Alter effects of rays.
	Decrease sensitivity of healthy tissue.
	Increase sensitivity of tumor.
Constraints:	Avoid damaging healthy tissue.
	Operation is not possible.

(1980, 1983) have investigated the use of such analogies in solving relatively ill-defined problems. The problem they studied most extensively was the "radiation problem" made famous by the Gestalt psychologist Karl Duncker (1945), which runs as follows: Suppose you are a doctor faced with a patient who has a malignant tumor in his stomach. It is impossible to operate on the patient, but unless the tumor is destroyed the patient will die. There is a kind of ray that at a sufficiently high intensity can destroy the tumor. Unfortunately, at this intensity the healthy tissue that the rays pass through on the way to the tumor will also be destroyed. At lower intensities the rays are harmless to healthy tissue but will not affect the tumor either. How can the rays be used to destroy the tumor without injuring the healthy tissue?

This problem is reasonably realistic, since it describes a situation similar to that which actually arises in radiation therapy. Table 10.1 sketches the kind of information that might be included in an initial model of the problem. Most of the problem components are reasonably well specified; the operators, however, are extremely vague. The problem solver might imagine the possibilities of altering the effects of the rays or altering the sensitivities of the healthy tissue and/or tumor. Not all of these might even be included in the initial representation, as no particular element in the hypothetical model is strictly necessary. In any case, none of these operators immediately specify realizable actions. As a result, the problem is seriously ill defined.

The problem model must therefore be transformed in some way. Analogy provides a mechanism for augmenting a problem model with new rules derived from a source analog. In terms of the kind of processing system described in chapter 2, there are no diachronic rules immediately available to construct a path from the initial problem state to a goal-satisfying state. Precisely because few strong rules will be available for dealing directly with an ill-defined problem, weaker synchronic rules that activate associations to the target may have an opportunity to direct processing.

Analogical Problem Solving
In the case of the radiation problem, an analogy might be used to generate rules that suggest more specific operators. This possibility was tested in the initial experiment performed by Gick and Holyoak (1980). The experimenters attempted to demonstrate that variations in the solution to an available source analog can lead subjects to generate qualitatively different solutions to the target. In order to provide subjects with a potential source analog, the experimenters first had them read a story about the predicament of a general who wished to capture a fortress located in the center of a country. Many roads radiated outward from the fortress, but these were mined so that although small groups could pass over them safely, any large group would detonate the mines. Yet the general needed to get his entire large army to the fortress in order to launch a successful attack. The general's situation was thus substantially parallel to that of the doctor in the radiation problem.

Several versions of the story were presented, describing various solutions to the military problem. For example, in one version the general discovered an unguarded road to the fortress and sent his entire army along it; in another version the general divided his men into small groups and dispatched them simultaneously down multiple roads to converge on the fortress. All subjects were then asked to suggest solutions to the radiation problem, using the military story to help them. Those who read the former version were especially likely to suggest sending the rays down an "open passage" such as the esophagus, so as to reach the tumor while avoiding contact with healthy tissue. Some subjects developed a more detailed version of this solution in which a "ray-proof tube" would first be inserted to ensure avoidance of contact (since the esophagus is of course not straight). As this example illustrates, the solution suggested by a source analog may need to be adapted and specialized to take account of important disanalogous aspects of the target, a point to which we will return.

Subjects who received the story about the general who divided his

army were especially likely to suggest a "convergence" solution—
directing multiple weak rays at the tumor from different directions.
Across many comparable experiments Gick and Holyoak found that
about 75 percent of tested college students generated the convergence
solution after receiving the corresponding military story and a hint to
apply it. In contrast, only about 10 percent of the students generated
this solution in the absence of a source analog, even though most subjects agreed that the solution is an effective one once it was described
to them. The mapping between source and target was occasionally
revealed in the protocols of subjects who spoke as they worked on the
problem: "Like in the first problem, the impenetrable fortress, the
guy had put bombs all around, and the bombs could be compared to
the healthy tissue. And so they had to, they couldn't go in en masse
through one road, they had to split up so as not to damage the healthy
tissue. Because if there's only a little bit of ray it doesn't damage the
tissue, but it's all focused on the same spot" (Gick and Holyoak 1980,
p. 327).

An important point to note is that subjects' ability to notice an
interdomain analogy can fall far short of their ability to make use of it
once it is pointed out. In the absence of a hint to apply it, only about
30 percent of the subjects in this experiment generated the convergence solution to the radiation problem immediately after having
read the "multiple approach routes" story. We will have more to say
later about factors influencing the spontaneous use of analogies.

Analogical Mapping and Schema Induction
Analogical problem solving involves four basic steps. These are
(1) constructing mental representations of the source and the target;
(2) selecting the source as a potentially relevant analog to the target;
(3) mapping the components of the source and the target (that is,
identifying components that play corresponding roles in the two situations); and (4) extending the mapping to generate rules that can be
applied to the target in order to achieve a solution. These steps need
not be carried out in a strictly serial order, and they will interact in
many ways. For example, a partial mapping with the target is typically required before one can select an appropriate source. Also,
because mapping can be conducted in a hierarchical manner, the
process may be iterated at various levels of abstraction. Nonetheless,
these four steps impose a useful conceptual organization on the overall
process.

The correspondences between the convergence version of the military story and the radiation problem are shown in table 10.2. Even

Table 10.2   Correspondences among two convergence problems
and their schema (after Gick and Holyoak 1983)

Military Problem

Initial state
Goal: Use army to capture fortress.
Resources: Sufficiently large army.
Operators: Divide army, move army, attack with army.
Constraints: Unable to send entire army along one road safely.

Solution plan: Send small groups along multiple roads
                simultaneously.

Outcome: Fortress captured by army.

Radiation problem

Initial state
Goal: Use rays to destroy tumor.
Resources: Sufficiently powerful rays.
Operators: Reduce ray intensity, move ray source, administer
                rays.
Constraints: Unable to administer high-intensity rays from one
                direction safely.

Solution plan: Administer low-intensity rays from multiple direc-
                tions simultaneously.

Outcome: Tumor destroyed by rays.

Convergence schema

Initial state
Goal: Use force to overcome a central target.
Resources: Sufficiently great force.
Operators: Reduce force intensity, move source of force, apply
                force.
Constraints: Unable to apply full force along one path safely.

Solution plan: Apply weak forces along multiple paths
                simultaneously.

Outcome: Central target overcome by force.

though the particular objects involved (army and rays, fortress and tumor, and so on) are very different, the relations that make the convergence solution possible are present in both. The goals, resources (and other objects), operators, and constraints can be mapped from one problem to the other. Because the military story provides clear operators ("divide the army", for instance), subjects are able to use the mapping to construct corresponding operators ("reduce ray intensity") that can be used to solve the ray problem.

The abstract structure common to the two problems can be viewed as a schema for convergence problems—a representation of the *type* of problem for which convergence solutions are possible. The convergence schema implicit in the two analogs is sketched at the bottom of table 10.2. The schema represents an abstract category of which the specific analogs are instances.

In fact, the implicit schema may become explicit in the course of using the analogy. Indeed, schema induction can be viewed as a fifth step in analogical transfer (in addition to the four listed above). The basic mechanism for such schema induction is to identify those elements of each model that (a) played roles in achieving the solution (that is, matched the conditions of rules that effected the transition from the initial problematic state to the final goal-satisfying state) and (b) were successfully mapped across the individual analogs. A generalization can then be formed using an intersection mechanism (Winston 1980). This type of induction may often be an important by-product of performing an analogical mapping. Because the information in a problem schema can be represented by a set of interrelated synchronic and diachronic rules, such schemas, like other categories, will correspond to clusters of rules.

Gick and Holyoak (1983), in their study of the use of analogies in solving the radiation problem, found evidence that schema induction is a major contributor to successful transfer across remote problem domains. These investigators had some groups of subjects first read two convergence stories: the military story described earlier and a firefighting story in which converging sources of fire retardant were used to extinguish a large blaze. Other groups read a single convergence story plus a disanalogous story. All subjects summarized each story and also wrote descriptions of how the two stories were similar. The latter task was intended to trigger a mapping between the two stories, which would have the incidental effect of leading to the induction of an explicit representation of the shared schematic structure. All subjects then attempted to solve the ray problem, both before and after a hint to consider the stories.

Gick and Holyoak found that subjects in the two-analog groups were significantly more likely to produce the convergence solution, both before and after the hint, than were subjects in the one-analog groups. Furthermore, more detailed analyses revealed that the more closely a subject's description of story similarities approximated a statement of the solution principle, the more likely it was that the subject would transfer the solution to the medical problem. Thus a subject who said that both stories illustrated the use of "many small forces applied together to add up to one large force necessary to destroy the object" was almost certain to give the convergence solution to the ray problem, without requiring any kind of hint. In contrast, one who said that "in both stories a hero was rewarded for his efforts" was unlikely to do so. Gick and Holyoak interpreted these and other more detailed results as indicating that induction of an explicit schema facilitates transfer.

As Gick and Holyoak (1983) argued, there are good theoretical reasons to expect an abstract problem schema to yield greater inter-domain transfer than would a single concrete source analog. The schema renders explicit the identities common to the source analog and the target, while effectively deleting their differences. An explicit problem schema will have attached rules for classifying novel instances, so that subsequent examples of the problem type can be categorized and solved by means of prestored general rules, rather than depending for a solution on execution of the less direct analogy mechanism.

It is important to realize that the schema in table 10.2 is not the only possible representation of the properties shared by convergence analogs. As is the case for categories in general, the set of rules that comprise a schema can vary across individuals and will depend on the overall default hierarchy in which the schema is embedded. As we have suggested, the initial use of an analogy defines a proto-category that will continue to evolve as new examples are assimilated to it, triggering further inductive changes. The evolution of a schema, like the initial noticing of a potential analogy, is intimately related to mechanisms that lead one situation to spontaneously remind the system of another situation or category of situations, even though the new situation is not strictly a member of the preexisting category (Schank 1982).

We have informally encountered numerous spontaneous remindings in response to the military and medical examples of convergence problems. For example, a sociologist was reminded of a patriarchal society in which anyone in the family who challenged the authority of the patriarch would incur his wrath. If family members wished to alter one of the patriarch's decisions, this could sometimes be achieved by having several people make the same mild suggestion to him, which might change his mind without arousing his ire (if a large force cannot be safely applied, try multiple converging weak forces). Note that this analog does not preserve the spatial aspects of the previous examples (the convergence is more abstract, simply involving the shared wishes of the family members), and the desired effect (changing the patriarch's mind) is no longer physical.

In another instance of analogical reminding, a colleague trained in physics was reminded of (a) a plan for getting a weapon through an airport metal detector, by bringing it through in multiple small pieces that would not trigger the alarm, and then reassembling the pieces on the other side; and (b) keeping two subcritical masses of fissionable material apart to safely transport an atomic bomb, and then bringing them together to trigger the explosion. Both of these examples include some schematic elements (for example, components that are innocuous in small separate pieces but powerful when combined); other elements, such as the goal of overcoming a centrally located target, are not preserved. In the metal detector analog the goal is to preserve the components of the weapon of attack from discovery, a generalized version of a component of the goal in the military problem (getting the soldiers safely to the fortress). As such additional analogs are considered, the convergence schema will presumably develop into a tangled default hierarchy of related variations of convergence situations. We believe that this is a typical pattern of development for abstract concepts rooted in analogies.

10.1.2 Problem Analogies as Second-Order Morphisms

What does it mean to develop an analogy between two situations? Given our focus on problem solving, we will begin by examining the more specific question of what it means to model one problem by analogy to another. Analogy involves "second-order" modeling—a model of the target problem is constructed by "modeling the model" after that used in the source problem. As schematized in figure 10.1, the model of the source problem is used as a model of the target problem, generating a new model that can be applied to the novel situation. (Compare figure 10.1 with figure 2.5.) In figure 10.1 the source model, with its associated categorization function P_A and transition function T_A', provides a morphism for some aspects of the world (labeled "World A"). A model of the aspects of the world involved in the target problem ("World B") is constructed by means of the ana-

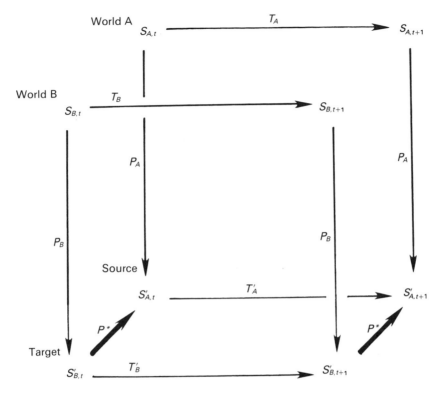

Figure 10.1
Analogy as a morphism between two mental models.

logical mapping P^* (indicated by dark arrows) from the target to the source. As indicated in figure 10.1, in an ideal case the resulting target model, with categorization function P_B and transition function T_B', will be isomorphic to the source model. That is, goals, objects, and constraints will be mapped in a one-to-one fashion so that corresponding operators preserve the transition function of the source (that is, the function T_B' in the target model mimics the function T_A' in the source).

Note that even in the ideal case not all elements of the source situation need be mapped. The most critical elements are those that were causally relevant to the achieved solution (that is, those that matched the condition of a diachronic rule involved in the solution sequence). In any problem model the components are directly relevant to the solution plan: the goal is a *reason* for it; the resources *enable* it; the constraints *prevent* alternative plans; and the outcome is the *result* of executing the solution plan. By defining analogy in terms of relationships between problem models, our framework provides a principled basis for delimiting the information transferred from source to target. (Hesse 1966 was the first to stress the central importance of causal elements in analogical transfer.)

In practice, however, the initial target model derived by analogy will be less than isomorphic to the source, and even an adequate target model typically will fall short of this ideal. Since the target problem will not be adequately modeled prior to the mapping process (otherwise the analogy would be superfluous), the initial mapping with the source will inevitably be partial. Initiation of the mapping process will depend on the problem solver having first identified *some* element of the target problem that is shared with the source model. In the case of interdomain analogies the similarities of the source and the target will primarily consist of abstract relations. Hence the initial mapping will necessarily involve detection of an abstract similarity between corresponding goals, constraints, object descriptions, or operators, which constitute the implicit schema common to the two analogs.

Elements of the implicit schema that are identified in the target can serve as retrieval cues to access relevant source analogs, as well as to initiate the mapping process once a source analog is available. We will have more to say about the retrieval of source analogs in section 10.2.1. Once the relevance of the source is considered and an initial partial mapping has been established, the analogical model of the target can be developed by extending the mapping. Since models are hierarchically structured and the mapping will usually be initiated at an abstract level, the extension process will typically proceed in a top-down fashion. That is, the goal of the source will be mapped with the goal of the target, constraints with constraints, and so on.

For example, a subject in one of Gick and Holyoak's experiments might first establish a mapping between the doctor's goal of using rays to destroy a tumor and the general's goal of using an army to capture a fortress, since both are instances of the implicit schema of using a force to overcome a target. The rays are now (tentatively) mapped onto the army; accordingly, the analogist will attempt to construct operators for acting on the rays that match those that act on the army in the source model. The procedure is to build new rules for the target domain by substituting mapped elements in the corresponding rules for the source domain. Since the large army could be divided into smaller groups, for example, it follows that the high-intensity rays could be divided into smaller parts as well. The mapping between the two domains in effect establishes new role-like categories of which mapped elements are members (the fortress and the tumor are categorized as a type of target, for example, and the army and the rays are categorized as a type of force). These emergent categories constitute the beginnings of a new higher-order problem schema of the sort described in the preceding section.

This process of model development will continue until an adequate target model is created or until a point is reached at which the analogy begins to "break down". What does it mean for an analogy to break down? Holyoak (1984) distinguishes between four types of mapping relations. *Identities* are those elements that are the same in both analogs (such as the generalized goal of using a force to overcome a target). The identities are equivalent to the implicit schema and play a direct role in the construction of rules for the target domain, as described above. *Indeterminate correspondences* are elements that the analogist has yet to map. These may eventually turn out to provide either useful extensions of the analogy or explanations of why an apparently analogous solution to the target problem failed when tested, but until they enter into the mapping process they simply will remain on the sideline, as it were.

The other two types of mappings involve known differences between the two analogs. For example, the mapped objects "rays" and "army" obviously will generate a host of differences when the concepts are analyzed. Differences do not necessarily impair the morphism, however; after all, the problems are only supposed to be analogous, not identical. *Structure-preserving differences* are differences that nevertheless allow construction of corresponding operators and hence maintain the transition function of the source model. For example, an army is visible whereas radiation is not; yet no operators necessary to achieving a solution are blocked simply because the rays are invisible. The property of visibility is irrelevant to the rules that comprise the new category of "army and ray forces". Consequently, this difference is structure preserving.

Other differences, however, will be *structure violating* because they prevent the construction of corresponding operators. For example, an army, unlike rays, consists of sentient beings. Accordingly, the general can simply tell his men to divide up, and the army can be expected to regroup appropriately without further intervention. Rays, of course, do not respond to such cavalier treatment. Although they can indeed be "divided", the requisite operator will be of a very different type. To accommodate this difference between the two analogs, subjects often introduce multiple "ray machines" (with no counterparts in the source analog) that can be modulated appropriately.

An analogy breaks down, then, roughly at the level of specificity at which differences prove to be predominantly of the structure-violating sort. Analogies vary in their *completeness*—their degree of approximation to an isomorphism in which all differences are structure preserving. The usefulness of an analogy, like the usefulness of any mental model, is determined by pragmatic factors. An imperfect analogy can be used to construct rules that provide a first approximation to a valid transition function for the target model. This approximate model will be useful if it can be refined by other inferential mechanisms.

The process of refining an approximate solution derived by analogy is conceptually the same as refining a q-morphism by the addition of new categories and diachronic rules, and can be viewed as an extension of the overall problem-solving task (Carbonell 1983). If a needed operator cannot be constructed by analogy, a different, viable operator with a comparable effect may be constructed by other means; if not, the analogy is a failure. In general, the relationship between a source model and a successful target model constructed from it will correspond to a q-morphism, as described in chapter 2. Analogical problem solving must be viewed as an integral part of the overall process of model construction. Inductive mechanisms can invoke the use of an analogous source model (if one is needed and available), and they can continue to improve an imperfect target model beyond the point at which the analogy itself "runs dry".

10.1.3 Syntactic and Pragmatic Factors in Analogical Transfer

An account of analogy in problem solving must address two related puzzles. First, how can a relevant source analog be found efficiently? Second, once a relevant analog is identified, what determines which of the properties of the source will be used to develop a model of the target problem? Given our overarching pragmatic framework, we naturally predict that the information transferred from a source to a target will be heavily influenced by the system's goals. The analogist will attempt to construct a set of diachronic rules for the target problem that embodies a transition function adequate to achieve the goal. Moreover, this fundamentally pragmatic principle is intimately related to syntactic aspects of analogical transfer, involved in finding a consistent mapping P^* between the source and the target.

Critique of the Purely Syntactic Approach
Our characterization of analogy thus differs sharply from approaches that attempt to predict the outcome of analogical transfer in terms of

purely formal analyses of the structures of the source and target analogs, without making reference to goals. Gentner (1983) is the most emphatic proponent of the syntactic approach. In her theory "the interpretation rules are characterized purely syntactically. That is, the processing mechanism that selects the initial candidate set of predicates to map attends only to the *structure* of the knowledge representations for the two analogs, and not to content" (p. 165). A critical examination of Gentner's analysis will illustrate some of the difficulties that beset purely syntactic accounts of inductive mechanisms, as discussed in chapter 1.

Gentner distinguishes between "attributes", which are one-place predicates, "first-order relations", which are multi-place predicates with objects as arguments, and "higher-order relations", which are multi-place predicates with propositions as arguments. The syntactic claim is that in using an analogy, people are most likely to map higher-order relations, next most likely to map first-order relations, and least likely to map attributes. For example, in the analogy between atomic structure and a solar system, the target and the source share the higher-order relation that "attraction depends on distance" and the first-order relation that "objects revolve around each other." However, attributes of the mapped objects, such as their absolute size, do not transfer. Gentner traces the preference for relations, especially higher-order relations, to what she terms a "systematicity" principle. This principle states that a highly interconnected predicate structure—one in which higher-order relations enforce connections among lower-order predicates—is most likely to be mapped.

In many ways Gentner's account appears quite similar to our own. Her concept of systematicity, for example, is closely related to our analysis of the syntactic constraints generated by an attempt to build a morphism connecting the source and the target. In the case of interdomain analogies such as that between atoms and solar systems, the primacy of relations in the mapping is virtually definitional. Furthermore, as Gentner acknowledges, the higher-order relations of interest typically are such predicates as "causes", "implies", and "depends on"—in other words, causal elements that are pragmatically important to goal attainment. Thus the pragmatic approach readily accounts for the phenomena cited as support for Gentner's theory, by defining systematicity in terms of morphisms linking models dominated by causal relations. In these terms, of course, systematicity is no longer a purely syntactic concept. Furthermore, it is defined in terms of relations *between* the source and the target, rather than in terms of relations within each, as in Gentner's theory.

It is by no means clear that the purely syntactic sense of systematicity advocated by Gentner effectively distinguishes relations that transfer from those that do not. For instance, in the analogy between solar systems and atoms, Gentner mentions "the sun is hotter than the planets" as an example of a relation that fails to transfer because it does not participate in an interconnected set of propositions. This claim is highly suspect. The relative heat of the sun and its planets is causally related to an indefinitely large number of other propositions, such as those describing why only the sun is a star, how the planets originated, the potential for life on the sun versus its planets, and so on. These interconnected propositions obviously have little or nothing to do with our understanding of the analogy with atomic structure, but the systematicity principle does not show why they are irrelevant.

Indeed, a basic problem with Gentner's analysis is that it seems to imply that the mappable propositions can be determined by a syntactic analysis of the source analog alone (since the relational status of propositions is defined independently of their participation in an analogy). It follows that the same information should be transferred in all analogies involving a given source. This is clearly false. As an example, let us take as our source analog the concept "elephant". Suppose we know a person of large girth with a penchant for stumbling over furniture. If one of us were to remark that "Sam is an elephant," the analogical basis of the metaphor would be quite clear. Now suppose that we tell you, "Induction is an elephant." You may be forgiven a moment of incomprehension, especially if you were misled into considering how induction might resemble our clumsy acquaintance Sam. You may grasp our meaning, however, if we remind you of the well-known story of the blind men who touched different parts of an elephant and then gave totally different descriptions of what the beast is like. Induction may be as much an elephant as Sam is, but only Sam has been insulted. Clearly, the basis of an analogy is intimately related not only to the source but also to the target and the context in which the analogy is used.

Finally, many analogies are more concrete than that between the solar system and the atom. Consider, for example, an analogy that four-year-old children can often use to help solve a problem. In a study by Holyoak, Junn, and Billman (1984), the target problem presented to the children required them to find a way to transfer a number of small balls from one bowl to another bowl that was out of reach. A variety of objects were available for possible use, including a rectangular sheet of paper. A source analog, presented prior to the target problem in the guise of an illustrated story, described how the television character Miss Piggy rolled up a carpet and used it as a tube to move her jewels from her jewel box to a safe. Many children were able to generate an analogous solution to the ball problem—rolling the paper to form a tube and then rolling the balls through the tube to the distant bowl.

In this simple analogy the successful mapping between the carpet and the piece of paper on the attribute of shape is important, because in each analog the shape enabled the critical "rolling" operator to be applied. In contrast, the relation of location failed to map: the paper was initially located on the table, whereas Miss Piggy's carpet was initially on the floor. This mapping failure, however, was irrelevant, because the initial location of the object to be rolled up was not causally related to the solution achieved in the source analog.

The syntactic approach might attempt to discount this example of attribute precedence in mapping by claiming that the story and the target problem used by the investigators were too similar to constitute a "real" analogy. The resulting restrictive definition of analogy would be quite arbitrary, however. The pragmatic approach admits of analogies that vary greatly in their degree of abstractness. Even objects that Gentner would term "literally similar"—those that share many attributes, in the sense of one-place predicates—can be analogically related if a goal is apparent. Because Gentner's theory is stated in terms of mappings between static propositions rather than in terms of rules, it misses the fundamental distinction between synchronic and diachronic relations, between the mapping and the transition function. An analogy, like any model, must bring with it rules for predicting state changes. Thus it is anomalous to say that "cats are analogous to dogs" (rather than "cats are *similar* to dogs"), because no clear predictive goal is apparent. In contrast, it is perfectly natural to consider whether cats and dogs are analogous *with respect to some specified predictive goal*, such as determining how it might be possible to get close to a cat given knowledge that dogs can be summoned by whistling (the misleading analogy that Jennifer explored in chapter 3).

A purely syntactic approach is unable to predict accurately the basis for analogical transfer, because it fails to take account of goals. Differing goals can lead to different mappings for what is putatively the "same" analogy (Holyoak 1984). The perceived structure of an analogy is heavily influenced by the pragmatic context of its use. The aspects of the source analog transferred to the target will be determined by a variety of factors, including knowledge of what aspects of the source are conventionally taken to be important or salient (Ortony 1979); the apparent goal in using the analogy—in other words, what aspects of the target need to be explained; the causal relations known to be central in the source (Winston 1980); and what aspects can in fact be mapped without generating structure-violating differences. These complex and interactive factors, which are obscured by purely syntactic analyses of analogy, can be investigated within a pragmatic framework.

Interactions between Pragmatic and Syntactic Constraints
The importance of contextual features and other pragmatic concerns is brought out particularly clearly in the Copycat project on analogy by Hofstadter and his colleagues (Hofstadter 1984; see also chapter 24 of Hofstadter 1985). A simple Copycat problem is *ABC* : *ABD* :: *PQRS* : *?*, to which a large number of answers are possible, among them *PQRD*, *PQST*, and *PQRT*, the last of which not only is most quickly generated by most people but also is preferred by most people when contrasted with other possibilities. Although in Copycat there is no direct source of environmental feedback that can validate this answer, it follows from an intuitive characterization of the problem, which runs roughly as follows. In the source domain, *ABC* has been changed into *ABD*. This change can be characterized in a more abstract way by the rule "Replace the *rightmost* letter in an *ascending sequence* by its alphabetic *successor.*" In the target domain, the initial state *PQRS* can also be characterized as an ascending sequence, which allows a natural mapping onto *ABC* (despite the fact that it is not one-to-one), so the rule can be reapplied, yielding *PQRT*.

Rather surprisingly, given the apparently arbitrary nature of this analogy problem, this simple characterization of its solution draws on pragmatic aspects of default hierarchies, categorization, and morphisms. First, the fact that it is natural to describe *ABC* as *changing* into *ABD* introduces a diachronic transition function into the analogy. As in figure 10.1, the mapping function *between* domains, *P**, is synchronic (both *ABC* and *PQRS* are characterized as "ascending sequences"); by contrast, the change *within* each domain is diachronic. In addition, note how compelling it is to characterize *C* and *S* as "rightmost letters of ascending sequences". Such categorizations derive from our background knowledge about linear orderings, which spans domains as diverse as rooms along a corridor, the days of the week, notes in a musical scale, and integer sequences. The categories that people will bring to bear in solving alphabetic analogies will be those that have emerged as useful general categories for dealing with linear structures in a myriad of experiences. We understand apparently unfamiliar situations so readily because they fit naturally into a preexisting default hierarchy of relevant synchronic and diachronic rules. And since these categories were built up in the service of past goals of the system, goals outside the immediate alphabetic analogy problem itself reenter the picture in a fundamental way.

Two further examples from the Copycat domain, both closely related to the previous one, serve to point out how the preferred characterization of elements in a particular situation depends not only on past experience but on relations among the elements. Consider first the following simple variant of the preceding analogy: *ABC* : *ABD* : : *PPQQRRSS* : *?*. Here, when the preceding rule ("Replace the rightmost letter by its successor") is mechanically applied, one gets *PPQQRRST*, which seems less than insightful. To generate a more elegant and deep solution, one must take notice of relations that have been ignored. In particular, the initial state in the target domain can be perceived as a series of *clusters* (where a cluster consists of multiple *tokens* of a single letter *type*): *PP-QQ-RR-SS*. A consistent mapping onto *ABC* can be made at that more abstract level. Specifically, when faced with this new situation, one perceives both *ABC* and *PPQQRRSS* as consisting of clusters, although in *ABC* they are degenerate clusters of length one. In both cases the letter types defining the clusters form ascending alphabetic sequences. With this shift in viewpoint the old formula can be applied again, but now to letter types rather than tokens. The rightmost letter type is *S*, and of course replacing it by *T* gives the esthetically satisfying answer *PPQQRRTT*. This example shows how the process of analogical mapping can force reperceptions of the entities and structures involved in an analogy, modifying the system's default hierarchy in the process.

As Hofstadter emphasizes, even in these alphabetic analogy problems having no apparent relevance beyond themselves, the analogical thought processes that take place are mediated by parallel interactions among categories that both compete with and complement each other. Analogies, like mental models in general, seldom achieve the pristine quality of isomorphisms. Rather, competing pressures create a problem of parallel constraint satisfaction, which must be resolved by violating relatively weak or isolated constraints, a process that Hofstadter calls "slippage". In this case the slippage was from letter tokens to letter types.

A subtler type of slippage that Hofstadter discusses is the process of activating a new category (or cluster of related categories) when a preliminary categorization has failed to bring about a satisfactory analogy, thus causing some kind of impasse. This is well illustrated by the Copycat problem *ABC* : *ABD* : : *XYZ* : *?*, another variant of the first example. Here, as with *PQRS*, one sees *XYZ* as an ascending sequence and is thus led to applying the default rule "Replace the rightmost letter in an ascending sequence by its successor". However, *Z* has no successor. This impasse should trigger some kind of slippage. One possible solution, disallowed in the Copycat domain, is to envision a circular alphabet in which the successor of *Z* is *A*. In that case there effectively is no impasse after all, and the default rule gives *XYA*. But if, following Hofstadter, one accepts the constraint that *Z* simply has no successor, then some kind of creative slippage will be necessary to find a satisfactory solution.

The critical clue is provided by the observation that *A* and *Z* are located at symmetric extremities of the alphabet, and moreover that the two structures in question, *ABC* and *XYZ*, are "wedged" against their respective ends of the alphabet, the *A* and the *Z* being each other's counterparts. This symmetric vision sets up pressure to bring in new categories linked to the old ones by symmetry. This is done by directed spreading activation carried out by synchronic rules representing associations among concepts. In particular, the relevance of such specific notions as "leftmost" and "predecessor" is suggested by the spreading of activation from "rightmost" and "successor", mediated by the activation of the more abstract notion of "symmetric-opposite". Thus, rather than acting on the rightmost letter to achieve a solution, one looks to the other end of the structure and finds *X*, which is now seen as the counterpart of *C* (at the far end of *its* structure from *A*). Moreover, the motion from *Z* toward *X* is leftward, and therefore *XYZ* is reperceived as a *descending* rather than an *ascending* sequence. The tight synchronic link between the concepts of "descending sequence" and "predecessor" further strengthens the estimated relevance of "predecessor". So the impasse has led us to a complete recasting of our vision of *XYZ*, according to which it now seems more natural to replace *X* by its predecessor *W* than by its successor *Y*. This yields *WYZ*, an esthetically pleasing answer.

Note that we have arrived at this answer by a *double* slippage of the default rule, in which "rightmost" is slipped into "leftmost" while at the same time "successor" is slipped into "predecessor". Simultaneous slippage seems necessary in this context, but there are other contexts in which the pressures would push for either one slippage or the other, but not both. An example is the analogy problem *ABC* : *ABD* : : *SRQP* : ?, in which it is acceptable either to replace the *leftmost* letter by its *successor*, yielding *TRQP*, or to replace the *rightmost* letter by its *predecessor*, yielding *SRQO*, but not to replace the leftmost letter by its predecessor, yielding *RRQP*. The many ways in which interacting pressures can activate synchronic rules to induce slippage according to context, and particularly the role of esthetics in such slippage, form the main area of study in the Copycat project.

10.2 Mechanisms of Analogical Transfer

In this section we will examine the mechanisms of analogical transfer in more detail. We suggested earlier that the process of using an analogy can be divided into four major steps—encoding of the target, selection of a source analog, mapping of the source and target, and transfer of knowledge to the target by generation of new rules. The first step, encoding, is in most respects not unique to analogy use. This is the general process of representing a problematic situation in terms of its basic components (forming descriptions of the initial state, the goal state, relevant operators, and path constraints). The encoding of the problem will be crucial in determining what potential source analogs (if any) are considered. Encoding the problem will initiate the basic categorization and search processes that the system uses in attempting to achieve its goals. The analogy mechanism is most likely to come into play when initial solution efforts based on available diachronic rules that describe the behavior of the target domain fail to generate an acceptable solution plan, resulting in an impasse. In such circumstances it may be necessary to attempt a less direct approach.

10.2.1 Selection of a Source Analog

Step 2, selection of a source analog, is the first step in the use of analogy per se. Empirical evidence indicates that candidate source analogs can be identified by two basic procedures, namely, *transformation* of the target problem and *retrieval* of a related situation stored in memory. Let us consider each of these procedures in turn.

Transforming the Target Problem
One way to select a source analog is to generate one by systematically transforming the target problem. A transformation is most likely to lead to the consideration of a source analog that is closely related to the target, differing from it in a constrained, specifiable way. For example, Polya (1957) suggested that a problem solver can approach a three-dimensional geometry problem by relating it to a corresponding two-dimensional problem. In this example the source can be generated by a systematic transformation of the target (reducing its dimensionality). The corresponding objects, for example a sphere and a circle, will otherwise be similar.

In many cases, including such geometrical examples, the source is *simpler* than the target, in the sense of having fewer elements. Most generally, a useful source will be one that (a) can itself be successfully modeled and (b) preserves the critical causal properties relevant to an adequate solution to the target problem. A simpler problem is quite likely to satisfy condition (a); it may well fail condition (b), however. The additional complexity of the target problem may demand a different type of solution, in which case the solution to a simpler problem may be unhelpful or even misleading. Many three-dimensional geometry problems, for example, have solutions quite different from those of their two-dimensional counterparts.

Research by Clement (1982b) provides clear illustrations of some of the types of problem transformations that can generate useful source analogs. Clement analyzed the protocols of two experienced problem solvers dealing with physics problems, and identified numerous cases of the spontaneous use of analogies. In his "spring coils" problem, subjects were asked to consider a spring with a weight hung on it; if the original spring were replaced with one made of the same kind of wire, with the same number of coils, but with coils twice as wide in diameter, would the spring now stretch more, less, or the same amount under the same weight, and why? (It will in fact stretch more.)

The protocols Clement obtained suggested that useful analogous variants of this problem were sometimes obtained by transforming the original problem through altering one of its properties. An important type of problem transformation was the generation of an *extreme case* by transforming a relevant quantitative dimension to its minimal or maximal value. For example, one subject imagined a very narrow spring, and decided that a spring with minimal material could not stretch very far. Extreme cases were typically created by varying a dimension, such as spring width, that was directly presented as relevant to the problem solution.

Both of Clement's subjects also varied qualitative features of the problem, which the statement had not suggested as variables. Both considered a problem variant in which the spring was reduced to a single coil (extreme case) and then unwound into a bending rod. The "bending rod" analogy may have been generated after rules involving "stretching"—the central relation in the representation of the target problem—activated the associated concept "bending", which could be applied to the extreme case of a single unwound coil. The concept "bending", which is conventionally a property of rods, was presumably attached to a richer set of diachronic rules than was "stretching".

The "bending rod" therefore proved to be a useful source analog for Clement's subjects. Further transformations were sometimes applied to generate a chain of source analogs that varied in their degree of similarity to the target. One subject went on to consider a coil as a square and then as a hexagon, in the process discovering the possibility that a torsion force (in addition to bending) might operate on the spring. The hexagon coil seemed to provide a kind of mediating bridge between a square coil and the original circular one, increasing the subject's confidence that the former situation indeed would preserve the relevant properties of the target.

Clement's protocols demonstrate that the problem transformations used to generate source analogs are highly systematic. The generation process is guided by relevant synchronic rules activated by concepts that are highly supported because of their centrality in the initial model of the target problem; for example, the concept "stretching" may have associations that activate "bending". As we will see below, associative rules play an even greater role in the case of source analogs that are retrieved from memory, rather than constructed by transformation. Inferential rules presumably guide the generation and analysis of extreme cases.

Retrieval of a Source Analog

Transformations of a target problem typically yield source analogs that are relatively similar to the target. In most circumstances this is desirable, since a solution plan appropriate to a source similar to the target is likely to succeed when transferred. In some cases, however, it will not prove possible to generate a useful source by a constrained transformation of the target. The alternative is to retrieve a known situation from memory to serve as a source. Often the retrieved source will be highly similar to the target. Social decisions afford many examples of the use of similar retrieved analogs. For example, a person considering how best to approach the boss for a raise is likely to be influenced by the manner in which the method of approach used by a friend apparently affected the boss's response to a comparable request. Such mundane analogies may scarcely be noticed as examples of analogy use.

The most interesting examples of retrieved source analogs are those in which a useful source is found in a domain that seems far removed from that of the target. Clement (1982b) observed several spontaneous references to interdomain analogies in the protocols discussed above. For example, one subject working on the spring problem made a deliberate effort to consider situations involving rubber bands, molecules, and polyesters. What the objects in this disparate collection seem to have in common are links to the key relation of "stretching", which is central to the goal of the target problem. The subject seemed to be searching memory for other, better-understood systems in which something like stretching occurs. This kind of focusing on critical relations as retrieval cues is central to the generation of interdomain analogies.

Interdomain analogies highlight the two key theoretical questions posed earlier. How are useful analogs retrieved from memory, and how are the relevant aspects of the source analog selected for mapping with the target? To answer these questions, we need to examine the mechanisms by which the cognitive system can find and use analogies.

10.2.2 Summation of Activation as a Retrieval Mechanism

Let us consider the four steps of analogy use—encoding of target, selection of a source analog, mapping, and rule transfer—in terms of the operations of cognitive systems described in chapters 2 through 4. When a target problem is established as the focus of processing, a rule-based search for a solution will ensue. Among the rules executed early in the problem-solving attempt will be synchronic rules (both associative and categorical) that send activation to concepts associated with those that are components of the representation of the target problem. In the case of Clement's "spring problem", for example, activation of the target concept "stretching" will in turn cause activation to pass to the associated concept "bending".

When rules that assign properties to concepts are executed, they will implicitly activate the concepts corresponding to the properties; these property concepts in turn will pass activation to other concepts associated with the properties. Thus the concept "spring" will tend to activate such property concepts as "thin", "flexible", "metallic", and "bendable", and hence tend to activate concepts with similar properties. Here the assumption that multiple sources of activation for a concept will sum together plays a critical role. A single shared property will likely yield only a small increment in activation for an associated concept; several shared properties, on the other hand, will tend to raise the activation level of an associate enough to allow it to begin to direct further processing. The PI program uses summation of activation to guide its search for stored source analogs relevant to solution of its current target problem.

The summation principle tends to ensure that source analogs that share multiple properties with the target will be activated. This principle is not sufficient, however, to account for the retrieval of inter-

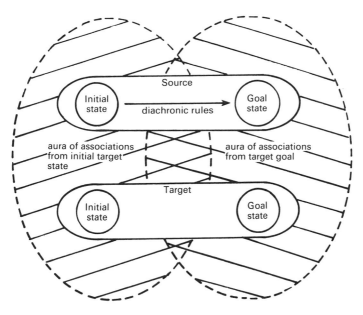

Figure 10.2
Pattern of activation indicating retrieval of a plausible source analog.

domain analogies, since it would appear more likely that concepts with many "superficial" similarities will be activated. As we will see, there is empirical evidence that surface similarities do play a role in analogical retrieval. The retrieval process, however, will tend to be dominated by shared properties that are *goal-related*. Note, first of all, that the goal in the target problem will help to determine which rules are executed, and hence which properties of concepts involved in the target actually will be activated. Second, plausible source analogs will be those that are related to multiple components of the target problem. In particular, a situation that is activated by both the initial state and the goal state in the target problem is likely to have associated diachronic rules relevant to transforming a corresponding initial state in the source into a corresponding goal state. A potential analogy has been found when synchronic rules connect the initial target state to an initial state in a source domain, diachronic rules in the source domain connect its initial state to a subsequent state, and the latter state in the source domain is in turn connected by synchronic rules to the target goal.

Figure 10.2 is a schematic illustration of the pattern of activation that signals retrieval of a plausible source analog. The concepts in the initial target model, especially the initial and goal states, create "auras" of associations via synchronic rules. A plausible source analog will meet two criteria. First, its constituent concepts will be highly activated by synchronic pathways from the target. Second, the source will have diachronic rules attached to it that connect concepts associated with the initial and goal states of the target. This second criterion will tend to exclude superficially associated concepts that do not carry relevant diachronic rules. In terms of the diagram in figure 10.1, at this point the system will have begun to develop the mapping $P*$ between the source and the target, and to identify diachronic rules that provide the transition function T_A' for the source.

It can be seen that the steps of selecting a source analog and those of performing a mapping between the target and the source actually merge. Once any potential source analog is well supported, it will become the focus of continued processing to extend and refine the mapping. This will set the stage for the fourth step in analogical transfer—the generation of new rules for the target by substituting mapped elements in the corresponding source rules. If the entire process is successful, these rules will provide a first approximation to an appropriate transition function T_B' for the target.

We should emphasize once again that none of the mechanisms of analogical transfer offers any guarantee that the target problem will be solved successfully or that the new rules generated will be useful ones. The new rules will be immediately subject to all the inductive pressures described in chapter 3, such as strength revision and specialization. An initially plausible source analog may ultimately be rejected altogether. Nonetheless, analogy is an especially powerful inductive mechanism because it allows an initially diffuse activation process to begin to focus on plausible sources of new ideas to bring to bear on problems for which any plausible idea may represent progress over none at all.

10.2.3 Similarity and Analogical Transfer

For an autonomous problem solver the most difficult step in the use of analogy is likely to be the retrieval of a plausible source. An interdomain analogy, by definition, is one in which the commonalities are relatively abstract, whereas the differences are blatant. As a result, it may be difficult for a problem solver to retrieve or notice the relevance of a source analog, unless a "teacher" calls attention to the analogy (Gick and Holyoak 1980).

The difficulty of noticing distant analogies is not surprising, since the underlying implicit schema is quite abstract, whereas the many superficial differences between the two cases are very obvious. Sometimes people are explicitly taught to think about one domain in terms of a very different one, so that the problem of noticing the analogy is avoided. For example, students often are told that electricity behaves like a hydraulic system. Gentner and Gentner (1983) have demonstrated that the ease with which high school and college students solve particular types of electricity problems depends on the degree to which the analogy they have been taught generates correct inferences about the relevant electrical concepts. In such cases instruction serves to establish synchronic association rules that cause problems in the target domain to activate a particular source analog.

The Role of Superficial Cues

We earlier described the roles of both synchronic and diachronic rules in the retrieval of source analogs, and pointed out that the requirement that the source carry relevant diachronic rules serves to exclude entirely superficial synchronic associates. This does not mean, however, that "surface-level" shared properties play no role in analogical transfer. On the contrary, any synchronic relation shared by the target and a source can potentially help to activate the source concept enough to allow its diachronic rules to be made available. Salient properties, even those that are functionally irrelevant to a solution to the target problem, may affect the solution plan indirectly by influencing the selection of a source analog. In other words, certain properties of a novel situation may serve to remind a person of a superficially similar prior situation, which, if it carries relevant diachronic rules, will in turn influence the plan generated for the target.

A study by Gilovich (1981) provides a demonstration of this possibility. Gilovich pointed out that modern American foreign policy has been heavily influenced by two salient historical analogies: the Munich analogy, referring to the misguided attempts to appease Hitler before World War II, and the Vietnam analogy, referring to American interference in a foreign country that led to disaster. Gilovich reasoned that if a new crisis were to arise that contained cues associated with Munich, people would tend to advocate intervention, whereas if the crisis cued Vietnam, people would tend to favor a hands-off policy. To test this hypothesis, he gave students in a political science course (dealing with conflict from World War I to the present) a description of a hypothetical crisis. The crisis involved a threatened attack by a large totalitarian country, Country A, against a small democratic country, Country B. The subjects were asked to select an option for the United States to follow, ranging from extreme appeasement of Country A to direct military intervention.

Gilovich constructed two versions of the crisis, intended to cue either the Munich or the Vietnam analogy. For example, the Munich version referred to the impending invasion as a "blitzkrieg", whereas the Vietnam version referred to it as a "quickstrike". The Munich version described how minority refugees were fleeing from Country A in boxcars on freight trains to Country G. In contrast, the Vietnam version indicated that minority refugees were fleeing from Country A in small boats that sailed up the "Gulf of C" to Country G. These alternative descriptions thus made the crisis seem superficially similar to either the situation prior to World War II or that prior to the Vietnam intervention. These cues, however, have no apparent functional relevance to a decision about how the U.S. should respond to the hypothetical crisis. Why should it matter, after all, whether refugees are fleeing in boxcars or in small boats? Nevertheless, Gilovich's subjects tended to make decisions of a more interventionist nature when they read the Munich version rather than the Vietnam version.

It might seem that Gilovich's subjects lacked normative justification for this influence of functionally irrelevant properties on their decisions about the target problem. From a broad perspective, however, their behavior was quite reasonable. The cues served to remind them of a source analog that might indeed suggest a plausible approach to the target problem; that is, either the Munich or the Vietnam situation might in fact provide useful information for someone engaged in assessing the consequences of foreign policy. Although the cues that activated one or the other were superficial, each is a plausible, goal-relevant analog. In the absence of any clearer basis for reaching a decision, the analogy at least supports *some* course of action. The danger, of course, is that superficial cues will favor the retrieval of particular source analogs over others that would be equally useful and would suggest alternative courses of action. Analogy, like all forms of induction, cannot be divorced from risk.

Surface and Structural Similarities
A major difficulty in retrieving interdomain analogies results from the relative dearth of superficial synchronic links between target and source. The trouble is that a remote analog by definition shares few of the salient surface features of the target. To the extent that the latter serve as retrieval cues, they will tend to activate competing associations that may block the retrieval of more remote analogs. The better able the problem solver is to identify and focus on the causally relevant aspects of the target problem, the greater the probability that a useful but remote analog will be retrieved.

It is possible, based on the taxonomy of mapping relations discussed earlier, to clarify the distinction between surface and structural similarities and dissimilarities. An identity between two problem situations that plays no causal role in determining the possible solutions to one or the other analog constitutes a surface similarity. (The cues used in the study by Gilovich were largely of this type.) Similarly, a structure-preserving difference, as defined earlier, constitutes a surface dissimilarity. In contrast, causally relevant identities constitute structural similarities, and structure-violating differences constitute structural dissimilarities.

Ideally, a problem solver would use only the structural properties of the target as retrieval cues, thus avoiding the activation of superficially similar but unhelpful situations. In reality, however, the problem solver's ability to distinguish surface from structural properties will be at best imperfect, since full knowledge of which properties of the target are structural depends on knowing the possible solutions—information clearly unavailable at the outset of a solution attempt. Consequently, surface properties that in fact are functionally irrelevant to a solution to the target problem may affect the solution plan indirectly by influencing the selection of a source analog, as suggested by Gilovich's results.

Once a source analog has been retrieved, surface properties should have less impact on the mapping process than structural ones. In particular, structure-violating differences will necessitate refinement of the initial solution plan generated by the mapping, whereas structure-preserving differences will not. Thus surface properties will tend to have a relatively greater impact on the selection of a source analog than on the subsequent mapping process. For example, it is much easier to learn to map an atom onto a solar system than to spontaneously link the two analogs in the first place. In contrast, structure-violating differences will diminish not only the probability of selecting the source analog but also the probability of using it successfully once mapping is initiated.

Of course, a test of the effects of types of dissimilarity on different steps in the transfer process requires a situation in which subjects do sometimes spontaneously notice analogies. A recent study by Holyoak and Koh (1986) provides such evidence, setting the stage for investigation of the influence of surface and structural properties on noticing and applying analogies. They investigated transfer between the radiation problem and another convergence situation, the "laser and lightbulb" problem. In the latter, the filament of a lightbulb in a physics lab is broken. Because the lightbulb is expensive, it would be worthwhile to repair rather than replace it. A strong laser could be used to fuse the filament; unfortunately, it would also break the surrounding glass bulb. The convergence solution, of course, is to use several weak lasers focused on the filament.

Relative to the low frequency of spontaneous transfer that Gick and Holyoak (1980, 1983) had found using the military analog described earlier, transfer between the radiation and lightbulb problems was excellent. One experiment involved students enrolled in introductory psychology classes. Seventeen experimental subjects were drawn from classes that used a textbook with a detailed discussion of the radiation problem, whereas ten control subjects were selected from classes that used texts that did not mention the problem. A few days after the experimental subjects had read about the radiation problem in their textbook as part of a regular assignment, all subjects participated in an experiment (out of class) in which the lightbulb problem was presented. About 80 percent of the subjects who had read about the radiation problem spontaneously generated the convergence solution, as contrasted with a scant 10 percent of the control subjects, who had not. Another experiment revealed that transfer was also good when the lightbulb problem was the source and the radiation problem the target.

The lightbulb analog differs from the military analog along many dimensions, so it is difficult to determine precisely why the former yields greater transfer. One obvious possibility is the difference in the degree of similarity between the instruments of force in the two analogs and in the radiation problem. Light from a laser is far more similar to X rays than an army is, a fact that provides a significant additional retrieval cue in the former case. Moreover, the deeper structural parallels between the lightbulb and radiation analogs make the analogy extremely complete. Both cases involve a target area enclosed within a fragile "container" at risk from a high-intensity force. Thus both a relatively surface-level similarity and a relatively complete structural mapping provide retrieval cues that can connect the lightbulb and radiation analogs.

In an attempt to disentangle the contributions of surface and structural similarity as retrieval cues, Holyoak and Koh generated variations of the lightbulb analog in which these factors were altered. To vary the surface similarity of the instruments to X rays, two of the new stories substituted "ultrasound waves" for lasers. The problem statement was also altered: instead of being described as broken apart, the filament was described as having fused together, and the ultrasound waves could repair it by jarring it apart. Thus in two stories the solution was to use a laser to fuse the filament, and in two it was to use an ultrasound wave to jar apart the filament. To the extent that the two types of action differ in their similarity to that required in the radiation problem (destroying a tumor), the latter appears more similar (since jarring apart seems more destructive than does fusing together). The more salient difference, however, is that ultrasound waves are far less associated with X rays than are lasers.

Independently of the variation in the instrument, the stories also varied in their structural similarity to the radiation problem. Specifically, the nature of the constraint preventing direct application of a large force was varied. In the versions with relatively complete mappings the constraint was as in the radiation problem—a high-intensity force would damage the surrounding area (fragile glass). In the versions with less complete mappings the constraint was simply that no single instrument of sufficient intensity (laser or ultrasound) was available. These latter versions thus removed a structural cue linking them to the radiation problem. Nonetheless, all four of the stories described essentially identical convergence solutions.

These two types of variations—of instruments and of constraints—yielded four alternative stories that were used as source analogs for different groups of subjects. Sixteen subjects served in each of the two fragile-glass conditions and fifteen served in each of the insufficient-intensity conditions. As the data in table 10.3 indicate, the versions differed greatly in their subsequent transfer to the target radiation problem. Table 10.3A presents the percentage of subjects in each of the four conditions who generated the convergence solution before receiving a hint to consider the story. When the source was the "laser and fragile glass" analog, which has both a similar instrument and a complete mapping, 69 percent of the subjects spontaneously generated the convergence solution. Transfer was significantly impaired if either the surface similarity of the instrument or the structural constraint similarity was reduced. If both changes were made (the "ultrasound of insufficient intensity" version), only 13 percent of the subjects generated the convergence solution. These results indicate that both surface similarities and deeper structural commonalities aid in the retrieval of source analogs, as our earlier account of retrieval mechanisms would predict.

As the data in table 10.3B indicate, a different transfer pattern was observed once a hint to use the story had been provided. Structural dissimilarity of the constraint significantly impaired total transfer (78 percent for the fragile-glass versions versus 54 percent for the insufficient-intensity versions), whereas surface dissimilarity of the in-

Table 10.3
Percentage of subjects producing convergence solution (from Holyoak and Koh 1986)

| Structural cue (constraint) | Surface cue (instrument) | | Mean |
	Similar (laser)	Dissimilar (ultrasound)	
A. Before hint			
Similar (fragile glass)	69	38	54
Dissimilar (insufficient intensity)	33	13	23
Mean	51	26	
B. Total (before and after hint)			
Similar (fragile glass)	75	81	78
Dissimilar (insufficient intensity)	60	47	54
Mean	68	64	

struments did not (68 percent for the laser versions versus 64 percent for the ultrasound versions). Thus although surface and structural similarity had comparable effects on spontaneous transfer, only the latter had a significant impact on total analogical transfer once a hint was provided. These results support the prediction that surface similarity will have a greater impact on retrieval of a source analog than on application of an analog once it is retrieved.

The results of Holyoak and Koh should not be construed as indicating that surface properties will *never* influence mapping once a source is selected. In their experiment only a single change was introduced to create the surface-dissimilarity condition. It might well be that the introduction of multiple surface dissimilarities would make it more difficult to map the components of the two analogs. In addition, surface differences will continue to impair transfer if the problem solver has difficulty discriminating them from structural differences even after a source analog is provided. In an experiment on analogical transfer performed with six-year-olds, with the ball problem mentioned earlier as the target, Holyoak, Junn, and Billman (1984) found that what appeared (to adults) to be a minor surface dissimilarity between the source and the target significantly decreased the percentage of children able to use the analogy. It may be that children, perhaps because they lack experience with a problem domain, have greater difficulty than adults in analyzing the causally relevant aspects of the source and target problems.

We now turn to a consideration of the development of ideas in science—a topic that illustrates the importance not only of analogy but of our entire framework for induction.

11

Scientific Discovery

In previous chapters we have discussed induction as it occurs in the everyday life of humans and other organisms. In this chapter we apply our framework for induction to the highest human inductive achievements. We will show that the notions we have discussed, such as default hierarchies and mental models, serve to illuminate the nature of the growth of scientific knowledge. In addition to illustrating our accounts of analogy, generalization, and concept formation with scientific examples, this chapter offers new perspectives on important problems in the philosophy of science, in particular those concerning the nature of scientific theories and explanations. Theories can naturally be understood as mental models of the sort described in chapter 2, and explanations can be analyzed as problem solutions. Moreover, the most sophisticated sort of inductive inference, in which a scientific theory is evaluated against its competitors, is based on criteria that are easily characterized within our framework.

We construe the topic of scientific discovery broadly to include processes by which laws and theories are initially conceived, as well as processes by which their acceptance is justified. Although our discussion is situated in a computational and psychological framework, it also addresses normative epistemological issues that are usually taken to lie within the province of philosophy of science. We do not regret this violation of the standard philosophical injunction to distinguish the "context of discovery" from the "context of justification" (Reichenbach 1938), for we see an intimate connection between descriptive issues of how science *is* done and normative issues of how it *ought* to be done. (For extensive treatments of the relationship between descriptive and normative epistemological concerns, see Goldman 1978; Stich and Nisbett 1980; Thagard 1982; Thagard and Nisbett 1983.)

We do not pretend to give a full account of the complexities of the development of scientific knowledge, which also has an important social dimension. Knowledge is developed by scientists working in communities, sharing methods and discoveries. In this chapter we are concerned with the inductive processes of the individual scientist.

11.1 The Structure of Scientific Knowledge

Philosophers have rarely discussed the structure of scientific knowledge in psychological or computational terms. The primary analytical tools used by twentieth-century philosophers have been syntactic. Scientific laws have been characterized as universal sentences in predicate calculus, having the general form $(x)(Fx \rightarrow Gx)$, which is read as, "For any x, if x is F then x is G" (see, for example, Hempel 1965). Theories are then taken to be sets of such sentences, ideally serving as axioms in a formal logistic system.

We offer an alternative, pragmatic account of the objects of scientific knowledge. In keeping with our discussion in chapter 2, scientific laws can be understood as rules within a processing system. Superficially, this coincides with the syntactic interpretation just described, since there is an obvious translation of universal sentences of the form "All F are G" into condition-action rules of the form "If x is F, then x is G". The key issue, however, is procedural: within the syntactic account of laws and theories, the only procedures available for applying laws in problem solving are deductive, whereas our discussion of processing systems described complex procedures by which relevant rules could be brought to bear on appropriate problems. These included directed spreading activation and competition among rules based on strength and other properties. Hence in characterizing the law "All copper conducts electricity" as the rule "If x is copper, then x conducts electricity", we are proposing more than a notational variant.

We suppose in particular that the rule just described is attached to the concept of "copper" (as in the system PI) and that the rule becomes available only when that concept is activated. Moreover, such concepts are linked together through pointers to superordinates and subordinates, so that the hierarchical organization of concepts plays a major role in determining the availability of rules about copper for particular problem-solving tasks. The diachronic relations concerning transitions in the world that scientific laws typically describe depend for their usefulness in problem solving on the existence of synchronic relations among concepts.

Scientific concepts are arrived at by the various processes described in earlier chapters; cases of category formation by analogy and conceptual combination are described in section 11.5. Theories must be thought of as much more than mere sets of rules, since the rules employed in a given theory will have important relations as the result of the hierarchical and associational structure of the concepts that contain them.

The structure of scientific knowledge can be understood within our framework as follows. Scientific laws are general rules. Scientific ideas are concepts that organize laws and other rules into useful bundles. Scientific theories are complexes of rules that function together computationally by virtue of the concepts that connect them. Moreover, these concepts are often of a special sort, making reference to entities and processes not directly observable by the scientific instruments of the day.

Although we are not assuming any strict division between what is observable and what is not, a relative distinction is important. When the properties under consideration are all observable, then bottom-up concept formation of the sort described in chapter 6 becomes possible; otherwise, conceptual combination, analogy, and other more top-down procedures must be used. We will call laws that deal only with observable things or processes "observational laws", contrasting them with theoretical laws that postulate nonobservables such as electrons and black holes. We must emphasize that this distinction is temporally relative: the concept of a gene, for example, was theoretical when first proposed, but with its reinterpretation in terms of molecules of DNA and the development of electron microscopes, genes are now observable entities. We will now discuss the growth of scientific knowledge in terms of the development of laws, ideas, and theories.

11.2 Scientific Laws

11.2.1 Laws and Defaults
According to one common view, a scientific law is a universal truth. The point of a law such as "Water boils at 212 degrees Fahrenheit" is to make a general statement about the world. The problem with this congenial view is that laws of nature taken this strictly tend to be false, since they fail to hold in at least some special situations. Under certain circumstances, such as when the water is contaminated or well above sea level, the boiling point of water is not 212 degrees Fahrenheit. Laws only hold when other things are equal, or, as we would say, under default conditions.

Cartwright (1983) makes the same point about Newton's law of gravitation, which says that two bodies exert a force between them that varies inversely as the square of the distance between them and varies directly as the product of their masses. The law $F = Gmm'/r^2$ is one of the most important ever discovered, but it does not truly describe how objects behave. If the two bodies have an electrical charge, for example, then the force between them will be affected by electrical forces as well as by the gravitational force. Thus the law of gravitation has an implicit qualification attached to it, stating that it is only expected to hold if other factors are absent. A more complete law would state that the force of gravitation is only a contributor to the total force, but such a law would be much more cumbersome to apply.

In our view, there is nothing paradoxical about such qualifications in scientific laws or about the consequence that laws lack strict generality. The point of a scientific law, like any other empirical rule, is to contribute to the development of a model that is q-morphic to the real system it represents. A full, exact representation is not to be expected; nor is it needed, since the hierarchical relations within the model should allow the handling of exceptions to general laws. In our discussion of default hierarchies in chapter 2, we discussed how special cases of general rules can be considered without violating the usefulness of the general rules. Similarly, scientific laws serve to establish powerful default expectations that can be overridden in special circumstances. Under ordinary circumstances we *should* expect water to boil at about 212 degrees, even though we know there are circumstances in which this is not true. Similarly, it is fine for an engineer to treat Newtonian mechanics as a default specification for the behavior of objects in the earth's atmosphere, even though it is known that Newton's laws break down, in ways predicted by the general theory of relativity, within intense gravitational fields close to stars.

11.2.2 The Discovery of Laws

How do scientists arrive at new laws? A common view, misattributed to Francis Bacon, is that scientists generally start with data and then by "induction" directly derive laws that describe those data. More typically, we will argue, the discovery of laws requires the kinds of reconceptualizations that are central to our account of problem solving; synchronic search among concepts is as important as the search for diachronic regularities. We will argue that this is true even for observational laws, or laws that cover observable events; it is even more obviously so for theoretical laws that require top-down concept formation.

The best-known computational work on the discovery of laws is the program BACON (Langley 1981; Simon, Langley, and Bradshaw 1981; Langley, Bradshaw, and Simon 1981, 1983). By contrasting the method by which BACON discovers Kepler's third law with Kepler's own methods, we hope to show the need for a more indirect and conceptually complex discovery process.

Kepler's third law states that for each planet the square of the period of revolution around the sun is directly proportional to the cube of the mean radius of the planet's orbit. BACON is given a set of data concerning the periods and locations of several planets and seeks to find a mathematical expression to account for these data. It notices which variables given to it are correlated, and uses sophisticated heuristics to arrive at the law that d^3/p^2 is a constant. Langley, Simon, and their colleagues have shown how similar heuristics can generate many important scientific laws, including those associated with the names of Coulomb, Ohm, and Snell. Nor are the laws limited to expressing only magnitudes given to them in the initial set of variables, since BACON can generate "intrinsic properties" expressing relations not directly derivable from the initial variables. For example, in generating Snell's law concerning the refraction of light, BACON develops an intrinsic property corresponding to the index of refraction of two substances.

Such performances, while very impressive, capture only part of the problem-solving activity crucial to scientific discovery. Contrast the relatively direct means by which BACON generates Kepler's third law with the immense labors attending Kepler's own discoveries (Koestler 1964; Hanson 1958). Although he started with relatively accurate data furnished by Tycho Brahe, Kepler's discovery of the three famous laws would have been impossible without several dramatic reconceptualizations of the problem domain. Much of his research was guided by metaphysical principles that now strike us as absurd: he expected the orbits of the planets to be spherically nested within each other exactly as the "perfect solids"—the pyramid, cube, octahedron, dodecahedron, and icosahedron—can be nested within each other. Thus Kepler's investigations began not only with a set of data but also with what was for him an equally important geometrical mental model of the relations among the planets.

Discovery of the laws became possible only when he began to develop a more physical approach to the problem, anticipating to some extent Newton's later development of the notions of force and inertia. The crude new model assumed that the sun was somehow the cause of the motion of the planets, paving the way for Kepler's second law (discovered before what we call the first). This law states that a planet moves in its orbit, not at a uniform speed as previously expected, but in a manner such that a line drawn from the planet to the sun always sweeps over equal areas in equal times. Now increasingly freed from the grips of the geometrical model, Kepler conceived what was later dubbed his first law: that the motions of the planets are elliptical rather than circular, with the sun occupying one focus of the ellipse. Much later, Kepler arrived at the formula expressing his third law, after what Koestler (1964, p. 400) describes as "patient, dogged trying". We saw that BACON too is capable of such dogged trying; but unlike Kepler, its trying is not in the least guided by mental models. The genesis of Kepler's views clearly shows the importance of having general models of the phenomena for which laws are sought. Without his reconceptualization of the motions of planets into physical rather than geometrical terms, and his substitution of the notion of an ellipse for that of a circle, Kepler's achievement would have been impossible. The development of qualitative notions such as "elliptical orbit" was as important as the generation of quantitative laws.

Our conclusion here is of a piece with that reached in chapter 8 concerning simpler kinds of generalization. We argued there that a generalization such as "All shreebles are blue" presupposes a mental model that generates estimates of variability. In cases such as Kepler's laws, the background mental model is essential not just for assessing the variability of kinds of objects but also for determining what sorts of hypotheses will be entertainable. The discovery of a scientific law is almost always an extremely ill-defined problem, insoluble by general heuristics without the direction of a mental model of the problem domain.

11.3 Theories as Mental Models

We usually speak of Kepler's *laws* of motion, but of Newton's *theory* of gravitation. What is the difference? Theories are distinguished from sets of laws by several important characteristics. First, whereas an observational law is expected to give an account of a set of observations, theories are often used to explain sets of *laws*, not merely particular observations. Thus one of the great achievements of Newtonian mechanics was to explain why Kepler's laws held. Second, theories are intended not merely to apply to phenomena in one domain but to unify phenomena in different domains. Newton's theory explained not only Kepler's laws of planetary motion but also Galileo's findings about the motions of objects on inclined planes, as well as numerous other phenomena, such as oceanic tides. Third, theories generally achieve their great unifications by postulating non-observable entities, as is evident in the following examples from physics, chemistry, biology, and psychology. Newton conceived of a force of gravitation existing between any two objects and producing the results observed by Kepler and Galileo. Dalton's atomic theory of chemistry postulated the existence of nonobservable atoms. Darwin proposed mechanisms of variation and natural selection that had yet to be observed, just as early geneticists postulated genes. Freud's ego, superego, and id were theoretical constructs that have not proved as fecund as force, atoms, natural selection, or genes.

The presence of terms denoting nonobservable objects has caused great consternation among philosophers of science and even practicing scientists. The logical positivists and their behaviorist cousins in psychology asserted that there could be no respectable place in science for such postulation. Although it is clear that these qualms must be ignored in the face of the impossibility of science without theoretical postulation, a serious problem arises for the study of scientific discovery: How could scientists ever arrive at concepts concerning things— such as electrons, black holes, and neutrinos—that they could not observe? Hume (1739/1888) proposed that ideas could be derived only from sense impressions or from definition in terms of other ideas, but concepts from Newtonian force to genes to mental models clearly require more complex processes of formation. We will argue that analogy is the primary means of theory construction, and that conceptual combination is the primary means for generating theoretical concepts. First, however, it is necessary to examine in more detail the nature and function of theories.

11.3.1 The Nature of Theories

Until recently, the standard view of scientific theories was that they are ideally sets of sentences in a formalized language such as predicate calculus, functioning as axioms in a logistic system (Hempel 1965). As we have frequently stated, we see little promise in purely syntactic approaches to describing the structure and growth of human knowledge. Instead, we will show how the ideas embodied in our framework can be used to develop a pragmatic conception of theories. We propose to understand a theory as a complex kind of computational system of the sort characterized in chapters 2 and 3; our claim, then, is that *theories can be understood as systems of rules furnishing mental models.*

The Set-Theoretic Notion of a Model

In the past decade a *semantic* conception of theories has become popular (see, for example, Suppe 1977; Stegmueller 1979; van Fraassen 1980). This conception takes from Tarskian semantics a set-theoretic notion of model that must be distinguished from ours. Tarskian semantics concerns the relations between symbols as syntactic entities and the world construed set-theoretically.

The essential notion is a *model*, which is a structure $\langle D, R \rangle$, where D is a domain consisting of a set of objects and R is a set of relations on those objects. A model *satisfies* a sentence under some interpretation I if the sentence, once interpreted, is true in the model. For example, consider the sentence "Jimmy is shorter than Gerald" and the model consisting of the domain {Jimmy Carter, Gerald Ford, Richard Nixon} and the relation consisting of the ordered pairs {(Carter, Ford), (Nixon, Ford)}. An interpretation consists of a mapping from the expression "Jimmy" to the object Carter, from "Gerald" to the object Ford, and from "is shorter than" to the relation characterized by the set of ordered pairs. Trivially, in this case, it turns out that the sentence is true in the model.

On the syntactic conception of theories, a theory is a set of sentences, and we can speak of the "models" of the theory, namely those models $\langle D, R \rangle$ that, given an interpretation of the sentences of the theory, render them all true. The semantic conception of theories avoids making a theory dependent on any particular language and takes a theory just to be a set of models, implicitly those models in which a theory in the old syntactic sense is true. On the semantic conception of theories, a theory is used to make claims about the world, not by saying that the theory is true, but by saying that certain substructures of the world are among those that constitute the theory. A theory is tested by checking this claim that the empirical substructures are among those picked out by the theory.

Mental Models in Science

In contrast to Tarski's set-theoretic notion of a model, our own notion of a mental model is essentially computational and dynamic. The key feature of mental models is that they include structures and processes that can simulate the transitions that occur in phenomena being modeled. Mental models can be part of the goal-driven psychological apparatus of practicing scientists, so that the conception of theories as mental models is essentially pragmatic. Yet, by virtue of its use of formalizable computational notions, our framework avoids much of the vagueness associated with previous attempts at pragmatic accounts of scientific knowledge. The highly influential account of Kuhn (1962) made telling points about the structure and growth of scientific knowledge, using the pragmatic notion of a "paradigm". Despite Kuhn's struggle to characterize paradigms both as exemplars of scientific achievement and as the disciplinary values built up from them, the notion of a paradigm remains beguilingly vague. Similarly, Laudan's (1977) frequently discussed pragmatic account of the role of theories as devices for problem solving does not contain a deep account of what it is to solve a problem. We will now outline how the central pragmatic functions of scientific theories can be understood in the pragmatic terms of our framework.

11.3.2 Prediction, Explanation, and Q-Morphisms

According to Popper (1959) and other prominent philosophers of science, the primary function of scientific laws and theories is prediction. A theory is tested by being used to make a prediction of an observable event: if the event occurs, then the theory is confirmed or corroborated; if the predicted event fails to be observed, then the theory is disconfirmed or falsified. Now, prediction is indeed important in science, but its role must be carefully appreciated. Often what is wanted is not merely prediction, but *explanation*.

The dominant view of explanation in philosophy of science has been syntactic. The *deductive-nomological* model asserts that explanation is essentially a deductive relation, in which a sentence is explained by being deduced from scientific laws plus statements of initial conditions (Hempel 1965). For example, we could *explain* an eclipse of the sun today by deducing a sentence describing its occurrence from laws of planetary motion plus statements of initial conditions concerning the location of the sun, earth, and moon yesterday. On the deductive-nomological account, explanation and prediction are symmetrical, since deductions yield both predictions and explanations.

As usually happens with elegant syntactic formulations, the deductive-nomological model has been met with a flood of counter-examples showing its pragmatic inadequacies (see, for example, Bromberger 1966). Consider how we might explain the fact that the flagpole in front of the county courthouse is 40 feet tall. It would be possible to deduce this fact from a measurement of the length of its shadow together with trigonometry and the law of the rectilinear propagation of light. But this calculation based on the length of the flagpole's shadow does not explain *why* it is 40 feet tall, even though it yields the deductive prediction that it is 40 feet tall. A genuine explanation would have to make reference to the reasons why the builders of the flagpole chose to make it 40 feet tall.

Similarly, we cannot use the law that anything that turns litmus paper red is an acid to explain why a given substance is an acid, even though we can deduce from the fact that it turns litmus paper red that it is an acid. Explanation of why something is acidic must be in terms of its molecular constituents, not in terms of the merely diagnostic information about its effect on litmus paper.

The deficiencies of the deductive-nomological account of explanation can be understood in terms of the importance of mental models and their q-morphic representations. Explanation is more than prediction, more than merely generating an answer. To explain something is to fit it into a general pattern of events, and syntactic relations such as deduction do not establish a sufficiently rich pattern. Mental models do. Applying a mental model to a puzzling event or fact removes puzzlement by locating it in several respects. Synchronically, a model identifies something as a particular kind of thing, locating it within a default hierarchy with all the attendant expectations. When you ask why the *flagpole* is 40 feet tall, the mental model you bring to bear will include the information that a flagpole is a kind of manufactured object serving particular purposes. That synchronic identification will make possible the use of a set of diachronic rules that can be used to generate an answer to why the flagpole is 40 feet tall, by bringing to bear pertinent facts about its design and manufacture. Without the synchronic features of the mental model, we have no way of knowing where to look for what is relevant. Similarly, our mental model of acids contains their categorization as a kind of chemical substance, so that we must look to the rules attached to concepts at that level to explain why something is an acid.

Thus scientific explanation of particular events, like the more everyday sort of explanation, involves locating a phenomenon within a model that uses synchronic and diachronic relations to provide a q-morphism, a layered set of rules providing default expectations and exceptions.

11.3.3 Theoretical Explanation and Unification

Although the prediction and explanation of particular facts is an important part of scientific activity, it pales in epistemic significance in comparison to the use of theories to explain and unify broad classes of facts. We value syntheses such as Newtonian mechanics, relativity theory, and Darwin's theory of evolution for the way in which they provide explanations of numerous laws of nature. Such syntheses can be understood as the development of a particularly powerful kind of mental model.

What does it gain a scientist to have a general theory for a whole domain rather than just a lot of isolated laws? Why do physicists look for explanations of why the laws of planetary motion hold, and why do non-behaviorist psychologists postulate processing mechanisms to account for observed empirical effects? At first glance it appears that we should be able to get a q-morphic representation of the world without recourse to postulation of anything nonobservable. But theories that postulate nonobservables can provide a particularly valuable kind of q-morphism, since they propose transitions that, although not themselves observable, play a crucial role in accounting for those transitions that are observable. Thus Newton needed the concept of gravitational force to tie together the motion of planets and the motion of earthly projectiles, and Darwin needed the hypothesis of a process of evolution by natural selection to tie together facts about the morphology and geographical distribution of related species. Without the postulation of gravitational force, for example, no commonality is evident between motions of planets and cannonballs.

In other words, a theory provides a powerful sort of default hierarchy, showing that phenomena thought previously to be disparate are in fact of the same kind. Newtonian theory can be thought of as defining a kind of mechanical system, and the achievement of Newton and his successors consisted in showing that planetary motion, projectile motion, the tides, the trajectories of comets, and so on are systems of just that kind (see Giere 1979). This synchronic relation has a striking consequence for problem solving, in that it makes available all the powerful mathematical rules of Newtonian theory for each previously isolated phenomenon. In terms of a processing system such as PI, activation of the concept of a Newtonian system, by associating the planetary system with it, provides access to all the diachronic rules useful for predicting and explaining the behavior of such systems. Whewell (1847) used the term "consilience" to describe this characteristic of a theory explaining and unifying a broad class of facts. A consilient theory is one that shows how disparate phenomena can be tied together, as when Newton showed that the motion of objects on earth is subject to the same kind of explanation as the motion of planets around the sun. In section 11.4.2 we will show how consilience plays a major role in inductive inference to scientific theories.

It must be stressed that the relation of the theory to the classes of facts it explains is not merely syntactic or semantic in the set-theoretic sense. From a syntactic point of view we could collapse all the sentences describing the phenomena explained by Newton into one long conjunction derivable from the theory. We avoid such trivialization by seeing that the notion of a class of facts is highly pragmatic, reflecting the organization of knowledge in the minds of scientists at a particular time. As we pointed out in chapter 1, any computational account is syntactic at some level, since a program is from the computer's point of view a purely syntactic entity. But inductive systems are not to be understood at that level, since reference must be made to their goals and context. Pragmatically and computationally, it is clear that a unifying theory is a tremendous achievement, extending techniques for problem solutions to a wide array of problems.

11.4 The Growth of Scientific Knowledge

11.4.1 Conservative versus Radical Views of Scientific Growth
The positivist account of the structure of scientific knowledge made possible a very conservative view of the nature of scientific development. The corpus of scientific knowledge could grow in a largely cumulative way, through the addition and subtraction of sentences. In contrast, Kuhn (1962) proposed a radical view of scientific growth, emphasizing revolutionary supersession of one paradigm by another incommensurable with it. Our own view of scientific knowledge as consisting of mental models charts a course between these two extremes.

If scientific knowledge consisted of mere sets of rules, then we could expect the same kind of cumulativeness that the positivists gained from having sets of sentences. Increases in our knowledge would consist of additions to the stock of rules available to the system. We assume, however, that the organized interrelations of rules are crucially important. In particular, in order to operate efficiently, rules must be organized into concepts that govern the accessibility of various rules. Thus two opposing theories can differ in more fundamental respects than merely having different rules, since the bundling of rules in the opposing theories can be very different. A high-level theory such as Newtonian mechanics or Darwin's theory of evolution organizes our thought processes in fundamental ways, shaping our approach to every problem that might fall under it. A new theory thus brings with it not only different declarative knowledge but different types of problem solutions and different patterns of activation of concepts.

Hence the growth of scientific knowledge is not neatly cumulative, piling truth upon truth. As Kuhn and others have pointed out, scientists often resist new theories that challenge existing favorites. They rarely react to disconfirmations of current theories with Popperian exultation over finding themselves refuted. We need not, however, view this reluctance to abandon functioning theories as an irrational, egotistical attachment, as Popper would have it. Because of their immense value in information processing, partially predictive mental models should not be readily abandoned. Their organization in default hierarchies implies that it is often quite appropriate to adjust them to accommodate exceptions, making it unnecessary to abandon the model as a whole. Thus for most of its history Newtonian mechanics failed to account for the perihelion of Mercury, yet its proponents considered no serious adjustments to their mental models. Even Ptolemaic astronomers should not be castigated for adding epicycles, so long as their model was the only plausible one available. The constraint on adding epicycles comes when a new, alternative theory that does not require special assumptions arises and offers to replace the existing theory.

The replacement of mental models by alternatives is indeed possible. Mental models are above all problem-solving mechanisms, and if scientists catch glimpses of alternatives that hold the promise of solving problems inaccessible from their current models, replacement may become a live option. Kuhn describes changes of paradigms as a kind of irreversible Gestalt switch, but this description is too radical. Although different mental models will carry with them very different organizations of rules and hence different approaches to problems, there is no reason to see these differences as total barriers to comprehension of a new theory by enthusiastic adherents of an older theory.

To be sure, comprehension of alternative models may often be quite difficult. Sometimes it will require instruction of the sophisticated sort we described in chapters 7 and 9. Just as novel sets of inferential rules cannot be learned by purely formal instruction, but require in addition substantial drill on concrete applications, so we expect that the procedural aspects of a new theory often will not be acquirable without considerable practice. Kuhn has a similar view of scientific education. He points out that a student who claims to know all the formulas but not to be able to apply them to problems is lacking what is most important in a theory. Scientific training requires work with standard examples of problem solutions. (This was the original meaning of "paradigm".) Through extensive practice the novice can acquire the ability to use deep categorizations of problems in terms of rules useful for solutions, an ability that is the central feature discriminating the expert from the novice (Chi, Feltovich, and Glaser 1981). As we saw in chapter 9, it is essential to learn both general rule systems and methods for applying those rules to particular situations.

A scientist can acquire a competing theory or mental model only by building it up through steps similar to those that a student would use—acquiring the novel concepts by learning a series of rules and problem solutions. Although we can understand how scientists committed to one model may be reluctant to invest much time in exploring a rival one, the key epistemological point is that parallel development of incompatible mental models in a single cognitive system is possible. It may not be possible for scientists to have the competing models simultaneously active, but at different times they can be run and their relative efficacy evaluated.

11.4.2 Theory Evaluation

The most important kind of inductive inference by scientists is the acceptance of a scientific theory. Although there is much more to acceptance than mere addition of some sentences to one's knowledge store, the complexity of the process of building mental models is consistent with the existence of objective criteria for assessing the worth of competing theories. Thagard (1978) proposed, on the basis of case studies from the history of science, that there are three main criteria—consilience, simplicity, and analogy—for judging a theory against its competitors. We will now show how these criteria can be understood in terms of our framework.

The principal criterion for evaluating scientific theories is consilience, the ability to unify many different classes of facts. Darwin (1859), for example, argued repeatedly that his theory of evolution by natural selection was superior to the theological theory of creation in that it could explain such diverse classes of facts as the geographical distribution of species, the existence of rudimentary organs, and so on. We have already discussed the processing advantages of a consilient theory, and shown how consilience can be understood pragmatically and computationally as establishing an extremely useful default hierarchy of problem solutions. From a set of competing theories we should prefer the theory that explains the most classes of facts, that is, applies its problem-solving apparatus to the most classes of problems.

A second criterion is *simplicity*. The ultimately consilient theory would explain everything, but only at the cost of triviality. How can we put a constraint on consilience? In order to explain new classes of facts, a theory often requires additional assumptions. For example, to explain refraction, the wave theory of light required the assumption that light waves slowed down when they entered denser bodies, an assumption that was not independently testable until several decades after the wave theory had been accepted. But we cannot fault the use of such assumptions in general, for the broad application of mental models would often be impossible without them. Nevertheless, scientists often contend that one theory is *simpler* in that it requires fewer special assumptions than do its competitors. (By a special assumption we mean one that is used in the explanation of only a single class of facts.) An example of a *non*-simple theory is creationism, which can explain the characteristics of any species given the assumption that God willed those characteristics, but which requires one special assumption for every fact explained. That God so designed us explains why people have two eyes, but another special assumption could have "explained" why we had seventeen.

In a default hierarchy, special assumptions appear as exception rules attached to concepts. They can arise in order to make possible the solution of particular problems. For example, whereas proponents of the wave theory of light had to assume that light slows down in denser media in order to explain refraction, proponents of particle theories made the assumption that light sped up in denser media. In the early nineteenth century there was no empirical support for either assumption. Theory evaluation will have to judge the simplicity of competitors by seeing which theory needs the fewest special assumptions to deal with particular classes of facts. Note that this is not necessarily *ontological* simplicity, concerning the number of kinds of entities postulated. There appears to be little basis for preference of a theory merely on the grounds that it proposes fewer entities. What matters is whether a theory achieves consilience at a lower cost in terms of special assumptions than do its competitors.

The third major criterion for theory evaluation is *analogy*. Darwin and the proponents of the wave theory of light not only used analogy as a guide to developing their theories, they also cited the same analogies as providing grounds for accepting their theories. From the pragmatic point of view, it is clear how analogy can be a mark for positive evaluation of a theory as well as a source of its ideas, for analogy is such a powerful aid to problem solving that a theory based on an established one will be more easily used and more broadly applied by scientists than will a radically new one. Analogies are not an absolutely essential part of a scientific theory, but when available they increase its problem-solving efficacy and hence its acceptability.

11.4.3 Induction and Holism

In our view, central problems in the philosophy of science are continuous with key issues in cognitive psychology and artificial intelligence. Fodor (1983) has also noted such connections, but where we see mutual illumination, he finds gloom. Using an argument based on the holistic character of inductive confirmation, he suggests that the aims of cognitive psychology and artificial intelligence for a general account of the central processes of thought may be unattainable. In reply, we contend that a sophisticated cognitive view of induction undermines such a skeptical assessment of the possibility of understanding mental processes.

According to Fodor, the cognitive sciences have had their greatest successes in dealing with encapsulated systems that analyze special kinds of input. He postulates that increased understanding of language acquisition and vision has been possible because these functions are performed by isolated modules. In contrast, he thinks that little progress has been made in understanding such general cognitive processes as problem solving. His diagnosis of this disparity relies on an analogy with scientific confirmation: The nondeductive fixation of belief in science is unencapsulated and holistic, so we should expect central cognitive processes to have the same features.

Fodor argues that confirmation is "isotropic" and "Quinean", meaning that the facts relevant to confirmation of a hypothesis may be drawn from anywhere in the field of previously confirmed truth and that the degree of confirmation of the hypothesis is sensitive to properties of the whole system. As described in our earlier discussions of confirmation theory, Hempel and others hoped to give a syntactic characterization of what it is for a hypothesis to be confirmed or disconfirmed by specific observations. In contrast, Quine (1961, p. 41) concluded that "our statements about the external world face the tribunal of sense experience not individually but only as a corporate body."

Such holism does indeed pose problems for the philosophy of induction and for the cognitive sciences. How can we go about evaluating a hypothesis if everything is potentially relevant? Fodor contends that the same problem arises with analogical problem solving: Any domain is a potential source of useful analogies. It is impossible to put prior restraints on what might turn out to be useful in solving a problem or in making a scientific discovery. Who could have predicted that Darwin's reading of Malthus's hoary political views would lead to dramatic advances in biology?

Our framework suggests a number of mechanisms for keeping the bogey of holism at bay. One can accept Quine's conclusion that everything is *potentially* relevant to confirming a hypothesis or solving a problem without making the numbing requirement that everything potentially relevant actually be taken into account. That global strategy is clearly computationally and psychologically impracticable. Needed instead are mechanisms for selectively searching through the potentially relevant domains, bringing to bear whatever information proves to be useful. We have discussed several such constraining mechanisms, most of them embodied in the problem-solving process of PI described in chapter 4. By tending to fire the strongest and most goal-appropriate rules, and by spreading activation only to the new concepts in fired rules, a constrained search through the space of relevant information can be carried out. The search for plausibly relevant source analogs, as we saw in chapter 10, can thus be guided by information already in place in existing concepts. Similarly, whereas a huge amount of information might be potentially relevant to evaluating the claim that all shreebles are blue, in practice the synchronic links that are part of the concept of "shreeble" will keep chains of association under control.

Thus a processing mechanism of the sort we favor circumvents the problem of the potential relevance of everything in the knowledge store by pragmatically selecting limited areas of information to explore. Because activation is constrained by the limited parallelism of rule selection, the system need not be paralyzed by the overwhelming Quinean problem of accessing everything at once.

Let us now see in more detail how the mechanisms for problem solving and induction we have discussed apply to scientific discovery.

11.5 Theory Formation

Within our framework theories are understood as sets of rules that generate explanations of general empirical facts, using concepts that denote nonobservable objects. We will show how theories can be discovered through the use of analogical problem solving, abduction, and conceptual combination. We will describe the operation of these mechanisms in PI's simulation of the discovery of a simple but important theory.

11.5.1 Analogy
The process by which an analogy serves to build up problem solutions in a new domain was described in chapter 10. Recall the fundamental

idea that analogy proceeds by transferring a network of rules from one domain to another, in such a way that a q-morphism is established in the second domain. Scientific theorists working in a problematic new domain often look to already understood areas as a source of transportable concepts and problem-solving techniques.

An excellent illustration is the wave theory of light. The developers of this theory, from Huygens to Young and Fresnel, often relied on analogies between light and sound, which was already understood in terms of waves. The structure of the analogy between light and sound can be understood as follows. We begin with a wave theory of sound, which provides a q-morphic representation of various phenomena of sound, and proceed to construct a higher-order q-morphism between the wave theory of sound and the developing wave theory of light, which in turn is intended to be q-morphic to observed phenomena involving light. From the theory of sound, the theory of light is able to take over variants of rules and concepts that will enable it to solve problems in its own domain. The theory of sound employs the synchronic rule that sound consists of waves, which can be used to predict that sound will propagate and reflect; the mapping to light generates the hypothesis that light also consists of waves, which then can be used to predict that light will propagate and reflect much like sound.

Similarly, Darwin (1887) often cited the analogy between natural selection and artificial selection performed by breeders as important to the development and justification of his theory of evolution. He argued that just as breeders can modify populations by selecting for traits produced by natural variations, so nature can produce new species by selection arising from the struggle for survival. Rules and concepts about the practice of breeding were thus carried over to a new domain.

Another well-documented use of analogy in theoretical discovery is what James Clerk Maxwell called his method of *physical analogy*: "that partial similarity between the laws of one science and those of another which makes each of them illustrate the other" (Maxwell 1952, p. 156; see also Nersessian 1984). Emulating Kelvin, who used analogies between heat and electrostatics and between light and the vibrations of an elastic medium, Maxwell used a mechanical analogy concerning stresses in a fluid medium to arrive at his celebrated equations for electromagnetic fields. By virtue of the use of such analogies, the theory or mental model for a new domain need not be built up from scratch but can derive fundamental aspects of its structure from other, already functioning mental models.

11.5.2 *Conceptual Combination*

Analogical problem solving provides a general context for theoretical discovery: many discoveries take place when problem solving leads to the association of a new problem domain with already understood ideas. Two important mechanisms for generating new theoretical rules and concepts in the context of analogical problem solving are abduction and conceptual combination. Abduction is evident in Huygens's postulation that light consists of waves, designed to explain the behavior of light using rules derived from the behavior of sound, and in Darwin's hypothesis of evolution by natural selection. In this section we will describe in more detail how conceptual combination can produce new theoretical concepts. A third mechanism, analogical schema formation, will be discussed in the next section.

The examples of conceptual combination given in chapters 3 and 4 were very ordinary: striped apple, feminist bank teller, and so on. What was important there was the idea that concepts have internal structure that enables them to enter into combinations more complex than could be achieved by merely adding them together. We described how it was possible to construct the concept of "feminist bank teller" by mingling rules taken from the donor concepts of "feminist" and "bank teller". The resulting concept was not *defined* in terms of the donor concepts, which yielded conflicting expectations. Rather, it amassed a collection of rules that could serve to generate expectations on its own. Scientific ideas also can be generated by combining rules present in existing ideas, with default expectations reconciled primarily by consideration of the problems with which the idea is intended to deal.

During the nineteenth century the dominant theory of light held that it consisted of waves, yet no one had ever observed a light wave. The concept of a light wave was developed by a conceptual combination of the notion of a wave familiar from water waves and sound waves (the latter a previous conceptual combination) with rules pertinent to light. Rules for the behavior of water and sound waves, such as their properties of rectilinear propagation and reflection, were naturally translated into rules that became part of the concept of a light wave. Of course transfer was not always simple, since some expectations generated by the donor wave concepts were hard to meet in the case of light. In particular, where it was easy to include a rule specifying the medium for water and sound waves, physicists were hard pressed to find an appropriate medium for light waves. As in the mundane examples of striped apple and feminist bank teller, resolution of the expectations generated by the donor concepts was required. In scientific cases such resolution will generally be goal directed, selecting a rule on the grounds that it increases the explanatory effectiveness of the theory that employs the concept.

Another fine example of concept formation by conceptual combination is Darwin's notion of natural selection as the mechanism for the evolution of species. As Darden (1983) has chronicled, Darwin's idea had two sources: the notion of artificial selection that was prevalent at the time through breeding experiments, and the notion, which Darwin had gained from reading Malthus, of a struggle for survival resulting from competition for food and other resources in the face of geometrically increasing population. Starting with a concept of selection that included a rule specifying humans as the selection agent, Darwin introduced a natural mechanism as the selection agent. At the time, conflict resolution was essential for this conceptual combination to occur, since the predominant assumption was that the degree of change that could be produced in a species by breeding was limited. Darwin devoted considerable space to arguing against limits to variation, paving the way for the goal-directed conceptual combination that produced the new concept of natural selection leading to new species.

11.5.3 Discovering the Wave Theory of Sound

Using conceptual combination and several kinds of inductive inference discussed in chapters 3 and 4, the program PI simulates the discovery of the wave theory of sound. The theory that sound consists of waves is very old, dating back to the Stoics (Samburski 1973). But it has the essential features of theories discussed earlier in this chapter. It unifies various observed phenomena, such as the propagation and reflection of sound, and it postulates a nonobserved kind of entity, namely, sound waves. The first systematic discussion of the wave theory of sound comes from the Roman architect Vitruvius, writing around the first century B.C. He set out to describe the acoustic principles that made the Greek amphitheater so effective in conveying sound from performers to an audience. Here is his conclusion about the fundamental nature of sound:

Voice is a flowing breath of air, perceptible to the hearing by contact. It moves in an endless number of circular rounds, like the innumerably increasing circular waves which appear when a stone is thrown into smooth water, and which keep on spreading indefinitely from the center unless interrupted by narrow limits, or by some obstruction which prevents such waves from reaching their end in due formation. When they are interrupted by obstructions, the first waves, flowing back, break up the formation of those which follow.

In the same manner the voice executes its movements in concentric circles; but while in the case of water the circles move horizontally on a plane surface, the voice not only proceeds horizontally, but also ascends vertically by regular stages. Therefore, as in the case of the waves formed in the water, so it is in the case of the voice: the first wave, when there is no obstruction to interrupt it, does not break up the second or the following waves, but they all reach the ears of the lowest and highest spectators without an echo. (Vitruvius 1926, pp. 138–139)

We have no detailed information about how Vitruvius or his predecessors actually discovered the wave theory of sound, but the above quotation suggests that it occurred in the context of trying to explain why sound propagates and reflects, and that it depended on noticing the crucial analogy with water waves. Similarly, PI is set the problem of explaining why sound propagates and reflects. In the latter case this amounts to starting with an arbitrary example of sound x and explaining why x reflects.

The discovery of the wave theory of sound depended on associating the phenomena of sound with the properties of waves already understood through the behavior of water. Here is one of the many ways in which this might have happened, as simulated in an actual run of PI. To get things going, the concepts "sound" and "reflection" are activated. Activation of the latter concept leads to activation of several rules concerning reflection, including the information that water waves reflect and rope waves reflect. The activation of these rules then triggers a condition-simplifying generalization that all waves reflect. This new rule then provides the basis for the abduction that x is a wave, since that in conjunction with the rule that all waves reflect would explain why x reflects. But now we have active messages that x is a wave and that x is sound, triggering both the generalization that all sounds are waves and the conceptual combination of sound-wave. Generalization succeeds because x was chosen arbitrarily, so that consideration of number of instances and variability is irrelevant.

The least plausible part of this simulation is the triggering of the condition-simplifying generalization that all waves reflect. That generalization might have come about more directly. It is possible that the only kind of waves that were at all familiar to the ancients were water waves. If so, more sophisticated procedures for analogical transfer would have been required as prerequisites for the abduction that sound is a wave.

The concept of nonobservable sound waves is produced by conceptual combination. Recall that in PI conceptual combination produces a new permanent concept only when combination requires the resolution of some conflict, as in the striped apple and feminist bank teller examples. The passage from Vitruvius shows that the combination of the concepts of sound and wave did require resolution of conflicting expectations. He remarks that sound spreads spherically whereas water waves spread out in a single plane. PI resolves this conflict by supposing that sound waves will inherit the actual property of sound. The result is the new, stored theoretical concept of a sound wave, containing the information that a sound wave is a kind of wave as well as numerous new rules formed from those attached to the concepts of sound and wave. Notice that there has also been an implicit change in the concept of wave. It still contains the default assumption that waves propagate in a single plane, but it now has a new subordinate, sound wave, which generates a different expectation. From a static, logistic point of view, there is a dangerous contradiction lurking here; but procedurally the problem is resolved by the mechanisms of rule competition and default-hierarchy traversal described in chapters 2 through 4.

Having formed the rule that sound consists of waves, PI is able to deduce why the arbitrary sound x reflects, so the problem of explaining why sound reflects is tentatively solved. Additional confidence that sound is a wave comes from the parallel abduction that the propagation of sound can also be explained by that hypothesis. Thus the wave theory of sound begins to become consilient in the sense of section 11.4.2, since it explains more than one class of facts.

This is clearly not the only way in which the fortunate confluence of ideas concerning sound and waves might have occurred. Another simulation takes into account the Greeks' strong interest in stringed instruments. PI is set the problems of explaining why sound reflects and propagates. In this case it reaches a solution via rule firing and spreading activation, via associations from sound to music to stringed instruments to vibrations to waves.

The wave theory of sound was not the only one that the Greeks constructed. Democritus recommended a particle theory of sound, which PI discovers using rules about the behavior of balls. Like most of the Greeks, however, PI rejects this theory because it cannot explain how sounds can pass through each other with little interruption.

In the simulations described, abduction and conceptual combination are the most important mechanisms, but it should also be possible to extend PI by developing more specific analogical mechanisms of the sort described in chapter 10. Suppose that the knowledge of the discoverer of the wave theory of sound was at the specific level of pond waves that had been observed to spread and reflect. Pursuit of the problem might lead to noticing the similarity between sound and pond waves. Abduction that sound *is* a pond wave would obviously be thwarted by the non-pondlike characteristics of sound, but a crude analogical notion of "sound wave" might nonetheless be formed by analogy to "pond wave". The highly important abstract concept of "wave" could then be formed by abstraction from "pond wave" and "sound wave". This new concept is like the analogical schemas of chapter 10, forming a bridge between the two previously unconnected domains. A similar kind of abstraction occurred following Darwin's discovery of natural selection (Darden 1983). From the concepts of natural selection and artificial selection a new abstract selection schema was formed, capable of being applied to other domains. This kind of analogical schema formation appears to be an important kind of inductive mechanism.

In this chapter we have argued that the use and discovery of scientific theories can be understood within our general framework. In the next chapter we evaluate our framework itself as a possible precursor to a theory of induction.

12

Epilogue: Toward a Theory of Induction

We have traveled a long distance, examining phenomena ranging from conditioning in rats to scientific discovery in humans. But the journey is not yet complete. To conclude the book, we will review briefly how the framework we have proposed has integrated and illuminated diverse phenomena, and we will describe how the result has fallen short of what we see as the ultimate aim of this enterprise. That aim is the development of a full *theory* of induction, a much more canonical and comprehensive description of mechanisms for problem solving and induction, with broader and more detailed empirical applications. We will sketch what such a theory would be like, and outline the research that appears to be needed to accomplish it. Clearly, our journey to this point has not been made alone, but in the company of many researchers, and we are eager to enlist still others.

12.1 Looking Backward

This book has two aims. The first is to establish a framework within which to view problems of inference and learning. The second is to establish the validity of several assertions about induction.

The framework is easily summarized by paraphrasing the principles we introduced in chapter 1. We view cognitive systems as constantly modeling their environments, with emphasis on local aspects that represent obstacles to the achievement of current goals. Models are best understood as assemblages of synchronic and diachronic rules organized into default hierarchies and clustered into categories. The rules comprising the model act in accord with a principle of limited parallelism, both competing with and supporting one another. Goal attainment often depends in part on flexible recategorization of the environment combined with the generation of new rules. New rules are generated via triggering conditions, most of which are best understood as responses to the success or failure of current model-based predictions.

In addition to providing a framework, we hope we have established the importance of a number of claims about the process of induction. Some of these claims are relatively narrow and are treated in only one chapter of the book. An example would be our claim, following Billman (1983), that multiple interrelated associations may be learned more readily than isolated associations. Some are broader but are highly speculative. An example would be our claim that categorizations at the most specific level of the default hierarchy typically override categorizations at more general levels. We wish to highlight here four claims that we believe to be of considerable importance and backed by substantial evidence. We believe they are well grounded empirically, and we are prepared to insist that they address important questions with which any satisfactory theory of induction must deal.

First, we believe that we have provided good evidence for the view that much inferential activity is best viewed as resulting from competition among rules and from the generation of new rules arising from that competition. We do not believe it is possible to understand either the animal conditioning literature or the work on lay understanding of the physical and social worlds without adopting the rules-in-competition perspective. For example, a rat in a conditioning box sometimes holds multiple hypotheses in mind as candidates for explaining the same class of events, and the interaction between those hypotheses or rules must be adjudicated in some way. Similarly, although it is possible to understand much of learning in terms of revision of rule strength, it is not possible to understand all of learning in that way. Somehow, at some point, those rules that are to undergo strength revision have to be *generated*. The particular rule-generation heuristics we have described may be questioned, but we believe that any comprehensive learning theory will require mechanisms for acquiring rules in a relatively quantum fashion.

We make similar claims with regard to the literature on modeling the physical and social worlds. It is very clear that people possess rules about the operation of the world that conflict with one another. This is true both across levels of the default hierarchy, as when rules of differing levels of generality conflict with one another, and for rules at approximately the same level of generality, as when people are taught general rules of physics or social behavior that conflict in their implications with rules that have been induced from living in the world. It is also clear that new rules emerge from the competition of established rules with one another, as when beginning physics students are found to have blended an old intuitive rule with one they have been taught, producing a hybrid that is different from either.

Second, we claim to have established that people represent the variability of the world and that they make use of their estimates of variability when making inferences. People do not merely understand that objects in a category can be variable with respect to their properties. They often have highly accurate representations of the dispersion of properties around their central tendencies. People make use of these dispersion estimates in making generalizations about categories of the type in question. We believe that our approach to the representation of variability in terms of default hierarchies and property-distribution rules has much to recommend it, but again we set less value on the specific mechanisms we have introduced than on the recognition that people do and machines must represent variability in some way, and that any future theories of induction must come to grips with the question of variability representation and processing.

A third claim we make is that many rules and categories are of a general and abstract nature. A great many contemporary viewpoints in psychology emphasize reasoning on the basis of concrete instances. While we do not wish to dispute the frequent importance of the specific and the concrete, we insist that we have established credible evidence for structures and processes at a high level of generality and abstractness. People possess inferential rules corresponding to at least a crude version of the law of large numbers, and they possess reasoning schemas corresponding to abstract notions about causal structures in the world and about contractual relations at the level of obligation and permission. These claims rest on evidence that people can reason effectively about situations described in terms of abstract but pragmatically important concepts and on evidence that it is possible to teach people rules at extremely high levels of abstraction quite directly. Furthermore, not only can knowledge acquired in this fashion be applied across essentially the full range of domains to which the rules are applicable, but it can be retained over substantial time intervals.

Our fourth major claim is related to the previous one. It is that the acquisition of new knowledge can be understood only in the light of the knowledge already possessed by the system. People are not blank slates on which just any kinds of rules can be written. Some rules will be quickly absorbed and clearly exhibited; others will have only faint consequences and will fail to be retained. There are two components to this claim. The first is that it is very difficult to teach rules that are not intrinsically similar to those the learner already possesses. It is vastly easier to extend a familiar rule system than to introduce a structurally novel one. The second component to the claim is that people must possess or be given rules for encoding the world in terms that make contact with the to-be-taught rule, or else the rule will simply not be applied. Even such inherently nonintuitive rule systems as formal logic can be taught if people are shown how to encode a domain and set of relations in such a way that the rule system can be applied. In contrast, it will be hard to extend even familiar rule systems to domains in which the individual lacks the necessary encoding procedures.

Behind these four claims is a deeper theme: Induction is a remarkably flexible process. New information is regularly and flexibly integrated into the pool of knowledge and procedures. Models are generated (and discarded) with ease. Hypotheses and plans concerned with everyday situations usually go from sketch to detailed expectations and execution with little difficulty. New situations as often as not give rise to several plausible hypotheses or plans. Overall, induction acts continually and pervasively on a tremendous diversity of material. This gracefulness in accepting new information and goals, with little disruption of extant capabilities, comes close to being a hallmark of induction. Such gracefulness depends on the ready emergence of plausible, but tentative, knowledge structures integrating categories, relations, procedures, and expectations—the structures we have formalized as quasi-homomorphisms. Regardless of the details of formalization, it is our firm belief that emergence, as mediated by the discovery and recombination of appropriate "building blocks", must be the central theme of any deep study of induction.

The above list should not be taken as evidence of a mood of unalloyed satisfaction with what has been accomplished. We have been fortunate in having critics who are sufficiently numerous and vocal to prevent such complacency. This book falls short of our aspirations in many important respects: theoretical integration, development of computational examples, and experimental tests. We faced tradeoffs between struggling toward a broad sketch of induction and developing detailed portraits of particular aspects of it. For better or worse we gave priority to the more general goal. There was and is much more to be done than we have been able to accomplish in our time together. Four is a large number of authors, but it is still a small number of investigators. In the section that follows we sketch the kind of progress we hope will be possible in the future.

12.2 Looking Forward

A genuine theory of induction would be both *unified*, using a single interrelated set of theoretical concepts and computational mechanisms, and *comprehensive*, applying to the broadest possible range of empirical phenomena. We will now sketch what would be required to develop such a theory within the framework we have outlined. The problems are indeed daunting, but even partial solutions would be immensely important for the understanding of mind.

12.2.1 Formal Developments

A deep understanding of problems in induction requires the aid—and constraint—of formal theoretical apparatus. Concepts described only in an intuitive framework remain malleable and uncertain in their implications. In contrast, when an intuitive concept, such as mass in physics, is embedded in a theory that describes its possible interactions and effects—its states and its transitions—we gain the highest level of comprehension that science has to offer. Because a formal theory constrains the derivation of consequences, reinterpretation of concepts as needed to fit observations is restricted.

A formal theory is very much a model, in the sense in which we have used that word throughout this book. It is also true that a well-conceived computer model—be it a model of a weather system or of cognition—can serve as a theory. The consequences of a theory defined via a computer model are indeed unambiguous, and computer "runs" can indeed provide predictions. Such a theory is typically unwieldy, however. It is difficult to relate computer models to one another because of the complexity of the syntax of the underlying language(s), and it is difficult to embed such a theory in a larger picture. As a consequence, much of the potential unifying effect of theory that we described in chapter 11 is lost. In short, a computer model is more an embodiment of a theory than a theory in itself. A particular run of a computer model gives only one specific outcome of the theory—it is more an experiment than an inference. For complex systems it is much better to have a mathematical theory working hand-in-hand with a computer model. The mathematical theory provides an overview and a relation to other theories (for example, theories of weather make extensive use of the physics of gases and fluids), while the computer model provides the possibility of detailed prediction and direct comparison with observation (the forecasts). So it should be with the study of induction.

What, then, are the possibilities for a mathematical theory that works within the framework we have been developing? There are two critical processes that take place within this framework. The first process involves the apportionment of credit to extant rules and building blocks on the basis of their observed usefulness in solving the problems the system encounters. The second process involves the discovery and recombination of multifunctional building blocks to generate plausible models of new situations. A relevant mathematics would provide guarantees that proposed apportionment-of-credit and recombination processes (algorithms) actually do what intuition suggest. Moreover, the mathematics should relate these processes to similar processes studied in other sciences. Once such relations are available, we can transfer models and related mathematics from one science to another. As chapter 11 points out, such transfer is a critical process in the development of science. Cross-disciplinary relations centered on induction should make possible deeper insights into the relation of the theory of induction to data provided by psychology, neurophysiology, and other complex systems.

Some pieces of mathematics are already in place. For models in general, we can begin to show mathematically the parsimony gained by loosening the technical requirement for a homomorphism (see appendix 2B). For apportionment of credit, the economic analogy used to describe the bucket brigade algorithm can be deepened so that some fixed-point theorems of economics show that the algorithm does indeed apportion credit appropriately in situations of interest. For recombination based on operators like crossover, we can prove that a sophisticated, efficient search for useful building blocks takes place as an implicit byproduct of the very process of generating candidate rules (see appendix 4B).

More generally, a mathematics appropriate to the study of induction holds many elements in common with the mathematics used to study other adaptive systems. An economy, in common with a cognitive system, exhibits (1) hierarchical organization, (2) retained earnings (strength) as a measure of past performance, (3) competition based on retained earnings, (4) distribution of earnings on the basis of local interactions of consumers and suppliers (the bucket brigade), (5) taxation as a control on efficiency, and (6) division of effort between production and research (exploitation versus exploration). Mathematical economics deals with many of these processes and much of that mathematics, with suitable alterations, is relevant to the study of induction.

As another example, in the genetics of ecologies we see (1) niche exploitation (models exploiting environmental opportunities), (2) phylogenetic hierarchies, polymorphism, and enforced diversity (competing models), (3) functional convergence (similarities of models enforced by environmental requirements on goal attainment), (4) symbiosis, parasitism, and mimicry (couplings and interactions in a default hierarchy, such as the protection of defaults by generated exceptions), (5) food chains, predator-prey relations, and other energy transfers (the bucket brigade), (6) recombination of multifunctional coadapted sets of genes (recombination of building blocks), (7) assortative mating (triggered recombination of building blocks), (8) phenotypic markers affecting interspecies and intraspecies interactions (tags), and (9) "founder" effects (general rules giving rise to specialist exceptions), among other parallels. Once again, though mathematical ecology is a young science, there is much in the mathematics that has been developed for it that is relevant to the study of induction.

These comparisons could be extended to other complex adaptive systems involving components interacting in a nonlinear fashion: the immune system, biochemical genetics, the central nervous system, physical systems far from equilibrium, and others. We can therefore hope to find useful analogies between theories drawn from these superficially disparate domains, allowing transfer of both qualitative ideas and formal models. For each of these domains there are mathematical developments, and where these developments overlap, there are substantial commonalities in the mathematics. All such systems, in one regime or another, exhibit all of the features described and others as well. A general mathematical theory of such adaptive systems would explain both the pervasiveness of these features and the relations between them. Such a theory, applied to the study of induction, would greatly enhance our chances of finding comprehensive, canonical descriptions of the mechanisms of model building and problem solving.

12.2.2 Computational Developments

While formal theory is a powerful tool, it typically encounters formidable barriers in complex domains such as the study of induction— barriers arising from the very complexity of the phenomena. It is at this point that computer models supply a vital bridge. Because a computer handles all the derivations, a computer model can be quite detailed and long sequences of transitions (state changes) can be carried out rapidly. Though each run is quite particular, valid only for the particular settings of parameters and initial state used, it gives a genuine, unambiguous prediction. Moreover, the model can be run time and time again with absolute control over the initial state and parameter settings. As a result one can develop related observations (sets of curves, for instance) suggesting regularities that can be used to advance formal theory. The fact that computer models themselves are presented in a formal, albeit complex, language aids in parsing out the origins of observed regularities.

Although theory supplies general results, its advance is often retarded by complexity. Observations of natural phenomena supply vital constraints, but except for the rare critical experiment that decides between theories, results remain particular and embedded in detail. Computer models supply a halfway house, yielding only particular results but with rigorous formulation and complete control of detail. The study of induction should benefit enormously from this bridge.

Perhaps the most basic issue to be addressed in future computational work on induction concerns mechanisms that might account for the emergence of high-level cognitive processes from more elementary subcognitive ones. Given an initial set of feature detectors, hard-wired response patterns, inductive operating principles, and other innate system components, how do abstract concepts and inferential rules eventually arise from experience? Current work on classifier systems and neural networks may help in addressing this complex question.

Such emergence is crucial if we are to avoid the arbitrariness of the symbols used in a cognitive model such as PI. We should not let PI's use of a LISP atom labeled SOUND, for example, mislead us into thinking that the program has a human-like understanding of sound. What is needed is a subcognitive underpinning linking such atoms to lower-level functions by means of the principle of inductive adequacy: The computational system should contain no structures that could not have been produced by the inductive mechanisms of the system. Much work remains to be done to construct a system that is inductively adequate yet representationally sufficient to describe the complexities of the world.

Even if the problem of emergence of the cognitive from the subcognitive can be handled, there remain innumerable problems of enhancing both subcognitive and cognitive mechanisms to account for a wider range of empirical phenomena. Our accounts of experimental results in chapters 5 through 10 have drawn heavily on the framework we propose, but we have rarely been able to present detailed simulations in which our programs reproduce the experimentally demonstrated learning of organisms. It would be highly desirable to have, for example, detailed computational reproductions of the focused-sampling results described in chapter 6, the learning and retention of erroneous physics principles discussed in chapter 7, the traversal of a default hierarchy to construct judgments of variability as described in chapter 8, the learning of inferential rules discussed in chapter 9, the formation of analogical schemas described in chapter 10, and the complex process of theory evaluation described in chapter 11. Moreover, myriad other empirical investigations of learning provide results that a full computational theory of induction should be able to simulate.

The full computational theory would not consist of a set of unconnected mechanisms, one for each kind of empirical application. Rather, it would have a theoretically unified set of inductive mechanisms that, given different goals and environmental inputs, could yield a wide range of observed phenomena. A full test of such a theory would require a large knowledge base, showing the feasibility of the triggering conditions and inductive mechanisms in realistic situations.

12.2.3 Experimental Developments

Not only do our computer implementations fall short of simulating all the empirical phenomena we have discussed, but it is obvious that empirical tests remain to be done for the psychological reality of many of the computational mechanisms we have postulated. Many principles central to our framework, such as the priority of rules, the role of default hierarchies in constructing mental models, and the prevalence and nature of triggering conditions, remain in need of more direct empirical tests. At a more specific level, we have provided little direct evidence for the psychological reality of such mechanisms as the bucket brigade, genetic operators, abduction, and conceptual combination.

Even in the areas where we do describe empirical results, there is obviously a wealth of experiments to be done. A list of unfinished projects might include the following:

1) Our account of classical conditioning suggests a wide range of empirical investigations contrasting our view with the Rescorla and Wagner account and its sequelae. For example, the two views lead to conflicting predictions concerning the circumstances under which new stimuli will be excitatory or inhibitory, concerning the extinguishability of inhibitory stimuli, and concerning the circumstances under which positive acceleration of learning will be observed.

2) It would be desirable to further examine how distributional parameters for properties are learned, that is, how systems come to learn

about variability. We have merely scratched the surface of questions that concern the role played by empirical rules about the particular kind of property in question, the role played by inferential rules in modeling variability, and the importance of a range of statistical and temporal aspects of information about the properties.

3) The powerful focused-sampling notion of Billman (1983), which seems capable in principle of accounting for why very complex sets of interrelationships are sometimes learned with ease, has been subjected only to very limited testing with a single type of input, an artificial grammar. The notion is capable of being examined for the full range of types of category formation, from perceptual learning to social stereotype acceptance.

4) The ideas offered in chapter 7 about how people model the social and physical worlds have been examined in only a small number of domains. The similarities we found between the errors made in social versus physical domains, together with our explanation for the similarities in terms of parochial circumstances of learning, remain speculations. The conflict between specific-level and general-level information has been examined in only a small number of studies. Prediction of the precise circumstances under which the one will dominate the other is of great importance, and may depend on any number of factors not yet identified.

5) The conditions that encourage appropriate generalization have been examined in only a small number of studies, almost exclusively in the social domain. The generalizations we have made about generalization badly need testing in other domains and require the examination of a much broader range of factors than we have examined.

6) We have identified only a small number of inferential rules and pragmatic reasoning schemas. We believe that such domain-independent tools of inference play a role in almost all kinds of reasoning, including causal analysis and analogy. We believe we have provided solid evidence for the existence of a set of rules for statistical reasoning and a set of rules for contractual relations such as permission and obligation. But these seem to us to represent only a fraction of the total number of abstract rule systems waiting to be identified. Other candidates might include certain fundamental mathematical concepts, such as one-to-one correspondence and elementary set theory (Greeno, Riley, and Gelman 1984). It is also important to understand how these rules are normally induced and how they can best be taught.

7) The strong view we have pressed concerning the irrelevance of various standard logical rules of inference is admittedly quite under-determined by the data we have generated. Much more needs to be done before this radical view can be considered well substantiated.

8) Our assertions about instruction in both empirical and inferential rules have been examined for only a very small number of rules and for only a very small number of domains. Questions about the role of encoding instruction, the teachability of certain rule types versus others, and the notion of competition between induced and instructed rules have been examined in a preliminary fashion only.

9) Our account of analogy in terms of q-morphisms and our assertions about the role of schema induction in successful analogical transfer have so far received only minimal empirical scrutiny. The many factors that likely influence the use of analogy, such as surface similarity, similarity of goal structures, and complexity of the mapping, clearly require further investigation.

12.2.4 Intellectual Variation: Phylogeny, Ontogeny, and Individual Differences

Beyond the above list of empirical projects, there is the need to pursue the implications of our approach to learning for comparative and developmental psychology and for the study of individual differences. Any general theory of learning should illuminate the broad phenomena of inference and intelligence that link these fields: members of different species vary widely in their capacity to learn, individuals of a given species exhibit common sequences of learning as they pass from infancy to adulthood, and individuals differ among themselves in qualitative and quantitative aspects of inference and learning.

In chapter 5 we stressed that even the simple forms of learning observed in lower animals can be understood in terms of rule-based default hierarchies. Induction in rats, however, falls far short of the generality and power of human induction. Where does the difference lie? This question may be directly related to the problem of explaining the emergence of cognitive from subcognitive mechanisms, in that species may differ in their capacity to build new layers of representation on top of more elementary ones. The myriad questions related to human language—how it is acquired and how it affects cognition— are connected to this same issue. To what extent does language depend on species-specific and domain-specific inductive mechanisms, and to what extent is it a complex instance of general inductive mechanisms at work? Such questions remain open.

The issue of emergence lies at the heart of human developmental psychology. In one theoretical approach that can be related to our framework, Halford and Wilson (1980) argued that levels of development can be defined in terms of symbol systems that constitute morphisms. Levels differ in the complexity of the concepts included in a morphism, ordered from unary predicates through n-ary relations. When development is viewed as change in morphisms or mental models, it is natural to expect variations in the rate of development across different domains and substantial continuity (rather than discontinuous stages) within domains.

In addition, our view of rules-in-competition suggests that strong rules learned in childhood will not be forgotten or replaced by subsequent learning. Instead, such rules will remain in the system, to be called up when later circumstances resemble those under which the rules were first learned. This view conflicts directly with the traditional Piagetian view, in which each new developmental stage represents a house cleaning, replacing the rules of the preceding stage with those of the more advanced stage. Traditional views of development allow that the child may be father to the man; our view suggests that the child will be found in the man—ready to compete with him in understanding the world.

Our framework is highly compatible with the notion of individual differences in inference and learning. Indeed, our approach *demands* that individuals differ in the rules they use to understand the world. The fact that rules are induced in particular problem-solving contexts and evolve within at least slightly different q-morphisms ensures that they will differ from individual to individual. In addition, the different goals that people have dictate that particular types of rules will be differentially important to different people. These points are well brought out in the pragmatic approach to intelligence characteristic of the work of Sternberg and his colleagues (Sternberg 1985; Sternberg and Suben 1986). An important task for the future is to relate Sternberg's analysis of intelligence in terms of the context in which it develops to a rule-based approach to understanding processes of inference and learning.

12.2.5 Normative Developments

Finally, a unified theory of induction cannot shy away from normative issues, concerning how induction *ought* to be done. We are confident that normative questions may be pursued within a computational and empirical framework. We do see normative questions as involving reflection at a higher level, however—reflection about how organisms might better accomplish their goals, and even about the appropriateness of those goals.

An essential tool in normative investigations is statistical theory, which has occasionally played a background role in our empirical discussions. A full theory of induction would further integrate statistics into a discussion of how organisms do and machines might learn, reflecting on the limitations of current mechanisms for learning and on strategies for improving them.

Our approach raises other fundamental normative questions. Based as it is on the notion of rules in competition, our framework makes clear that a certain degree of inconsistency and incoherence are inevitable. Just how much incoherence is permissible or desirable and how hard one should work to eradicate it, either from oneself or from a flexible machine system, are normative questions that our framework raises but does not yet answer.

12.2.6 Envoi

Although we are aware of the limitations of what we have so far accomplished, we hope that other investigators will find the framework we have evolved useful. There is clearly an enormous amount of work to be done by psychologists, computer scientists, and philosophers, as well as researchers from cognate fields such as linguistics, biology, and statistics. We end with an ecumenical homily. Our collaboration in this enterprise of trying to provide an integrative framework for induction has required all of us to enmesh ourselves in computational, psychological, *and* philosophical concerns. We firmly believe that the progress we envision will require other researchers similarly to breach traditional intellectual boundaries.

References

Abramowitz, C. V., and Dokecki, P. (1977). The politics of clinical judgment: Early empirical returns. *Psychological Bulletin, 84*, 460–476.

Ackley, D. H., Hinton, G. E., and Sejnowski, T. J. (1985). A learning algorithm for Boltzmann machines. *Cognitive Science, 9*, 147–169.

Anderson, J. R. (1976). *Language, memory, and thought.* Hillsdale, New Jersey: Lawrence Erlbaum.

Anderson, J. R. (1983). *The architecture of cognition.* Cambridge, Massachusetts: Harvard University Press.

Anderson, J. R., Greeno, J. G., Kline, P. J., and Neves, D. M. (1981). Acquisition of problem-solving skill. In J. R. Anderson (ed.), *Cognitive skills and their acquisition.* Hillsdale, New Jersey: Lawrence Erlbaum.

Anderson, J. R., Kline, P. J., and Beasley, C. M. (1979). A general learning theory and its application to schema abstraction. In G. H. Bower (ed.), *The psychology of learning and motivation,* vol. 13. New York: Academic Press.

Axelrod, R. (1984). *The evolution of cooperation.* New York: Basic Books.

Bartlett, F. C. (1932). *Remembering.* Cambridge: Cambridge University Press.

Battig, W. F., and Montague, W. E. (1969). Category norms for verbal items in 56 categories: A replication and extension of the Connecticut category norms. *Journal of Experimental Psychology Monograph, 80* (3, part 2).

Berlin, B., and Kay, P. (1969). *Basic color terms: Their universality and evolution.* Berkeley and Los Angeles: University of California Press.

Bethke, A. D. (1980). Genetic algorithms as function optimizers. Ph.D. dissertation, University of Michigan.

Billman, D. (1983). Inductive learning of syntactic categories. Ph.D. dissertation, University of Michigan.

Blodgett, H. C. (1929). The effect of the introduction of reward upon the maze performance of rats. *University of California Publications in Psychology, 4,* 113–134.

Bodenhausen, G. V., and Wyer, R. S., Jr. (1985). Effects of stereotypes on decision-making and information-processing strategies. *Journal of Personality and Social Psychology, 48*, 267–282.

Booker, L. (1982). Intelligent behavior as an adaptation to the task environment. Ph.D. dissertation, University of Michigan.

Borgida, E., Locksley, A., and Brekke, N. (1981). Social stereotypes and social judgment. In N. Cantor and J. F. Kihlstrom (eds.), *Personality, cognition, and social interaction*. Hillsdale, New Jersey: Lawrence Erlbaum.

Braine, M. D. S. (1978). On the relation between the natural logic of reasoning and standard logic. *Psychological Review, 85,* 1–21.

Braine, M. D. S., Reiser, B. J., and Rumain, B. (1984). Some empirical justification for a theory of natural propositional logic. In G. H. Bower (ed.), *The psychology of learning and motivation,* vol. 18. New York: Academic Press.

Bromberger, S. (1966). Why questions. In R. Colodny (ed.), *Mind and cosmos.* Pittsburgh: University of Pittsburgh Press.

Broverman, I., Vogel, S., Broverman, D., Clarkson, F., and Rosenkrantz, P. (1972). Sex-role stereotypes: A current appraisal. *Journal of Social Issues, 28,* 59–78.

Brown, J. S., and Van Lehn, K. (1980). Repair theory: A generative theory of bugs in procedural skills. *Cognitive Science, 4,* 379–426.

Brown, R. (1958). How shall a thing be called? *Psychological Review, 65,* 14–21.

Brown, R. (1973). *A first language.* Cambridge, Massachusetts: Harvard University Press.

Bruner, J. S., Goodnow, J. J., and Austin, G. A. (1956). *A study of thinking.* New York: Wiley.

Brunswik, E. (1952). The conceptual framework of psychology. *International encyclopedia of social science, 1.* Chicago: University of Chicago Press.

Buchanan, B., and Shortliffe, E. (1984). *Rule-based expert systems.* Reading, Massachusetts: Addison-Wesley.

Bush, R. R., and Mosteller, F. (1955). *Stochastic models for learning.* New York: Wiley.

Campbell, D. (1974a). Evolutionary epistemology. In P. Schillp (ed.), *The philosophy of Karl Popper.* La Salle, Illinois: Open Court.

Campbell, D. (1974b). Unjustified variation and selective retention in scientific discovery. In F. Ayala and T. Dobzhansky (eds.), *Studies in the philosophy of biology.* Berkeley: University of California Press.

Carbonell, J. (1983). Learning by analogy: Formulating and generalizing plans from past experience. In R. Michalski, J. Carbonell, and T. Mitchell (eds.), *Machine learning: An artificial intelligence approach.* Palo Alto: Tioga Press.

Carnap, R. (1950). *Logical foundations of probability.* Chicago: University of Chicago Press.

Carnap, R., and Jeffrey, R. (eds.) (1971. *Studies in inductive logic and probability.* Berkeley: University of California Press.

Cartwright, D. (ed.) (1951). *Field theory in social science,* by Kurt Lewin. New York: Harper and Row.

Cartwright, N. (1983). *How the laws of physics lie.* Oxford: Clarendon Press.

Champagne, A. B., Klopfer, L. E., and Anderson, J. H. (1980). Factors influencing the learning of classical mechanics. *American Journal of Physics, 48,* 1074–1079.

Chapman, L. J. (1967). Illusory correlation in observational report. *Journal of Verbal Learning and Verbal Behavior, 6,* 151–155.

Chapman, L. J., and Chapman, J. P. (1967). Genesis of popular but erroneous diagnostic observations. *Journal of Abnormal Psychology, 72,* 193–204.

Chapman, L. J., and Chapman, J. P. (1969). Illusory correlation as an obstacle to the use of valid psychodiagnostic signs. *Journal of Abnormal Psychology, 74,* 271–280.

Chase, W. G., and Simon, H. A. (1973). The mind's eye in chess. In W. G. Chase (ed.), *Visual information processing.* New York: Academic Press.

Cheng, P. W. (1985). Restructuring versus automaticity: Alternative accounts of skill acquisition. *Psychological Review, 92,* 414–423.

Cheng, P. W., and Holyoak, K. J. (1985). Pragmatic reasoning schemas. *Cognitive Psychology, 17,* 391–416.

Cheng, P. W., Holyoak, K. J., Nisbett, R. E., and Oliver, L. M. (1986). Pragmatic versus syntactic approaches to training deductive reasoning. *Cognitive Psychology, 18.*

Chi, M., Feltovich, P., and Glaser, R. (1981). Categorization and representation of physics problems by experts and novices. *Cognitive Science, 5,* 121–152.

Clement, J. (1982a). Students' preconceptions in introductory mechanics. *American Journal of Physics, 50,* 66–71.

Clement, J. (1982b). Spontaneous analogies in problem solving: The progressive construction of mental models. Paper presented at the meeting of the American Education Research Association, New York.

Collins, A. M., and Loftus, E. F. (1975). A spreading-activation theory of semantic processing. *Psychological Review, 82,* 407–428.

Craik, K. (1943). *The nature of explanation.* Cambridge: Cambridge University Press.

D'Andrade, R. (1982). Reason versus logic. Paper presented at the Symposium on the Ecology of Cognition: Biological, Cultural, and Historical Perspectives, Greensboro, North Carolina.

Darden, L. (1983). Artificial intelligence and philosophy of science: Reasoning by analogy in theory construction. In P. Asquith and T. Nickles (eds.), *PSA 1982,* vol. 2. East Lansing: Philosophy of Science Association.

Darley, J., and Batson, C. D. (1973). From Jerusalem to Jericho: A study of situational and dispositional variables in helping behavior. *Journal of Personality and Social Psychology, 27,* 100–119.

Darwin, C. (1859). *The origin of species.* London: Murray.

Darwin, C. (1887). *The autobiography of Charles Darwin and selected letters,* edited by F. Darwin. London: John Murray (edited by N. Barlow). Reprinted New York: Dover, 1958.

Davis, R., and King, J. (1977). An overview of production systems. In E. W. Elcock and D. Michie (eds.), *Machine Intelligence, 8*. Chichester: Ellis Horwood.

de Groot, A. M. B. (1983). The range of automatic spreading activation in word priming. *Journal of Verbal Learning and Verbal Behavior, 22*, 417–436.

DeJong, K. A. (1980). Adaptive system design—a genetic approach. *IEEE Transactions: Systems, Man and Cybernetics, 10*.

Dietterich, T., and Michalski, R. (1983). A comparative review of selected methods for learning from examples. In R. Michalski, J. Carbonell, and T. Mitchell (eds.), *Machine learning: An artificial intelligence approach*. Palo Alto: Tioga Press.

Duncker, K. (1945). On problem solving. *Psychological Monographs, 58* (no. 270).

Elio, R., and Anderson, J. R. (1981). The effects of category generalizations and instance similarity on schema abstraction. *Journal of Experimental Psychology: Human Learning and Memory, 7*, 397–417.

Erman, L. D., Hayes-Roth, F., Lesser, V. R., and Reddy, D. R. (1980). The Hearsay-II speech-understanding system: Integrating knowledge to resolve uncertainty. *Computing Surveys, 12*, 213–253.

Evans, J. St. B. T. (1982). *The psychology of deductive reasoning*. London: Routledge and Kegan Paul.

Evans, S. N. (1967). A brief statement of schema theory. *Psychonomic Science, 8*, 87–88.

Fahlman, S. (1979). *NETL: A system for representing and using real-world knowledge*. Cambridge, Massachusetts: MIT Press.

Fillenbaum, S. (1975). If: Some uses. *Psychological Research, 37*, 245–260.

Fillenbaum, S. (1976). Inducements: On phrasing and logic of conditional promises, threats and warnings. *Psychological Research, 38*, 231–250.

Fischler, I. (1977). Semantic facilitation without association in a lexical decision task. *Memory & Cognition, 5*, 335–339.

Flannagan, M. J., Fried, L. S., and Holyoak, K. J. (1986). Distributional expectations and the induction of category structure. *Journal of Experimental Psychology: Learning, Memory, and Cognition, 12*.

Fodor, J. (1983). *The modularity of mind*. Cambridge, Massachusetts: MIT Press.

Fong, G. T., Krantz, D. H., and Nisbett, R. E. (1986). The effects of statistical training on thinking about everyday problems. *Cognitive Psychology, 18*.

Fong, G. T., and Nisbett, R. E. (1986). The effects of statistical training: Domain independent and long-lived. Unpublished manuscript, Northwestern University.

Fowler, C. A., Wolford, G., Slade, R., and Tassinary, L. (1981). Lexical access with and without awareness. *Journal of Experimental Psychology: General, 110*, 341–362.

Fried, L. S., and Holyoak, K. J. (1984). Induction of category distributions:

A framework for classification learning. *Journal of Experimental Psychology: Learning, Memory, and Cognition, 10*, 234–257.

Garcia, J., McGowan, B. K., Ervin, F., and Koelling, R. (1968). Cues: Their relative effectiveness as reinforcers. *Science, 160*, 794–795.

Garcia, J., McGowan, B. K., and Green, K. F. (1972). Sensory quality and integration: Constraints on conditioning. In A. H. Black and W. F. Prokasy (eds.), *Classicial conditioning II: Current research and theory*. New York: Appleton-Century-Crofts.

Geis, M. C., and Zwicky, A. M. (1971). On invited inferences. *Linguistic Inquiry, 2*, 561–566.

Gelman, S. A., and Markman, E. M. (1983). Natural kind terms and children's ability to draw inferences. Paper presented at the meeting of the Western Psychological Association, San Francisco.

Gentner, D. (1982). Are scientific analogies metaphors? In D. S. Miall (ed.), *Metaphor: Problems and perspectives*. Brighton, Sussex: Harvester Press.

Gentner, D. (1983). Structure-mapping: A theoretical framework for analogy. *Cognitive Science, 7*, 155–170.

Gentner, D., and Gentner, D. R. (1983). Flowing waters or teeming crowds: Mental models of electricity. In D. Gentner and A. L. Stevens (eds.), *Mental models*. Hillsdale, New Jersey: Lawrence Erlbaum.

Gentner, D., and Stevens, A. L. (eds.) (1983). *Mental models*. Hillsdale, New Jersey: Lawrence Erlbaum.

Gibson, J. J., and Gibson, E. J. (1955). Perceptual learning: Differentiation or enrichment? *Psychological Review, 62*, 32–41.

Gick, M. L., and Holyoak, K. J. (1980). Analogical problem solving. *Cognitive Psychology, 12*, 306–355.

Gick, M. L., and Holyoak, K. J. (1983). Schema induction and analogical transfer. *Cognitive Psychology, 15*, 1–38.

Giere, R. (1979). *Understanding scientific reasoning*. New York: Holt, Rinehart and Winston.

Gilovich, T. (1981). Seeing the past in the present: The effect of associations to familiar events on judgments and decisions. *Journal of Personality and Social Psychology, 40*, 797–808.

Ginsberg, M. L. (1985). Counterfactuals. In *Proceedings of the Ninth Joint Conference on Artificial Intelligence*. Los Altos, California: Kaufmann.

Glass, A. L., and Holyoak, K. J. (1975). Alternative conceptions of semantic memory. *Cognition, 3*, 313–339.

Glass, A. L., and Holyoak, K. J. (1986). *Cognition* (2nd edition). New York: Random House.

Glass, A. L., Holyoak, K. J., and O'Dell, C. (1974). Production frequency and the verification of quantified statements. *Journal of Verbal Learning and Verbal Behavior, 13*, 237–254.

Goldberg, D. (1983). Computer-aided gas pipeline operation using genetic algorithms and rule learning. Ph.D. dissertation, University of Michigan.

Golding, E. (1981). The effect of past experience on problem solving. Paper presented at the Annual Conference of the British Psychological Association, Surrey.

Goldman, A. I. (1978). Epistemics: The regulative theory of cognition. *Journal of Philosophy, 75*, 509–523.

Goodman, N. (1965). *Fact, fiction and forecast* (2nd edition). Indianapolis: Bobbs-Merrill.

Granger, R. H., and Schlimmer, J. J. (1985). Learning salience among features through contingency in the CEL framework. In *Proceedings of the Seventh Annual Conference of the Cognitive Science Society*.

Greeno, J. G., Riley, M. S., and Gelman, R. (1984). Conceptual competence and children's counting. *Cognitive Psychology, 16*, 94–143.

Griggs, R. A., and Cox, J. R. (1982). The elusive thematic-materials effect in Wason's selection task. *British Journal of Psychology, 73*, 407–420.

Halford, G. A., and Wilson, W. H. (1980). A category theory approach to cognitive deveopment. *Cognitive Psychology, 12*, 356–441.

Hanson, N. R. (1958). *Patterns of discovery*. Cambridge: Cambridge University Press.

Hayes-Roth, B., and Hayes-Roth, F. (1977). Concept learning and the recognition and classification of exemplars. *Journal of Verbal Learning and Verbal Behavior, 16*, 321–338.

Hayes-Roth, R., and McDermott, J. (1978). An interference matching technique for inducing abstractions. *Communications of the ACM, 21*, 401–410.

Hebb, D. O. (1949). *The organization of behavior*. New York: Wiley.

Heider, F. (1958). *The psychology of interpersonal relations*. New York: Wiley.

Hempel, C. G. (1965). *Aspects of scientific explanation*. New York: The Free Press.

Henle, M. (1962). On the relation between logic and thinking. *Psychological Review, 69*, 366–378.

Hesse, M. B. (1966). *Models and analogies in science*. Notre Dame, Indiana: University of Notre Dame Press.

Hewitt, C. E. (1977). Viewing control structures as patterns of passing messages. *Artificial Intelligence, 8*, 323–364.

Hinton, G. E., and Anderson, J. (eds.) (1981). *Parallel models of associative memory*. Hillsdale, New Jersey: Lawrence Erlbaum.

Hofstadter, D. R. (1979). *Godel, Escher, Bach: An eternal golden braid*. New York: Basic Books.

Hofstadter, D. R. (1984). The Copycat project: An experiment in nondeterminism and creative analogies. A. I. Memo 755. Cambridge, Massachusetts: MIT Artificial Intelligence Laboratory.

Hofstadter, D. R. (1985). *Metamagical themas*. New York: Basic Books.

Holland, J. H. (1975). *Adaptation in natural and artificial systems*. Ann Arbor: University of Michigan Press.

Holland, J. H. (1986). Escaping brittleness: The possibilities of general purpose machine learning algorithms applied to parallel rule-based systems. In R. S. Michalski, J. G. Carbonell, and T. M. Mitchell (eds.), *Machine learning: An artificial intelligence approach*, vol. 2. Los Altos, California: Kaufmann.

Holland, J. H., and Reitman, J. (1978). Cognitive systems based on adaptive algorithms. In D. Waterman and F. Hayes-Roth (eds.), *Pattern-directed inference systems*. New York: Academic Press.

Holyoak, K. J. (1982). An analogical framework for literary interpretation. *Poetics, 11*, 105–126.

Holyoak, K. J. (1984). Analogical thinking and human intelligence. In R. J. Sternberg (ed.), *Advances in the psychology of human intelligence*, vol. 2. Hillsdale, New Jersey: Lawrence Erlbaum.

Holyoak, K. J., and Gordon, P. C. (1984). Information processing and social cognition. In R. S. Wyer, Jr., and T. K. Srull (eds.), *Handbook of social cognition*, vol. 1. Hillsdale, New Jersey: Lawrence Erlbaum.

Holyoak, K. J., Junn, E. N., and Billman, D. (1984). Development of analogical problem-solving skill. *Child Development, 55*, 2042–2055.

Holyoak, K. J., and Koh, K. (1986). Analogical problem solving: Effects of surface and structural similarity. Paper presented at the Annual Meeting of the Midwestern Psychological Association, Chicago.

Holyoak, K. J., Koh, K., and Nisbett, R. E. (1986). An adaptive default-hierarchy theory of classical conditioning. Manuscript in preparation, University of Michigan.

Homa, D., and Vosburgh, R. (1976). Category breadth and the abstraction of prototypical information. *Journal of Experimental Psychology: Human Learning and Memory, 2*, 322–330.

Horwich, P. (1982). *Probability and evidence*. Cambridge: Cambridge University Press.

Hull, C. L. (1932). The goal-gradient hypothesis and maze learning. *Psychological Review, 39*, 25–43.

Hull, C. L. (1934). The concept of the habit-family hierarchy and maze learning: Part 1. *Psychological Review, 41*, 33–54.

Hull, C. L. (1943). *Principles of behavior*. New York: Appleton-Century-Crofts.

Hume, D. (1739/1888). *A treatise of human nature*, edited by L. A. Selby Brigge. London: Oxford University Press.

Jain, R. (1981). Dynamic scene analysis using pixel-based processes. *Computer*, August, 12–18.

Jennings, D., Amabile, T. M., and Ross, L. (1982). Informal covariation assessment: Data-based vs. theory-based judgments. In A. Tversky, D. Kahneman, and P. Slovic (eds.), *Judgment under uncertainty: Heuristics and biases*. New York: Cambridge University Press.

Jepson, C., Krantz, D. H., and Nisbett, R. E. (1983). Inductive reasoning: Competence or skill? *Behavioral and Brain Sciences, 6*, 494–501.

Johnson-Laird, P. N. (1982). Ninth Bartlett memorial lecture. Thinking as a skill. *Quarterly Journal of Experimental Psychology, 34A*, 1–29.

Johnson-Laird, P. N. (1983). *Mental models.* Cambridge, Massachusetts: Harvard University Press.

Johnson-Laird, P. N., Legrenzi, P., and Legrenzi, M. (1972). Reasoning and a sense of reality. *British Journal of Psychology, 63*, 395–400.

Jolicoeur, P., Gluck, M. A., and Kosslyn, S. M. (1984). Pictures and names: Making the connection. *Cognitive Psychology, 16*, 243–275.

Jones, E. E., and Davis, K. E. (1965). From acts to dispositions: The attribution process in person perception. In L. Berkowitz (ed.), *Advances in experimental psychology, 2.* New York: Academic Press.

Jones, E. E., and Harris, V. A. (1967). The attribution of attitudes. *Journal of Experimental Social Psychology, 3*, 1–24.

Jones, E. E., and Nisbett, R. E. (1972). The actor and the observer: Divergent perceptions of the causes of behavior. In E. E. Jones, D. E. Kanouse, H. H. Kelley, R. E. Nisbett, S. Valins, and B. Weiner (eds.), *Attribution: Perceiving the causes of behavior.* Morristown, New Jersey: General Learning Press.

Kahneman, D., Slovic, P., and Tversky, A. (1982). *Judgment under uncertainty: Heuristics and biases.* New York: Cambridge University Press.

Kahneman, D., and Tversky, A. (1973). On the psychology of prediction. *Psychological Review, 80*, 237–251.

Kaiser, M. K., Jonides, J., and Alexander, J. (1986). Intuitive physics reasoning on abstract and common sense problems *Memory & Cognition,* in press.

Kaiser, M. K., McCloskey, M., and Proffitt, D. R. (1986). Development of intuitive theories of motion: Curvilinear motion in the absence of external forces. *Developmental Psychology,* in press.

Kaiser, M., Proffitt, D. R., and McCloskey, M. (1986). The development of beliefs about falling objects. *Perception & Psychophysics,* in press.

Kamin, L. J. (1969). Predictability, surprise, attention, and conditioning. In B. A. Campbell and R. M. Church (eds.), *Punishment.* New York: Appleton.

Kelley, H. H. (1972). Causal schemata and the attribution process. In E. E. Jones, D. E. Kanouse, H. H. Kelley, R. E. Nisbett, S. Valins, and B. Weiner (eds.), *Attribution: Perceiving the causes of behavior.* Morristown, New Jersey: General Learning Press.

Kelley, H. H. (1973). The process of causal attribution. *American Psychologist, 28*, 107–128.

Kimble, G. A. (1961). *Hilgard and Marquis' conditioning and learning.* New York: Appleton-Century-Crofts.

Koestler, A. (1964). *The sleepwalkers.* Harmondsworth: Penguin.

Kuhn, T. S. (1962). *The structure of scientific revolutions.* Chicago: University of Chicago Press.

Kuhn, T. S. (1970). Logic of discovery or psychology of research. In I.

Lakatos and A. Musgrave (eds.), *Criticism and the growth of knowledge*. Cambridge: Cambridge University Press.

Kuhn, T. S. (1977). *The essential tension*. Chicago: Univerity of Chicago Press.

Kunda, Z. (1985). Motivation and inference: Self-serving generation and evaluation of causal theories. Ph.D. dissertation, University of Michigan.

Kunda, Z., and Nisbett, R. E. (1986). The psychometrics of everyday life. *Cognitive Psychology, 18*.

Kyburg, H. (1974). *Logical foundations of statistical inference*. Dordrecht: Reidel.

Lakoff, G., and Johnson, M. (1980). *Metaphors we live by*. Chicago: University of Chicago Press.

Langley, P. (1981). Data-driven discovery of physical laws. *Cognitive Science, 5*, 31–54.

Langley, P. (1985). Learning to search: From weak methods to domain-specific heuristics. *Cognitive Science, 9*, 217–260.

Langley, P., Bradshaw, G., and Simon, H. (1981). BACON.5: The discovery of conservation laws. *CIP Working Paper* no. 430, Carnegie-Mellon University.

Langley, P., Bradshaw, G., and Simon, H. (1983). Rediscovering chemistry with the BACON system. In R. Michalski, J. Carbonell, and T. Mitchell (eds.), *Machine learning: An artificial intelligence approach*. Palo Alto: Tioga Press.

Larkin, J. H., McDermott, J., Simon, D., and Simon, H. A. (1980). Expert and novice performance in solving physics problems. *Science, 208*, 1335–1342.

Lashley, K. (1951). The problem of serial order in behavior. In L. A. Jeffries (ed.), *Cerebral mechanisms in behavior*. New York: Wiley.

Laudan, L. (1977). *Progress and its problems*. Berkeley: University of California Press.

Lehman, D., Lempert, R., and Nisbett, R. E. (1986). The effects of graduate education on reasoning. Manuscript in preparation, University of Michigan.

Lehman D., and Nisbett, R. E. (1986). Does social science training influence reasoning about social events? Manuscript in preparation, University of Michigan.

Lenat, D. (1983). The role of heuristics in learning by discovery: Three case studies. In R. Michalski, J. Carbonell, and T. Mitchell (eds.), *Machine learning: An artificial intelligence approach*. Palo Alto: Tioga Press.

Levi, I. (1980). *The enterprise of knowledge*. Cambridge, Massachusetts: MIT Press.

Lewin, K. (1935). *A dynamic theory of personality*. New York: McGraw-Hill.

Lewis, D. (1973). *Counterfactuals*. Oxford: Blackwell.

Locksley, A., Borgida, E., Brekke, N., and Hepburn, C. (1980). Sex stereotypes and social judgment. *Journal of Personality and Social Psychology, 39*, 821–831.

Locksley, A., Hepburn, C., and Ortiz, V. (1982). Social stereotypes and judgments of individuals: An instance of the base-rate fallacy. *Journal of Experimental Social Psychology, 18*, 23–42.

Luchins, A. (1942). Mechanization in problem solving. *Psychological Monographs, 54* (no. 248).

McClelland, J. L., and Rumelhart, D. E. (1981). An interactive activation model of context effects in letter perception: Part 1. An account of basic findings. *Psychological Review, 88,* 375–407.

McCloskey, M. (1983). Intuitive physics. *Scientific American, 24,* 122–130.

McCloskey, M., and Kaiser, M. K. (1984). Children's intuitive physics. *The Sciences, 24,* 40–45.

Mackintosh, N. J. (1974). *The psychology of animal learning.* New York: Academic Press.

Manktelow, K. I., and Evans, J. St. B. T. (1979). Facilitation of reasoning by realism: Effect or non-effect? *British Journal of Psychology, 70,* 477–488.

Maratsos, M., and Chalkley, A. (1980). The internal language of children's syntax: The ontogenesis and representation of syntactic categories. In K. E. Nelson (ed.), *Children's language,* vol. 2. New York: Gardner Press.

Marcel, A. J. (1983). Conscious and unconscious perception: Experiments on visual masking and word recognition. *Cognitive Psychology, 15,* 197–237.

Maxwell, J. C. (1952). *The scientific papers of James Clerk Maxwell,* vol. 1, W. D. Niven (ed.). New York: Dover.

Medin, D. L., Altom, M. W., Edelson, S. M., and Freko, D. (1982). Correlated symptoms and simulated medical classification. *Journal of Experimental Psychology: Learning, Memory, and Cognition, 8,* 37–50.

Medin, D. L., and Schaffer, M. M. (1978). Context theory of classification learning. *Psychological Review, 85,* 207–238.

Meyer, D. E., and Schvaneveldt, R. W. (1971). Facilitation in recognizing pairs of words: Evidence of a dependence between retrieval operations. *Journal of Experimental Psychology, 90,* 227–334.

Milgram, S. (1963). Behavioral study of obedience. *Journal of Abnormal and Social Psychology, 67,* 371–378.

Mill, J. S. (1843/1974). *A system of logic ratiocinative and inductive.* Toronto: University of Toronto Press.

Millenson, J. R. (1967). *Principles of behavioral analysis.* New York: Macmillan.

Miller, G. A. (1979). Images and models, similes and metaphors. In A. Ortony (ed.), *Metaphor and thought.* Cambridge: Cambridge University Press.

Minsky, M. (1975). A framework for representing knowledge. In P. H. Winston (ed.), *The psychology of computer vision.* New York: McGraw-Hill.

Mitchell, T. M. (1977). Version spaces: A candidate elimination approach to rule learning. In *Proceedings of the Fifth International Joint Conference on Artificial Intelligence.* Los Altos, California: Kaufmann.

Mitchell, T. M. (1979). An analysis of generalization as a search problem. In *Proceedings of the Sixth International Joint Conference on Artificial Intelligence.* Los Altos, California: Kaufmann.

Mitchell, T. M. (1982). Generalization as search. *Artificial Intelligence, 18,* 203–226.

Mitchell, T. M. (1983). Learning and problem solving. In *Proceedings of the Eighth International Joint Conference on Artificial Intelligence*. Los Altos, California: Kaufmann.

Murphy, G. L., and Medin, D. L. (1985). The role of theories in conceptual coherence. *Psychological Review, 92,* 289–316.

Neely, J. H. (1977). Semantic priming and retrieval from lexical memory: Role of inhibitionless spreading activation and limited capacity attention. *Journal of Experimental Psychology: General, 106,* 226–254.

Nersessian, N. (1984). Aether/or: The creation of scientific concepts. *Studies in the History and Philosophy of Science, 15,* 175–212.

Neumann, P. G. (1977). Visual prototype formation with discontinuous representation of dimensions of variability. *Memory & Cognition, 5,* 187–197.

Newell, A. (1969). Heuristic programming: Ill-structured problems. In J. S. Aronofsky (ed.), *Progress in operations research,* vol. 3. New York: Wiley.

Newell, A. (1973). Production systems: Models of control structures. In W. G. Chase, (ed.), *Visual information processing.* New York: Academic Press.

Newell, A., and Simon, H. A. (1972). *Human problem solving.* Englewood Cliffs, New Jersey: Prentice-Hall.

Nisbett, R. E., Caputo, C., Legant, P., and Marecek, J. (1973). Behavior as seen by the actor and as seen by the observer. *Journal of Personality and Social Psychology, 27,* 154–164.

Nisbett, R. E., Krantz, D. H., Jepson, D., and Kunda, Z. (1983). The use of statistical heuristics in everyday inductive reasoning. *Psychological Review, 90,* 339–363.

Nisbett, R. E., and Kunda, Z. (1985). Perception of social distributions. *Journal of Personality and Social Psychology, 48,* 297–311.

Nisbett, R. E., and Ross, L. (1980). *Human inference: Strategies and shortcomings of social judgment.* Englewood Cliffs, New Jersey: Prentice-Hall.

Nisbett, R. E., and Wilson, T. D. (1977). Telling more than we can know: Verbal reports on mental processes. *Psychological Review, 84,* 231–259.

Nisbett, R. E., Zukier, H., and Lemley, R. (1981). The dilution effect: Nondiagnostic information weakens the implications of diagnostic information. *Cognitive Psychology, 13,* 248–277.

Ortony, A. (1979). Beyond literal similarity. *Psychological Review, 87,* 161–180.

Osherson, D. N., and Smith, E. E. (1981). On the adequacy of prototype theory as a theory of concepts. *Cognition, 9,* 35–58.

Paap, K. R., and Ogden, W. C. (1981). Letter encoding is an obligatory but capacity-demanding operation. *Journal of Experimental Psychology: Human Perception and Performance, 7,* 518–527.

Peirce, C. S. (1931–1958). *Collected papers,* 8 vols. Edited by C. Hartshorne, P. Weiss, and A. Burks. Cambridge, Massachusetts: Harvard University Press.

Piaget, J. (1936). *La naissance de l'intelligence chez l'enfant.* Neuchâtel and Paris: Delachau et Niestle.

Piaget, J., and Inhelder, B. (1951/1975). *The origin of the idea of chance in children.* New York: Norton.

Pietromonaco, P. R., and Nisbett, R. E. (1982). Swimming upstream against the fundamental attribution error: Subjects' weak generalizations from the Darley and Batson study. *Social Behavior and Personality, 10,* 1–4.

Pirolli, P. L., and Anderson, J. R. (1985). The role of learning from examples in the acquisition of recursive programming skills. *Canadian Journal of Psychology, 39,* 240–272.

Polya, G. (1957). *How to solve it.* Princeton, New Jersey: Princeton University Press.

Popper, K. (1959). *The logic of scientific discovery.* London: Hutchinson.

Posner, M. I., and Keele, S. W. (1968). On the genesis of abstract ideas. *Journal of Experimental Psychology, 77,* 353–363.

Posner, M. I., and Keele, S. W. (1970). Retention of abstract ideas. *Journal of Experimental Psychology, 83,* 304–308.

Posner, M. I., and Synder, C. R. R. (1975). Attention and cognitive control. In R. Solso (ed.), *Information processing and cognition: The Loyola Symposium.* Hillsdale, New Jersey: Lawrence Erlbaum.

Quattrone, G., and Jones, E. (1980). The perception of variability within in-groups and out-groups: Implications for the law of large numbers. *Journal of Personality and Social Psychology, 38,* 141–152.

Quine, W. V. O. (1961). *From a logical point of view* (2nd edition). New York: Harper Torchbooks.

Quine, W. V. O. (1969). *Ontological relativity and other essays.* New York: Columbia University Press.

Reber, A. S., and Allen, R. (1978). Analogic and abstraction strategies in synthetic grammar learning: A functionalist interpretation. *Cognition, 6,* 189–221.

Reber, A. S., Kassin, S. M., Lewis, S., and Cantor, G. (1980). On the relationship between implicit and explicit modes in the learning of a complex rule structure. *Journal of Experimental Psychology: Human Learning and Memory, 6,* 492–502.

Reed, S. K. (1972). Pattern recognition and categorization. *Cognitive Psychology, 3,* 383–407.

Reich, S. S., and Ruth, P. (1982). Wason's selection task: Verification, falsification and matching. *British Journal of Psychology, 73,* 395–405.

Reichenbach, H. (1938). *Experience and prediction.* Chicago: University of Chicago Press.

Reitman, J. S., and Bower, G. H. (1973). Storage and later recognition of exemplars of concepts. *Cognitive Psychology, 4,* 194–206.

Reitman, W. (1964). Heuristic decision procedures, open constraints and the structure of ill-defined problems. In M. W. Shelley and G. L. Bryan (eds.), *Human judgments and optimality.* New York: Wiley.

Rescorla, R. A. (1968). Probability of shock in the presence and absence of

CS in fear conditioning. *Journal of Comparative and Physiological Psychology, 66*, 1–5.

Rescorla, R. A. (1972). Informational variables in Pavlovian conditioning. In G. H. Bower (ed.), *The psychology of learning and motivation.* New York: Academic Press.

Rescorla, R. A., and Wagner, A. R. (1972). A theory of Pavlovian conditioning: Variations in the effectiveness of reinforcement and nonreinforcement. In A. H. Black and W. F. Prokasy (eds.), *Classical conditioning II: Current theory and research.* New York: Appleton.

Rips, L. J. (1983). Cognitive processes in propositional reasoning. *Psychological Review, 90*, 38–71.

Rips, L. J., Shoben, E. J., and Smith, E. E. (1973). Semantic distance and the verification of semantic relations. *Journal of Verbal Learning and Verbal Behavior, 12*, 1–20.

Rosch, E. (1973). On the internal structure of perceptual and semantic categories. In T. E. Moore (ed.), *Cognitive development and the acquisition of language.* New York: Academic Press.

Rosch, E. (1978). Principles of categorization. In E. Rosch and B. B. Lloyd (eds.), *Cognition and categorization.* Hillsdale, New Jersey: Lawrence Erlbaum.

Rosch, E. Mervis, C. B., Gray, W., Johnson, D., and Boyes-Braem, P. (1976). Basic objects in natural categories. *Cognitive Psychology, 7*, 573–605.

Rosenbloom, P. S., and Newell, A. (1986). The chunking of goal hierarchies: A generalized model of practice. In R. S. Michalski, J. G. Carbonell, and T. M. Mitchell (eds.), *Machine learning: An artificial intelligence approach*, vol. 2. Los Altos, California: Kaufmann.

Ross, L. (1977). The intuitive psychologist and his shortcomings. In L. Berkowitz (ed.), *Advances in experimental social psychology, 10.* New York: Academic Press.

Rumelhart, D. (1980). Schemata: The building blocks of cognition. In R. Spiro, B. Brucc, and W. Brewer (eds.), *Theoretical issues in reading comprehension.* Hillsdale, New Jersey: Lawrence Erlbaum.

Rumelhart, D. E., McClelland, J. R., and the PDP Research Group (1986). *Parallel distributed processing: Explorations in the microstructure of cognition*, vol. 1. Cambridge, Massachusetts: MIT Press.

Safer, M. A. (1980). Attributing evil to the subject, not the situation: Student reaction to Milgram's film on obedience. *Personality and Social Psychology Bulletin, 6*, 205–209.

Salmon, W. (1967). *The foundations of scientific inference.* Pittsburgh: University of Pittsburgh Press.

Salzberg, S. (1985). Heuristics for inductive learning. In *Proceedings of the Ninth Joint Conference on Artificial Intelligence.* Los Altos, California: Kaufmann.

Samburski, S. (1973). *Physics of the stoics.* Westport, Connecticut: Greenwood Press.

Samuel, A. L. (1959). Some studies in machine learning using the game of checkers. *IBM Journal of Research and Development, 3*, 210–229.

Schank, R. C. (1982). *Dynamic memory*. Cambridge: Cambridge University Press.

Schank, R., and Abelson, R. P. (1977). *Scripts, plans, goals, and understanding: An inquiry into human knowledge structures*. Hillsdale, New Jersey: Lawrence Erlbaum.

Schleidt, W. M. (1962). Die historische Entwicklung der Begriffe 'Angeborenes Auslösendes Schema' und 'Angeborener Auslösemechanismus'. *Zeitschrift für Tierpsychologie, 21*, 235–256.

Schneider, W., and Shiffrin, R. M. (1977). Controlled and automatic human information processing: I. Detection, search, and attention. *Psychological Review, 84*, 1–66.

Schwartz, B. (1978). *Psychology of learning and behavior*. New York: Norton.

Seligman, M. E. P. (1970). On the generality of the laws of learning. *Psychological Review, 77*, 406–418.

Shiffrin, R. M., and Schneider, W. (1977). Controlled and automatic human information processing: II. Perceptual learning, automatic attending, and a general theory. *Psychological Review, 84*, 127–190.

Siegler, R. S. (1983a). How knowledge influences learning. *American Scientist, 71*, 631–638.

Siegler, R. S. (1983b). Five generalizations about cognitive development. *American Psychologist*, March, 263–277.

Siegler, R. S., and Shrager, J. (1984). Strategy choices in addition and subtraction: How do children know what to do? In C. Sophian (ed.), *Origins of cognitive skills*. Hillsdale, New Jersey: Lawrence Erlbaum.

Simon, H. A. (1956). Rational choice and the structure of the environment. *Psychological Review, 63*, 129–138.

Simon, H. A., Langley, P., and Bradshaw, G. (1981). Scientific discovery as problem solving. *Synthese, 47*, 1–27.

Skinner, B. F. (1938). *The behavior of organisms*. New York: Appleton-Century.

Sleeman, D., Langley, P., and Mitchell, T. (1982). Learning from solution paths: An approach to the credit assignment problem. *AI Magazine, 3*, 48–52.

Smith, E. E., and Medin, D. (1981). *Categories and concepts*. Cambridge, Massachusetts: Harvard University Press.

Smith, E. E., and Osherson, D. (1984). Conceptual combination with prototype concepts. *Cognitive Science, 8*, 337–361.

Smith, S. (1980). A learning system based on genetic algorithms. Ph.D. dissertation, University of Pittsburgh.

Stegmueller, W. (1979). *The structuralist view of theories*. New York: Springer-Verlag.

Sternberg, R. J. (1985). *Beyond IQ.* New York: Cambridge University Press.

Sternberg, R. J., and Suben, J. G. (1986). The socialization of intelligence. Unpublished manuscript, Yale University.

Stich, S., and Nisbett, R. E. (1980). Justification and the psychology of human reasoning. *Philosophy of Science, 47*, 188–202.

Stricker, G. (1977). Implications of research for psychotherapeutic treatment of women. *American Psychologist, 32*, 14–22.

Suppe, F. (1977). *The structure of scientific theories* (2nd edition). Urbana: University of Illinois Press.

Sutton, R. S., and Barto, A. G. (1981). Toward a modern theory of adaptive networks: Expectation and prediction. *Psychological Review, 88*, 135–170.

Thagard, P. (1978). The best explanation: Criteria for theory choice. *Journal of Philosophy, 75*, 76–92.

Thagard, P. (1982). From the descriptive to the normative in psychology and logic. *Philosophy of Science, 49*, 24–42.

Thagard, P. (1984). Conceptual combination and scientific discovery. In P. Asquith and P. Kitcher (eds.), *PSA 1984*, vol. 1. East Lansing, Michigan: Philosophy of Science Association.

Thagard, P., and Holyoak, K. J. (1985). Discovering the wave theory of sound. In *Proceedings of the Ninth International Joint Conference on Artificial Intelligence*. Los Altos, California: Kaufmann.

Thagard, P., and Nisbett, R. E. (1982). Variability and confirmation. *Philosophical Studies, 42*, 379–394.

Thagard, P., and Nisbett, R. E. (1983). Rationality and charity. *Philosophy of Science, 50*, 250–267.

Thibadeau, R., Just, M. A., and Carpenter, P. A. (1982). A model of the time course and content of reading. *Cognitive Science, 6*, 157–203.

Thistlethwaite, D. (1951). A critical review of latent learning and related experiments. *Psychological Bulletin, 48*, 97–129.

Tolman, E. C. (1932). *Purposive behavior in animals and men.* New York: Century.

Tolman, E. C. (1948). Cognitive maps in rats and men. *Psychological Review, 55*, 189–208.

Tolman, E. C. (1959). Principles of purposive behavior. In S. Koch (ed.), *Psychology: A study of a science*, Vol. 2. New York: McGraw-Hill.

Tolman, E. C., and Honzik, C. H. (1930). Introduction and removal of reward, and maze performance in rats. *University of California Publications in Psychology, 4*, 257–275.

Tversky, A., and Kahneman, D. (1971). Belief in the law of small numbers. *Psychological Bulletin, 2*, 105–110.

Tversky, A., and Kahneman, D. (1983). Extensional versus intensional reasoning: The conjunction fallacy in probability judgments. *Psychological Review, 90*, 293–315.

van Fraassen, B. (1980). *The scientific image.* Oxford: Clarendon Press.

Vitruvius (1926). *The ten books on architecture*, trans. M. H. Morgan. Cambridge, Massachusetts: Harvard University Press.

Wagner, A. R., Logan, F. A., Haberlandt, K., and Price, T. (1968). Stimulus selection in animal discrimination learning. *Journal of Experimental Psychology, 76*, 171–180.

Wason, P. C. (1966). Reasoning. In B. M. Foss (ed.), *New horizons in psychology*. Harmondsworth: Penguin.

Waterman, D. (1970). Generalized learning techniques for automating the learning of heuristics. *Artificial Intelligence, 1*, 121–170.

Waterman, D., and Hayes-Roth, F. (eds.) (1978). *Pattern-directed inference systems*. New York: Academic Press.

Watson, J. B. (1924). *Behaviorism*. Chicago: University of Chicago Press.

Whewell, W. (1847). *The philosophy of the inductive sciences*. New York: Johnson Reprint Corp.

Wilson, S. (1982). Adaptive "cortical" pattern recognition. Interval report, Research Laboratories, Polaroid Corporation.

Winston, P. H. (1975). Learning structural descriptions from examples. In P. H. Winston (ed.), *The psychology of computer vision*. New York: McGraw-Hill.

Winston, P. H. (1980). Learning and reasoning by analogy. *Communications of the ACM, 23*, 689–703.

Winston, P. H., and Horn, B. (1981). *LISP*. Reading, Massachusetts: Addison-Wesley.

Wittgenstein, L. (1958). *Philosophical investigations* (2nd edition, trans. G. E. M. Anscombe). Oxford: Blackwell.

Zimmer-Hart, C. L., and Rescorla, R. A. (1974). Extinction of Pavlovian conditioned inhibition. *Journal of Comparative and Physiological Psychology, 86*, 837–845.

Zukier, H. (1982). The dilution effect: The role of the correlation and the dispersion of predictor variables in the use of nondiagnostic information. *Journal of Personality and Social Psychology, 43*, 1163–1174.

Zukier, H., and Jennings, D. L. (1984). Nondiagnosticity and typicality effects in prediction. *Social Cognition, 2*, 187–198.

Index

Abduction
  forms of, 89
  multiple abductions, 89
  and PI, 136–138
Abelson, R. P., 12
Abramowitz, C. V., 221
Ackley, D. H., 27
Alexander, J., 209
Allen, R., 199
Altom, M. W., 190
Amabile, T. M., 177
Analogy
  and abstract categorization, 388
  breakdown in, 299–300
  and categorization, 294
  and convergence solutions, 292, 296
  Copycat project on, 304–307
  and default hierarchies, 305
  diachronic transition function of, 303–304
  formation of
    and diachronic rules, 311–312
    and goal-related properties, 311
    mapping characteristics of, 310, 311
  function of, 287
  interdomain analogies, 289, 295, 303, 311–312
  and mental model construction 297–298
  pragmatic nature of, 300–304
  and problem solving, 98, 287–288, 290, 294, 296, 300
  and q-morphisms, 38–39, 95
  and the radiation problem, 289–296
  refinement of, 300

  and rule generation, 94
  and schema induction, 292–296
  as a "second-order morphism," 296–297
  selection of, 307–310
    retrieval of a source analogue, 310
    transforming target problems, 307–309
  and slippage, 305–307
  and source and target analogs, 291, 292, 296–298
  spontaneous generation, 292, 295, 303, 308, 316, 317
  structure of, 289–300
  syntactic account of, 300–304
  transfer in
    and hints, 317–318
    mechanisms of, 307, 312–314
    "surface-level" properties of, 313
    utility of, 313
Anderson, J. R., 8, 14, 23, 24, 25, 48, 56, 58, 77, 130, 198, 202, 209, 225, 289
Apportionment of credit, 70–71. *See also* Rule refinement
  and bidding, 71
  and causal analogies, 76
  and conditioning, 152, 154
  local techniques of
    and the bucket brigade algorithm, 72, 75
    and prediction-based mechanisms, 76
  nonlocal techniques of, 71, 76
    and causal analysis, 76–78
    and problem solving, 348
    and rule strength, 70–71